Raising the Devil

Raising the Devil

Satanism, New Religions, and the Media

Bill Ellis

THE UNIVERSITY PRESS OF KENTUCKY

Scholarly publisher for the Commonwealth,
serving Bellarmine College, Berea College, Centre
College of Kentucky, Eastern Kentucky University,
The Filson Club Historical Society, Georgetown College,
Kentucky Historical Society, Kentucky State University,
Morehead State University, Transylvania University,
University of Kentucky, University of Louisville,
and Western Kentucky University.
All rights reserved.

Editorial and Sales Offices: The University Press of Kentucky
663 South Limestone Street, Lexington, Kentucky 40508–4008

04 03 02 01 00   5 4 3 2 1

Library of Congress Cataloging-in-Publication Data

Ellis, Bill, 1950-
    Raising the devil : Satanism, new religions, and the media / Bill Ellis.
        p. cm.
    Includes bibliographical references and index.
    ISBN 0-8131-2170-1 (alk. paper)
    1. Satanism. I. Title.
    BF1548 .E45   2000
    133.4'22—dc21   00-035928

For Elizabeth,

*in hopes that she will inherit
a better world*

There is nothing new under the sun.
Is there a thing of which it is said, "See, this is new"?
It has been already in the ages before us.
There is no remembrance of former things,
nor will there be any remembrance of later things
yet to happen among those who come after.

—Ecclesiastes 1:9–11

I raised the Devil,
and the Devil raised me,
I never shall forget
when the Devil raised me.

—19th-century Derbyshire
conjuring charm

Contents

Acknowledgments

This book is the result of an intellectual quest that began in October 1983, when I saw a popular news article describing the murder of two teenagers in a rural area in southeastern Ohio. The article reported local speculations that a "satanic cult" was responsible, and in some of the theories expressed I recognized elements from a number of adolescent legends that I had been studying. The area, like many others, had circulated stories about mysterious groups that met at night for occult ceremonies and sacrificed those unwary enough to spy on them. I followed the case (which was never officially solved), and so began a long, dark, and often lonely journey. The reader may well wonder what motivated me to study this bizarre and often appalling subject.

Primarily, I felt that the subject deserved to be addressed by trained folklorists. Much of the information being circulated on both sides of the debate over Satanism, I saw, was based on profound misunderstandings of folk traditions. In some cases, magical healing traditions that had been carefully studied by ethnographers were being demonized as satanic in nature. In other cases, adolescent rituals having nothing intrinsic to do with Satanism were misunderstood as signs of cult activity. And the previously unstudied phenomenon of rumor panics seemed to be an opportunity for folklorists both to observe myths and beliefs in contemporary action and to help institutions respond to rumors about Satanism in an accurate, productive way. Overall, I thought studying and responding to the scare would be a way of demonstrating that the discipline of folklore was not the quaint study of the past but the dynamic study of the emerging present. Such were my *professional* motives, quixotic as they were.

Folklorist David Hufford, who has also chosen to study elements of religious belief and practices that impact contemporary policy decisions, has argued (1995) that it is misleading for researchers to imply an attitude of total impartiality. The crusade against Satanism scare has important social consequences, and so a completely detached response is simply not possible. Following his suggestions, I would also like to lay out my *personal* views at the outset. I do not do so to accuse or try to convert my readers, but to acknowledge that I hold beliefs as an individual that have influenced the course of my academic study. Knowing these, the reader can better see in what ways the book is biased.

I am a member of the Evangelical Lutheran Church of America (ELCA) who has taken leadership positions and on occasion taught adult Sunday school and led services. I am regularly called on to publicly "reject sin, the devil, and all his empty promises." Therefore I am inclined to respect those who express and act on faith in Jesus Christ and follow his commandments to love God and neighbor. In addition, I do not disparage belief in the devil as a force promoting evil, though I do not hold it as a central tenet of my own faith. Far more important to me is the need to acknowledge and try to reform my own tendencies toward sin.

As an academic folklorist, I regularly collaborate with people of other faiths, and I find their personal integrity and good will far more important to me than any creed their religious expression may include. I hope they feel the same way toward me. Some of my close professional friends are in fact participants in the Neo-Pagan movement, and I respect both their beliefs and the actions they have taken based on them. This does not contradict my own faith in Jesus Christ, for my understanding is that Jesus likewise honored the integrity and faith of those who practiced other faiths and instructed his disciples to do so as well. For if we respect only those of our own faith, Jesus taught, then we are doing no more than the xenophobic pagans of his day did (Matthew 5:47).

I have also been personally involved in cases when people holding rank within Christianity used their position to hurt others whom I held dear. Such events initially shook my faith, and once when I was deeply troubled over such an incident, I was invited to join a Wiccan congregation. I declined, choosing to continue in the faith in which I was raised and which I still find rewarding. But the experiences have left me with a strong distrust of the *institution* of Christianity, which I feel often allows individuals to advance their own political agenda instead of the values of the church's founder. Such experiences have given me a personal insight into the legitimate reasons why some individuals may find such a new religion more rewarding than traditional Christianity. On the other hand, I see from my research that individuals in the neo-pagan movement may at times fall prey to the same institutional temptations as do some Christians.

This is why the book stresses that the intensity of the Satanism Scare may often lead its participants into sins of their own. Often teenagers' actions that could readily be understood in the context of sound ethnographic research are misunderstood by attributing "Satanic" motives to them. Often those who lead crusades against folk devils—Christian, Pagan, and secular—have reasons for doing so that have more to do with deflecting criticism of their own religious agendas than with any widespread social or spiritual threat. Often age-old conspiracy theories—including some once used against the early Church—have been recycled to exaggerate the importance of occult movements and attribute their motives to innocent people. When such things happen, truth suffers, and whatever else we may say about Satan—whether a real spiritual entity or a traditional name for a universal human defect—we know he is the father of deception.

Such were the *personal* motivations of this work. I therefore owe a debt to all those who helped me, even though they knew that such assistance might be misconstrued as lending support to a book that may outrage many religious sensibilities. First, Penn State University made basic groundwork for this research possible with a one-semester sabbatical in the spring of 1992 that allowed me to visit a number of folklore archives and locate many ephemeral sources from the 1960s and 1970s. Travel funds also allowed me both to present early versions of several chapters at conferences and to visit archives on the West Coast and in Great Britain, most importantly the British Library's local newspaper collection in Colindale.

Richard Tyce and Kathy Stone of the Penn State Hazleton Library were both untiring in locating many rare books and periodicals through interlibrary loan. The late Charles Mann was kind in allowing me to access many books in the Occult Collection of the Rare Books Department of the Pattee Library. Penn State provided a one-course reduction in my writing courses in spring 1993 and 1997 to help me finish parts of the manuscript. This, combined with the loan of a laptop computer, helped me bring many drafts into a common format, making it possible to submit the manuscript.

A number of colleagues and friends assisted me materially in finding rare sources and making it possible to visit archives on an extremely limited budget by sharing their homes and sofas with me. Daniel Barnes and Linda Milligan of Ohio State, Janet Langlois of Wayne State, Steve Roud of Croydon, England, Bill Thompson of Reading, England, and Ruth Stotter of Dominican College, San Francisco, provided help at especially needful times. D. Hudson Frew and Nikki Bado, priests of the Covenant of the Goddess, were kind in granting interviews and directing me to important early sources that might have been overlooked. Jeff Mazo and Philip Jenkins of the Religious Studies Program at University Park were also kind in sharing with me many clippings and ephemera documenting the rise of interest in Satanism in Great Britain.

Even with the material in hand, this book would not have been completed had it not been for the constant encouragement given me by others. Some are fellow analysts of the Satanism Scare, particularly Jeffrey S. Victor, Phillips Stevens Jr., and Sherrill Mulhem, all of whom gave me needed reactions to my early efforts. Others were fellow folklorists interested in seeing me bring a difficult project to term, particularly my Penn State colleague David Hufford who provided important guidance at a critical moment in the book's progress.

And some are former participants in the events. Particular thanks go to David Farrant and Sean Manchester, both of whom provided many detailed memories of the Highgate Cemetery affair, along with copies of documents from the period. The chapter on the U.S. cattle mutilation panic would be much less detailed had it not been for the willingness of both Jerome Clark and Loren Colemen to share clippings and photocopies of rare documents from this period.

None of the individuals or institutions mentioned above should be held responsible for the opinions I present or the conclusions I reach. These are mine alone, and beyond the assistance openly acknowledged above I have not been offered, given, or promised any consideration whatsoever from any organization, be it academic, political, religious, or occult.

Some of the material that appears in this book appeared in tentative form in the following articles and is reprinted with permission: "Kurt E. Koch and the 'Civitas Diaboli': Germanic Folk Healing as Satanic Ritual Abuse of Children." *Western Folklore* 54.2 (1995): 77–94; "Speak to the Devil: Ouija Board Rituals among American Adolescents." *Contemporary Legend* 4 (1994): 61–90; and "Cattle Mutilation: Contemporary Legends and Contemporary Mythologies." *Contemporary Legend* 1 (1991): 39–80.

Introduction

Demonizing Folklore

On May 16, 1985, the ABC television "newsmagazine" *20/20* gave national attention to claims that thousands of Satanic cults across the United States were practicing bizarre rituals including animal mutilation, ritual murders, and even cannibalism. Such claims had circulated previously within isolated communities and among specialized networks of law enforcement agents. But from this point on, Satanism became a major national crisis, and the *20/20* feature was followed by several other national exposés, including a 1988 Geraldo Rivera special that proved the highest-rated two-hour documentary in history. Media events like this were powerful because at the time there was no organized scholarly counterresponse pointing out their excesses.

In 1989 anthropologist Philips Stevens Jr. surveyed racist elements in this corpus and called for folklorists to take more decisive action to counter it. Some have followed his lead, but the bulk of data and the paucity of adequate folkloristic concepts have hampered coherent discussion of this phenomenon. Proponents referenced many cases supporting the existence of cults from 1980 on, and many verifiable cases of vandalism, animal mutilations, and even murders suggested that ritual devil worship was a fact of life. There seemed to be too much evidence to rebut case by case. To gain perspective on the phenomenon, it is necessary to move backward in time, to a period when cases were few but influential and when the case for Satanism as a social threat was still being made.

In 1951 the occultist Manly Palmer Hall commented that the "modern" world had eliminated superstition from medicine, law, and economics, adding,

for the most part, orthodox religious groups are emphasizing the

importance of character development, and there are fewer
references to theological abstractions. We no longer believe that
our misfortunes are due to malevolent spirits or that our neighbors are practicing Satanism. Except in a few remote communities, demonology and witchcraft survive only as lore, and the
sprites and goblins of the past are remembered only at Halloween
festivals. (42)

A few years later, British criminologist Henry T.F. Rhodes surveyed
what he accepted as good evidence for the existence of Satanic "black
masses" in past centuries. But he concluded that "Satanism no longer
looms large and terrible because it no longer exists as a kind of public
mischief. . . . Having no longer the anti-theological and anti-social influence of its hey-day, it has degenerated into a commercial racket." He concluded, "Contemporary Satanism (if it can be called that)" exists only
"for the benefit of visitors and tourists" credulous enough to witness
pornographic shows displayed as "age-old ceremonies . . . in the great
tradition of ancient devil worship. . . . The strong sexual emphasis of this
singular form of amusement is the explanation of its popularity"
(1954:210–12).

The Devil himself seemed ready to concede defeat: in 1960 businessman Clyde B. Clason published *I Am Lucifer:Confessions of the Devil*, a
book that he said was inspired by a vision he had in a railroad sleeping car
on the way to Chicago. While preparing for sleep, Clason relates, he heard
a voice: "I am Lucifer . . . I have won. I am about to take full possession of
this planet." He saw history spread itself out in the form of a continuous
struggle between Lucifer and God, and, returning home, he found himself
compelled to the typewriter by "Some force I could neither understand
nor withstand" to type the Devil's memoirs by dictation (1960:ix-xii).

Despite the diabolical boast, the book showed Lucifer decidedly on
the defensive. Not since medieval times had anyone worshiped him in
the old fashion, he complained, and "man's original religion . . . had defi-
nitely lost its attraction for the masses." The old religion, Satan admitted,
was preserved only "by scattered covins [*sic*] of witches" and the Black
Mass only by the occasional lunatic "in somebody's basement with the
blinds pulled down and the windows carefully shuttered" (1960:203).
His only hope lay in disguising his agenda in the form of Communism
and Rationalism. British journalist Pennethorne Hughes also conceded
in 1964 that some people *might* still be practicing black magic in Great

Britain, "with the eating of babies and desecrations of the Cross." He added, nonchalantly, "the importance seems negligible. . . . It is a revolt against reason and humanity. It is depravity. But it is not very interesting" (1965:216–17).

If in the 1960s Satanism was at best a not-terribly-interesting survival from medieval days, then how was the case for it as a major social problem fought and won by 1980? How can the discipline of *folklore* help us to understand how this happened?

Folklore is the knowledge that the members of small groups choose to preserve and circulate, outside of social institutions such as churches and formal organizations. It is a functional, conservative element in cultures. It helps individuals and groups to construct beliefs, concepts, scenarios, and paradigms for experiences that otherwise would prove ambiguous and thus psychologically threatening.

Folklore grows out of social contexts, which it intends to alter. It may present itself as news freshly arisen from the teller's social setting. Of course, its motifs and structure may be quite old, but its impact depends on being directly relevant to the audience's past, present, and future. Their primary *meaning* in performance arises not from literal factuality, that is, but from the specific point that the performer wants to make. Likewise, audiences have expectations they want fulfilled. Folklore thus embodies a complex social event, in which the performer attempts to gain social control over an ambiguous situation. The best performers—and the most influential folklore—have the potential to transform social structures for better or worse. Hence, the act of passing on folk knowledge is often a fundamentally political act.

One role of folklore is to redefine reality in a way that restores the narrator's control over chaotic situations. In the Grimm Brothers' fairy tale, "Rumpelstiltzkin," an uncanny creature claims a right to a young woman's newborn baby unless she can guess his name. The tale describes how she learns the name and exorcises the creature. According to what I have termed "The Rumpelstiltzkin Principle," the act of *naming* such a social threat allows people to put a name, a face, and an agenda onto a poorly defined problem. Translating it into words allows individuals to gain control over these threatening social stresses. In fact, the word for performing a story—"telling," "*erzählen*," "recounting," "*reconter*"—is in many European languages related to the concept of counting or enumerating, likewise a magical means of reducing the unknown into cultural language and so gaining control over it.

So contemporary folklore often defines an *emergency*—a social problem that urgently needs social action. In some cases, though, folklore itself served as the target of action. That is, common folk beliefs and rituals were misunderstood as evidence for "devil worship." In other cases, folk narratives and rituals themselves were used to combat the supernatural and helped construct the means crusaders used to combat "Satanism." In either case, we find folklore progressively "demonized": beliefs and activities originally formed for other purposes are polarized so that they fit cultural models of existential good and evil.

This book will examine the process by which this craze was launched by looking closely at the role the Devil and Satanism played in three of its constitutive elements—Anglo-American magical folklore, the practice of exorcism, and the subversion myths that had previously scapegoated cultural outsiders such as Jews and Communists. Then we will examine two processes: the appearance of "confessing Satanists," influential works that claimed to portray an insider's view of cults, and the rumor panics over graveyard desecrations and cattle mutilations. These helped fuse and communicate the image of Satanism to a mass public.

When contemporary folklore about social dangers circulates widely, it tends, paradoxically, to help bring these dangers into a reality of their own. Stories about Satanism, that is, have a way of coming true. Whether or not Satanists have been operating undercover for centuries, the current controversy has created real "satanic" activities, through the process of *ostension*.

Semiotician Umberto Eco first used this term to refer to moments in oral communication when, instead of using words, people substitute actions: "Would you like a cigarette?" might be signaled by waving a pack. Hungarian-born folklorists Linda Dégh and Andrew Vázsonyi appropriated the term to refer to ways in which "the reality itself, the thing, the situation or event itself functions in the role of message" (1983:6). Entire legend plots can, for instance, be reduced to an allusive action. Freshmen living in dormitories often pass around a common legend in which a girl is attacked by a mysterious "hatchet man" and dies scratching at her roommate's door. Sylvia Grider, one of Dégh's students, found that for weeks after the story circulated, girls would frighten each other by scratching, rather than knocking, at each others' doors (Grider 1973).

Through ostension, cultural traditions may function like a silent conspiracy that motivates similar acts in widely separated locations. That is, if a narrative is widely known through oral or media transmission, individuals may become involved in real-life activities based on all or part of that narrative, even if there is no organization that is physically coordinating these people's actions. Like Hughes, I do not deny that individuals and even groups have practiced what they themselves define as Satanic rituals. I describe the adolescent custom of legend-tripping, which lends itself to ritual acts of vandalism and desecration. Further, culturally available accounts of "Black Masses" and "Satanic sacrifices" may well provide patterns for criminal acts, even murders. In fact, anti-Satanism workshops and lectures may do much more to network directions on how to carry out a "Satanic" ritual than any underground group of devil-worshippers. Joel Best (1991) has rightly cautioned us not to overestimate the power of ostension, and he has also noted that in many panics in which people allegedly "acted out" rumors, the vast majority of cases subsequently proved to be hoaxes (Best and Horiuchi 1985). Not all stories induce people to act them out in real life, but we still need to keep this possibility in mind in interpreting real-life events involving Satanism.

This work is therefore written not to "debunk" the crusade against Satanism but to give readers access to information that will help shed light on its origins and its rationale. Much of the material covered deals with matters such as graveyard desecrations, animal mutilations, and overt statements of racial, gender, and ethnic hatred. Occultists, self-defined Satan-worshippers, and key figures in the neo-pagan movement contributed to the modern Satanism Scare, as did many proponents of mainstream and fringe Christianity. I find all sides responsible in some way for the alarm that developed. Not surprisingly, I have already received harsh letters from both neo-pagans and Christians, insisting that if I did not advocate their position, I surely must be giving aid and comfort to the extremists on the other side.

The intensity of the debate among those already in the field may be one reason why relatively few scholarly studies exist. This work makes no claims to be "the truth," but only a step toward a reasoned middle ground. I hope that surveying the origins of the Satanism Scare will allow readers to assess more accurately the reasons why people engage in occult practices and to reflect more carefully on the motives some people have for exaggerating the danger of these practices.

Christian Magic and Diabolical Medicine

The Theory behind the Scare

In the most civilized countries the priest is still but a
Powwow, and the physician a Great Medicine
—Henry David Thoreau,
A Week on the Concord and Merrimac Rivers

Folklore by definition is the part of culture characterized by small-group choice in the face of institutions who impose formal creeds, rules, and laws. Institutions such as religions remain stable over centuries, though obviously they include mechanisms for change so they can adapt to new situations. By contrast, folklore has no necessary means of ensuring its own survival: being transmitted orally or at best in some ephemeral medium, it simply disappears if it no longer provides some immediate function. Nevertheless, as folklorists have noted, it can preserve some kinds of lore in a conservative way for centuries in a way that superficially mimics the means by which institutions maintain their own traditions.

When anti-Satanism crusaders find witchcraft beliefs in circulation over a long period of time and in many different locations, it is logical for them to suspect some underground institution, similar to Christianity but devoted to opposite aims. However, to the extent that Satanism does exist in folklore, it exists as an "antiworld," a deliberate protest against institutional norms. This means that whatever structure exists in folk Satanism derives from institutional structures, which they adopt in mirror image.

So we must be careful to distinguish folklore *of* witchcraft and Satanism (i.e., what witches and Satanists *do* believe) from folklore *about* witches and Satanists (what anti-occult crusaders *think* witches and Satanists believe). This distinction has always existed, even during the historic witch trials, as folklorist Gustav Henningsen (1980) has noted. In his study of a seventeenth-century panic in the Basque provinces of Spain, he found that oral traditions concerning the devil and witchcraft were part of a community's normal cultural language. Such traditions may be dangerous at times but on the whole served useful functions in maintaining group identity and coping with internal conflicts.

The other tradition, folklore *about* witches, was made up of intense but short-lived beliefs circulated only at the time of witch crazes. These, Henningsen observes, constitute "an explosive amplification" of the fears expressed by folk beliefs "caused by a temporary syncretism of the witch beliefs of the common people with those of the more specialized or educated classes." When religious or secular authorities used these beliefs to detect "conspiracies," they had the potential to set off crusades implicating as much as half the population of some areas. Such a body of beliefs, he concludes, "could only exist over a shorter period [than folk witchcraft beliefs], as it would otherwise lead to the complete breakdown of society." So every time a witch craze is mounted, Henningsen found, these beliefs had to be reintroduced and made credible. Even during the centuries when such crusades were widespread, participants "had to be instructed through preachers or secular agitators before a new mass persecution could be initiated" (1980:390–92).

It was this function that demonologists' manuals fulfilled in historical witch-hunts. Studies of witch crazes in Early Modern times have noted the role played by such manuals as Henry Kraemer and Jacob Sprenger's *Malleus Maleficarum* (1486), F.M. Guazzo's *Compendium Maleficarum* (1609), and, for Anglo-American culture, King James I's *Demonologie* (1597) and Cotton Mather's *Late Memorable Providences Relating to Witchcrafts and Possessions* (1689). Folklorists have described how these works were based fundamentally on internationally distributed legends and folk beliefs (Kittridge 1929, Hole 1947, Dorson 1973). Yet social historian Leland E. Estes (1986) has cautioned against drawing a direct cause/effect relationship between witch-hunters' manuals and crazes. In fact, such panics often broke out decades after these works were published. And the explicit targets of such works—the village folk healer or curser and the dabbler in ceremonial magick—usually escaped prosecution. Rather, people who were deviant in economic, political, and gender roles bore the brunt of such crazes.

But the diabolization of folklore served as a warrant for a subversive conspiracy of evil. Since folk practices are ubiquitous, it superficially makes sense that a secret underground institution is infecting cultures with them. Belief in such conspiracies, Henningsen notes, is *not* central to folk beliefs, but it constitutes the cornerstone of witch-hunting manuals produced by representatives of religious and secular authorities. Hence, we have two bodies of knowledge that draw from each other but are essentially inimical to each other: one preserved orally as part of folk culture, the other made up of folk beliefs given a new meaning in institutionally generated and preserved publications.

This chapter and the next discuss such bodies of knowledge that came to motivate the Satanism Scare. The information developed among a tightly networked group of Charismatic Christians. A faction of a much larger religious movement, this movement sought to revive the Charismatic gifts exercised by the early Christian church in modern-day practice. Among these gifts were magical healing by identifying and casting out demons that dwelt within otherwise normal individuals. In so doing, these movements developed rituals that were, in the eyes of rival sects, perilously close to witchcraft. Even within the ranks of the Charismatics, bitter disputes arose about the proper use and interpretation of these gifts. The need to distinguish their practices from devil worship, together with the practical knowledge gained through exorcisms, soon made participants of this movement experts on demonology. However, the Charismatic movement was not without its bitter internal differences, and as they began to be aired, we find participants deflecting criticism from themselves and their practices and giving the earliest warnings against Satanism.

Folk and Institutional Mythologies

Folk traditions of witchcraft and the Devil have a structure of their own, made up of narratives about real or allegedly real contacts with evil. These are constructed with the help of broader structures which are not themselves legends but global concepts that subsume story elements and observable behavior and phenomena. These global concepts give meaning to old legends and impetus to emerging ones. Narratives make up only part of the cultural language used to construct a community's definition of reality, and they are difficult to understand unless we also pay attention to the broader units of thought that give them meaning.

To extend an analogy from the introduction: a legend is like a name, or word, in that it expresses, or "tells" an anxiety specific to a particular place and time. Legends are part of a cultural "belief-language" that helps individuals make sense of disorienting and stressful experiences. As unexpressed anxieties build up, pressure will likewise build toward the development of a new legend type that will adequately "name" these discordant elements. The cathartic effect of this "naming" function partially explains contemporary legends' intense but short-lived careers in communities. While active, the legend process generates heated debate between believers and skeptics, and even among groups of believers who interpret events in different ways. Whether conducted orally or in popular media, this debate shows competition among alternative ways of constructing contemporary events into culturally "grammatical" interpretations.

But legends, like words, do not carry meaning in isolation; rather they are given primary meaning by the role they play in larger expressions of thought, analogous to the role words play in sentences. Consequently, clusters of legends, rumors, and beliefs often collaborate with other kinds of stories or bits of information to form global traditions. These broader "scenarios" provide contexts for individual facts: the scenario may suggest ways of interpreting the event; the event may help flesh out the scenario. These scenarios may give meaning to experience even when they do not have any direct point of contact with the events they describe.

What do we call these bodies of lore? Gillian Bennett (1987a, 1987b) has suggested the concept "traditions of belief" for such clusters of personal experience, secondhand information, media reports, and religious interpretations. Traditions like these are not homogeneous: they may in fact subsume sharp debates or skeptical opinions. They make it possible for people to share puzzling opinions about or apparent contacts with the supernatural world without defining the speaker as deviant. But since they are global in nature, these traditions frequently include references to supernatural or superscientific forces and are generally acknowledged by their proponents to be unverifiable by science; they must be *mythic* in nature. In the hands of highly motivated subcultures, they can become organized into self-aware *mythologies*.[1] These informal definitions of reality assume ongoing penetration of this world by supernatural forces. They are verbalized, and indeed hotly debated, at times of perceived crisis. I therefore suggest that we use the term *contemporary mythologies* to refer to these global scenarios accepted on faith by the members of subcultures who use them to link and give ultimate meaning to puzzling events.

The standard folkloristic definition of myth (Bascom 1964), assumes that the events related are "considered to be truthful accounts of what happened in the remote past," while accounts of more recent events have traditionally been called "legends." But many narratives alluding to ancient "mythological times" also explain present events and in fact impact the tellers' own lives (Georges 1971). Even institutionalized myths, in the traditional sense of the word, are used to explain and validate contemporary social practices (Berger and Luckman 1967). Therefore, the difference between "mythic" and "legendary" events is far less divergent than usually assumed. The distinction is simply one of levels of abstraction: beliefs are combined and linked in legends; legends are combined and linked in myths.[2] *Contemporary mythologies* thus are scenarios made up of many beliefs and narratives which are accepted on faith and used then to link and give meaning to stressful events in terms of continuous penetration of this world by otherworldly forces.

Witchcraft mythologies, Henningsen argues, are a historically stable safety valve for social aggression. Groups may use them to justify scapegoating deviant individuals, but such beliefs do not lead to panics. Over the long term, they play a positive role in the moral systems of communities.[3] Phillips Stevens Jr. (1991), by contrast, terms witch scares *demonologies*. They may give credence to some folk traditions but they combine them with quite other sets of beliefs drawn from intellectual or political institutions. As Henningsen shows, this linking of folklore to politics can lead to an explosive development in which the occasional scapegoating of deviant individuals through folk traditions may grow into a mass persecution. The contemporary Satanism Scare was such a social phenomenon, exactly parallel to the earlier witch scares.

This is not to deny that traditions involving malicious magic remain in practice in contemporary times. What can be challenged is the belief that these practices survived only because of a well-concealed but ubiquitous satanic movement. Such a belief more likely documents the emerging need of certain movements to legitimate themselves by launching a crusade against a movement that mirrored their own concerns, a diabolical enemy. And new crusades had to be founded on a new set of demonological manuals that educated religious and secular leaders on the marks of satanic conspiracies.

The initial development of Satanism schemes was couched in terms of medicine, not superstition. Estes notes that the intellectual basis of the earlier demonologies was the considerable turmoil caused by the overthrow of medieval theories of medicine, and that witch-hunts were in fact motivated by procedures based in the "new science" of medicine. Where earlier procedures treated illness by examining only a limited set of symptoms, the increasingly empirical newer medicine proposed a much more complex set of diagnoses. One side effect of this expanded scope of medicine was that physicians could now recognize a greater range of ailments, particularly mental ones. Medical theory, however, could not expand quickly enough to propose scientific causes for such complex or puzzling conditions.

Ironically, advances in medicine actually led to a resurgence of belief in magic. When confronted with a puzzling illness that did not respond to natural treatment, as one physician reasoned, the obvious conclusion was to define its etiology as supernatural. An ailment could be traced to witchcraft, he said, if "natural remedies or means according unto art and due discretion applied, do extraordinarily or miraculously either lose their manifest inevitable nature, use and operation, or else produce effects and consequences, against or above their nature" (qtd. in Estes 1986:204). In other words, such logic ran, if "scientific" treatment did not lead to a cure, the medical theory being used was not at fault; rather, the Devil was at work to frustrate the doctor.

In a second irony noted by Estes, a medieval physician diagnosing a "diabolical ailment" would have assumed that demons induced natural symptoms and would have prescribed a natural cure. Such practices built on the herbal cures followed by the majority of wise women and "white witches" to our day. But a "new science" physician confronted with an illness that his theories could not explain thought it inappropriate to treat such a patient medically. Instead he would rely on the older folk methods of punishing the person thought to be the witch. Rather than using the various rituals intended to "turn the trick" on the implicit witch, physicians would notify religious and secular authorities, who in turn would trace, arrest, prosecute, and, if necessary, execute the person thought to be guilty.

Finally, Estes notes, older paradigms of witch-caused illness might have convinced enough people in a rural community to cause the scapegoating of deviant individuals. Such individuals might well have turned this scapegoating to their social advantage by adopting the title "witch" and promising to cause illnesses for a fee. But actually prosecuting even a self-proclaimed witch was unlikely to convince a local magistrate and even less likely to impress a judge coming from a literate urban background. Thus, to convict a witch before a court of law, Estes argues, the prosecution's case would have to find support both in local rumor and folklore and, more importantly, in the great medical tradition with which the "judicial classes" were closely in touch. That is, the charges would have to make sense in terms of the latest and best medical opinion, as supported and taught by the universities and propagated in the scholarly literature of that period (1986:207).

We therefore expect modern demonologies to syncretize older folk medical beliefs with learned medical theories. The result would be a "diabolical medicine" intended to give a supernatural diagnosis of an ailment not easily explained in natural terms. Such a theory would help religious and legal authorities to detect individuals who caused such illnesses. To be credible, the diagnosis would need to be based not just in folk mythologies, but also in the most learned of institutional mythologies.

The Rise of the Modern Charismatic Movement

This connection developed through the deliverance ministry as it developed from a small-scale, uncoordinated movement into a highly coordinated *conduit* of ideas and information. It is an oversimplification to treat Christian fundamentalism per se as a folk group; this movement is a mass culture centered on the central mythic belief in the infallibility of the Old and New Testaments, both as history and as codes of behavior. And, while most within this culture would concede the Bible's supernatural character, they would object to linking "magic" with "religion." But let's accept as normative Aleister Crowley's famous definition of ceremonial magick as "the Science and Art of causing change to occur in conformity with Will" (qtd. in Adler 1986:8).

Clearly, the use of prayer in a Christian context is close to a form of ceremonial magick, in which priests and their followers collectively request changes to occur in one's world in accordance with will. The majority of fundamentalist Christians may and do ask for healing of medically incurable illnesses, for instance. But most theologians argue that asking for change is not the same as causing change: God may or may not grant such requests in accordance with His will. When a person claims to carry out such healing directly with the help of a special gift from or through God, many conservative Christians would consider such a claim blasphemous.

But there were conduits within fundamentalism that believed that Christians could actually make claims to powers that were in fact, if not in name, magical. The Pentecostal movement of Protestant Christianity arose around interest in reviving the "gifts of the Spirit," the miraculous powers exercised by the original apostles during the first century A.D. Among these were the ability to speak in foreign or heavenly languages and to receive insights about individuals' personalities and prophecies concerning their future. Again, Pentecostalism as a whole did not constitute a folk religion, but well-defined factions did construct methodologies of dealing with mental or physical illness in terms of identifying and casting out oppressing demons. Such practices were often held in deep suspicion by other factions within fundamentalist Christianity, and indeed within Pentecostalism, because, objectively speaking, their gifts often were indistinguishable from magical practices.

The Pentecostal movement had its modern origin in nineteenth-century Great Britain. In 1830 a Presbyterian group led by the Reverend Edward Irving became convinced that the end of the world was imminent. The Christian community needed to find apostles, equipped with the original spiritual gifts, to usher in the new age. The movement, which eventually was called the Catholic Apostolic Church, provoked controversy, especially for its emphasis on tongue-speaking, and its activity virtually ceased around the turn of the century when the last of the self-proclaimed apostles of the church died. A similar movement broke out in the United States at a Kansas bible college in 1901 and soon after spread to a largely black and ethnic mission in Azuza, California. A number of organized denominations, such as the Assembly of God, trace their origins to this movement, but after the initial excitement, tongue-speaking and similar gifts became associated mainly with marginal cultures and areas.

But starting around 1960, the Pentecostal movement began to make inroads into mainstream sects as well, both among Protestants and Catholics. Informal "bible groups" sprang up within existing denominations to focus on these gifts, which were often termed the "charismata" and those who practiced them, "Charismatics." By 1975, theologian James Hitchcock said, the Charismatic movement within the Roman Catholic Church had become "the most formidable religious movement on the American scene" (1982:38). Relying on Ronald Knox's 1950 work *Enthusiasm*, he characterized the modern Charismatic movements in terms of three common features.

First, faith needed continual reaffirmation through contact with the divine world. Indeed, Hitchcock noted, any intensely meaningful experience was assumed to be divine in nature. As described by participants, the most common experience involved being filled with the power of an entity associated with the Biblical Holy Spirit. Believers might fall into an ecstatic trance—"slain in the Spirit"—or, more commonly, speak in an inspired voice. At times these utterances were revelations in English, but most often they were interpreted as messages expressed in celestial language.

Second, they held that God's direct intervention superseded ordinary means of worship. "The devotee does not apply ordinary prudential skepticism to allegedly supernatural manifestations," Hitchcock says, adding, "a certain pride . . . causes the individual to assume that everything which happens in his or her life is supernaturally caused."

Third, believers who are motivated spontaneously by the Spirit were impatient about comparing these revelations with established theologies. It followed that since enthusiasts saw themselves as extraordinary people, they must have an extraordinary mission, which means that God was using them for some immediate great purpose, presumably to prepare society for the Second Coming (1982:16–23, 125–32, 156).

Those who were instrumental in publicizing such beliefs were often criticized by conservative religious figures as being themselves tools of the Devil (e.g., Hoekema 1972). Spiritual healing and tongue-speaking were both attacked as being at best unnecessary for Christian growth and at worst a form of supernaturalism that equated grace with the miraculous. Nevertheless, the movement flourished, particularly in nonwestern cultures, where converts from traditional religions focusing on spirit possession found it more congenial than doctrinally focused missionary movements. Glossolalia, or tongue-speaking, and trance states, indeed, have been recognized as central to shamanic religions across the world, and research by Felicitas A. Goodman, among others, has argued that spirit possession is a universal human experience (Tippett 1976, Goodman 1988).

It was this persistent and ultimately successful attempt to reintroduce spirit possession into the mainstream Anglo-American Christian tradition that led to the need for Pentecostals to construct an evil satanic counterpart. Pentecostals needed to justify their revival of spiritual gifts that the theology-based European religious tradition had suppressed for centuries. And, as Goodman has pointed out, signs of possession by benevolent spirits is difficult to distinguish from signs of demonic possession. A number of critics within fundamentalism, as we shall see, used this very point to attack Charismatics.

Media-Enhanced Conduits

Such a link, however, presented no surprise to Pentecostals. Even more so than mainstream fundamentalism movement, their mythology required there to be demons in order for the divine magic of tongues to be valid. But it therefore became essential for factions of Pentecostals that came particularly under attack to collect and network information among themselves about how to distinguish genuinely divine supernaturalism from its diabolical counterfeit. As this ministry became more tightly networked, rituals that originally were practiced within folk groups became formalized and validated in terms of an increasingly complex demonology that relied on human scapegoats.

Hence, the Pentecostal community relied on specialized networks similar to those that folklorists Linda Dégh and Andrew Vázsonyi have termed *conduits* (Dégh and Vázsonyi 1975; Dégh 1979). In several contexts they observed that persons did not communicate information to everyone they knew; rather, they formed specific alliances based on shared beliefs and interests, and selectively passed on messages through this conduit. Describing one such network, observed during the 1940s in a Hungarian military labor company, they observed: "The resulting conduit was not the product of necessity, neither was it created by lack of choice; it was naturally and genuinely formed. Those who were interested in hearing and telling it passed on the message. Members of the company knew each other quite well after having spent many months together. They knew each other's taste, orientation, field of interest and knew well to whom to turn, whom to avoid" (1975:221–22). Similar dynamics inform many groups that have grown up around controversial beliefs. Observers of the vast numbers of New Age quasi-religious groups, including the Wiccan or neo-pagan movement, have noted the vital role played by small-scale newsletters and other forms of networking (Melton 1990:315–20). Such conduits have also been documented linking private investigators of the Kennedy assassination (Lewis and Schiller 1967:64–92), of UFO encounters (Milligan 1983), and of evidence for Sasquatch or Bigfoot (Milligan 1990).

These networks generate close personal relationships among participants, have a high sense of self-identity, and share specialized information, so they are identical to conduits typical of folk groups, even though they augment traditional face-to-face oral transmission with modern communication media such as telephones, newsletters, and personal computers. This form of networking, which in fact is normal among folk groups in technological societies, I term *media-enhanced conduits*. Because of their special interests, combined with their shared suspicion of mainstream denominations and their official channels, the Pentecostal movements developed and relied on highly organized conduits to share information. Linda Dégh (1990; 1994:110–52) has shown that testimonies given in one Pentecostal church and circulated on audiotape show the characteristics of legend.

But Charismatics complemented face-to-face performance with use of the mass media in highly specialized ways. Charismatics spread illustrations of God's power nationwide and indeed internationally through newsletters, small-run booklets, taped sermons, and, beginning in the 1970s, videotapes. And the material circulated comprised far more than legends: it also included beliefs, interpretations of Scripture, and practices of healing and discerning demonic influence. Thus, the movement's conduits disseminated material central to maintaining the contemporary mythology that supported Charismatics' identity. The esoteric, ephemeral nature of the material circulated also deflected opposition from hostile factions, since it often went unnoticed outside the conduit.

The deliverance ministry was one such small but influential media-enhanced conduit. It stressed the power of believers, individually or collectively, to heal diseases, cast out demons, and perform other apparently miraculous acts. This network linked Protestants who practiced supernatural healing through discerning and casting out demons. In orthodox Judaic and Catholic traditions, this magical practice was known as exorcism, and many of the elements of this body of knowledge became public knowledge during the publicity over William Peter Blatty's

The Exorcist, a best selling book of 1971 and award-winning movie of 1973. But the Judaic-Catholic tradition was not as influential in this conduit as the knowledge and tactics that arose from the grassroots prayer groups that developed and networked in the wake of the Charismatic movement. In contemporary reports, we can see three distinctive elements that became part of this movement:

1. Increasing emphasis on hymns, prayers, and protective charms based on "The Blood."
2. Public confession as a necessary first stage in receiving Holy Spirit baptism.
3. Integration of some form of supernatural experience into the group's rites of passage.

Each of these three elements needs to be examined closely.

1. *Blood-Pleading.* One tradition specific to the deliverance ministry focused on "pleading the Blood," or making a special appeal to the power of Jesus' blood shed during the Crucifixion. The immediate source of this tradition, Catherine Price, was not a cleric but a London housewife who met weekly with a group of four other women to pray for a revivalistic outpouring of the Holy Spirit. In 1907, she was busy preparing a meal "when she was constrained by the Spirit to leave everything and go to wait upon the Lord. As she waited, Jesus came to her in person." Price at once received the power to speak in tongues and became for a time a London celebrity who spoke at revival meetings and received prayer groups at her home. At one meeting, she cried out, "Oh, how can you sing so listlessly, so apathetically, so carelessly about the Blood of Jesus Christ!" and broke into glossolalia. The result electrified the audience, and Price later found that appeals to The Blood produced similar effects in meetings (Whyte 1973a:7–8).

Price's example sparked imitations in Scotland, where in January 1908 a worshipper at a Kilsyth meeting hall rose and began repeating, "Blood, Blood, Blood!" whereupon the participants at once began speaking in tongues (Whyte 1973a:87–88). The participants in the London and Kilsyth revivals spread "pleading the Blood" as a means of invoking spiritual gifts to other congregations, and pilgrims from as far afield as the United States came to witness the miracles performed.

2. *Confession.* One feature of public evangelical meetings has often

been a mania of public confession. Some evangelists argued that even one person's failure to confess could block the outpouring of spirit for the whole community. Canadian Oswald Smith, for instance, preached:

> This has been the history of revival work all down the centuries. Night after night sermons have been preached and no results obtained, until some elder or deacon bursts out in an agony of confession, and, going to the one whom he has wronged, craves forgiveness. . . . Then when confession and restitution have been made, the fallow ground broken up, sin uncovered and acknowledged, then and not until then, the Spirit of God comes upon the audience and a Revival sweeps over the community.
>
> Generally there is but one sin, one hindering thing. . . . And God will put His finger directly on the spot. Nor will he take it off until that one obstacle has been dealt with. . . . And no sooner will the obstacle of sin be taken out of the way than God will come in mighty revival power. (1933:66)

Typically, the sins confessed are normal breaches of social behavior, often petty ones: anger, gossip, dishonesty in business, indulgence in gambling or sports. One witness noted that merchants found that many old debts long abandoned as uncollectable were paid off at last; others received sums anonymously, labeled "Conscience money" (Johnson 1906:369). The deliverance ministry inherited this insistence on confession as a first step toward religious experience. In time, it focused specifically on *occult* sins and argued that unofficial use of magic was an infraction of the first commandment against worshipping other gods. Such an infraction, in fact, gave Satan the quasi-legal right to send one of his spirits to occupy the personalities of Christians or to oppress them with illnesses, mental or physical. Only by bringing the specific occult sin to mind and renouncing it by name could Christians free themselves to enjoy a direct, ecstatic religious experience.

3. *Supernatural Experience.* The deliverance ministry inherited its stress on personal religious experience from the Methodist tradition of evangelism. This process of "conversion" featured a dramatic psychological process, in which the believer vacillates between periods of intense self-doubt and ecstatic contacts with the divine. Often this process climaxes in a dramatic moment of emotional collapse. The confession of sins and absolution have always been central tenets of Christianity. In

the deliverance ministry, however, this ethical concept was mythologized: that is, the effects of sins were defined as malign external personalities, demons in short. Thus, compulsive patterns of behavior or even physical illnesses were diagnosed as caused by an alien personality opposed to Christians' normal mode of thought. What the deliverance ministry added was a ritualized way of allowing the afflicted person's normal personality to become passive, allowing (even forcing) the alien personalities to identify themselves and explain their origins.

These three mythological elements—blood-pleading, confession, and supernaturalism—would become the basis for defining and describing the satanic threat against whom the deliverance ministry was committed to war. By the early 1960s, so many informal groups both in England and the United States had taken up exorcism as a procedure that mainstream denominations were beginning to take interest. In 1963, *Christian Life* published a series of articles entitled "Victory over Demonism Today." These detailed counselors' experiences with apparently possessed individuals and argued that "deliverance" should be revived (Meade 1963). The following year in Great Britain, the Reverend Dom Robert Petitpierre, O.S.B., organized a Church of England Study Group on Exorcism committed to reviving similar rituals (Petitpierre 1972). Growing theological sympathy toward belief in demon possession, in short, created an atmosphere favorable for the growth of informal media-enhanced conduits founded on a diabolical theory of mental illness.

A detailed history of the movement is beyond the scope of this book, so I will focus on three important individuals from three distinct backgrounds who influenced deliverance. In this chapter, I will discuss Kurt E. Koch, a Lutheran pastor from the German/Swiss border region, and H.A. Maxwell Whyte, a Briton transplanted to Toronto, Canada. These two men developed highly elaborated theologies that explained why satanic power was a massive threat to fellow Charismatics. In the next chapter, I will discuss Don Basham, an American fundamentalist turned exorcist, who used ideas from both Maxwell Whyte and Koch to develop a practical ritual of allowing demonic personalities to emerge from otherwise normal individuals. The histories and interplay of these three illustrate and encapsulate many of the international dynamics of this complex movement.

⎰ealing and ⎅emonization

The most frequently cited authority in the first generation of demonologists was the Lutheran Charismatic, Kurt E. Koch. Born in November 1913 in Berghausen, a town located in the German province of Baden, near the Black Forest and the Swiss border, Koch received his Doctor of Theology degree from the University of Tübingen, specializing in mental health counseling. Returning to Baden in the 1930s as a pastor and youth counselor, he found the area afflicted by "a flood of magic." In fact, the chaotic period between the two World Wars was marked by a revival of many forms of occultism. The focus of many of these magical practices was *The Sixth and Seventh Books of Moses*, an early analog of 'Anton LaVey's *Satanic Bible* describing how to perform black magic.

Koch himself was sensitive to mental problems linked to occultism, since as a child he found that whenever he visited his grandparents he would wake up in the night and see "a huge beast with glowing eyes." These visions puzzled him for years, until his father mentioned that he had had similar night visitations during his own youth. Koch continues:

> The bombshell dropped when my father related how his grandmother, while raising her children, had practiced magic with the Sixth and Seventh Books of Moses. This, then, was my great-grandmother. At one stroke I understood why the experiences of my father and his siblings were similar to those of my own childhood. My grandmother, about whom there had been many rumors, was the demon-oppressed daughter of an enchantress [*die belastete Tochter einer Besprecherin*]....[3] Now I could see how my grandmother and great-grandmother were responsible both for my father's frightening experiences and also for my own terrifying moments of fear. This insight motivated me as pastor and evangelist to conduct thousands of conversations with soul-sick, occult-oppressed persons and come to hear similar things, time and time again. (1980a:20–21; my translation)

Beginning in the 1930s, Koch specialized in counseling individuals suffering from depression and other signs of mental illness. He noted that such patients inevitably had had contact with folk healers like his great-grandmother, or had themselves practiced some form of folk magic.

By 1949 he had developed a relationship with Wiesbaden psychoanalyst Alfred Lechler, one of a group of Christian therapists in Germany who accepted demonic influence as a valid diagnosis for some mental problems. Lechler, too, assumed that involvement in folk magic could lead to such demonization. He argued:

> What then must we regard as the cause of demonic enslavement and of possession? If we enquire closely from such people . . . we very often find in their background the use of magic means such as are employed in black magic, viz. acts of charming or being charmed, the sin of fortune telling or visits to fortune tellers and card layers, and participation in spiritist sessions. Black magic is much more prevalent than is ordinarily assumed. . . . Together with spiritist activities, magic stands in a class of its own in relation to other sins, when it includes an appeal to Satan's services or even a formal *pact with Satan* [emphasis his]. . . . For by invoking Satan man yields himself unequivocally to powers of darkness, in that he attempts by magic and the help of Satanic power to gain something that God has forbidden or withheld. (Qtd. in Koch 1972:156)

Following Lechler, Koch developed a "demonic" clinical psychology based on his belief that *Brauche*, or Germanic folk healing, was a dangerous ritual that derived its power from evil sources and so constituted an *implicit* pact with Satan. Koch used narratives and beliefs drawn from folk healing to demonstrate the evils of the occult. Indirectly they contributed a model for a theory that children were most at risk, as they could be demonized directly by being healed, and they also could inherit demons from occult-involved ancestors.

Koch developed a huge file of cases from his ministry in Germany, Switzerland, and Austria, which he organized under types of occult involvement. This file eventually formed the basis for a series of works for Christian counselors on how to deal with mental and spiritual problems, the first of which were published in the 1950s. These books include many accounts, anecdotal and firsthand, of cases involving what he defined as demonic activity. Koch interpreted these cases as evidence that Satan continues to oppose good in this world. "The Civitas Dei, the Kingdom of God," he said, "is confronted by the civitas diaboli, the kingdom of Satan" (Koch and Lechler 1970:25).

When Koch's *Between Christ and Satan* appeared in English in 1962, he immediately found himself in demand outside of Germany. That year he came to the United States for the first time to give talks on demonology at the Moody Bible College in Chicago and the Dallas Theological Seminary. Soon after, he was involved in a series of world tours, visiting fundamentalist seminaries in Latin America, Australia, and Asia.

Within ten years, all of Koch's demonological works were available in English, including *Der Aberglaube* (trans. *The Devil's Alphabet*, 1970), *Demonology, Past and Present* (1973a), a collection of popular lectures, and his technical manual, *Seelsorge und Okkultismus* (trans. *Christian Counseling and Occultism*, 1972). Also translated was *Belastung und Befreiung* (trans. *Occult Bondage and Deliverance*, 1970), a collaborative effort with Dr. Lechler. On the whole, he seems to have been more popular in the Anglo-American camp than in his native Germany. In his last demonological work, *Okkultes ABC* (trans. *Satan's Devices*, 1978), he apologized to his German audience for the inclusion of "movements with strange-sounding names," as the book was being prepared specifically for translation into English (1978:1).

Koch's works on discerning and remedying demonic possession were cited as authoritative within the deliverance ministry. Three of his ideas became essential to the deliverance mythology, and so his key arguments formed a theoretical base for much of the anti-Satanism propaganda that followed. First, he argued that the charms and procedures used in Germanic folk healing, even when they appeared to help the patient, were *always* satanic in nature. Such diabolical charms left "engrams," or concealed psychic injuries, in the personality of the person healed, which later emerged as physical or mental illnesses of demonic origin. Most importantly, these engrams were multigenerational in nature, inherited by children and even grandchildren from relatives who were in league with demons.

As his first contribution, Koch built a theological argument identifying Germanic magical healing as a satanic parody of spirit-filled ministry. This tradition is often called "*Brauche*" ("using" occult powers) or "pow-wow" in areas of the United States where it is still actively practiced. Healers, as folklorists have observed, do in fact resemble priests as channels of superhuman powers that drive away evil forces causing the illness. While no two powwowers use the same or even similar motions, their rituals are often analogous to those of a priest's blessing. Koch also notes this similarity (1962:76) and argues that the healing ritual was in fact a close counterfeit of institutional Christian liturgy. The healer's conventional invocation of the Trinity or "three holy names" corresponded to addressing God in prayer; use of a charm was equivalent to use of the Scriptures; symbolic actions such as drawing the ailment to the healer matched sacramental laying on of hands; and the fetish often used related to holy water or the Sacrament (1962:85).

Folklorists also have noted that the healing ritual has a strong element of counseling, in that the healer typically begins by encouraging patients to talk about their problems. Thomas E. Graves stresses that the powwower is "a caring person to whom troubles and anxieties may be told and thus lessened." Similarly, patients are usually given opportunities to discuss their fears in between repetitions of the ritual (1992:638–40). In short, folk healers in the Germanic tradition often function as exorcists, banishing not only the ailment but also the evil spirits that caused it. Through this image of healing and through the informal discussions that accompany the ritual, healers may also function as folk counterparts to religious/psychological counselors such as Koch. When one recognizes, too, that such folk traditions were often passed on and practiced by females in the face of a patriarchal religious institution, we see how the powwower could be considered a serious folk rival to the institutionally ordained pastor or priest. This may be why the subversive essayist Henry David Thoreau commented in 1849, "In the most civilized countries the priest is still but a Powwow, and the physician a Great Medicine. . . . Priests and physicians should never look one another in the face. They have no common ground, nor is there any to mediate between them" (Thoreau 1985:209).

Koch was hardly original in attacking folk healing: many pastors before him had denounced it as superstitious and ignorant. But Koch believed that it was more than superstition; indeed it worked all too well. Rather than simply calling it irrational, he conceded that powwowers could produce medically valid cures. But he argued that such magical healing only appeared to have a beneficial effect. Healers usurped the priest's legitimate roles of counselor, psychiatrist, exorcist, and custodian of the Christian liturgy. Koch conceded that there was a direct relationship between the holy words of a prayer uttered by a priest and a holy power that empowers the miracle. But, he argued, "when a charmer uses biblical phrases, in doing so he severs them from God." When this occurs, the words, despite their holy origin, fall into the hands of the Devil. "The mechanical and magical usage of the words of the Bible," Koch argues, "is thus demonic and occult in nature" (1962:87–88).

It is often difficult to distinguish between miraculous healing as the result of prayer and charming, but he explains, "In the true prayer of faith, the person concerned submits completely to the will of God. In white magic the ideal is to compel God to act. With true prayer God is really involved, whereas in white magic the name of God is only used by way of a technical formula. Genuine prayer is inspired by the Holy Spirit. The white magician is inspired by the powers of darkness" (1962:76). In fact, such treatment secretly left spiritual wounds whose effect was, in Koch's system, far more damaging than the physical ailments that were cured. Such unfortunate after-effects were the logical consequence of engaging in a craft forbidden by God. "The compensation is far in excess of the help one apparently experiences," he argued. "Satan cheats his victims every time" (1962:89–90).

His second major contribution lay in his use of existing psychological terminology to define the mechanism by which this spiritual harm was caused. It is well known, Koch notes, that disorders in the mental realm could lead to physical, "psychosomatic" illnesses. But he argued that the reverse was also true: magical cures of organic illnesses were actually curses that could lead to mental disorders. This explained why those who apparently had been healed successfully by charming later on fell prey to mental illnesses. In some cases, the problems could be traced to conscious guilt over having dabbled in sorcery. In other instances, as when a child was charmed at birth, the effects of the magic healing led to otherwise inexplicable physical and mental problems, as in one case cited by Koch:

During the birth of a baby girl the midwife noticed that the child had a rupture. This was not treated at once but the midwife advised the family to take some of the excrement of the child and to bury it in a place which was out of reach of the light of both the sun and the moon. They took this strange advice and the infant's rupture disappeared. However, as the child grew up she developed a festering of her nasal bone. A purulent discharge constantly drained from her nose. No medical treatment helped. By her late twenties the trouble had still not cleared up, and in addition to this complaint the girl suffered from a compulsion to swear. She often had to scream and curse and she would shake for no apparent reason. (1962:90)

Koch's psychoanalytical model was derived from the work of Alfred Brauchel, a Swiss naturopath. Brauchel had relied on the concept of engrams to show how traumas caused by physical illnesses could later resurface in the form of mental problems (1972:138–42).[4] Koch argued that when magical healing took place, the physical trauma was not in fact exorcised; rather, it moved to the "organic unconsciousness" and became an engram that could later produce mental disorders. "Magical healings are therefore not really healings at all," he concludes, "but merely transferences from the organic to the psychic level" (1973a:121).

Such engrams might go unnoticed for years, Koch conceded, but the effect of magic "cuts a person off from God and turns him toward the worship of idols." Occult bondage allowed most people to live quite peacefully in the world, but it blocked their spiritual development. As a Charismatic Lutheran, this development was crucial for Koch. In one tract he wrote:

> I confess ... that through God's grace I belong to the communio
> sanctorum, to the Body of Jesus Christ. This Church of Christ is
> drawn from all denominations. A Catholic who has been born
> again or a brother of the Pentecostal movement who is scriptur-
> ally sound in faith is closer to me than a minister of my own
> Lutheran persuasion who is not a disciple of Christ. . . . A sectar-
> ian is a person who is cut off from the Body of Christ. A Lutheran
> is a sectarian if he is not a born again Christian. (1969:36)

Thus, like most Charismatics, Koch saw the need for intense religious experience as more crucial to Christian faith than official church doctrines. When a person experienced difficulty or misgivings about being born again, then, Koch saw symptoms of satanic interference with the "communio sanctorum." Mental instability during a quest for conversion was especially likely to be caused by demon-implanted engrams. The psychological agitation was itself a satanic trick because uninformed secular doctors often diagnosed the problem as religious mania when in fact the problem was the believer's inability to experience a full surrender to God. "The rule is quite simple," Koch concluded, "the devil will not trouble a person so long as he remains his servant. Only when his victim wants to leave his 'school' does the resistance begin" (Koch and Lechler 1970:33–35).

It is for this reason that Koch insisted that those he counseled search their minds for every form of folk magic they might have practiced and confess it as a sin. "Every form of sorcery," Koch argued, "is in reality a contract with the powers of darkness. The devil therefore accepts this as his right to take people captive, and will resist strongly at the first hint of his having to lose his victim." In this, Koch reinforced the deliverance ministry's emphasis that full baptism in the Holy Spirit was hindered or blocked by unconfessed sins. The crucial difference, though, was that the earlier emphasis focused on venial sins such as unpaid debts or drinking habits. Koch, by focusing on widespread traditions of folk magic, made it nearly certain that those seeking revival would have participated in "occult sins" in some way. In short, Koch made *folklore* the door through which Satan entered.

And even if individuals had had only trivial contact with magic, chronic mental problems could also be traced to demon possession through folklore. Koch's third and most long-lasting contribution to the deliverance mythology was his argument that the effects of "occult sins" were multigenerational. That is, mental illness could be caused by individuals' own dabbling with the occult or, equally, to the use of folk magic by parents or grandparents. One reason underlying this argument was the belief that white magic was as satanic as black, and the same persons who promised to help patients could and often did use their powers aggressively to harm them.

The interaction of "good" and "bad" healing powers, often wielded by the same individual, is a regular and presumably functional part of this tradition of belief. Certainly the dual role of healers has been amply described in other cultures' traditions of belief, notably that of the African Diaspora (e.g., Jackson 1976). Koch, with reason, took stories showing the dark side of *Brauchers* as proving the evil source of their power, and he was fond of stories in which apparently innocent practices were later exposed as evidence of a satanic pact.

Koch relied on widespread folk traditions of becoming a witch through some sort of ritual demonic pact.[5] Likewise, he accepted stories that described the effect of such pacts on the children of such sorcerers. One woman, who claimed to have subscribed both herself and her unborn child to the Devil, later saw the child suffer early senility (1970:25–26). And a man who contracted with the Devil to gain a wife from a higher social class later fathered twins that were born "horribly disfigured" (1962:93).[6]

Stories and rumors current among American healers frequently assume that a witch is likely to—perhaps even obligated to—cause the death of a child or other family member in exchange for her magical gifts (Randolph 1947:268; Yoder 1962:34; Stewart 1976:16). Hence, in traditional witchcraft stories, the gaining of supernatural powers accomplishes the exact reverse of healing and making the community whole. Koch adopted this belief in his own theory: even when children seem at first to be unaffected or unaware of their parents' occult powers, they still suffer in later life. His contribution lies in redefining this traditional legend format with psychological concepts.

Alfred Brauchel, Koch's mentor, had agreed with Jung that humans shared a collective subconscious, in which the history of the species is passed on from parent to child. They also inherited a family subconscious, he reasoned, in which the experiences of ancestors enter and "find their way, as the runes of fate, into the hereditary chain and are retained in the following generation." Psychoanalyst Alfred Lechler agreed that one need not actively dabble in magic to become oppressed by demons. If parents or grandparents were occultists and tried to transfer their powers to their relatives, they too would "fall under the ban of the devil" (Koch and Lechler 1970:138–39).

Koch extended this concept: when parents practiced healing, they created engrams in this middle level of the subconscious. These "enter the hereditary chain and constitute a latent breeding ground and efficient cause for psychological disorders in the next generation." No overt ceremony was necessary to pass the mental effects of occultism to children; indeed, children may be totally unaware of their parents' satanic involvement. Such engrams may fade rapidly if the children avoid occult activity; on the other hand, they may reappear as serious mental problems when children or grandchildren dabble with magic (1972:138). Or problems may appear when individuals seriously become involved in revivalist religion, for, as Koch observed, "The powers of darkness continue to claim their right of ownership although quite often the descendents remain completely unaware of the fact, perhaps since they have had no contact with sorcery themselves. Nevertheless immediately a person in this situation is converted, Satan very soon makes his claim felt" (Koch and Lechler 1970:100).

In cases in which mental problems could not be traced to any occult activity on the part of the victims themselves, Koch encouraged them to investigate the backgrounds of their friends. He warned any person determined to be suffering from occult oppression to "break off relationships with any of his friends who continues to practice occultism, or who is affected by it, even if the person is his best friend" (1973a:152). If such a search proved fruitless, then one should look to parents or grand-parents for the source of demonic influence. If blood relatives proved to be practitioners of folk healing or other occult practices, Koch insisted, those whom he counseled should demand that they renounce their activities. If they refused, they should break off contact with them. In one case, he told a woman undergoing counseling to leave home, as "the evil powers which dwelt in her parent's house would surely make her life into hell if she tried to follow Jesus." The young girl did so, but found herself mentally attacked whenever she remembered her mother in her prayers. Koch advised her to stop praying for her mother. "Sometimes," he adds, "I advise the children of spiritistic families not to pray for their parents at all if they are still engaged in occult practices. . . . This is not a form of pious egotism. I cannot hope to help others spiritually, until I myself have been saved" (Koch and Lechler 1970:93).

Blood-Pleading as Ritual Magic

While Koch built his ministry around opposition to folk healing, other Charismatics freely introduced practices from *Brauche* into their ministry. H.A. Maxwell Whyte came from a British family that was fascinated by fringe religion and the occult. His mother was a follower of Joanna Southcott, the nineteenth-century "female Christ" of Manchester, and several aunts and uncles participated in table-turning, automatic writing, séances, and medium trances. In 1939, however, Maxwell Whyte converted to Pentecostalism through a prayer group that traced its origin to Catherine Price's 1907 London revival, which induced exorcism and glossolalia through "pleading the Blood." In this group, The Blood first functioned as a kind of initiation into the Holy Spirit: when Maxwell Whyte found himself unable to pronounce the word, his companions then pled the Blood on his behalf. Maxwell Whyte recalls that he immediately fell flat on his face, stiffened like a board. "It was years later," he wrote, "when I realized that, at that moment, an evil spirit . . . had left me, by the honouring of the Blood of Jesus" (1973c:23–24). A week later he returned to the meeting, pled The Blood freely, and at once was able to speak in tongues. Interestingly, his mother joined him in Charismatic worship, likewise speaking freely in tongues. "I know all about these things!" she told her baffled son, and staunchly refused to burn her Southcott books. "What she really meant," Maxwell Whyte commented later, "was that she was familiar with Satan's counterfeits" (1973a: 23–24).

After World War II, Maxwell Whyte emigrated to Canada and set up a Charismatic ministry in Toronto. By 1948 he had begun to use deliverance as a means of dealing with parishioners' problems such as arthritis, homosexuality, and addiction to cigarettes. He describes one member who had severe asthma and was also a heavy smoker, even though the church had prayed to relieve him of this habit. One day, Maxwell Whyte suggested an experiment: "It is possible that you may have a smoking demon." A reformed Catholic, the member agreed to an exorcism, during which he, his wife, and Maxwell Whyte sang choruses of hymns that emphasized the Blood of Jesus, then demanded that the demon come out. The result was a lengthy bout of coughing and vomiting, during which the floor became covered with sputum-soaked handkerchiefs. But in the end, says Maxwell Whyte, the man was healed: years later, he could breathe normally and no longer had the urge to smoke (1973b:37–38).

Maxwell Whyte initially seems to follow the traditional line that gifts of the spirit, such as tongues and prophecy, are not magical in that they come freely from God, not as a result of humans' desire for change to occur in conformity with their will. "We do not think [tongues] up at all," he argued; "we simply receive them through our spirits. Any so-called gift which comes only from the human mind is a counterfeit gift." Similarly, he says, when a minister is given prophetic insight during prayer, such a revelation "is not sought after" but is "word of knowledge given by God." Therefore, one should not ask even spirit-filled persons to utter prophecy on demand, as they might be tempted to abuse the gift and so "attract to themselves another spirit" (1973a:44).

Nevertheless, Maxwell Whyte claims that once man truly uses his spirit, "he has opened the door into the spiritual realm. . . . *By the operation of his own free will*, he can have *free* converse with Almighty God and with the angels from time to time" [emphasis mine]. This comes remarkably close to Crowley's credo, that magick is "causing change to occur in conformity with Will." Such a practice is dangerous, Maxwell Whyte concedes. Unless the believer maintains his righteousness in the face of God, "he can easily be seduced by an angel of light . . . who will come to woo him in much the same way an immoral woman would endeavor to win the affections of a married man" (1973b:19–20).

So it was essential for the faithful Christian to recognize and avoid immoral supernatural practices. Like many Pentecostals who renounced a spiritualist background, Maxwell Whyte considered non-Christian magic not merely a delusion but a genuine threat. Therefore, the phenomena produced during séances and their folk counterparts such as Ouija board rituals were not bogus or imaginary. Maxwell Whyte stresses: "*They are real, but they are not of God* [emphasis his]. They are brought about through demon powers. . . . and if we open our lives, through disobedience to God's Holy Word, we then become the servants of these same demon powers" (1973b:89).

Given the omnipresence of demonic influence, some simple means was needed to shield spirit-filled Christians from the prostitute-like "angels of light" who otherwise would try to seduce them during their spiritual quest. So Maxwell Whyte's *The Power of the Blood*, written in 1959, proved his most influential work. The book is a lengthy description of the theory and practice of pleading the Blood to defeat demonic influences and gain spiritual power. "As New Testament believer-priests," he argues, "we are to take the living Blood of Jesus and 'sprinkle' it with our tongues before the Lord by repeating the word 'Blood.' Immediately, we begin to bring Satan's work into bondage and nullify his evil workings" (1973a:79–80). He refused to set rules for pleading the Blood, except that it be done "in simple believing faith." While some fellow pastors reiterated the whole phrase, "I plead the Blood of Jesus," Maxwell Whyte seems to have preferred simply to say "The Blood" three times, and he noted that still others found that repeating the one word "Blood" worked just as well (1973a:74).

Reference to The Blood provided a miraculous tool for casting out evil spirits and making contact with the divine. "The devil hates the mention of the Blood of Jesus," Maxwell Whyte observes; nothing disturbed evil personalities more than its mention (1973a:19–20). Thus, many deliverance ceremonies used explicit reference to Jesus' Blood as the ultimate weapon in forcing demons to leave victims. Conversely, to summon the Holy Spirit to baptize groups in the spirit, Maxwell Whyte explains, "I have simply instructed them to start repeating the word 'Blood,' and within a matter of seconds they have begun to speak in tongues. Usually I then call over another worker and suggest that he or she praise God *with* them so that they do not stop speaking in tongues. They are now entering another spiritual dimension, and it is wonderfully strange! It is important that they do not begin to doubt at this point" (1973a:83; emphasis his). Strange indeed, since the constant repetition of the word "blood" at some level must bring to mind, consciously or preconsciously, the many cultural taboos against contact with animal or human blood. Given Maxwell Whyte's British background, also, the verbal use of "blood" as a blessing must be seen against the vulgar use of "bloody" as a curse word. Thus, the concept of using divine blood, however intellectualized, during magical rituals must be seen against the context of ancient and culturally universal beliefs about real blood.

Anthropologists and folklorists have identified several levels of widespread beliefs concerning blood. Most immediately it is thought to contain or even constitute the life force of an animal or human. Therefore, sacrifice or consumption of blood in some sense makes use of the spirit of a sacrificed being through an act of ceremonial magick. Maxwell Whyte, like others in his camp, is quite aware of the primitive underpinnings of this concept. He points to the huge spiritual value placed on blood in Old Testament times, when "the priests offered physical sacrifices of animals. The flesh was burned with fire, but the blood was drained into basins and was USED by being sprinkled" (1973a:79). The Biblical emphasis on ritual blood sprinkling—often in huge amounts—is a reminder of "the tremendous value that God puts on blood" (1973a:58–59).[7]

However, he adds, after Jesus' crucifixion, the limitless river of His spiritual Blood freed humans from the need to sacrifice animals for the sake of using their literal blood. The central Christian ritual of the Eucharist, nevertheless, continues this older tradition by associating the drinking of wine with literal consumption of Jesus' blood. However theologized, such an act falls in line with a universal practice of absorbing the soul of a divine entity by consuming its blood, a form of ritual cannibalism.

Particularly powerful taboos insisted that magical blood be defined as male in origin; otherwise, it risked being thought of as parallel to female, or menstrual blood. Before modern understanding of the nature of conception, the fetus was thought to develop partially from the nurturing blood provided by the female. Hence, menstrual blood was thought too charged with magical power to be touched, particularly by males, and most cultures, both western and non-western, have surrounded the topic with extraordinarily powerful cultural barriers.

Significantly, Maxwell Whyte devoted one of his most complex discussions to explaining why female blood was totally irrelevant to the power of (patriarchal) Blood—because Jesus' conception was unique and miraculous. He adopts the modern understanding of childbirth, admitting that a normal conception would involve a female ovum. But in Jesus' case, he says, this ovum, though itself bloodless, would still carry the genetic heritage of "Adamic blood" and so would be conceived with the stain of sin. Even if God had miraculously created a sperm that fertilized Mary's ovum, the resulting fetus would be an entity "conceived with mixed blood, part of Adam and part of God." But Jesus' body, Maxwell Whyte says, was miraculously placed as a living entity in Mary's womb, so His blood type was not dependent in any way on a female's genetic code. "As the Blood type of the Son of God was a separate and precious type," he concludes, "it is inconceivable that Mary would have supplied any of her Adamic blood for the spotless Lamb of God. All the Child's Blood came from His Father in Heaven by a supernatural creative act of God."

Eve's sin tainted the blood line of Adam, as patriarchal theologians remind us, but Jesus' blood, by divine intervention, was wholly male-derived and, as Maxwell Whyte points out, was "thereafter protected by the placenta from any flow of the mother's blood into the fetus" (1973a:15–16). To paraphrase the argument, "Adamic blood," permanently corrupted by female influence, is like menstrual blood, bringing sickness and death to those who contact it. Divine Blood, by contrast, is wholly distinct from female blood and thus alone can cleanse Christians' souls and protect their bodies from demon-caused diseases.

Maxwell Whyte's testimonies and illustrations describe a wide range of supernatural results brought about by blood-pleading. Many of these represent continuations of the very folk magical practices decried by Koch: for instance, using The Blood to stop bleeding or to "put out the fire" of accidental burns and accelerate healing (1973a:52–53, 84; 1973b:71). In fact, Maxwell Whyte managed to link the folk tradition of magical healing practices with his theological concept of Jesus' Blood. His pleading the Blood to cause supernatural healing is similar in many ways to the mechanism of *Brauche*, as described by folklorists. Conceding that germs are the immediate cause of illness, he adds:

> We may well ask ourselves if God does not have some way of
> protecting his people from these germs. God is omnipotent, and
> nothing is beyond His power. Certainly, He can send His
> ministering spirits to protect us and to prevent evil spirits from

putting the germs (or spores) into our bodies, if we pray for
protection and keep God's laws. Remember that nothing
happens by "chance" or luck, but all is ordered by God. Demons
are merely agents in the hands of Satan to do his work at his
bidding in the same way that soldiers obey their officers.
(1973b:70–71)

Elsewhere, he stresses, "We must realize that Satan is the author of all
damage to the body. Demons try to attack any injured part of our body
and permit germs, which are always around us, to impinge on the injured flesh and do their work of destruction and poisoning. But when
the Blood of Jesus is applied in faith, it acts as a covering which prevents
Satan from attacking us with germs" (1973a:53). Germs, Maxwell Whyte
adds, will be destroyed at the Second Coming. In the meantime, he says,
"When boiling water has been spilt on human flesh, immediate 'pleading of the Blood' over such an injured person has prevented inflamma-
tion, showing clearly that it is the demons which visit the germs on the
injured part of the body." The Blood of Christ, Maxwell Whyte concludes,
is "the finest disinfectant in the world" (1973b:71–72). So even in cases
of physical injury, some form of demonization is necessary in order for
infection to occur, according to Maxwell Whyte's scheme. Blood-pleading banishes the demon associated with the injury, allowing the body of
the believer to heal itself.

Such a concept would have been quite familiar to Brauchers and
powwowers. Most charms, folklorist Don Yoder has observed, are magical conjurations addressing the affliction and demanding that it cease
its action or leave the body. They define the healing ritual as a kind of
exorcism, Yoder notes: "Disease is believed to be demonic, 'sent' by evil
forces into the person or animal; hence, it has to be removed by a
'counterspell.'. . ." Defining medicine in such terms, he concludes, links
it with exorcism as parallel forms of transference of evil (1972:203). Indeed, Maxwell Whyte defined demons as incorporate beings possessing
a "malign intelligence" and swarming around the unwitting Christian
"like mosquitos in northern Canada" (1973b: 52–53). He believed that
"the primary causes of such death-dealing sicknesses as cancer [and]
heart failure" were seemingly innocent acts such as reading syndicated
daily horoscopes. Such a habit was akin to "Russian roulette," he argued,
for "By seeking knowledge from these sources we can open ourselves to
demons that may cause arthritis and other crippling diseases" (1973c:80).

Because they have a personality, they can be rebuked, placed under the power of The Blood, and ordered to leave the victim's body.

Maxwell Whyte's use of The Blood also included magical protections from danger at home or during travel. Every night during the Blitz, he recalled, he ritually covered himself and his family with The Blood. Consequently, even though one night thirteen block busters landed close by, their home suffered only minor damage, and none of his family was hurt (1973a:23). Maxwell Whyte also describes his use of The Blood to ensure safety while traveling by plane or car, and notes that an English brother, faced with a car that would not start, pled The Blood and got it to turn over (1973a:87).

And Blood pleading also promised financial rewards to some believers. On one instance, a church member complained that she was losing money because she could not rent out an apartment she owned. "The Lord showed us," Maxwell Whyte says, "that this was . . . the work of Satan to withhold money, to disturb, frustrate and impoverish." After a group pled the Blood in every room and closet, the apartment was rented within two days (1973b:54–55). Although he noted that "carnal-minded Christians" might scorn such testimony, he records that two American believers chose to sprinkle The Blood over their paychecks and soon after received unexpected bonuses in cash (1973a:87).

"We are convinced," Maxwell Whyte says, "that the whole Church has yet to learn the value of *using* the Blood of Jesus [emphasis his]. To those who have discovered this secret, the whole realm of God's power is opened" (1973a:32). Such statements are difficult to distinguish from the philosophy of ceremonial magicians like Crowley. Indeed, Maxwell Whyte's "Blood work" represents a patriarchal Christian appropriation of a folk mythology that provided many females with counseling and spiritual healing powers equivalent to those possessed by priests. It is therefore no surprise that the threat of female witchcraft was a special concern of his. In a series of booklets, among them *The Kiss of Satan*, he attacked a wide range of occult practices, ranging from eastern religions to astrology. But his emphasis was often focused on female magic, understandably, given his family's focus on Joanna Southcott's feminist revision of Christianity. By 1973 he was convinced that there was a practicing adolescent "witch" in every American high school (1973b:85). He described challenging many young "witches" who did not appear evil, but when faced with The Blood, the demons inside these women responded, twisting the subjects' bodies and often speaking or laughing eerily from their lips (1973c:91; cf. Basham 1972:111). The testimony of these demons, in turn, powerfully reinforced Maxwell Whyte's conviction that only The Blood stood between the true Christian and total domination by satanic powers.

Conclusions

Both theologians, in their ways, presented deliverance both as a necessary first step to personal conversion and as a type of medicine. Maxwell Whyte was the most literal here, showing how demons could be responsible for ailments ranging from smoking to arthritis. But Koch, while he mainly deals with mental illness, implies that demons cause physical ailments such as the persistent nasal infections of the charmed baby. Even in cases where no physical ailment is obvious, the concept of the engram or hidden psychic injury implies a literal "mark of the devil" left by magical healing. And both agreed that any and all forms of folk magic were forms of closet Satanism that placed the practitioner in bondage to demons. Such bondage was not just individual but could be passed on, consciously or unconsciously, to children.

Ironically, this belief in fact demonstrates that the techniques the deliverance ministry appropriated from folklore were a form of "Christian magic." By reintroducing the scapegoat element of traditional witchcraft into his mythology, Koch simplified the path to absolution. Rather than locate the fault within oneself, one need only identify the individual or group responsible for causing the trouble. Blood-pleading, as it developed under Maxwell Whyte, was an all-encompassing form of occult self-defense similar to *Brauche*. By defining virtually any difficulty or disease as caused by demons, it confirmed Satan's influence as ubiquitous. Thus, active use of magical phrases and rituals were necessary in order to fight this pervasively diabolical influence.

If Maxwell Whyte was the most dramatic advocate for the reality of good and evil magic within the practice of deliverance, Koch deserves credit as its principal theorist who explained in psychological terms exactly what was happening. He produced a "demonic psychiatry" that showed how parents' participation in magical practices would lead to mental disorders in their children. In so doing, Koch laid the groundwork for what became a standard diagnosis in some forms of Christian psychiatry: tracing a patient's mental problems to ritual magic practiced by blood relatives. He also was the earliest and most widely cited authority who defined non-authorized magic—even charms in the name of the Trinity —as a form of occult child abuse. The concepts of engrams and multigenerational demonization formed a "diabolical medicine" that would later be developed into the essential theory of satanic ritual abuse.

2

The Jesus of Satan

Deliverance and Spiritualism

If you ask for the Holy Spirit, you'll get the Holy
Spirit. No one has ever asked the Father for
the Holy Spirit and received an unholy spirit.
—H.A. Maxwell Whyte, *Demons and Deliverance*

To this point, we have focused on the theology that motivated this movement's opposition to the occult. H.A. Maxwell Whyte and Kurt E. Koch provided a theoretical background for the deliverance ministry, showing how Satan gained power over otherwise devout individuals through their sins or those of their blood relatives. They also described how believers could avoid or minimize the chance of demonic attack, through using magic phrases and rituals. Given the terms of this institutional mythology, though, it was practically impossible to dwell in this world without giving in to some venial or trivially occult sin such as reading one's newspaper horoscope or opening a fortune cookie. For this reason, even born-again Christians were obsessed by one or more personal demons. To rid themselves of these forces, participants in deliverance needed some way to confront and banish these internal personalities.

The passion of this crusade, therefore, was not based on intellectual issues but the sense that one was directly experiencing contact with existential good and evil. The goal was what Koch termed the "true surrender," the experience of being overshadowed by the Holy Spirit, without which one could never be a true Christian. And to gain victory over satanic power, one needed to experience both the ecstasy of the Holy Spirit and the agony of deliverance. Thus, it is essential to look objectively at both these experiences, the holy and the blasphemous, and understand how they were intimately related.

Traditional folklorists looking at what they traditionally defined as "folk beliefs" or "folk religion" have tended to look at witchcraft, glossolalia, or exorcism as practices of people who were irrational or at least uncritical about the nature of observed events. A person raised in a culture that believed in demons, for example, would interpret readily explainable events in terms of demonic influence. In short, the perceived experience is no more than a reflection of what a culture persuades an individual to view. Hence, it would be tempting to look at the religious practice of exorcism as a projection of ideas circulated among credulous persons by theologians such as Maxwell Whyte and Koch.

This approach has been effectively challenged by David Hufford in his work on "the Old Hag." He argues that demon possession, as well as other extraordinary events, should be studied not as reflections of culture but on their own terms, as experiences widely shared among many different people. Culture, of course, puts a name and an interpretation on these experiences, but Hufford argues that many of them are universal, found in essentially the same form among societies widely separated by time and space. His student, James McClenon (1994), has documented this theory in detail, finding widespread evidence that hauntings, precognition, near-death experiences, and other forms of the "paranormal" actually appear to be normal elements of cultures from the earliest records to modern day industrialized societies. Thomas Bullard (1989, 1995, 1998) has taken a similar approach to UFO abductions, showing that in spite of wide differences among the ways in which they were remembered and documented, they appear to reflect a common structure and thus a common experience.

This experiential approach to extraordinary events does not commit the researcher to "believe in" experiences such as demon possession in the sense that one feels constrained by a specific *interpretation* of them. Even in the literature one finds widely varying interpretations. Alternate "selves" arising within an individual may be seen as caused by demons, benevolent spirit guides, traumatic splits within the personality, or the souls of people tragically killed or otherwise "earthbound." What seems constant is the dramatic sense that the "usual" personality of the individual has somehow been replaced by another. D. Martyn Lloyd-Jones, a prominent British Methodist minister with medical training, gives an especially clear description of this state.

One clear diagnostic point is that one becomes aware of a dual personality. There is another person. You see it in the face, hear it in the voice. It is an unnatural and quite different voice and can very often be accompanied by horrifying facial expressions. There is also—a most important point—an alternation between what we may call a normal and an abnormal element. These persons can be one moment quite normal and can discuss things quite readily for a time; then suddenly they change. The "other" person seems to take charge. They will tell you that they are conscious of suggestions and voices; and frequently that they have come to have abnormal powers. (1988:165–66)

Before deliverance emerged, a large quantity of popular and scholarly literature on demon possession already existed, including descriptions of what was even then known as "multiple personality."[1] As early as 1886, French psychologist Pierre Janet had experimented with a form of exorcism in his clinical work in Paris, though he assumed that the "demonic" personalities he was able to evoke in his patients were fragments of the patient's primary personality, not objective beings. In 1895, American missionary John Nevius published *Demon Possession and Allied Themes*, an account of native exorcisms he and other missionaries had witnessed in China. Shortly after giving a lecture on the topic in 1896, American psychologist William James wrote to Nevius's editor, promising to promote the book. He commented,

I am not as positive as you are . . . in the belief that the obsessing agency is really demonic individuals. I am perfectly willing to adopt that theory if the facts lend themselves best to it, for who can trace limits to the hierarchies of personal existence in the world? . . . I am convinced that we stand with all these things at the threshold of a long enquiry, of which the end appears as yet to no one, least of all myself. . . . The first thing is to start the medical profession out of its idiotically *conceited ignorance* [emphasis his] of all such matters—matters which have everywhere and at all times played a vital part in human history." (Taylor 1984:109–10)

In 1968, Nevius's book was reprinted by Kregel Publishers, Kurt E. Koch's American publisher, and it became a standard reference for the deliverance movement.

Further, both Catholic and Protestant exorcists described a ritual with a specific structure. The normal ritual begins with a series of prayers that *invoke* the power of God and then force the possessing demon to *name* itself. A ritualized *dialogue* follows in which the exorcist seeks to determine when and how the spirits entered and demands to know the time of their departure. In the normal rite, after such information is determined, a *confrontation* follows in which the demons usually curse and threaten the exorcist or the person they claim to possess. Many exorcisms end with some sort of "sign" that the demon has in fact been expelled, after which the ritual is *terminated*.[2]

One need not prove that the alternate personality has a reality outside the person displaying it in order to accept that deliverance is an objectively real experience. As McClenon points out, if a significant part of a subculture accepts both these events and a given religious interpretation, then they have real effects on the believer. Further, if we can show that similar events have similar features, then we can further accept that these experiences are not unique to believers in deliverance but are probably ubiquitous (1994:7–10). Indeed, Felicitas D. Goodman (1988) has found similar rites and experiences among many world cultures. Further, she has found that the experience of glossolalia is closely allied with demon possession in some cultures, in some cases indistinguishable from it. This is a link that was clear to those within the deliverance ministry. Indeed, both seem to be two sides of a common coin—an induced experience that brought about a voluntary dissociation of personalities. Over and over, we find situations in which individuals, under hypnosis or through some other alternate state of consciousness, allow their dominant personalities to be passive, thus allowing the indwelling "spirits" to speak, identify themselves, and perform in public.

Don Basham: The Practical Exorcist

Don Basham (1926–1989) was strongly influenced by personal contacts with Maxwell Whyte but also incorporated Koch's theories into his own practice. Born in Wichita Falls, Texas, Basham first became a commercial artist, then left this field in 1951 to become a minister. During his studies at Phillips University, a Christian college in Oklahoma, he became interested in the Charismatic movement, and together with his wife he formed a weekly prayer group. However, after several group participants had received Holy Spirit baptism and practiced speaking in tongues and faith healing, rumors about his prayer group began to spread among the more conservative members of this college. "We were accused of holding séances and practicing voodoo," he recalled. "Some claimed we were experimenting with hypnotism and were putting one another into trances. It was even said that we turned out all the lights and held wild sex parties" (1967:78; cf. 1986:138–39).

There was, to be sure, a grain of truth to these libels, as Basham admits. Like Maxwell Whyte, Basham came from a background strongly influenced by spiritualism. While in seminary, he also attended a Spiritualist church led by a trance medium who gave advice to her followers in the persona of "Minnie Marie Blackburn." The Sunday evening services, he recalls, attracted ten to fifteen people, who would each place a folded-up question in a basket. After "an old-fashioned gospel hymn" was sung, the medium went into a trance and answered the questions, without, however, touching the papers or the basket. Although the medium was blindfolded, Basham stresses, "The meetings were all conducted in the open, in bright light, where the proceedings could be viewed clearly" (1972:130–33).

Basham also confessed that he was once invited to a private séance with the famous Canadian medium Arthur Ford, and was so excited that he could not sleep the night before (Basham and Leggatt 1974:85). Unwilling to become a medium himself, however, Basham turned away from the practice and eventually recognized it as "a lie-world of the supernatural, a whole realm of counterfeit spiritual experience. Oh, real enough in the sense of being authentically supernatural! But a deadly counterfeit in that it places the innocent seeker, not in touch with God, or the spirits of departed loved ones, as he supposes, but with the very powers of darkness themselves" (1972:130). Like Maxwell Whyte, he confessed his occult background as a sin, formally renounced it, and eventually cast out the demon who had been encouraging his spiritualist interests. His "benign toleration" for occultism then turned abruptly to "acute loathing and disgust" (1972:135–36).

After being ordained, Basham moved to Toronto, where he headed a Disciples of Christ church and became friends with Maxwell Whyte. His ministry focused on tongue-speaking and healing, but his work was daunted by a series of failures and conflicts with parishioners, first in Toronto, then in Sharon, Pennsylvania. Forsaking a regular ministry,

Basham and his wife traveled to Florida, where he chose to make his living writing and giving lectures on Holy Spirit baptism.

Basham's uses of The Blood were not as ceremonial as Maxwell Whyte's, although he reprints testimony from one couple who successfully used a method given on one of Basham's "television seminars" to rebuke a "demon of infirmity" that caused their five-year-old's nosebleeds (Basham & Leggatt 1974:103). Such a practice incorporated *Brauche* methods for "stopping the blood" through a magical transference of evil. More influential were Maxwell Whyte's methods of treating illnesses by naming and expelling demons. In Cleveland to take part in a Charismatic workshop, Basham re-encountered Maxwell Whyte, who was there to talk on casting out demons. Asked to assist at a counseling session following one of Maxwell Whyte's lectures, Basham was present when a young woman challenged his patriarchal views on occultism, "I consider myself a Christian," she began, "yet I feel I've been greatly helped by some of the very practices you condemned in your talk. I believe in extrasensory perception. I read my horoscope daily, and at times spirits from the other side have communicated with me, giving me helpful advice. I cannot accept the authority of the Bible the way you do. It was written by men and some of its teachings are cruel and judgmental." However, after Maxwell Whyte's first exorcism, Basham saw the same woman utter a piercing scream and go into convulsions. The climax of the crisis convinced him that he was confronting evil forces: "Now from her lips came an eerie laugh, more sinister than anything I had ever heard. It sent shivers all the way down my spine. I didn't know what to do but hang onto her arm. I was shaken to my very depths. 'That laugh!' Maxwell Whyte exclaimed. 'I'd recognize it anywhere. Witchcraft!'" Indeed, when Maxwell Whyte addressed the "demon of witchcraft" and commanded it to leave, she went limp and after regaining her composure apologized, admitting that "some power" had been compelling her to read "strange books" (1972:111–12).

Basham at once applied Maxwell Whyte's practices to those he counseled in Florida. The results were dramatic on more than one level. When he challenged the demons inside Stella, the first woman he counseled, a "demon of hate" manifested itself in a gaze of "crafty intelligence" that nearly hypnotized Basham and spoke in a "metallic tone" quite different from the woman's own. After this demon left, Stella claimed she could hear more voices arguing inside her, and Basham demanded that they name themselves. "Vanity" then spoke in "a high, whiny voice" different from the other two. In the following two hours, twenty evil spirits named themselves and left, bitterly complaining. Basham commented, "If Stella had been the greatest character actress of the century and if she had rehearsed her role for a year, she could not have played half so many parts half so convincingly. Some of the distorted expressions her face assumed, some of the exaggerated voices, had to be seen and heard to be believed" (1972:116–18).

Basham's own contribution to the deliverance ministry was twofold. First, he made multiple deliverance, unusual in the older exorcism tradition, the norm in his work. Testimonials published by Basham describe instances in which dozens of demons were cast out, over a hundred in one case. And these demons were self-named by the person undergoing deliverance, mainly physical conditions or weaknesses that had bothered them. Where the older tradition required the naming of the afflicting demon in a standard demonological hierarchy, Basham's system allowed victims to identify their own circles of hell.

For instance, Basham reprints one letter from J. Lawton Smith, M.D., a member of the University of Miami School of Medicine. Trained as an ophthalmologist, Dr. Smith received Holy Spirit baptism in October 1969. Soon after, he had "an evil dream" and inferred that it must have come from an evil spirit that manifested itself while he was asleep. Smith's testimony does not specify the nature of this dream, but as he later tells how "unclean sex spirits" were cast out, it is likely that the experience was an incubus, or involuntary sexual stimulation.

He went to two local evangelists, who in the usual way instructed him to confess all his sins. When one of the evangelists commanded a demon to name itself, Dr. Smith recalls, "I heard a voice speak out of my own larynx, (but with an entirely different tone and inflection than my own voice!) and say 'Finger nail biting!'" This was, he admits, a childhood habit that he had never been able to break, even as an adult. The ministers cast this and many other demons out during the next hours, including "allergy, sinusitis, [and] post-nasal drip." Many of them, he notes, "had prepubertal, adolescent voices and had come in when I was only a small child." Over the next five days, over a hundred demons revealed themselves, including those of gluttony, migraine headache, fear, and others. Subsequently, Dr. Smith learned how to pray in tongues to repel any returning demons, and his letter testified to his lasting victory. Smith concludes that demons try to keep Christians from believing in them; failing that, they try to make believers think they do not have a demon. The growing popularity of deliverance, he concluded, proves that "The Lord is cleaning up the believers so that they will be without spot or blemish and this is simply another sign of the lateness of the hour and the impending return of our Saviour" (1971a:88–90).[3]

This points to Basham's second contribution. The earlier Catholic-derived process of exorcism put a professional demon-hunter in charge of the process and assumed a grueling ordeal of ten to twelve hours— perhaps days or weeks (Martin 1976:16–17). Basham developed a less formal procedure that could be carried out by practically anyone in a matter of minutes. In his workshops, Basham practiced group deliverance, in which whole roomfuls of participants named and cast out their demons (1972:190–93). Indeed, Basham discovered, most afflicted Christians did not need to consult an exorcist, but they could initiate the process of deliverance in the privacy of their own homes, just like the experiences of Holy Spirit baptism and glossolalia. In a series of manuals, he described simple procedures that could be used by individuals who sought to speak in tongues or drive out demons in solitary. "We believe that no Christian's spiritual progress can be complete without this empowering," he concluded. "Therefore, no book dealing with the power of God can be complete without endeavoring to help the seeking Christian personally to experience the fullness of the Holy Spirit in his [sic] life" (1967:176). Believers could repeat Basham's recommended procedure in private as often as necessary, as the complete act of deliverance may take several days or weeks. Nevertheless, they could continue a normal life between self-deliverance sessions. Repeat episodes could be avoided by reading Scripture, maintaining a prayer life, submitting to spiritual authority, and avoiding contact with the occult. "All temptation to dabble again in any form of psychic or occult activity must be sternly resisted," Basham cautioned. "It is as foolish for a person who has been delivered from astrology to take a peek at the horoscope in the daily newspaper as it is for the reformed alcoholic to stop in at a bar for 'just one drink'" (Basham & Leggatt 1974:81–94; cf. Basham 1972:202–8).

Basham's Pennsylvania pastorate led him into association with Robert E. Whitaker, international director of the Full Gospel Business Men's Fellowship, one of the largest networks of secular Pentecostals and informal prayer groups, for whom Basham's do-it-yourself approach was ideal. Whitaker also ran a small press, which not only published several of Basham's manuals but also republished Maxwell Whyte's demonological works, making them widely available in the United States. Shortly after relocating in Florida, Basham joined the "Fort Lauderdale Five," an informal coalition of Charismatic ministers. His partners included Derek Prince, a British Cambridge-trained Charismatic who had relocated in the United States and was circulating his teachings in booklets and taped sermons. The others were Episcopalian Bob Mumford, Southern Baptist Charles Simpson, and W.J. "Ern" Baxter, an associate of the controversial faith-healing evangelist William Branham. Their common interest in Pentecostalism, they found, transcended their denominational differences.

Eventually joining the Fort Lauderdale Shepherd's Church, they founded the Christian Growth Ministries, which with its publication, *New Wine,* initiated what became known as the Shepherding Movement. Insisting that its participants meet weekly in closed meetings under the strict leadership of a "shepherd" chosen by God, the group often described itself in militaristic terms, fighting the Lord's battle against an alien world and expecting opposition from other denominations. Such was the concern raised by this group that in 1975 Pat Robertson, already a leading figure in the Christian Broadcasting Network, denounced the movement as a "cult." A meeting between the Five and other fundamentalist leaders that year resulted in a reconciliation, but even within the Charismatic movement many continued to criticize the leaders' "hypersensitivity and secrecy . . . even to the point of disallowing discussion of its doctrines and practices with others outside the group" (Shepherding Movement 1999).

Together, the coalition developed a library of audiotaped and videotaped ministries on a whole range of spiritual gifts including deliverance (1972:209–13). These formed the focus of an extremely influential Charismatic conduit. In early March 1970, Basham spoke one night in Schenectady, New York. Shortly afterwards, Pat Brooks, later an influential evangelist in her own right, wrote Basham two letters praising his preaching and workshops. She concluded, "The one tape we bought from those made the night you spoke here has been copied thirteen times. Copies are now in Pennsylvania, New Jersey, California, Nebraska, and Maryland. Every evangelical pastor in this area of any consequence has heard it! Far more people have heard you since your visit than heard you while you were here" (1971a:85–86).[4]

Tongues and Demons

The popularity of Basham's tracts and tapes, however, brought troublesome criticisms from within the very Christian communities that supported the deliverance conduits. Basham notes with surprise that even Pentecostals who endorsed glossolalia criticized his deliverance work, saying he "was demon-possessed and . . . glorifying Satan in [his] ministry" (1986:170). Worse, he had to contend with allegations of closet Satanism from within the deliverance ministry, for Koch himself frequently asserted that involvement in tongue-speaking was occultism disguised as religion. Thus, a bitter debate erupted in the early 1970s over which spiritual gifts should be practiced by spirit-filled Christians. The debate was intensified by the growing popularity of grassroots prayer groups, which often encouraged tongue-speaking and/or deliverance in networks outside of major denominations. When religious revivals developed, like the one that affected much of Western Canada in the early 1970s, vocal disagreements took place among and within these networks.

Like many other fundamentalists, Koch took a dim view of tongue-speaking. From his missionary work he observed that glossolalia was found among non-Christian religions, particularly in Third World countries; further, he had also learned that British secular spiritualists like Maxwell Whyte's mother had spoken in tongues (1973b:32–33). He conceded that there might be some instances in which this practice might be a sign of grace, especially when it was used as a form of private prayer. But perhaps 95 percent of the tongues movement, he concluded, was "mediumistic" in nature. Using his counseling records, he estimated that about 8 to 10 percent of Europeans were mediumistically inclined.

This tendency might originate through acts of sorcery such as folk magic, but, Koch argued, more often it was the result of multigenerational demonism. Using a version of his "family engram" theory, he reasoned:

> Latent mediumistic powers can be caused by the parents or
> grand-parents of a person committing sins connected with
> sorcery. Dabbling with fortune telling, magic, or spiritism
> develops such mediumistic powers and they then become heredi-
> tary factors. The children of such people are mediumistic, even
> when they do not realize it. This mediumism is not a sin of the

one who inherits, but it is a burden. Some people are also mediumistic because they were charmed magically when they were very young. . . . in almost all cases mediumism is an open door for the demonic. . . . A person carries his latent mediumistic powers over into his Christian life. Later he discovers that he can speak in tongues and he reckons this to be a gift of the Holy Spirit. In reality it is only a mediumistic gift and such gifts are not used by the Holy Spirit. (1969:34–35)

Koch also made another complaint that we have encountered before: the movement flouted traditional patriarchal limits on women's roles in religion. St. Paul's taboo on letting women speak in tongues, Koch noted, was "not heeded anywhere in the new tongues movement today" (1969:39). He was even more upset by some of the practices among Catholic-oriented Charismatics. He relates a case in which a woman, frustrated by her inability to speak in tongues, prayed, "If You do not give me the baptism of the Spirit, I will speak to Your mother about it" and at once received the gift. And Koch quotes another Charismatic who asserted that spirit baptism led to greater love of the Virgin Mary. A Lutheran enemy of Mary-worship, Koch commented, "The Holy Spirit leads us into all truth, not into false doctrines" (1978:32). Spirits that encouraged appeals or devotion to the Virgin Mary, in short, by definition must come from Satan, not from God.

In addition, Koch objected to practices that smacked more of spiritualism than of traditional Christianity. One Charismatic minister, he reported, advised his followers to repeat a short prayer "five to eight hundred times" to alter one's consciousness and begin speaking in tongues (1969:24), a variation on Maxwell Whyte's repetition of the word "blood" to induce glossolalia. In other Pentecostal meetings, he noticed, participants were encouraged to form a human chain by touching each other, or by placing their hands on the radio or television over which a Charismatic preacher was giving a message. "These are the same proceedings," he said, "that one finds associated with spiritistic table-lifting and glass-moving" (1969:46–47). When healing was offered by the same linking of hands, he felt, it "often has the same by-products as magic charming" (1970:43). In short, Koch accused tongue-speakers of exercising a gift that was genuine enough, but which derived from Satan, not from the Holy Spirit.

Koch had previously encountered cases in which speaking in tongues proved to be linked to demonic possession, but on visiting Canada during a revivalistic movement, he learned of a large number of such incidents. For instance, he heard of an Edmonton eighteen-year-old who insisted on praying in tongues. When he was asked to pray in English, he explained that he could not do so, but always went straight into tongues. One of the revivalist ministers commanded the boy's demon to speak in English, whereupon the boy immediately began to blaspheme and curse God (1973b:83–84). Others found that after Pentecostals had helped them pray in tongues, they found themselves plagued by troublesome voices. In another attack on "fanaticism," Koch applied the "devil baby" motif to Charismatics, telling of a pregnant woman who had a deformed child after attending a Pentecostal service (1970:51).

Most dramatic, however, was the testimony Koch elicited from the demons themselves, who often freely admitted during exorcisms that they had entered during Pentecostal rituals. Koch cites several incidents in which speaking in tongues proved to be demonically inspired. In one instance, which circulated on a cassette tape distributed by the Toccoa Bible Institute, a girl obsessed by speaking in tongues was tested. The spirit that spoke through her admitted that it hated Christ and got into the girl "By the laying on of hands of a Pentecostal preacher." The missionary ordered the spirit to leave, and since then, Koch says, she has not spoken in tongues (1973b:84).

Koch's ministry during the 1970s brought more extreme discoveries: another missionary told him that when a woman began speaking in tongues, he challenged the spirit in Jesus' name, and the spirit said, "'I belong to a church.'" The missionary did not leave it at that, Koch continues. "'Which church?' he asked. 'The Church of Satan,' came the astonishing reply" (1978:207). Even more dramatic was the case of "Mark," who attended a Pentecostal meeting, was "slain in the spirit," and revived speaking in tongues and praising Jesus in a loud voice. He continued to do so until a counselor suspected the demonic nature of his tongue and commanded the controlling spirit to speak. The spirit identified itself, appropriately, as "Jesus." "What Jesus?" the counselor persisted. "Jesus of the devil," the spirit replied (1978:33–34). In a "guide to practical supernatural healing," two of Koch's American disciples cautioned exorcists not to be fooled when they elicited an alternate personality who said "I believe in Jesus," for, they say, "there have been demons with the names of 'Jesus,' 'Holy Spirit,' and even 'Yahweh'" (Ensign and Lowe 1984:298).

"Jesus" was an ordinary biblical name that demons could and often did adopt, Koch notes, adding that still other spirits had revealed themselves under challenge as "the unholy Jesus" or "the Jesus of Satan." Thus, from cases such as these he concludes "that the so-called baptism of the Spirit in the Charismatic movement is usually an opportunity for demons to enter" (1978:209). There were some Pentecostals whom he admired, Koch candidly admitted, adding that he did accept invitations to give seminars on demon possession in Charismatic churches. "One day, in eternity, there will be Pentecostals in heaven and Lutherans in hell," he commented, though he added characteristically, "the reverse will also be true" (1973b:85). A vocal critic of post-war "demythologizing" trends in the church, Koch added that "tens of thousands" of Charismatics would inherit heaven, but "there will not be a single modernist theologian in Heaven, unless he repents . . . and throws his theology overboard" (1978:31).

Elsewhere, Koch was less charitable: that some people are converted at Pentecostal meetings proves only "that God can even save a person through an erroneous movement. God's saving grace reaches even to the depths of hell" (1970:52). Those who practice "pseudocharismatic" gifts, Koch argued, "are the élite, the advance guard of Satan" (1978:31). The only good that the movement accomplishes, he argues, "is only caused by the fact that real Christians have been drawn into the movement, when really they belong outside it" (1969:13). In order to keep their lives in order, he concluded, Christians must renounce contact with the tongues movement (Koch and Lechler 1970:95–96).

Can a Christian Have a Demon?

Because his works were so effective in identifying causes of demonization, Koch's argument that tongue-speakers were closet "spiritualists" gained considerable acceptance within the deliverance ministry in North America. Traveling preachers within this camp frequently came into conflict with Charismatics who accepted both tongues and deliverance as valid gifts of the spirit. The latter were thus put in a difficult position: the gift of speaking in tongues was repeatedly cited as the primary sign that believers had experienced genuine spirit baptism. If glossolalia were defined as diabolical in origin, then the religious experience that underlay the entire movement was really a form of Satanism.

The president of a Midwestern Full Gospel Business Men's Fellowship chapter wrote to Don Basham in alarm, describing an event that occurred during an evangelical seminar conducted by a visiting evangelist:

> This man has a real ministry of casting out demons. He writes articles and books against speaking in tongues. I sat in on several seminars and here is what he does: When a Pentecostal doubts his experience in tongues, while he is speaking, this man "tests the spirit." He asks the spirit its name. In one case the English words came forth, "I won't tell you my name." After prodding, the words came forth, "My name is Jesus." As the person continued to speak in tongues the minister asked the spirit if he could confess that Jesus Christ, the Lord, came in the flesh. The words came back, "No! No!" The minister then proceeded to command the demon to go and the woman began to shout, "Yes, come out! Oh, Jesus, set me free!" Of course, this woman no longer speaks in tongues.
> ... *What is this? What is happening here? I need an answer!*
> (1971a:64; emphasis in original)

Basham responded judiciously in *Can a Christian Have a Demon?* (1971a), one of his most closely argued theological works. He connected the evangelist's theories with Koch's deliverance ministry, which he warmly endorsed, "especially in regard to people who have been involved in occult practices." But he noted that the minister in question, like Koch, had come into the deliverance ministry without first learning to speak in tongues. "As a result," he said, "he is using a valid ministry in an attempt to discredit a genuine spiritual experience, namely the baptism in the Holy Spirit" (1971a:65).

Defenders of glossolalia such as Don Basham did not claim that receiving the Spirit cleansed Christians of the tendency to sin; indeed he admitted that some ministers who exercised tongues and other spiritual gifts also fell prey to temptations such as sexual immorality. However, being able to use gifts such as discerning and casting out demons proved only that divine gifts could flow through fallible human channels, though Basham remarked, "If I were God I might have chosen to do it another way" (1971b:29). He had often cast out demons that *prevented* people from speaking in tongues, and added, sadly, that people might take Koch's valid ministry in deliverance as proof of his mistaken theology about tongues. Basham concluded, "if people believe a lie, they will be bound by the power of it" (1971a:65).

Consequently, he insisted that seeking spirit baptism was still the logical first step in individual Christians' quest for sanctification, "We cannot dogmatically say that everyone must speak in tongues in order to have the baptism, we merely point out that it is the normative experience. It is said that the baptism in the Holy Spirit is the doorway into the supernatural realm of the Christian life. And since speaking in tongues is a supernatural way of praying it is often considered the doorway to the other supernatural gifts such as interpretation and prophecy" (1971b:34). Ironically, he felt, the "demon of tongues" that had been cast out of the woman mentioned in the letter quoted earlier was indeed a demon that had been hindering the woman's spiritual progress. Now she should be able to speak in tongues even more freely than ever; "but she's been badly frightened by her experience and now has the fear that her speaking in tongues was of the devil. And unless someone comes along to straighten her out, she may remain in bondage to that fear for the rest of her life" (1971a:68).

But there was a deeper issue involved: not only did Holy Spirit baptism fail to eliminate the tendency toward sin, in fact Basham found that 75 percent of those he found demon-possessed had also received the Holy Spirit through tongue-speaking. Demon possession and glossolalia, Basham conceded, were often difficult to distinguish. He described a case in which he watched a woman praising Jesus at a midwestern worship service, when suddenly "a demon spirit manifested itself. . . . As her minister and I watched, her face twisted into an ugly mask and the most vile blasphemies and curses began to spill from her lips. Her minister turned pale. 'My God!' he cried, clutching [Basham's] arm. 'That woman is one of my most devoted deaconesses.'" The demon was cast out, and moments later the woman resumed her praise of Jesus (1971a:47).

Such a link between spirit baptism and demons had been noted by others, who found it difficult to explain how the same individuals could by turns express a heavenly language motivated by the Spirit and then, without obvious backsliding, admit that foul-speaking demons were living inside their personalities. Hobart E. Freeman, whose *Angels of Light?* (1969) was an influential defense of the deliverance ministry, also noted that the vast majority of persons found to be demonized were Christians, many of whom had experienced Holy Spirit baptism. He suggested a distinction between "absolute demon possession," in which the demon controls the person's everyday life, and demonic oppression or infestation, in which demons influenced or hindered the believer's work. The latter condition was especially severe if the Christian had not confessed "occult sins."

The same question had arisen as early as the 1962 *Christian Life* series on demon possession, where the editor, Russell Meade, concluded, "There is no Bible proof that the Holy Spirit and a demon cannot inhabit the same body." After a discussion of several scriptural passages, though, he relied on Dr. V. Raymond Edman, president of the fundamentalist Wheaton College and an early supporter of Koch. Edman argued that the theological issue was irrelevant: "Theory says, no; but the facts say, yes." According to standard Christian theology, it is true that a demon could not remain in the body of a Christian who has received the Holy Spirit. "However I *know* true Christians who were *truly* demon possessed," he continues, "and who were delivered in answer to prayer given in the name of the Lord Jesus" (Meade 1963:34–35; emphasis mine). As is common in the Pentecostal movement, direct religious experience has an evidential value far greater than traditional theology.

If it was not easy to dismiss the personal experiences in which sincere Christians experienced both spirit baptism and demon possession, neither was it easy to refute the claim that spirit baptism *caused* demonization. Critics called tongues a doorway into a satanic supernatural realm, and that the prevalence of demon possession among tongue-speakers proved that the two were either one and the same or else linked by a cause-effect process. It was, in fact, difficult to say when a given action was inspired by the Spirit and when it was motivated by an indwelling demon. Maxwell Whyte tells of an argument that he had with "a Christian lady (so called)." Provoked by her rebukes, he ordered the demon that was obviously inspiring her to criticize him to come out. "It did (at least one of them did)," Maxwell Whyte relates, "and caught me by the throat and started to strangle me. I cried 'The Blood,' three times, and it went back into her. But while it had been trying to throttle me, the demon in the lady said, 'There you are, *you* have a demon!'" "It was a lie of Satan," Maxwell Whyte countered (1973b:48–49), but in conflicts such as this it was never clear who was speaking, the Holy Spirit or Satan.

Indeed, both Maxwell Whyte and Basham, in their own ways, conceded that there could be some truth to Koch's claim that tongue-speaking could be demonic. In fact, knowledge of unfamiliar languages has been a traditional sign of demon possession in the Catholic tradition (Martin 1976: 460). A demon, Maxwell Whyte said, could be "a created living being" from long before man was created. So it might have possessed a man in China long ago and thus learned Chinese during his sojourn. On this man's death, the demon might move to, say, an Indian and would learn his language as well. Over time, Maxwell Whyte says, the demon "might well live in the human bodies of many men and women of different nationalities. And he would learn all of their languages." No wonder, then, that a person with a "multilingual demon" might arrive at a Pentecostal church and speak fluently in several different languages. Thus tongue-speaking, in and of itself, was not always a token of the Holy Spirit (1973b:33–34).

The crux of the problem, according to Basham, was that deliverance was not a straightforward process of casting out all the demons present and inviting the Holy Spirit in. Another of his cases involved a young man who spoke in tongues yet felt strangely depressed afterwards. Basham encouraged him to speak in the spirit, but he at once sensed that the "hoarse, guttural sounds" that came forth were demonic in nature. He cast the strange spirit out, then prayed for "the genuine article," and the man began to worship "fluently in a clear heavenly language." During counseling, the young man told Basham "a typical story of involvement in drugs, witchcraft and eastern cults," and Basham inferred that because he had not yet confessed his occult dabbling, he could not receive the genuine Holy Spirit. Instead, the demonic activity already present in his life made him *think* he was speaking in tongues (1971b:52–53).

Moreover, Basham reasoned, individuals could continue to be plagued by evil thoughts and afflictions even after renouncing sins, ordering demons to leave, and experiencing the genuine ecstasy of the Holy Spirit. Even after he had become established in his tongues and deliverance ministry, Basham recognized that he had been partially controlled by a "spirit of fear" that, he suddenly recalled, had entered when his older brother had forced him to go with him to a vampire movie. Naming the spirit, Basham felt himself doubled over in convulsions, "as if [he] were some kind of sponge filled with dirty water being twisted and wrung out by a pair of giant loving hands." Finally, he vomited, and, he relates, "I could sense I was in physical contact with the true nature of the filthy beast which had lodged within me" (1972:181–84).

The genuine Holy Spirit thus could come into believers' personalities, according to Basham, even when a "filthy beast" also dwelt within. Basham suggested that there might be latent demons that entered not through sin but through moments of anxiety and stress. These also needed to perhaps be reexperienced in a cathartic moment of "flashback" memory before the demon could be named and cast out. He also relates an instance in which he was taken to a young woman who repeatedly woke up in the middle of the night gasping for air for reasons no doctor could diagnose. In the following deliverance session, a "choking demon" was identified, which explained that it had entered when the woman was only three years old. Her mother had given her a spoonful of peanut butter, which had temporarily blocked the child's windpipe. "That's when I came in!" the demon exclaimed. "I was waiting for my chance! . . . I wanted to kill her!" (1972:141–42).

Only a minor extension of this principle would suggest that such latent demons could enter during infancy or, as in Koch's multigenerational theory, even be inherited from blood relatives. Basham continued to stress the need for continual self-examination and confession. It is only through retrospection that one can recognize the many ways in which Satan can claim one's soul and block direct genuine contact with mythological experience.

But even if the quest for spirit baptism was complicated by counterfeit tongues and latent demons, still he stressed "*no Christian seeking the baptism in the Holy Spirit with speaking in tongues needs to be afraid* [emphasis his]. When we ask in the name of Jesus, what we get, we get from God. If in the process of our seeking, the Holy Spirit reveals some demonic influence and we get rid of that, so much the better" (1971b:53). For much the same reason, Maxwell Whyte found incomprehensible the idea that tongues were a satanic gift. Citing Luke 11:11–13, he argues

> Jesus clearly said that we need not fear getting something we didn't ask for, or something evil. If you ask for bread, you'll get bread. If you ask for an egg, you'll get an egg. If you ask for the Holy Spirit, you'll get the Holy Spirit. No one has ever asked the Father for the Holy Spirit and received an unholy spirit. . . . Do you think, then, that a Christian could earnestly ask for the power of the Spirit and receive an unholy, devil-inspired tongue? Certainly not! (1989:106)

Maxwell Whyte also identified the chink in Koch's spiritual armor: in combating the dangers of mediumistic powers, he had accepted as valid a ministry based on information "discovered" by holding dialogues with demons. These, he logically observed, "should be open to serious

question! ... Demons are all liars and will use the most nonsensical statements in order to confuse the unwary and the novices in this ministry.
... I do not recommend forming doctrines based on the word of a lying
spirit" (1989:125–26). In brief, for all his hostility to spiritualism, Koch
had received and accepted as authoritative a theology that relied on evidence derived from self-defined evil spirits speaking through persons in
a ritually induced trance. If Basham and Maxwell Whyte were guilty of
using "mediumistic" techniques in their ministries, Koch was no stranger
to the same tactics. The whole dispute was less an indictment of supernaturalism than a falling out among Christian magicians.

The Alternate State of Consciousness

As early as 1896, William James had theorized that the controlling mechanisms in demon possession and in spiritualism were analogous, perhaps
even one and the same (Taylor 1984:108–9). Felicitas Goodman (1988)
has brought an impressive body of medical and anthropological data to
argue that glossolalia and exorcism involve identical mental processes. If
we add to this the testimony of those who worked in the deliverance
ministry, we see that the gift of tongues is closely related to and often
indistinguishable from the gift of discerning and casting out demons.
The position of those involved in deliverance is that spiritualism is a
"satanic counterfeit" of Charismatic religion; Koch and his followers
would add that most glossolalia would also fit this category.

A simple conclusion to draw from these perceived connections is
that phenomena in both categories are so closely linked that they must
rely on similar mental processes, which may manifest as either "divine"
or "diabolical," or may vacillate between the two poles. The traditional
antagonism between Charismatic Christianity and spiritualism implies
that both are rival forms of ritually inducing an altered state of consciousness.

It is therefore useful to survey objectively what a variety of observers have seen as distinctive about alternate states of consciousness. Hilary Evans, a historian of psychic research, has brought together accounts
of such cases, both spontaneous and ritually induced, and found remarkable similarities that cross historic and cultural boundaries (1989). He
suggests that an alternate state of consciousness is characterized by the
following:

Diminished Awareness of Reality. Or rather, as Evans notes, participants become aware of having entered an altered or a heightened state of consciousness. Typical indications of this include reduced reality-testing, attention to surroundings, or awareness of passing time.

Diminished Sense of Personal Control. Participants gain the sense of some other agency controlling their bodies: they speak syllables or words seemingly coming from someone else.

Improved Performance of Certain Tasks. Evans notes that in a wide variety of cases, participants find their abilities to discern tiny differences or clues are enhanced. Participants' mental and even physical abilities often become enhanced in a seemingly paranormal fashion.

Increased Suggestibility. As perhaps an extension of the above, those undergoing an alternate state of consciousness often become extraordinarily responsive to suggestions made, even unintentionally, by those around them.

Depersonalization and Role-Playing. The participants' personalities may sometimes be submerged or replaced by personalities quite different from their everyday personas. They also have a talent for defining others' roles and making them part of the performance. (Based on Evans 1989:34–48)

Evans illustrates these characteristics from a variety of traditions, ranging among religious enthusiastic movements, anthropological studies of shamans and spirit possession cults, and personal experiences reported to paranormal study organizations such as the British Society for Psychic Studies. He observes, too, that his checklist has much in common with the Stanford Hypnotic Susceptibility Scales, a standard guide to gauge the depth of a clinically induced trance. These include characteristics such as "narrower focus of attention," "increased suggestibility," and "tendency to role behavior" (111). Such clinically induced states of mind, he suggests, are not intrinsically different from those entered into voluntarily as parts of other rituals.

In fact, there are considerable points of contact between messages obtained under hypnosis and those volunteered by mediums and by demons speaking through people during exorcism. As we shall see, there are reasons to believe that people in alternate states of consciousness are more likely to fabricate events that fit the roles they are asked to play than to recall memories of actual events in a truthful and photographic fashion. But first let us survey the ways in which Evans's characteristics fit the material already surveyed.

Diminished Awareness of Reality

Many of the cases Evans describes show individuals entering such a state spontaneously and without warning, the encounter seeming to be an uninvited beatific or diabolical experience. In folk traditions, there is usually some ritual process in which consciousness is altered. Among the elements are narrating stories that provide role models for the individual experience, narrowing the focus of senses by darkening the room and repeating a chant, a supportive group of peers sustaining a suspenseful context, waiting for "something" to happen.

The techniques advocated by Maxwell Whyte and Basham for speaking in tongues or discerning demons likewise induce altered consciousness in group contexts in similar ways: testimonies by the minister or supporters that prepare for future experiences, repetition of words or phrases such as "Blood," a tensely expectant group setting. While Koch was suspicious of such tactics, he placed a premium on the religious experience of conversion, which occurs in a similarly altered state of consciousness. His methods of lengthy introspective counseling produced a similar state of alertness in which identification of the "right" occult sin triggered the conversion experience.

Such a process underlies the distinctive methods of revival meetings, in which participants frequently lost track of time and continued in meetings long into the night or early morning. Koch, a supporter of these methods, presents in detail the model testimony of a Canadian official, who arrived a sympathetic but unmoved spectator five days after the beginning of a Canadian revival. Asked to give some remarks toward the end of the group meeting, the official responded politely, but privately found some of the testimonies given exaggerated and "doubted whether what the people were saying was true." The evangelist hosting the revival called over several of his helpers, asking what they thought of the official's statement: they then asked "several pointed questions, intended to expose what it was that held [the official] back from being a Spirit-filled man."

As a result, the man was invited to the "afterglow" meetings, and when he still had no extraordinary reaction, to the next day's meeting. The official was still untouched on Thursday evening, even after he had answered an altar call and attended a second all-night afterglow meeting in which his resistance to the Spirit was the focus of collective prayer and "group therapy." The official notes, "Then someone in the circle asked me to put my chair in the middle of the circle. This is the usual method. . . . I did it and then knelt down. They asked God to break down whatever stood as a hindrance in my way. It was now already five o'clock in the morning and I was still not touched. [One of the participating ministers] declared: 'There must be some barrier. My advice to him is: go into a room and battle it out with God on your own.'" This proved crucial: after a brief moment of sleep, the official awoke convinced that he had to ask several persons for forgiveness and make financial reparations, and soon after experienced the ecstatic feeling of being converted (1973b:60–63). While the religious experience was, in the end, one experienced in private, there is no question in the official's mind that the methods used by the revivalists were responsible for inducing this change.

Diminished Personal Control and Improved Performance

These two characteristics often merge into a state of mind in which "something" external to the personality is responsible for actions that the individual feels s/he could not possibly have been able to do in a normal state of mind. In one directly visible manifestation of this, Evans presents several cases in which persons undergoing an ecstatic alternate state of consciousness spontaneously exhibit physical strength far beyond their ordinary powers. In one case, a man was lost for half an hour in a vision of angels and heaven. When he returned to his normal consciousness, his workmates told him he had picked up and loaded several barrels of flour "with the ease of a giant," a task ordinarily impossible for a single man (1989:98). Preternatural strength is also a commonly cited symptom of demon possession (Martin 1976: 460), and in one of Basham's cases, a "quite tiny" woman expressing a demon had no trouble dragging Basham and Maxwell Whyte around the room "as if we were small children."

Maxwell Whyte warned that the young adolescent game of "Levitation" was an invitation to demons. In it, young children are able to display far greater strength than they would in a non-ritual context, and it seems to rely on creating an alternate state of consciousness through a repetitious chant and group reinforcement. Or this game may be based on a physical illusion, in which the "levitated" persons are raised in a way that equally distributes their weight. In any case, the impression is created that the group has somehow gained supernatural power either to make the volunteer weightless or to make their strength superhuman. Maxwell Whyte was so impressed by the ease with which such groups could lift people that he concluded that "demons . . . lend their strength and do the levitation" (1973a: 54).

And the complexity of messages so received often seems itself paranormal. In 1842, a short-lived "preaching epidemic" swept rural Sweden. Though church officials called it mass hysteria, participants experienced it as a miracle because previously untutored participants suddenly became skilled at preaching and leading prayer meetings. An investigating Bishop observed that many would fall into a trance so deep that not even a needle thrust into their bodies would arouse them. Yet at the same time they would be "given" messages phrased in eloquent, lively language, in a much purer style "than was usual, or apparently possible, in their natural state." In particular, a young girl of about ten adopted a saintlike persona in which her normal hoarse voice was replaced by a wonderfully clear tone that gave an edifying homily in theological language "which, when awake, it would have been impossible for her to use" (Evans 1989:68–70).

This last talent recalls, too, the case of "Hélène Smith," a nineteenth-century Swiss psychic who claimed that her alter ego frequently traveled to the planet Mars. She supported this claim by writing, speaking, and translating an unknown language that she said was "Martian." In fact, it was an artificial language based on her native French, but her ability to create it and consistently use it over a long period of time as a living tongue impressed researchers, who noted that otherwise the woman showed no unusual creative talents (Rogo 1985:11–14). The connection here with tongue-speaking is clear, even if we grant that recorded examples of glossolalia seem to be similarly based on the speaker's native language. The ability to speak and "interpret" tongues is similar to the ability to compose hymns and devotional material spontaneously, using talents quite different from those employed in the conscious composing of such works.

And, though documented examples of glossolalia recorded on tape display no language of record, anecdotal accounts suggest that use of unfamiliar languages is possible under such circumstances. An individual who was personally known to Don Basham spoke in tongues at a meeting, then had another person interpret the message. Afterwards, a bystander told the friend that he had recognized the tongue spoken as his native language, French. He also affirmed that the interpretation was "a perfect translation," even though neither person knew any French (1971b:49). Without audiotape documentation, it is easy to disregard such stories as apocryphal, but similar anecdotes show up in accounts of exorcisms. Douglass Deen, the young boy in the case later fictionalized in *The Exorcist*, likewise was said to have spoken to the priests who attended him in Latin, a language he had never studied (Ebon 1974:17). Such cases suggest, at least, that persons in an alternate state of consciousness can gain an uncanny ability to pick up (or invent) and use a foreign language in a way that they would find impossible in their normal state.

One common claim is that during an alternate state of consciousness, persons' abilities to "read others' minds" become heightened. Knowledge of "things that are distant or hidden" has been noted as a diagnostic symptom of possession in the Catholic tradition. Malachi Martin says that demons typically know "the most secret and intimate details of the lives of everyone in the room" and warns that the exorcist must be prepared to have his secret sins shouted out loud for all to hear (1976: 19, 460). In a similar way, the Canadian Charismatic healer Katherine Kuhlman was notorious for her ability to point to unfamiliar persons during her meetings and describe in detail the symptoms of their illnesses. "And sometimes I can tell the sin in that life," she added (Spraggett 1967:170–71).

This talent is matched in a divine way by Charismatics who have the ability to utter "prophecies"—not in the sense of predicting the future but rather of speaking to some unspoken or unknown fact in the immediate situation. Basham, for instance, recalls finding himself drawn into spirit-led prophecy during a missionary trip to Hungary. He heard his voice say that God had sent him and his companions "to take the place of others I called but who failed to go." Later that day Basham found that the church that had invited them to Hungary had been disappointed when two other young missionaries who had promised to visit them had never showed up (1971b:121–22).

Overall, we note in all these traditions both a sense of "another person" taking charge, which is matched by heightened perceptive, creative, or even clairvoyant powers. We may question the scientific legitimacy of "ESP" abilities and suggest that what appears psychic may in fact be a heightened ability to notice and pick up on non-verbal behavior. Professional fortune-tellers, after all, rely on their clients' reactions to tell them if they are on the right track in "reading their minds." Still, such a talent emerges spontaneously, without training, and apparently in a way different from the usual learning/composing process of the conscious mind. The precise details of this skill, unfortunately, are not well understood, even by psychics.

Suggestibility and Role-Playing

These characteristics, as Evans notes, also fit together in an intricate way. On the one hand, the normal identity and ability to initiate conscious actions are depressed, perhaps even suppressed. Some persons experiencing an alternate state of consciousness have no awareness of their actions during the altered state; others retain their consciousness but sense that their lips or hands are behaving in an autonomic fashion. Thus, the participant seems to be yielding control to an external personality. A number of nineteenth-century spiritualists commented on this sensation: Emma Hardinge Britten often felt herself "to be two individuals," one her normal self, functioning as a bystander, the other an active speaker expressing thoughts that were often "new and strange." Elizabeth d'Espérance, a professional medium, also expressed this sense while describing her perception of a séance, "It is a horrible feeling, thus losing hold of one's identity. I long to put out one of these hands that are lying so helplessly, and touch someone just to know if I am myself or only a dream—if "Anna" [her spirit guide] be I, or I am lost as it were, in her identity.... How long will there be two of us? Which will it be in the end? Shall I be "Anna" or "Anna" be I?" (qtd. in Owen 1990:224–25).

On the other hand, Evans indicates, persons undergoing an alternate state of consciousness do not take on random and wholly individualistic identities. While they *feel* themselves to have lost control of what they are doing, their behavior conforms to a pattern based on events recognized by their culture and context. "Beneath all these experiences we can trace a common pattern of depersonalization," Evans notes. "Individuals cease to be their ordinary selves—and role-playing—they identify themselves with a culturally accepted stereotype. Their behaviour reflects a universal need, which is satisfied in pretty much the same kind of way" (1989:171–72). This indicates that, on some level, such events are controlled and therefore purposeful; as Evans puts it, "there is some part of the mind which is very much aware of what is going on and very capable of actively controlling the situation" (1989:158–59).

Though intellectually and morally the "weaker" sex, through traffic with the Devil, women threaten to exploit such roles and gain significant power over males and male- focused institutions. I.M. Lewis (1989), studying third-world traditional religions, notes that frequently women are central in cults that spring up around apparent cases of possession. Indeed, he suggests that such groups are "thinly disguised protest movements directed against the dominant sex." In such groups, possession is initially treated as an illness, in which essentially amoral spirits randomly afflict women. As the spirits are held to originate outside the afflicted persons' personalities, such persons cannot possibly be blamed for the language or violent actions they enact during the cure: "They are thus totally blameless; responsibility lies not with them, but with the spirits." Significantly, Lewis notes, the groups that spring up around such cases often do not simply expel the possessing spirit, but rather tame and domesticate it, turning what was initially a diabolical illness into a means of communicating with a divine world.

In cultures in which women lack direct means of expressing their views, Lewis concludes, such cults "protect women from the exactions of men, and offer an effective vehicle for manipulating husbands and male relatives." Such a point, he adds, is supported by the orthodox Christian historian Ronald Knox, who calls enthusiastic movements in the church "largely a history of female emancipation" (1989:26–27). Indeed, the three male theologians we have studied locate their work in traditionally patriarchal denominations, and their strongest links in these institutional networks are with other males. Maxwell Whyte's closely argued argument for the 100 percent masculine nature of The Blood counters the occult world that is dominated by females whom these Charismatics see as grasping for illicit power. This is true not only of the "witches" described by all three as being at the core of Satan's contemporary threat, but, paradoxically, it is also true of the majority of their followers. And it is not difficult to find implicit protest elements, such as I.M. Lewis would have predicted, in the antiworlds these women created in their exorcisms.

For instance, one woman who attended a demonstration of deliverance sent Basham a testimonial of her deliverance. She reported that even on the way home after the service, she continued to identify and cast out demons "until my companions became . . . perturbed by their quantity and nastiness." Three especially strong ones were dominance, aggression, and intellectualism; two weaker but unfamiliar ones were calumny and tautology, and the woman noted that she "required a dictionary to find out what had come out of me." In the end, she expelled fifty-three named demons and concluded, "I marvel that the Lord has been able to use me up to now, with all that filth and nastiness in me" (1971a:77–78).

Given the difficult position that females face in fundamentalist religious groups, one does not need a dictionary to see that this woman's personal demons reflect ambivalence about her education and the potential empowerment it represented. And, although her desire for dominance and aggression are cast out as "filthy" demons, nevertheless her exorcism allowed her to express them in ways in which she could escape personal responsibility. Basham, like the others, also counseled male converts, but his methods offered females a particular opportunity both to express the inexpressible through an antiworld personality and also to gain status within their groups with a dramatic story of deliverance.

Pat Brooks, one of Basham's few female associates to lead a deliverance ministry under her own name rather than her husband's, addressed this issue of women's roles most directly. An active workshop leader and author, she perhaps needed to balance her Charismatic power with a firmly patriarchal mythology. Despondent after a frustrating missionary stint in Nigeria, she read the 1966 *Christian Life* series on deliverance and found there a possible explanation for her depression. Her conviction strengthened by a terrifying spiritual attack that night, she contacted a prayer group in New York State. The group's directors, a lay preacher and his wife, questioned her closely about her past involvement in the occult; she admitted that she had used a Ouija board as a youth and still prayed for "future leadings," just as many spiritualists call on spirit guides for advice.

The leaders identified this tendency as evidence for a "lying spirit of prophecy" in the woman and offered to exorcise it:

I knelt down between the man and his wife. She began to pray and repeat the phrase "the blood of Jesus" over and over again, while he amazed me with a direct verbal attack on Satan and this demon that had plagued me for so long.

Finally he said, "You lying spirit of prophecy come out of her in Jesus name!"

Immediately a horrible shudder went through my whole body, and convulsive sobs came up from deep within. I could hardly believe that the uncontrollable weeping I heard was mine at all. In actuality, it was not. (Brooks 1972:59–61)

Later, she led exorcisms of her own and describes the three-day deliverance of "Heidi," a woman afflicted by hate, sex demons, lesbianism, and masturbation. At the end, Brooks records, her assistant Stella warned the woman, "Be sure to submit to your husband." When Heidi objected that sometimes he might be wrong, Stella insisted, "Submit to anything but sin. You know as well as I do, the usual faults men make are not in that category. . . . God keeps your head and mind covered by him in some wonderful way I don't pretend to understand" (1972:143). Later, Brooks found Biblical passages that indicated to her that a woman who wanted to protect her personality against the influence of demons had to submit to authority: "For a married woman this means she must submit to the headship of her husband." Recognizing this, she at once turned her checkbook and the direction of her prayer meetings over to her spouse. As before, though, she continued to exorcise, write, and network under her own authority (1972:214–15).

Conclusions

All three of the crusaders discussed faced criticism outside the Pentecostal ranks. Koch had his *Christian Counselling and Occultism* placed on an index of forbidden books by the head of the Beatenberg Bible School. More understandably, an associate in South Germany created pandemonium when he preached a sermon against the local *Braucher* who had performed charming for most of the farms in the area; the minister was ostracized and forced to leave his church. Koch comments, "Those who make their witness against sins of sorcery must expect counterattacks from Satan and his helpers" (1978:2–3, 286). Similarly, Maxwell Whyte was "misunderstood, ridiculed, and ostracized by the Christian community" during his early years in Toronto (1989:iii). Basham recalled accusations of "fanaticism, heresy, mental instability, or being in league with Satan" (1986:170). As the deliverance movement grew, one might expect the only check to come from such outside forces—skeptics, occultists, and liberal Christians—whose resistance could safely be explained as satanically inspired.

But when attack came instead from *within* the Pentecostal community, the deliverance movement had to defend both the gift of tongues and the ministry of exorcism against the charge of being forms of devil worship. Even Koch found his work criticized by fundamentalists for giving the Devil too much honor. Anthropologists have consistently found glossolalia and demon possession related to the same rituals. The best evidence, in fact, attributes both phenomena to similar neurological processes. Practicing the positive spiritual gifts therefore required contact with the forces of evil. In order to justify the gifts of the Spirit, Satanism had to be carefully defined as something recognizably distinct from charisma, but in fact neither glossolalia nor demon possession could exist in an institutionalized mythology without the other.

The psychological, sociological, and religious mechanisms that underlie these interrelated phenomena are not well understood, but the ritual creation of an alternate state of mind is in fact commonplace, not only in non-western cultures but among Anglo-American folk groups and religious media-enhanced conduits such as the deliverance ministry. Ironically, as Evans points out, many people *use* the alternate state of consciousness to participate directly in cultural mythology, to express personal or political frustrations, or simply to create excitement in an otherwise repressive context. But the ubiquity of the process does not mean that any of the participants come close to *understanding* or *controlling* what happens (1989:227). Indeed, the perceived loss of personal control and emergence of autonomic behavior encourages the sense that what is happening is marvelous by definition.

This factor, along with the obscenity, threat of violence, and real psychological and physical risks involved, has meant that few objective studies exist of the consciousness-altering traditions we have surveyed. For this reason, whatever the etiology and neurological mechanism of the state we are studying, we do not as yet have the objective data that would let us propose a "scientific" theory of such traditions. And we cannot disregard as intrinsically absurd the idea that they are caused by cunning supernatural entities external to the participants, who have extraordinary abilities to deceive. Such a claim, though extraordinary, in fact is a simpler way of making sense out of the phenomena than to hold that stories obtained through alternate states of consciousness are reliable versions of past events.

In the often-bitter debate that emerged over their use of the supernatural, Charismatics were frequently characterized as nothing less than satanic recruiters. And indeed the deliverance ministry used techniques and rituals derived from spiritualism and folk magic, even as it defined the latter traditions as diabolical. For both tongues and demons, as real psychological phenomena, have much in common with trance mediumship and associated folk rituals. In the end, none of the participants in this debate could fully cut their ties with the occult, for without the "satanic counterfeit" they could not justify their own activities as "genuine."

This debate is not only logical to expect, it is inevitable. Koch and Maxwell Whyte represent two extremes of this debate, and Basham's perspective is a realistic, streetwise compromise. But such a debate profited no one, as it called attention to the ways in which both participants drew their power from contact with supernatural powers. In fact, the anecdotes and discussions used to carry on the debate dramatized the ways in which positive uses of charisma resembled, indeed were difficult to distinguish from, those "satanic counterfeits" that Charismatics felt they were combating. Indeed, the three major figures used many of the techniques of spiritualism and folk magic; they differed only to the degree that one should cause "change to occur in conformity with Will."

Faced with direct accusations of worshipping "the Jesus of Satan," not all Charismatics were as honest as Basham in admitting that the same person could speak in tongues and be simultaneously influenced by demons. But it was equally unprofitable to counterattack Koch's camp directly, for fear of discrediting the "diabolical medicine" of exorcism that they all valued. They found it more effective to shift attention from their internal dispute to convenient scapegoats, whom no one could deny were truly part of "the church of Satan." Demons, and their fellow travelers, the shadowy black magic rings that encouraged dabbling in occultism as part of a satanic scheme, were therefore theologically necessary for the deliverance movement.

3

Speak to the Devil

Ouija Boards and Deliverance

The demons have a better theology
than the modern theologians.
—Kurt A. Koch,
Occult: The Christian Perspective

In February 1978, psychiatrist Lawrence Pazder traveled from Victoria, British Columbia, to the Vatican City with one of his patients, Michelle Smith, to seek approval for an official investigation of the story she had told. Over the past eighteen months, Pazder's therapy had helped her recall, first vaguely, then with increasing detail, how her mother had involved her in a satanic cult at the age of five. The study, eventually approved by the Vatican secretary of state, marked one of the first formal investigations of what Pazder soon termed "ritual abuse." Michelle's story, first published in the popular magazines *Macleans* and *People*, became an influential book, *Michelle Remembers* (1981). This work subsequently became the catalyst for a series of crusades against alleged incidents of "Satanic Ritual Abuse," or SRA. Throughout the 1980s, an increasing number of professionals found their patients recovering similar memories from early childhood, describing horrifying forms of physical and sexual abuse inflicted on them by their parents or other adults. When a number of children also appeared to report the same kinds of activities, a growing number of therapists concluded that there was a large underground conspiracy of devil-worshippers who were carrying out these acts. The agenda was to inflict such psychological damage on the victims that they would grow up to perpetuate the cult activity. Hence, this activity was multigenerational in nature.

Investigation of this incident revealed little hard evidence for Michelle's claim that she had been sexually and psychologically abused for nearly a year. Interviews with her father, her neighbors, her family doctor, her former teacher, and her ex-husband revealed no suggestions that such events had occurred, nor had she undergone any unusual stress until entering therapy with Dr. Pazder (Allen and Midwinter 1990; Nathan and Snedeker 1995:45). Similarly, investigations of the memories of subsequent "survivors" of ritual abuse found no grounds for claims that underground cults were regularly meeting to torture and murder young children. Skeptics such as Kenneth Lanning (1989) pointed out that such a claim flew in the face of law enforcement knowledge of criminal conspiracies. Sex rings based on child sexual abuse and circulation of pornography certainly have existed—and still do exist—in circumstances of extreme secrecy. However, the fantastic allegations that such stories contained were not typical of prosecuted cases where evidence was found to document the crimes. For this reason and others, Jeffrey S. Victor (1993) called the ritual abuse claim a "contemporary legend."

Therapists countered that their patients' memories do not match widely observed characteristics of "contemporary legend." Clinical psychologist George Greaves finds several areas in which legends and SRA memories contrast. Legends, he notes, are brief, focused on a single event, told mainly for entertainment and end with a conventional "punch line," in which (for instance) a couple parking drive home and find the hook of a homicidal maniac dangling in the door. They circulate "through the entire culture" and cannot be documented but always happen to a "friend of a friend." Ritual abuse narratives, by contrast, are multilayered personal narratives, "told as true with genuine emotional involvement," sometimes taking hours to relate. Told only to a therapist or support group, they can be corroborated by scars and other medical evidence (qtd. in Vargo 1993:3).

There is merit to Greaves's argument: traditionally "legend" has been taken to mean "clearly fictitious." Such an attitude goes back at least as far as Swedish folklorist C.W. von Sydow, who coined the term "fabulate" in 1934 to refer to narratives that contained unbelievable elements. The events of the fabulate, he said, "*could not have actually happened* in the form that they take in the telling; they were shaped much more by the creative art of the folk" (1978; emphasis mine). Until recently, most folklorists' understanding of "legend" as a whole is that they, like fabulates, are believed by the teller but are actually untrue. Certainly claims like

Jeffrey S. Victor's that the Satanism scare was a "contemporary legend" implies that, on some level, it *has* to be a conscious fiction. But if these memories were not deliberate efforts to mislead, then where did they come from?

Most of Greaves's descriptions of "contemporary legend" describe only one form of narrative tradition, and not often accurately: like ritual abuse narratives, many legends are told in first person, with genuine emotional involvement, and combine to form lengthy, multilayered series of stories that may take hours to present. And unlike traditionally defined legends, they may well refer to directly observable proof and end without any clear "punch line." Even if the specific details in one performance may be told only to its immediate audience, its motifs (or distinctive story elements) may well circulate widely, if not through an entire culture, at least through the media-enhanced conduit in which the teller participates. Greaves's analysis ultimately evades the central issue: do the stories that analysts obtain from their patients reflect a broader cultural tradition?

This chapter and the next will argue that they do: further, these stories reflect a tradition that has been closely associated with contact with the diabolical. The supernatural emphasis in the deliverance ministry strongly allied it with spiritualism and other folk traditions of achieving an alternate state of consciousness; hence, to maintain its legitimacy in the Christian community it had to diabolize these traditions. This is especially true for those traditions that entailed constructing narratives while being in such a state. The world of the Charismatic movement needed to include demons as part of their institutional mythology. The last chapter has argued that the deliverance ministry in particular founded itself on repeatable religious experiences that involved inducing an alternate state of consciousness. During this alternate state, demons manifested and told narratives that explained the possessed person's mental and physical ailments in terms of spiritual traumas. Expressing such traumas was frequently a transcendent experience on the part of those undergoing deliverance, and their manifest improvement in health was further proof of the demons' objective existence.

Almost since its invention in the late nineteenth century, the Ouija board has been associated with the threat of demon possession. Both experiences—the Ouija ritual and deliverance—share a common structure and share so many elements that they must rely on a similar experiential mechanism. In both, the personality or personalities of those present appear to be overshadowed by alternate "selves," which often have horrifying stories to tell. This is not to say that the Ouija ritual and deliverance are identical or equally significant; or that they always have the same form or origin; or that either is intrinsically good or evil. Each tradition has unique elements, and participants' experiences in both range from self-transforming to psychotic. Yet each tradition has involved many of the same risks of "bad trips," and participation in one apparently enhances participants' abilities in the others. So it is not surprising to find both a high rate of tongue-speakers among those found to be demon-possessed as well as a surprising number of deliverance ministers who in youth participated in spiritualism or used a Ouija board.

Further, we find that during the decade before the first ritual abuse narratives were elicited, a number of psychologists were experimenting with exorcism as a therapeutic technique for disturbed patients. The results of these experiments produced "memories" that were as detailed and as compelling as the first SRA stories. Although the therapists found these memories often misleading and ultimately fictitious, their work provided an important link between the folk world of the Ouija, the theological world of the exorcism, and the secular world of satanic cult-hunting.

The Ouija Ritual

Practically since its invention a century ago, mainstream Christian religions, including Catholicism, have warned against using Ouija boards, claiming that they are a means of dabbling with Satanism (Hunt 1985:93–95). Occultists, interestingly, are divided on the Ouija board's value. Jane Roberts (1966) and Gina Covina (1979) express confidence that it is a device for positive transformation and they provide detailed instructions on how to use it to contact spirits and map the other world. But some occultists have echoed Christian warnings, cautioning inexperienced persons away from it. On the other hand, most adolescents consider the Ouija board as a party game, and most accounts describe nothing more than playful speculation about boyfriends and future events. Yet enough personal experience stories circulate that seem to validate the fears of adults: some teens do admit that evil spirits and even Satan himself take over the board. In fact, according to some such descriptions, adolescents deliberately invite demons to communicate through the Ouija board.

Such contacts are followed by messages that threaten death, injury, and demonic possession, and the contact is capped by some physical manifestation that proves the demon's power.

Are religious and occult experts correct in saying that the ritual is spiritually and psychologically dangerous, since it invites evil to take over the participants? Do we minimize the significance of the practice by calling it merely a party game? We need to distinguish between serious modes of religious experience and the adolescent patterns of playlike deviance that mimic them. There are important differences between occultists' approach to this device and that of the adventure-seeking teenager. In particular, the sincere occultist may perceive it as a way to create an *alternative* world to that of official science and religion. Rather than accepting religious verities secondhand, the occultist constructs his or her own supernatural worldview. The adolescent, however, will use it to create an *antiworld* to challenge and reject. Nonetheless, both approaches allow participants to participate *directly* in myth. In much the same way, the device allows teens a two-way dialogue with the Devil. In official religion the concept of Satan can be used to threaten adolescents; with the Ouija board they can talk back to him.

Religious critics universally condemn use of this "toy." Fundamentalist Jess Pedigo, for instance, relates with some horror how a group of students at one of the United State's strictest evangelical colleges used a homemade Ouija board, to contact "Mephistopheles." After asking questions about their futures, they eventually turned to questions about Christ and salvation. But one student asked a question "with a deliberate intent to ridicule the power behind the Ouija board." At once he "was picked up from the floor by an invisible force, suspended for a second, and then with terrific violence was thrown heavily across the room and into a wall. That ended the fun and games in that group." But Pedigo noted that this did not end the evil influence over the group: one convert who had previously attempted suicide made a second abortive attempt after the Ouija ritual (1971:58–59).

Such messages demonstrate to crusaders that the board is essentially a form of Satanism. Even seemingly benign and truthful messages must be diabolical in nature, Pedigo adds, since "if there are only two sources of power who can reveal these hidden secrets and if God is not the power that moves . . . the planchette, it must, of necessity, be Satan." (1971:54–55). Likewise, youth evangelist Gary A. Wilburn noted that serious belief was necessary to make the Ouija board work. "As it requires faith in God through Jesus Christ for man to live in true spiritual union with God," he argued, "so it requires faith to align oneself with the evil spirits—spirits which cause the triangle to glide across the face of the Ouija Board." Such reliance on blasphemous faith makes the device "deadly" and the user "easy prey for evil spirits" (1973:194–95).

A representative sample gathered from the traditions of teenagers in folklore archives in Ohio, Michigan, and Pennsylvania at first seems to confirm this evil image of the Ouija board. Violent, foul-speaking spirits frequently manifest, threatening to possess or harm the participants. And while some accounts describe trivial fortune-telling questions, some include the elements of sadistic sexual harassment. Nevertheless, it is also clear that they fit into a structured pattern. However improvised the ritual or board session may be, common narrative elements recur that fit it into a set of expectations. If "demons" manifest, their presence is neither surprising nor uncontrollable. The following narrative pattern seems to underlie the adolescent "success stories" consulted:

1. The users *invoke* a spirit.
2. They then *name* the spirit and determine its background.
3. Participants *test* the spirit by asking it questions with known or knowable answers.
4. The messages take on the character of a *dialogue* between the "spirit" and the users, in which the "spirit's" contribution is less and less predictable.
5. The users *confront* the spirit, challenging its statements and demanding a *sign* of its reality.
6. The users *terminate* contact.

Although not all accounts of successful Ouija board rituals give or elaborate all elements in this list, still all the texts consulted can be subsumed in this scheme. And the concepts seem implicit in observers' comments on the experience and on its significance to them. The nature of these elements can be illustrated in examples from these collections.

1. Invocation. Typically, the Ouija is used by a small group of teens in private, normally in a bedroom, though surprisingly often parents are included in the "game." Generating the right atmosphere for "spirits" was important: as in séances, lights were dimmed and candles lit to accentuate the uncanny atmosphere. Usually, participants began the session by asking out loud if a spirit was present, then, with two members touching the indicator, they quietly waited for it to move. One occultist who used the board to gain closer contact with "the spirit world" insisted on beginning with a protective prayer and opened with the question "Is there a spirit here who loves the Lord?" (OSUFA: Salvato 1987). But as with personalities who said they "believed in Jesus" during exorcism, this informant found that spirits contacted in this way still gave all kinds of "misleading crap."

2. Naming. Once "contact" has been made, users often begin, like exorcists, by asking for a name. One informant said that as soon as a spirit was contacted, they would ask if it was male or female, what it preferred to be called, when it had been alive, how old it was when it died, and similar questions about its past life. The answers determined what course the Ouija board session took (OSUFA: Weichel 1982). This process may be extended in follow-up questions that generate a history of the spirit's past life. The archival accounts show that the personalities tend to fall into one of two broad categories. One commonly found type of spirit, normally a "good" one, is that of a small child or woman who has died in an accident. In many other cases, however, such "good" spirits alternate with self-consciously evil ones. In addition to Satan and "the Devil" himself, teens described contacting spirits who identified themselves as "Evil," "Legion," and "Mark a.k.a. Lucifer."[1] In general, an "evil" spirit signaled its presence by moving the indicator "the wrong way," or counterclockwise (IUFA: Gans 1970:6–7; cited in Pimple 1985) or in "the Satan way . . . like a snake slither[ing] across the board" (OSUFA: Swartzel 1974; Keiser 1978). Obscene language also suggested evil spirits, as did refusing to spell out words like "God" or "cross," except in unusual ways. One account that includes several of these elements came from an Ohio youngster:

> Well, we kept saying that we wanted to talk to Satan 'cause everybody kept say, all the spirits kept saying that that was who the power really came from. And we kept pushing for it. And the messengers kept saying, "Ya—you know you're really going to be in trouble if you do. You're really going to make him mad."
>
> So finally it, it like stopped, then it started, it, it moved in a snake ["S" movements with the hands], in a writhing kind of thing. And it went around the board writhing like that. And then it, it kept circling the "S." And we asked who it was and finally it would say "Satan."

And it wouldn't spell, couldn't spell "God." It would spell "G,"
then it would go to the alphabet to spell "G." But then it would go
to the word "Good-bye" to pick out the "O" and then it would
come back to the alphabet to get "D." It couldn't use all the letters
out of the alphabet to spell "God" or "cross" or anything like that.
(OSUFA: Keiser 1978:15–16)

This stage seems clearly parallel to the practice of deliverance, which not
only sought a name for the indwelling spirit but also a distinctive character with a history. In any case, the messages coming from the board are
not disembodied answers to questions but expressions of an alternative
personality with mannerisms and moods of its own.

   3. *Testing.* However compelling these signs may be, users are not
satisfied until they have seen some evidence of the board's uncanny nature. Since two persons hold the planchette, it is possible that one may be
consciously or unconsciously directing its motions, so to eliminate (or at
least complicate) this theory, the group will try to prove that an independent personality is in control. In some cases, the action of the indicator
itself will prove its supernatural nature by flying off the table or doing
something else unexpectedly. Normally participants will test spirits by
asking it questions that have verifiable answers. The group could ask for
an answer known to one or another of the persons touching the indicator, but since that person could then direct it to the right answer, users
usually give the "spirit" a harder test. One would be to ask a question
known to someone who is in the room but is not touching the planchette.
In another instance, the person conducting the test chose not to say the
question out loud, yet received an appropriate answer (IUFA: Herman
and Cully 1970:10; cited by Pimple 1985). And on occasion the test involves information that no one in the room knows, but is verifiable.

Then I said, well, let's test this thing, R———. Let's see how truthful it is. See, I lost my yearbook and I said, "Could you tell me
where my yearbook is?" And they looked all over the house for it.
   It said, "coffee table," right, so I went out in the living room
and me and R———like ripped the coffee table apart. We like
threw everything everywhere, and I looked—I lifted up the coffee
table and underneath it was the—because you can't see underneath the coffee table—underneath it was my yearbook.
   I don't know what the heck it was doing underneath the

coffee table, and like I never looked there. So I didn't subconsciously know it was there, though. So like you can't say my subconscious did it because I didn't even think that it would be there, you know. (PSUHFA:Watkins 1988)

This phase can include a limited form of divination: participants may ask about important events in the immediate future. Other requests deal with upcoming events in the users' life. In such cases, the answers are not known, but will soon be made clear by future events. Some may involve romantic relationships: who will go with him/her to the prom, how long will a girl/boyfriend relationship last. Or the questions may include academic or sports events: what courses will the user fail, who will win the World Series, and the like.

Many accounts of Ouija rituals are limited to the first three elements, which constitute a slightly eerie form of play with divination. Even when sinister elements intrude, often the participants do not emphasize them. In one session taped in Columbus, Ohio, users began by asking the spirit where it came from. It responded, "H-E-L-L," but the participants gave a weak, "Oh, wow," reaction and continued by asking for the results of upcoming elections and basketball tournaments (OSUFA: Hilinski 1991). For many people, especially those in the twelve- to seventeen-year-old range, the Ouija ritual is not taken very seriously, and elements like those following are the exception rather than the rule.

4. *Dialogue.* However, if the users choose to pursue this activity, particularly past an introductory session, the interaction between them and the "spirits" contacted becomes more complex. The result is what we could now term a dialogue, since the initiative often shifts from the participants' questions to direct, often surprising comments from the "spirits." That is, the "spirit" who dominates the board now appears to take on an agenda of its own, and the participants now are forced to react to these messages. Both critics and users note that it is usually at this point that the rhetoric of spirits summoned becomes increasingly obscene and violent. Such indications suggest that at this phase in the ritual the participants are constructing an "antiworld." In this case, the medium used is language alone, of course, so the inversion results in a sarcastic, adversarial tone, combined with obscenities and antireligious elements. A sinister strain enters when questions about death are asked: who in the user's family will die next, or even how long will the users live. Some participants caution against asking such questions, saying that spirits

will lie or refuse to answer. But the topic may emerge from the dialogue spontaneously: the spirit contacted may indicate that they or their friends will come to some harm or even die.

5. *Confrontation.* Paradoxically, such threats rarely seem to frighten the users. More often, what follows is a verbal confrontation in which the adolescents deny the spirit's power: " . . . she like told [the spirit] off, you know, and it said, 'I'm going to kill you tonight, R—' and she goes, 'That's bull.' You know, she goes, 'A spirit cannot kill you, especially no Ouija board.' She says, 'What are you going to do, like fly this thing at my heart?' She was being really sarcastic to it. It said, 'Okay, fine. I'll just scare you then.' R— goes, 'Yeah, yeah, right,' you know" (PSUHFA: Watkins 1988).

At times this confrontation climaxes with some spontaneous sign that the messages are real and not figments of the users' imagination, often a result of the participants' refusal to take the threat seriously. In some cases, the sign is left to be fulfilled later in an unspecified way, as in the quote above. A near accident in a car, an unexplained noise, a queer dream, or even a phone call with no one on the other end could serve as the fulfillment of the "sign." Archival accounts suggest that, while many signs may be spontaneous, some are also the result of well-planned ostensive hoaxes.[2]

But many users demand an *immediate* sign to prove the spirit's power. In the most dramatic experiences, the verbal confrontation and the physical sign combine into a dramatic scene in which human and supernatural forces dispute in an almost tangible way. This account describes one version of "wrestling with the devil":

> And we kept provoking [the spirit], saying, "I don't believe in your power, and I don't believe you exist.". . . I remember saying things like, "You think you have all this strength and power, yet we can keep you from talking to us by just holding down on this dial and you can't talk to us." And we would use all of our mights and to the point where, to the point where that thing was cracking, and it would still move. And at one point we even stood up. We were standing up and the sides of, we pushed down in the middle, and the sides of the board as if someone were underneath it were folding up and creaking. And the board, honest, if we'd have kept going would have snapped. It was just rising out of our laps and the sides were curling, and it's wood. And it was just creaking and crawling up around the sides, as we were pushing

down. And then I think that we decided that that was about *enough.* (OSUFA: Keiser 1978:16)

This stage forms a climax to the ritual in two ways: the nature of the "spirit's" communications first forces a reaction from the participants, and their response then demands something extraordinary from the "spirit." This makes literal sense if we assume that the two sides of the dialogue are in fact distinct sides in the conversation. But the confrontation and particularly the literal sign make even more sense if we consider that the messages are consciously or subconsciously constructed by the users. If no such stage took place, the stories about the board's use are weird but nothing more, and participants may find themselves blamed for the irreligious and vulgar messages. The more violently obscene the language, the more extravagantly evil the entity, and the more spectacular the sign, then, the less likely those who actually spelled out the messages with the indicator will be held responsible for their content.

We could see the participants as doubly insulated from the "spirit" messages by the Ouija ritual. First, since two persons normally move the indicator, it is impossible to say for certain which one might have consciously spelled out the words. Second, a successful "test" and particularly an impressive sign both "prove" that a supernatural entity outside of the two users is responsible for the communications.

6. *Termination.* In most cases, once the sign is described, participants abruptly give up the ritual. Typical comments include, "That scared us so much that we stopped right then and we got rid of the Ouija board," and "Yeah, that was the last time we used it. We said, 'All right, that's enough!' and we turned on the lights, and we burnt the board." "It's like if you don't want to get a phone call, why have a phone?" one participant said. "It's just like get rid of it" (OSUFA: Keiser 1978). Again there seemed to be a contrast between cautionary fabulates and the more realistic personal experience stories reflecting actual Ouija sessions. Fabulates describe boards that refused to burn (OSUFA: Keiser 1978), or that would not burn completely, leaving the number "6" (for 666, the Devil's number) or the letters "H-E-L" (OSUFA: Hunt 1989).[3] But no personal experience stories described any difficulty in disposing of the device—or indeed in getting another one when the group got bored again.

Overall, anti-occult crusaders and serious occultists see the device as a means of opening up a sustained and permanent link with the other world, for good or ill; but adolescents see it as a part of a transient state to be approached, touched, then abandoned. The "fun" of activities like these rely on participants' faith that the trip they are taking through an alternative world that they have created has a secure starting point and a safe means of conclusion.

Whether this faith is justified, however, is another question. Even if the messages come not from a supernatural world but from the participants' imaginations, clearly the Ouija board ritual encourages the expression of powerful emotions in raw, frightening form. And the corpus analyzed here is made up of accounts volunteered only by those users who found the experience scary but enjoyable in the same sense as a well-constructed horror movie. Experiences that did lead to more prolonged mental difficulties are more likely to be told to more experienced occultists or Christian counselors. Overall, we can say that the Ouija ritual plays with creating an alternate state of consciousness that in an unstructured, uncontrolled state could be intensely frightening and possibly unhealthy. To this extent, the fears of crusaders and occultists are justified. However, the form of the ritual recognizes these dangers and attempts to channel this phenomenon in ways that most (but not all) participants find enjoyable and healthy. One commented, "I'm glad I got to experience it when I did."

Exorcism and Ouija as Parallel Experiences

Don Basham's simplified procedure for deliverance follows a format very similar to that of adolescents' Ouija rituals. In a handbook, he described how believers could cast out their own demons in private without the need of an exorcist. This required a quiet *preparation* in which believers confessed the satanic nature of occultism practices and reviewed their specific sins and resentments. Then the believer read out loud an itemized statement to Jesus renouncing any practice considered magical in nature, followed by a command for any demons present to identify themselves by *name*. A name would most likely come to mind, Basham advised his readers, or come spontaneously out of the believer's lips. Alternatively, one might feel some physical sensation or trembling: this "just means you've made contact, and you should proceed." Whatever name comes to mind should be accepted, even if it is embarrassing or shocking. Indeed, he assures his followers not to be concerned if this leads to a *confrontation* with "a particularly repulsive or violent demon," often giving its name as a heinous sin. Believers may not be guilty of committing this sin, but the demon would have eventually led them into committing it. After renouncing the demon by name and commanding it to leave, two or three times if necessary, Basham tells his readers to open their mouths and expel it. The physical act may be dramatic: a scream, gagging, or coughing attack; or it may be as gentle as a long sigh or yawn. Whatever followed, would be a physical *sign* that the exorcism was successful and the contact with the indwelling demon *terminated* (Basham 1972:202–8; Basham & Leggatt 1974:81–94).[4]

Basham does not advise the solitary self-exorcist to engage in *dialogue* with one's own demons, but his own accounts indicate that deliverance could frequently involve extended discussions with these alternate personalities. Other accounts make clear that such dialogues often tempted exorcists to use their contacts with spirits for spiritualistic purposes. Exorcists are warned against asking unnecessary questions because spirits often give deceptive answers, particularly when they reveal alleged details of crimes and how they might be solved. The desire to use such "spirit" personalities to validate doctrinal points or to challenge and taunt them remains so strong among exorcists that the Catholic rite specifically forbids priests to engage in frivolous talk with demons (MacHovec 1973:13; Martin 1976: 461; Richards 1974:224; Masters 1978:180–81).

The reason for this taboo is plain: using an exorcism as an opportunity to talk to demons makes exorcism into a sort of séance, with the demon-possessed person functioning as a kind of medium. When the dialogue, not the banishing of the spirit, becomes the focus of the event, it then can be prolonged past the point of safety. In Germany, a twenty-three-year-old Bavarian university student, Anneliese Michel, showed signs of possession, and in September 1975, the local Catholic diocese authorized a team of exorcists to treat her. Although several demons were cast out that fall, the team persisted in their efforts and even began taping the sessions because the demons "had so many fascinating things to say, especially about the reforms introduced as a result of the decisions of the [liberalizing] Second Vatican Council" (Goodman 1988:121). As a result, the woman fell into a deep depression and died on July 1, 1976, of anorexia, still under the supervision of the official exorcists. While defended by many within the Catholic Church, the tapes eventually became public during a widely publicized trial in 1978, when the girl's parents and two priests were found guilty of negligent homicide. The presiding priest affirmed his belief that he had done the right thing, and that the girl had "died willingly to atone for the sins of others."[5]

A similar phenomenon—dissociation of personality and the temporary emergence of alternative "selves"—has been observed in a wide range of contexts, including spiritualism and the psychological disorder of multiple personality. Mediums frequently used trance states in which they spoke in the persona of the "earth-bound spirit" afflicting a mentally ill patient. What is distinctive about exorcism is that the demons do not speak through a medium who has gained experience in "channeling" alternative personalities. Rather, the ritual encourages otherwise inexperienced individuals to let their dominant personalities give way abruptly to their own demons, who speak directly through their lips.

As such, exorcism more immediately resembles the dynamics of the Ouija ritual, with the exorcist serving as the analog of the necessary second person holding the planchette. Indeed, several of the evangelists who reacted most strongly against the Ouija ritual told of holding extended dialogues with demonic spirits during exorcism. Even though demons by their nature could be deceptive, Koch and his American followers held that they could be forced to speak the literal truth by using a verbal formula that was a "test for truth." This act of "commanding" demons involved rebuking the demon in the name of Jesus Christ, then demanding, "You must speak only the truth before Almighty God" or asking "Will that statement stand as truth before the true and living God?" This procedure theoretically eliminated the chance that demons would deceive the exorcist; of course, it simultaneously turned exorcism into a form of séance in which the exorcist could expect to receive supernatural answers to any question he might ask.[6]

The number of authorities who have connected the Ouija ritual and the rite of exorcism (e.g., Richards 1974:59–66; Watkins 1984:53–72) seems too persistent to be accidental. The act of casting out demons follows the same ritual structure as adolescents' Ouija rituals of *invoking* demons. They focus on inducing the same set of alternate states of consciousness, and we can expect similar features to emerge in accounts of both. Further, both rituals are founded on a genuinely extraordinary experience that induces an alternate state of consciousness. True, the mechanism by which the planchette seems to move by itself is probably a tactile illusion. Scientist Michael Faraday found an explanation for the apparently paranormal motions of table-tipping: even though participants *believe* they are pressing directly downward on an object,

Faraday demonstrated that in fact they are also pushing it to one side or the other. When two or more persons combine such a lateral pressure, the object underneath will appear to move by itself (Hunt 1985:20–21). The movements of the Ouija planchette apparently rely on the same illusion.

Even if we understand the physical *means* by which Ouija users move the indicator around the board, we are still far from understanding how it is that they construct messages. Often, the ways in which the words are spelled out suggest powers beyond those that the participants display in their everyday life. For instance, research done early in the century by Sir William F. Barrett showed that the Ouija board could spell out meaningful messages even when those who held the indicator were blindfolded and the letters were rearranged on the board in a random fashion (Barrett 1914). In a similar 1918 Canadian experiment, Dr. Horace Westwood found that his eleven-year-old daughter Anna could also produce messages on a homemade scrambled alphabet while blindfolded (1949:23–24). This talent suggests, at the very least, an unusual ability to discern (through verbal or non-verbal clues) and retain a mental image of the locations of the letters. While not every Ouija experience may involve such phenomena, narrators persistently give accounts of how spirits gave inexplicably correct answers to personal questions.

Even when a number of spirits manifest within the same possessed person or at the same Ouija session, they tend to fall into three consistent categories that have been identified in other phenomena involving alternate states of consciousness. Evans (1989:80–82) classifies these personality types into three groups. One common type is a timid, introverted *Self-1* who shows little initiative. Ouija users note that the first spirit to show up frequently identifies itself as a small child who died at an early age. We recall, too, that self-identified demons that manifest during deliverance will sometimes have childlike voices and claim to have entered when the victim was very young. This spirit alternates with a much more aggressive and reckless *Self-2* that advocates activities that the normal self would not consider. Hence, extreme vulgarity and threats of violence appear in an "antiself" that is the analog to the "antiworld" self that we have seen as central to adolescents' rebellious folklore. Many "demons," both in Ouija rituals and exorcisms, seem to be extreme extensions of Self-2 personalities. Finally, Evans notes a mediating "prudent and wise" *Self-3* that attempts to integrate the timid Self-1 and the potentially self-destructive Self-2. Such a type presumably underlies personalities such as the more sophisticated "spirit guides" developed by experienced mediums and occultists who use the Ouija.

Finally, we observe that both rituals involve a great deal of role-playing. The spirits that Ouija users contact are not unfamiliar types, and they and the users play similar kinds of games of mutual aggression. Interestingly, tongue-speakers confronted by an exorcist in Koch's camp, after an initial moment of confrontation, readily come around to admitting that the Charismatic activities they have previously enjoyed were inspired by Satan. This implies that participants in rituals in which they are expected to express alternate personalities will accommodate the person conducting the ritual, even when it means expressing ideas antagonistic to their previous behavior. A similar phenomenon was noted by the second-century Christian apologist Tertullian, who belonged to a sect that practiced exorcism and other spirit-led activities. In his justification of his religion, he described what must have been a spectacular yet reliable confrontation with the equivalent of "mediums" who advertised their ability to speak in the voice of a "daemon" or pagan divinity:

> Produce someone before your tribunals, who is admittedly demon-possessed. Let any Christian you please bid him speak, and the spirit in the man will own himself a demon—and truly—just as he will elsewhere call himself a god, falsely. . . . if they do not confess they are demons, not daring to lie to a Christian, then shed that impudent Christian's blood on the spot! What could be plainer than such a deed? What proof more reliable? The simplicity of the truth is plain to see. Its own power is in it. . . . If on the one hand they really are gods, why do they lie and say they are demons? To oblige us? (1931:125, 127)

Tertullian's ironic comment holds true in one sense: the extreme suggestibility shown by such mediums demonstrates that the controlling entities could not be "gods" if a simple change in context could induce such a turnabout. Further, such a reversal must have been predictable indeed if the exorcist could bet his life on the results before a hostile pagan tribunal.

But his closing remark points to a final factor: when one party in an alternate state of consciousness engages in role-playing, others engaging in the same activity may also adopt other personalities in a way that may not be consciously controlled by either party. In a precisely analogous process, two persons normally move the indicator in the Ouija ritual, but neither feels responsible for fabricating or constructing the message. Such a process, in fact, is probably facilitated if both persons are participating in alternate state of consciousness, which may also explain why those conducting deliverance may speak in tongues while the patient is simultaneously expressing demonic voices. Basham, in fact, observes that demons were in fact as stirred up by tongues as they were by mention of "The Blood" (1972:197–98).

If we accept that deliverance relies on many of the same mental processes as spiritualism and the Ouija ritual, we can see why authors within the deliverance ministry often come from a background in which they had experimented with spiritualism or at least with the Ouija. Such parallel traditions may well be ways of cultivating the means of altering one's consciousness and at least channeling it for a defined positive religious purpose. However, as both spiritualists and Ouija users have cautioned, it is impossible to avoid "bad trips," and the emergence of self-defined mischievous or destructive personalities can be both dangerous and stubborn to treat. For this reason, any tradition that relies on training its participants to create and use alternative states of consciousness must somehow define and neutralize these Self-2 manifestations. Believers, in short, may find that the same techniques that allow them to tap the extraordinary perceptive and creative talents uncovered during such alternative states may also create, or at least bring them in contact with, startlingly obscene and violent personalities.

In short, exorcism and the Ouija ritual are mirror-image forms of calling and dismissing demons and hence participating directly in myth. Christian, spiritualist, and diabolical contacts with spirits, in short, comprise similar dynamics and could be equally dangerous. Whatever the precise etiology of these alternate states of consciousness, participants usually define their nature as involving personal control over supernatural forces, which is a form of magic. And any mythology that involves good magic must also construct rituals to neutralize bad magic. It follows that spiritualists' and Ouija users' means of confronting and banishing "bad spirits" parallel the deliverance ministry's parallel means of identifying and exorcising demons.

Ouija and Exorcism as Mythmaking

Further, both activities are alike in their goals—to allow participants to participate in the Christian myth directly. In most denominations, believers are passive, with acts of power—prayer, healing, the consecration of the Eucharist—reserved for priests and other institutionally designated specialists. Bible reading and reflection on doctrinal issues may satisfy many believers, but others seek a more direct experience of the divine. Deliverance and the Ouija are parallel paths to this close encounter with the world of angels and demons. Deliverance, to be sure, is an intensely ideological battlefield, in which even the slightest dip into heresy, even within closely related fundamentalist Christian sects, can be defined as demon-inspired. By contrast, a religious ideology is difficult to find in accounts of adolescents' board experiences. Most Ouija board rituals conducted by adolescents, in fact, can hardly be called "satanic," because the information revealed by spirits invariably confirms the dogmas of mainstream Christianity. Such warnings also seem not to deter others from engaging in their own rituals. The more seriously the board is described as dangerous, the more attractive it becomes in some teens' minds. The enormous success of the movie *The Exorcist* hardly affected youngsters' use of the Ouija board; indeed, some informants claimed that seeing the movie inspired them to try one out to see what would happen. And in years to come, *Witchboard*, a horror movie allegedly illustrating the demonic nature of the Ouija ritual, likewise encouraged use of it among some teens. What elements in the ritual account for this paradoxical traffic with Satan among groups who could otherwise be most expected to reject him?

Popular occult movements, however they differ from Christianity, are like orthodox religion by having ideologies that subordinate individual initiative to dogma, whether quasi-religious or scientific. The Ouija board ritual, being a folk ritual by definition, allows the participants to act as if they were in an alternative world outside of all such ideologies. For all of its gamelike elements, it is a modest kind of shamanistic quest, in which individuals or small groups seek out their own personal definitions of the mythic world, often in the face of priestly institutions. Occultist Gina Covina seems to come closest to this angle of the ritual: "Ouija is a tool through which we enter into conversation with the parts of ourselves that are God, the parts of us that reach beyond our conscious selves into the infinite one reality that is God. Ouija is a tool through which we become more and more conscious that we are God. Let's say it in the bluntest way possible: The Ouija board is a tool through which we become God" (Covina 1979:153). Institutionalized religions, however, have been jealous of such conversations with the divine, and have sought to limit such power to professional priests and holy men. So legends about invoking *angels* are few, and (as with apparitions of the Virgin Mary) are usually described as being initiated by the angel or divine being, not humans. The Charismatic movement constructed rituals to allow the common person to be overcome by divine spirits, and so provided such an avenue for direct involvement in myth. For other Christians wanting to contact mythic forces directly, the only social alternatives have been spiritualism or means of invoking specifically diabolical spirits, as with the Ouija. As these three were rival ways of accomplishing the same end, it now becomes clear why both Charismatics and spiritualists both actively campaigned against use of the Ouija board.

The Ouija experience thus can be seen as an exact parallel to exorcism, in which an evil spirit or devil is invoked, questioned, then confronted and, after some kind of frightening sign, sent away. Furthermore, there seems to be a strong element of role-playing on both sides, such that successful Ouija board experiences, like dramatic exorcisms, take on the quality of improvised morality plays. The Devil and his demons, when questioned, do not disguise their evil nature but play their traditional roles to the hilts. Indeed, the image of the Devil that emerges is an unattractive figure that practically asks to be rejected, and participants show no hesitation in challenging him and, eventually, terminating contact. So both rituals are literal enactments of the baptismal rite in which the believer (or his sponsors) are asked to reject the Devil and all of his works.

The strictly orthodox nature of this devil is illustrated by a student's account of one dialogue. When asked if it was afraid of those in the room, it responded that it did fear all those who were wearing crucifixes, and was especially afraid of "my dad because it said that he had the gift of the Holy Spirit." (PSUHFA: Shaller 1990.) In another session attended by a student studying to be a minister, the indicator refused to move, citing "SON OF GOD" as the reason (OSUFA: Swartzel 1974). This probably explains why the ritual seems especially popular among adolescents who otherwise display a strongly fundamentalist worldview. Edmond C. Gruss found that fully half of the students at his Baptist-run college/seminary had either used a Ouija board or knew a close friend or relative who had done so, a surprisingly high figure since most students had come from Christian families that rejected fortune-telling (1975:59, 174–75). Other religious writers note with some horror that even "spirit-filled" students at the strictest religious schools could be found using or improvising a Ouija board (Pedigo 1971:58).

An experience reported to Gruss by "a Christian young man" is typical of these "holy" Ouija rituals. One evening after attending church, Gruss relates, the believer and three friends lit candles and called spirits on their Ouija board. After awhile

> they became quite bold and said, "May we have Satan in our presence." Nothing happened, but the pointer began to go in circles. All of a sudden the pointer flew out of their hands and went off the table. They put it back on the board and asked if Satan was present. The indicator went to YES. They asked several questions and became more frightened, as the answers were too accurate for comfort. The young man stated that fear gripped them all, as the candles dimmed, and a feeling of evil pervaded the room. One of the fellows threw his pocket New Testament on the Ouija board, only to have it scoot off in a different direction. They all joined in prayer at this point, asking for the evil presence to leave. . . . This experience ended their use of the Ouija board.

It would be condescending to describe this as a "game," since Gruss notes that even after the Devil was rejected, all four of the participants experienced religious crises, one even developing what Gruss called "different personalities." The ritual required a second rite of termination, in which under Gruss's direction the board was located, formally renounced, then destroyed. After this, at least two of the participants found their religious faith restored (1975:91–92).

This conclusion should not be surprising: adolescents talking to demons on the Ouija board or evangelists provoking demons during a Charismatic religious meeting are not really looking for an alternative ideology; they want to know if the one they already accept is valid. Simply accepting theological credos passively is for many not enough: they need to test and directly participate in events that demonstrate their truth in terms of direct religious experience. The Ouija ritual, for adolescents, sets up a temporary anti-ideology that mirrors mainstream Christianity so that they can participate actively in mythmaking without themselves challenging traditional Christian dogma. Even if the ritual contains playlike elements, at heart it is not play, but ritual. It provides direct confirmation for adolescents' religious worldviews, which they are in the process of testing and internalizing. The "sign" that they demand from the Devil is also a powerful demonstration of the existence of a traditional God. This suggests that even though it is Satan whom the teens call and with whom they converse, they are really intending to contact God.

For the deliverance ministry, however, the intention of exorcism was slightly different. Their anti-ideology was, like their own, a real challenge to mainstream denominations. Without such ongoing, dramatic contacts with the supernatural, they believed, Christianity was passive in the face of satanic threat. Thus, this movement was committed to regular confrontations with the demonic world. And such confrontations did not occur entirely on the psychic plane. Oral tradition includes many stories about magical duels that take place in the real world when one occultist maliciously tries to harm another person but is instead harmed himself when it turns out that the stranger is a more powerful witch. Harry Hyatt collected a terse German American variant in Quincy, Illinois, during the 1930s: "A man was going down the street, driving a team of horses. A man standing on the corner laugh[sic] at him, and one of his horses fell down and broke his leg. The man on the wagon said, 'You are not so smart.' He crack [sic] his whip, and the man on the sidewalk fell down and broke his leg. It was *a witch meeting a witch* "(1965:847, no. 16235; emphasis his).

And as a type of testimony, the "witch meeting a witch" pattern shows up in many anecdotes circulated by the deliverance ministry. As early as 1948, ex-spiritualist Victor Ernest interpreted unusual mental stress during a service as a satanic attack and asked his congregation to plead the Blood with him. Soon afterward, he took the confession of a woman who claimed that she and a companion were the witches responsible: when their attack failed, she attempted suicide and her companion was committed to an insane asylum (1970:59–60). Similarly, Koch relates the experience of a friend who crusaded against occult books. One day a physician called to admit that he had himself used such books in his practice. "Because of this," the doctor said, "I tried to use my magical powers against you but they didn't work. I find that there's a power around you and protecting you which is greater than mine." Concluding, "I must carry the consequences of this now myself," the doctor committed suicide the next day (Koch and Lechler 1970:127).

Koch did not deny the validity of faith healing within a Christian context. In fact, he attributed his miraculous recovery from satanically inspired illnesses to the prayers of his supporters. And, beginning in 1932, he both advocated and practiced a form of faith healing that combined confession of past sins with anointing with oil and prayers by church elders (see Ensign and Lowe 1984). But he felt that faith healing could also be a diabolical gift, too close to *Brauche* for comfort, and compared many forms of it with healing practiced in spiritualist circles. In particular, he denounced several prominent Christian healers as "mediumistic," using powers derived from the Devil. Those who went to such healers, Koch claimed, were subjected to occult bondage just like those who were charmed by folk healers. Oral Roberts, for instance, was an example of a Christian who mistook his own "mediumistic" abilities as power given by the Holy Spirit. His suspicions were further aroused when the evangelist visited Germany in 1966.[7] At the Congress he attended, a rumor circulated that Roberts had once been charmed by an "old Indian," who had presumably communicated diabolical powers to him,[8] but Koch was unsuccessful in convincing other fundamentalists to denounce him.

So Koch describes he and his supporters attended one of his prayer meetings, first praying "Lord Jesus, if this man is working for you then bless his ministry and use him. If, however, he is opposing your work then hinder his ministry tonight." The healer, according to Koch, found himself mysteriously unable to do healings and commented to the audience that "there are some counter-forces at work in the meeting tonight" (1972:12). Thus, in an ironic inversion, Koch took on the role of the witches who tried to hinder Victor Ernest's preaching. In this case, though, Koch's success in supernaturally disrupting the meeting meant that he, and his power, represented the stronger form of Christian magic

This approach could come close indeed to the parallel traditions of spiritualism and the Ouija ritual. One of Koch's favorite narratives (1971)[9] tells of Pat Tolosa, a student at the Lutheran Theological Seminary in Manila. He came one day to the president, a Dr. Hufstetler, complaining of a terrible headache and asking the man to pray for him. When the president did so, Tolosa went into a trance and began to speak in strange voices. Hufstetler sent for Koch, who was visiting on a lecture tour. Koch at once recognized the case as one of demonic possession and asked the voices to identify themselves. There were "fifty demons" possessing him "because he didn't make the full surrender." It seemed that Tolosa had not undergone the experience of conversion and so, in Koch's view, was still a sectarian. Besides, his mother was an active "sorceress" in the native religion. Koch commented, "This is a warning for us: every incomplete surrender is an open door for the power of demons."

The fifty demons came out one by one, each expressing individual personalities. "We had to deal with demons from all over the world," Koch recalled, "therefore they spoke in different languages." They frequently lied to the exorcists but gave themselves away "with derisive laughter." Anyway, he adds, "they were forced to tell the truth" when they were commanded in the name of the Lord. The usual suspects appeared. One demon admitted coming from "an occult circle" in Holland; another was a "Russian demon" who explained that a group of communists in Manila were shadowing Pat, looking for a chance to murder him. A spiritual threat now had become a literal one, and so local police were notified to investigate and arrest this group. One unusually cooperative voice identified itself as "Rakrek" from Communist China. By this time, practical issues of how to dispossess Tolosa had faded to the background, as Koch eagerly conversed with the demon about the Devil's theological agenda:

> "What do you want in our schools?"
>
> "I will confuse the minds of the students and then bring modernism and liberalism to the schools."
>
> ... "Why do you wish to bring modernism and liberalism to the school?"
>
> The voice answered, "You have a good school. We bring to you the modernists and liberalists because they are our companions."
>
> I wish all modern theologians had heard this: "The modernists and liberalists are our companions." That means that companions of the demons are standing on the pulpit to preach the Gospel. (1971; cf. 1973b:143–44)

Other demons confirmed that the second coming of Jesus Christ was indeed immanent. "That is interesting," Koch commented ironically, "modern theologians deny the second coming of the Lord, and the demons know it—and fear it. The demons have a better theology than the modern theologians" (1971; cf. 1973b:146; 1980b:35).

The exorcism came to a climax when one demon began to attack Koch and his writings, leading to a direct confrontation:

The demon declared, "Doctor Koch, you commanded us in France, you commanded us in Switzerland, and now you command us in the Philippines. Leave us alone." A second time he accused me: "We are destroyed by your books. Some of my companions in Europe are not satisfied. Leave us alone." Until then I had not realized that books could have such an effect. . . .

In another phase of the battle I was attacked again. The demon said, "With the strongest hypnosis of Sumatra, fall asleep." In this moment his eyes were flashing in a horrible fire, so that I hardly could stand his glance. In my heart, I looked at Jesus and replied, "In the name of the Lord, I laugh at your hypnosis. I stand under the protection of the Blood of Jesus."

The demon repeated his attack and screamed, "With the strongest black magic of Egypt and the most powerful black magic of Tibet I will kill you." I replied like before: "In the name of the Lord I laugh at your threats. You are ridiculous folly; you have nothing to offer."

He threatened again and screamed at me, "With the strongest black magic of Mexico and Africa, I will kill you." Again, I gave him the same answer: "I laugh at you in the name of Jesus." (1971; cf. 1973b:14; 1980b:34–35)

Eventually, even this demon was forced to give up and was cast out. All the participants, Koch concluded, were overwhelmed by the experience and compelled to repentance and prayer.

Conclusions

Obviously, this narrative and the Ouija ritual parallel each other. Both involve a face-to-face confrontation with evil spirits, not so much to worship Satan but to taunt and reject him. Meantime, the "antiworld" nature of the event paradoxically confirms the religious values of the participants. The demons, ritually commanded to speak the truth and nothing but the truth, admit that communists, "occult circles," and modernist theologians are their friends. Hence, Koch is justified in using information obtained from demons to expose those people who are secretly part of Satan's plot to take over the world. Tolosa proves to be only partially to blame: he had failed to make "the complete surrender." But his own mother was the far more serious factor because, as Koch pointed out at the end of his account, she was a "sorceress" in a non-Christian sect. Her occult sins actually *caused* Tolosa's demon possession, much as Koch's childhood terrors were caused by his great-grandmother's use of *The Sixth and Seventh Books of Moses*.

Most importantly, the exorcism proved a stunning validation for Koch's ministry. Just as the Ouija ritual subjects demons to teenagers' manipulation, so too Koch was able to command Tolosa's demons and prove that his ministry was a threat to the satanic plot. His ability to withstand the strongest spells that the demons could try to cast proved that his supernatural power was greater than that wielded by all fifty demons. While Koch made no pretensions to being or wanting to become God, certainly the experience and similar ones allowed him to claim Jesus' divine power to perform miracles on the same level. And in so doing he gave the world inspired testimony from truth-speaking demons that he was the superior magus who could command them all. For both adolescents and for deliverance circles like those advised by Koch, the demons' theology was indeed better than the beliefs that underlay the sterile, intellectual world of mainstream sects. For invoking and commanding demons allowed them to participate directly in the Christian mythos and carry out the work of God in a more dramatic way than Sunday liturgies.

One difference, though, is that for adolescents the confrontation is an end in itself. By challenging a demon's power and receiving a sign, they demonstrate for themselves the power of God, crosses, pocket testaments, and other symbols of faith. Once this is tested, for virtually all participants the Ouija becomes irrelevant and is set aside. For the deliverance ministry, exorcism only begins a long process of avoiding and countering the many sources of demonization. Those delivered must now learn to recognize and fight Satan's presence on earth. Koch's use of the Tolosa exorcism to diabolize liberalism, communism, and occultism was only the first in an effort to locate real-life "satanic networks." More importantly, such pronouncements made in trance could then be used to identify the source of others' occult affliction. Since human representatives of demons made such psychic attacks, these co-workers of Satan could be identified in this world, not the next. Such a mythic activity thus tends to shade into the secular realms of therapy and law enforcement.

4

Putting the Pieces Together

MPD and Ritual Abuse Narratives

> Do not cast it aside, for your child may be next!
> —Veronica Lueken, *The Incredible Bayside Prophecies
> on the United States and Canada!*

We now turn to the role of investigators who, through persistent interrogation, helped patients recover from mental illnesses by recognizing and reconstructing childhood traumas. A number of excellent critiques exist of the techniques that were used to piece together the stories of allegedly abused children and adult "survivors" of ritual abuse.[1] These discussions focus on the controversy that emerged publicly in the late 1980s and early 1990s, but this practice descended directly from a much earlier tradition that blamed a variety of mental and physical ills on the influence of demonic spirits. Kurt E. Koch's synthesis of psychology with folk healing proved attractive to a growing Christian mental health movement in Great Britain and the United States. The two major British discussions of demon possession, Michael Harper's *Spiritual Warfare* (1970) and John Richards's *But Deliver Us from Evil* (1974) repeatedly cite Koch's case histories as authoritative. In the United States, Koch was endorsed by fundamentalist theologian Merrill F. Unger in his *Demons in the World Today* (1971). Unger's work was followed in 1972 by two popular books: Gary Wilburn's *The Fortune Sellers* and the best-seller, *Satan Is Alive and Well on Planet Earth*, written by Unger's student, Hal Lindsey.[2]

This theological acceptance soon led to practical manuals on how to counsel the occult-oppressed Christian: Kent Philpott's *Manual of Demonology and the Occult* (1973) and Peter Anderson's *Talk About the Devil* (1973) applied Koch's ideas to show Christian counselors how to recognize and exorcise demons caused by occultism. This complex of ideas soon influenced secular psychological medicine as Koch and his mentor Alfred Lechler inspired respect from professionals. When John Warwick Montgomery organized a symposium on demon possession at the University of Notre Dame under the auspices of the Christian Medical Association (1976), participating clinical psychologists were often skeptical of demon possession as a diagnosis. Nevertheless, they cited Koch and Lechler more frequently than any other resources.

In particular, Dr. John White, Associate Professor of Psychiatry at the University of Manitoba, endorsed Lechler's diagnostic description of demon possession, noting cases from his own practice. One woman in particular failed to respond, either to standard antipsychotic drug therapy or to White's own polite version of exorcism. Returning from vacation, however, he found the patient visibly improved. In his absence, he learned, she had visited another exorcist whose teaching White felt was a jumble of "psychological insightfulness and wild inaccuracy." The exorcist claimed, for instance, that fully 25 percent of the North American population was affected by demon possession, a figure White found fantastic. Yet he could not deny that this exorcist's ritual had helped his patient while his own therapy had not; the woman remained symptom-free under later observation (1976:292–94).

Although Koch warns counselors to exclude obvious mental illness before proceeding to exorcism, the broad range of activities he defines as occult makes demonization nearly impossible to rule out. And when he factored in the occult activities of blood relatives, the range of mental illnesses that could be blamed on the occult became virtually universal. After some misgivings, Basham too accepted multigenerational demonization as real. In one exorcism, a demon claimed it had a right to stay in a young girl's body because "I was here when she was born." At first Basham assumed that the demon was lying. "But it was as if the Holy Spirit brought to mind," he countered, "just as children can be born with physical birth defects such as crossed eyes and club feet, they can also be born with a form of demonic torment" (1971a:23). Maxwell Whyte also endorsed this concept, claiming that he continuously received letters describing "cases of people bound in wheel chairs because their mother or father (or both) were involved in occultism in some form or another." Citing Exodus 20:5, he maintained that occult practices could lead to both mental and physical disorders, as far down the family tree as great-grandchildren (1973c:72–73). It was but a short step from this religious practice to the secular practice of psychological therapy, during which patients, often under hypnosis or in a meditative state of mind, would recover repressed memories of the occult that in turn explained their present difficulties. Indeed, Charismatics' belief that the role of family members bound their children to demons through occult practices seems to have inspired the claim that now emerged, that parents literally involved their children in blood sacrifices to Satan.

As a number of scholars have noted, the period of the 1970s, during which the deliverance ministry developed, coincided with a social move to combat sexual abuse of women and particularly of small children.[3] Such a move was on the whole beneficial, as it allowed topics previously tabooed to emerge into both academic and political discussion. However, this social dialogue coincided with secular therapists' interest in the techniques of exorcism. As a third factor, the clinical condition called "multiple personality disorder," or MPD, in which alternate "selves" emerge and succeed each other outside of trance states, also became a popular research topic during the 1970s. Again, this study had a rationale: some persons diagnosed with this disorder spontaneously change "selves" and behavior patterns much like persons undergoing exorcism.

These three elements developed among some networks of therapists into a core set of beliefs and practices, which became for secular psychiatry the analog of the "diabolical medicine" created by Koch and his followers. That is, many different puzzling mental disorders were now diagnosed as resulting from multiple personalities. Intensive therapy, often involving clinical hypnosis, attempted to get the patient to recall memories of childhood trauma, thought to be the cause of the disorder. These memories at first seemed bizarre and disconnected. To piece them together into a narrative that would explain what had happened and why, patients and therapists collaborated to construct them in terms of current social demonologies. Over time, these traumas were identified as evidence for real acts of "ritual abuse" carried out by members of satanic cults. The detail with which patients described such rituals and the clinical improvement they experienced after disclosing them attested to the authenticity of these memories. However, as we will see, the nature by which these memories were recovered and put together actually links them far more closely to the existing traditions of exorcism and the Ouija board rather than to principles of criminal investigation.

Therapy and Spiritualism

In translating what had been an essentially religious experience to the secular world of psychotherapy, those involved lost sight of a number of factors that might otherwise have made them cautious. First, therapy often involved techniques similar to those used to induce alternative states of consciousness. Dissociation and role-playing are characteristics of such states, so the personalities that emerged were similar to those previously identified as typical of spiritualism trances, Ouija board dialogues, and exorcisms. Second, persons in these alternative states seem passive, but in fact they appear to develop skills of observing others' non-verbal signals and are also enabled to construct detailed stories seemingly without preparation or labor. Finally, a common element in such accounts involves recovering memory of an event, often experienced as satanic in nature, that closely parallels the sexual harassment and rape of women. Hence, therapy sessions (and, later, police investigations) may have recreated conditions similar to ritual events in folk and religious culture, during which persons were encouraged to dissociate and express alternative personalities.

1. Many of the techniques of therapy can lead to an alternate state of consciousness. Hypnotism has frequently been used to regress patients to states during which they could relive accounts of traumas that might relieve their mental problems. However, this technique shows up in many of the spiritualistic phenomena discussed in the previous chapter.[4] Not surprisingly, the literature of the deliverance ministry repeatedly portrays it as an evil craft. Hobart Freeman called it "one of the most subtle and potentially dangerous forms of magical practice," and, in a claim current since the early days of mesmerism, suggested that hypnotists used it to gain sexual favors from female patients. Worse, once hypnotized, patients became more susceptible to trance states and even to invasion by evil spirits. Indeed, he found, demons had confessed during exorcisms that "the power behind the hypnotist is Satan himself" (1969:36–38). Maxwell Whyte was equally explicit: "One who practices hypnotism is a witch!" In fact, he warned, the trance is induced when "familiar spirits" in control of the hypnotist take over the patient's mind. The power of hypnotism is the same as that behind "the evil eye," he says, which is why many demon-possessed persons have "narrow pupils" that are naturally hypnotic. In addition, even after the trance is over, the demons remain latent in the victim's personality (1973c:59, 63–65).

Such an antipathy did not prevent a number of ministers from using hypnosis during their own counseling sessions, with results similar to those seen by deliverance ministers. Again, it seems likely that this diabolization of hypnotism derives from a recognition that its tactics comprise yet another "satanic counterfeit" of those being used by Christians to get in touch with their inner demons. And hypnotism in fact gained some following among some fundamentalists: a tape recording distributed in 1968 by the Reverend David Lawson told of how he counseled "Judy," a young woman suffering from emotional problems, by inducing a hypnotic trance so that he could talk to an "Inner Judy." One day a harsh voice unlike either Judy intruded, calling itself a demon and boasting that he and his fellows would try to kill her. Indeed, the voice became more intrusive, sometimes suppressing Judy's own personality entirely, until during one session she attempted suicide. Rev. Lawson also found that the demons inhabiting Judy had the ability to give "intimate details of [his] private life which no other human being could possibly know." In desperation, Rev. Lawson called in a relative who was a minister in a small Pentecostal church, who came and over several sessions managed to expel a series of demons, after which Judy led a normal "victorious Christian life." While Basham retold this story as a valid example of deliverance, he warned in a footnote, "Hypnosis itself can lead to demonic activity" (1972:138–40).

But alternate states of consciousness can be induced by means other than hypnosis. Sigmund Freud was initially convinced that the women he diagnosed as suffering from hysteria had experienced perverse sexual abuse during their childhood, as nearly all related detailed accounts of their fathers committing incest with them. When he eventually concluded that most of these accounts were not literally true, he wrote, "the result at first was hopeless bewilderment. Analysis had led by the right paths back to these sexual traumas, and yet they were not true. Reality was lost from under one's feet. At that time I would gladly have given up the whole thing [psychoanalysis]. . . . Perhaps I persevered only because I had no choice and could not then begin again at anything else" (qtd. in Sargant 1961:192). An unintentional alternate state of consciousness may result from the fatigue, repetition, and sensory deprivation of intensive counseling. Psychologist William Sargant, describing the process of "brainwashing," or forcing involuntary conversions among political prisoners, notes in passing that such tactics have been used accidentally during police interrogations. It was very easy, he warned, to induce a state in which prisoners could be led to believe (at least temporarily) that they had committed the crimes to which they were confessing. The situation is made more complex when the interrogators were unaware that they were being affected by the same factors that were altering the prisoners' state of mind. Hence, they too were led into an alternate state of consciousness during which, in good faith, they collaborated in constructing confessions that both sides felt were sincere and truthful. Clearly, therapists who lack Freud's skepticism can unintentionally participate in the process of reconstructing ritual abuse accounts, even when they feel that they are not *verbally* coaching the patient.

2. *During such alternate states, people can develop unusual capabilities for constructing stories.* Freud's initial belief reflects the surprising facility with which persons in an alternate state of consciousness can "remember" convincing stories. Martin Orne, a Pennsylvania University psychiatrist, showed that hypnosis could produce especially convincing testimony. He regressed a patient to the age of six and asked him to make typical drawings. In response, the patient produced pictures that genuinely looked like child's artwork: "It seemed as if he actually relived [his life]." However, Orne was able to obtain some actual drawings the patient had done at that age and compare them to those he had done under hypnosis. They proved to be quite different; yet Orne commented, "If you didn't have the real thing, it would have looked as if it were an actual recollection and reliving" (qtd. in Evans 1989:189–90).

A similar experiment conducted on a twenty-three-year-old English woman produced what seemed to be even more convincing evidence. When she was regressed past her birth date, she spontaneously recalled being tried for witchcraft in 1556. Speaking in archaic language, she described many precise details of her trial and of her everyday life, details that were confirmed when the researcher located a rare publication on British witch trials that mentioned the very trial in the woman's memories. Outside of hypnotic trance, the woman had no recollection of reading about the subject, and her behavior in trance seemed sincere and compelling beyond any talent she might have had for playacting. But further research found reason to doubt the authenticity of these past-life memories: the rare publication had in fact made factual errors discovered when the court records were located, errors that also occurred in the woman's "memories." Analysis of her archaic-seeming language, too, showed that it did not preserve the actual language and patterns of sixteenth-century English but owed more to modern media images of "Elizabethan" English. Somehow, researchers concluded, she must have read the witchcraft story and stored it away in her deep memories, even though it was now beyond her ability to consciously bring it to memory (Victor 1993:87–89).

Sargant suggests a possible function for such fabrications when he treated patients suffering from mental problems caused by traumatic experiences during World War II. First he found that sedating such patients, then encouraging them to "relive" the terror of the event, significantly improved their mental health. But further experience showed that *better* results could be obtained by suggesting to patients some imaginary situation that involved analogous fears. Though this situation was pure fantasy, he reasoned, the fear that it might happen could be at the root of these patients' disorder. A methodology was developed in which patients were brought to a suggestive state of mind, then stimulated to imagine being involved in a terrifying scenario.

Often, Sargant says, this process climaxed in a sudden emotional collapse, after which many of such patients' nervous symptoms dramatically disappeared. "If, however, little emotion had been released, and [the patient] had only had his intellectual memory of some horrible episode refreshed," he stressed, "little benefit could be expected. *But a falsely implanted memory might create a larger emotional discharge than the real and induce the physiological effects needed for psychological relief*" (1961:xxv; emphasis mine).[5] In a similar way, Sargant continues, psychologists counseling patients may induce a similar process "by believing and conveying to his patient, for instance, that certain childhood traumata have caused his symptoms." After a process of thought and anxiety, the patient "may come up with detailed and complicated accounts of emotional damage done him on this or that occasion." It seems rash to claim any special status of accuracy for stories obtained through hypnosis. Dr. Pierre Janet, the French psychologist who made some of the first clinical descriptions of patients with multiple personalities or with indwelling demons, once heard a colleague say that "he has never come across a hypnotised subject who tells lies." He commented ironically, "If so, he's been very lucky" (qtd. in Evans 1989:115).

Unless the process of counseling is carefully controlled, Sargant concludes, such accounts may emerge with enough conviction that they are sincerely believed to be real memories by both patient and therapist (1961:191). This kind of warning clearly should have been heard about the early ritual abuse stories. Therapists saw that patients relating them clearly improved, and the way in which they were told suggested memories sincerely recalled rather than attempts to fabricate stories or deceive the listener. Further, the contents of these accounts, often graphic and bizarre, suggested something that no one would choose to invent under therapy. But in fact many therapists actively help their patients construct their narratives. Daniel Ryder, a social worker and head of a codependency treatment program for ritual abuse survivors, claims that his patients typically have no clear memories of the abuse when they enter treatment. Rather, they display one of a set of very general symptoms, such as fear of being the center of attention or vague memories of childhood. The actual memories, he explains, emerge only gradually, often in the form of bad dreams or flashbacks, and Ryder advises therapists to "prime" their patients with generalized articles on Satanism, exorcism, and others' ritual abuse narratives before encouraging them to tell their own stories (1992:esp. 89–92).

Even when efforts were made not to coach patients, though, we have seen that in an alternate state of consciousness people develop skills of heightened perceptivity. Many patients claiming to have multiple personalities also have a "chameleon-like manipulative personality" that tends to produce the kinds of narratives they sense therapists want to hear (Victor 1993:93). Under such conditions, there may have been no way to avoid non-verbal signals between patient and therapist that would unintentionally shape the direction of a story, just as Ouija board users often can answer questions correctly even when the person who knows the correct answer is not touching the planchette. Still, such an interpretation may partially beg the question: where did the horrifying elements of child sexual abuse come from in the first place?

3. Elements of violence, demonology, and sexual abuse are intrinsic to the alternate state of consciousness. In the nineteenth century, trance mediums and spiritualists who used automatic writing often received messages that were blasphemous and even obscene. One psychic researcher commented that participants were called "names which they had never even heard of until they saw them spelled out on paper, and which are of such a nature that I cannot give them here" (Owen 1990:214). Warnings about the Ouija board have expressed a similar concern that users might awaken sexually aggressive personalities that would be difficult or impossible to contain. In his 1918 attack on the Ouija board, Catholic theologian J. Godfrey Raupert warned that "spirits" contacted often turned mischievous, ridiculing Christianity and appealing to the users' baser instincts. The Ouija board dabbler finds, he said, "that while it was an easy thing for him to *open* the mental door by which the mind could be invaded, it is a difficult, if not an impossible thing, to *shut* that door and to expel the invader" (1918:463, 475; emphasis his).

As with deliverance, a number of case histories show that in some cases the "spirit" contacted engages in a sort of war within the user's personality, in which the everyday consciousness is assaulted in a quasi-sexual manner by a sadistic alter ego. In a book otherwise sympathetic to spiritualism and the occult, Harold Sherman, head of an ESP research group, warned his readers not to use the Ouija board. This activity can involve casual users, he said, in "an invasion of their minds by thoughts and feelings so foreign to their natures as to cause them great concern and often panic." As a warning to readers, he presented a series of cases on which he had advised, all "people of character and refinement . . . from intelligent, educated, and cultured backgrounds" who had fallen victim to such invasions. The syndrome that he identified began benignly enough with "spiritual and philosophic messages," then changed to messages that were insultingly obscene. In a second phase, the user heard such messages directly within the mind, often accompanied by "sensual feelings of such a revolting nature as to terrorize those so influenced" (1969:118–19).[6]

In one case history, a woman regularly spoke to a spirit claiming to be a deceased friend. However, as time went on, the communications "became sexier and sexier," and when the Ouija board suggested that the woman try automatic writing, she found herself writing in a strange hand "I am a new spirit from hell." One of her daughters found that she too could communicate with the spirit by asking it to lift one of her fingers for "yes" and two for "no." The experience came to a crisis when the mother began hearing a voice in her head claiming to be the same spirit. After several days of listening to this voice, it "became harsh and loud and started to curse," threatening that on days when she would be home alone she "would be at his mercy all day, to do his bidding." After a brief respite, the woman experienced a series of frightening psychic rapes:

> After I had shut this thing out of my mind, I went to bed a few nights later and was prevented from sleeping the entire night. I was subjected to the most powerful sexual stimulation that I had ever known, and I could do nothing to stop it. . . .
> On Palm Sunday morning, I awakened, and again I was

experiencing this sexual stimulation. My body was turning violently from one side to another. Then I was on my back, and it was as if I was being attacked, only there was not anyone there— that I could see. (1969:129–30)

Sherman published two other equally explicit cases involving women who experienced similar psychic sexual assaults, commenting,

Of course this evil entity enjoys using this kind of language, and feeling that you react to it, because he is attached to your subconscious, and every time you have a sexual experience, he also senses it, even though you may succeed in putting it out of your mind for the time being. . . .

I am sure there are many "earthbound entities" of an extremely low character, like him, seeking contact with living mortals, so as to get vicarious sex thrills through them. This is a fact science is going to have to recognize, one of these days.[7] (1969:124)

Such experiences are independently attested, and we can grant that some individuals develop a talent of using the Ouija board to induce an alternate state of consciousness. In some cases, as with talented mediums like Pearl Curren and Jane Roberts, this talent can be channeled into messages that are positive, or at least not indecent. Likewise, others could find the process of hypnosis beneficial in allowing themselves to see inner selves that would not be expressed during their everyday lives. However, in both traditions we find the risk of sexual abuse. In the case of hypnosis, the therapist could take advantage of women in such a state and get them to perform sexual acts to which they would not otherwise consent. With the Ouija, the risk came when users became unable to control their contact with spirits and became the victims of a kind of spiritual rape.

In the context of exorcisms, too, these elements sometimes emerge, and experienced ministers regularly report that patients utter horrifying vulgarities and may attempt to attack the exorcist, others present, or themselves. And, like the Ouija, once inner demons have been allowed to surface, care must be taken to contain them and channel their activities into socially acceptable activities. The scandal created by things that Christian women would say during exorcism was one of the most troubling problems for exorcists. And worse could happen. In 1974 a horrific case emerged in the press concerning a young man, Michael Taylor, who murdered his wife after engaging in an exorcism.[8] Taylor, who had previously expressed no particular interest in religious experience, had joined a Christian Fellowship Group led by a lay preacher, Marie Robinson. Within days, Robinson was able to get Taylor to speak in tongues at meetings, but events began to go wrong when his wife, Christine Taylor, expressed suspicions at one meeting that his relationship with Robinson was more carnal than at first seemed. Suddenly, Taylor later explained, it appeared that he and Robinson were both naked. "I felt evil with me," he said. "I fought it—but it overcame me. I had sought knowledge of myself and my being on earth and she tried to give it to me but this is not the way."

The result was a series of violent encounters. Taylor first physically attacked Robinson in a kind of Charismatic rage. "I did not know what to say," she recalled. "I started speaking in a tongue.... Mike also screamed at me in a tongue. We just screamed at each other." Physically restrained, Taylor was calmed down, and he received absolution at the next meeting of the group. However, his behavior became more and more erratic until the local vicar called in other ministers with experience in deliverance. In an all-night ceremony, the group invoked and cast out at least forty demons, including those of incest, bestiality, blasphemy, and lewdness. At the end, exhausted, they allowed Taylor to go home, although they felt that at least three demons—insanity, murder, and violence—were still left in him. A few hours later he was found naked in the town's streets, covered with blood. "It is the blood of Satan," he told police, who found Christine Taylor's mutilated body inside his house. The trial that followed, in which Michael Taylor was found not guilty but insane, led to a public backlash against the deliverance ministry in Great Britain. The vicar who had presided over the event, like the priest who presided over Anneliese Michel's fatal exorcism, expressed confidence that he had done the right thing in trying to exorcise Taylor's demons and that in the end "God will bring good out of this in His own way."

Minds in Pieces: Ralph B. Allison

A crucial figure in the development of this therapy was UCLA-trained psychiatrist Ralph B. Allison, an early specialist in multiple personality cases. In his 1980 autobiography, titled *Minds in Many Pieces: The Mak-*

ing of a Very Special Doctor, Allison described how in 1972 he had begun to encounter patients with puzzling disorders that could be best understood in terms of alternating personalities. In some cases, these "alters" emerged spontaneously out of therapy, but Allison soon learned that clinical hypnosis was a more effective way of identifying them. "Hypnosis," he explained, "simply means that the mind is more open to suggestion than usual.... The subject's imagination can be stimulated far more readily than in the normal waking state. There is a heightened awareness, and it is possible to break through to the subconscious mind. Thus, experiences that have been repressed can be remembered under hypnosis" (1980:45). Using information gained from these alters during trance states, he found that they were often "means of coping with an emotion or situation that the patient cannot handle" (1980:184).

One direction of therapy, therefore, was to pinpoint the "birth" of such alters in a particularly traumatic incident. Often, this involved repeated acts of rape or molestation: Allison's first patient, Janette, recalled being first sexually assaulted by the minister of the fundamentalist church to which her family belonged, then raped by a schoolmate at the age of eleven (60). Carrie, one of his most important patients, recovered a memory of being gang-raped by a motorcycle gang at an early age, then forced into sex by her first boyfriend. In addition, she also claimed that the doctor running the alcohol treatment center where she worked regularly forced her to perform oral sex in his office (1980:71–73). Finding such memories too painful to recollect, such patients split off personalities at such moments, and the events could only be brought to light by contacting these alters under hypnosis.

Allison also used hypnosis to contact an "Inner Self Helper," or ISH, to advise him in the proper course of therapy. The ISH, he found, was "the best part of the individual," a part of the mind that always used good judgment and had "a conscious awareness of God" (1980:56–57). By engaging a patient's ISH in dialogue, he felt, he could gain insight into the causes of her illness and help the alters reintegrate into a normal personality. The son and grandson of Presbyterian ministers, Allison chose not to argue that the ISH was supernatural in nature, but in many of his descriptions, this element of the personality resembles the Christian Holy Spirit. ISHs "feel only love and express both awareness of and belief in God," he says, adding, "They serve as a conduit for God's healing power and love. When they find themselves weaker than anticipated, they can call on a higher power to help" (1980:131). Elsewhere, he calls the ISH "that part of the mind through which God is revealed to the individual" and notes that patients could come to access their own ISHs "through visions, automatic writing, speech, and the presence of an inner voice" (1980:109). Thus, this personality in essence proved to be nothing other than the mysterious "spirit guide" contacted by spiritualists and some devoted Ouija board users.

It is not surprising that Allison and some of his supporters (see Rosik 1992) came to believe that ISHs could accurately predict future events and also warn of demonic plans to harm the patient. Other therapists did not observe such paranormal features and suggested that they were fabricated to please Christian therapists. "While this can certainly be true," an Allison supporter responded, "it is equally plausible that paranormal phenomena may be withheld from disbelieving therapists" (Rosik 1992:222). The principle is presumably the same invoked by many parapsychologists to explain why anomalous effects such as ESP tend to disappear when subjected to close, experimental scrutiny (McClenon 1994:201–3).

However, in other patients, self-consciously demonic personalities emerged, apparently without any discernable point of origin or purpose. This was particularly pronounced in the case of Carrie, whose four multiple personalities appeared early on in therapy. Allison's treatment took an unusual turn when his nurse, who had taken a weekend course on developing psychic abilities, told him that she had asked her instructor to "visit" Carrie's mind during a trance state. On breaking off the trance, the instructor told the nurse that Carrie had been taken over by the evil spirit of a drug user who had died five years previously. Allison was skeptical but concerned that Carrie's condition was beginning to deteriorate. He also had determined, in an earlier session, that "she had once experimented with witchcraft while in high school" and had once had a boyfriend who had dabbled in "black magic." Accordingly, he felt that an exorcism was in order. "Essentially, I was bringing mental health full circle," he reasoned, "combining the best of medicine and religion. Since my family has produced a long line of ministers, it seemed quite natural for me to mix a religious act with my psychiatry since this seemed to be in the best interest of my patient" (1980:83).

In determining when a spirit had successfully been exorcised from Carrie, Allison used a process of semi-automatic finger movements under hypnosis, which later became a standard method used in clinical hypnosis. "The raising of the finger had nothing to do with the exorcism," he explained, "but is a standard device in hypnosis. By designating one finger as a 'yes' finger and another as a 'no' finger, the patient can answer questions easily since speech is often an effort during hypnosis" (1980:85). The "yes/no" method of answering questions, however, is another link between MPD therapy and the Ouija and its predecessors, which relied on a similar "yes/no" pattern of answers. Similar finger-raisings under trance were later widely used by therapists to recover memories of alleged satanic ritual abuse (Nathan and Snedeker 1995:50).

This exorcism went well, and others followed in which Allison asked Carrie to project her negative feelings into symbolic objects, which were then thrown into water or the town dump. Unfortunately, as in the case of Michael Taylor, the alternate personalities were not as easy to banish as they were to raise: Carrie fell into manic-depressive episodes and committed suicide a little over a year after entering therapy. However, Allison was able to improve the mental health of some of his other patients by calling in religious specialists and eventually conducting a form of exorcism that he had adapted from his readings of Biblical rites.

By 1974, he was publishing his experiences with the ISH in *The American Journal of Clinical Hypnosis,* and two years later he made a presentation before the American Psychiatric Association on the ability of MPD patients to "zap" therapists by psychically draining energy from them. Allison related how "Gail" remarked one day that she wished she could draw on some of the psychiatrist's strength. He took this as an innocent compliment, but later he was called from a social dinner by a frantic phone call. Rushing to Gail's residence, he found that she had made an effort to slash her wrists. Holding her gently for comfort, he took her to a hospital, where she was treated, then, with the crisis apparently over, he returned to the dinner. There he found that he could barely lift the fork to his mouth and in fact "had barely enough energy to breathe." It took Allison more than a day to recover, and he insisted that the psychic draining had been much more profound than a simple emotional reaction to Gail's crisis. Interviewed by psychic investigator D. Scott Rogo, Allison felt that he had also been "telepathically attacked" by other patients.[9] In another case, a diabolical entity expressed by another of his female MPD patients who had "liked to dabble in the occult" boastfully claimed responsibility for a bleeding ulcer that Allison had developed, an act of revenge for trying to expel him from her mind (Rogo 1987:260–61)

Allison's experiences directly parallel those circulated by Charismatics about brushes with satanic power. We recall, for instance,

Victor H. Ernest's strange mental attacks during his ministry against the occult, which he later learned were caused by Satanists attending his church and using their powers to hinder his preaching. Similar stories were told by Koch, Basham, and Maxwell Whyte about demonic efforts to silence their ministries. And Evangelist Nicky Cruz knew a colleague who counseled a female college student who had contacted a strange entity by using a Ouija board. Its fascinating answers led them further and further, until she and her friends "made a pact with the devil." Cruz's friend was successful in leading the girl into a religious fellowship group, but the effort of praying with her left him so weak, he recalled, "that he had to drink a whole bottle of Coca-Cola before he had enough energy to walk away" (1973:46–47).

By 1978, Allison was reporting to the American Psychiatric Society on a standard process of reintegrating multiple personality patients. He used their ISHs to neutralize potentially violent elements, then banished them in a ritual that recalls both deliverance and its immediate ancestor, *Brauche* or powwow:

> I put a bottle in the patient's hand, ask her to close her eyes and go up to the level of the ISH. Then I ask the patient to join with the ISH, to become one with its power and to bring the ISH down to cast out the negative energy of the bad personality. Then I put my hand on top of her head and move my cupped hand down her head, neck, shoulder and arm out to the bottle, all the time telling the patient that I am helping by pushing out the negative energy from each part of the body I touch into the bottle. The patient, when cooperative, goes through quite a contortion as if really pushing something down her arm and out her fingers. Some patients need no object and just extend their fingers. One "spoke in tongues" to do it. (1978)

Allison also told his colleagues that, in such a process, they should tell their MPD patients to "get off the moral fence and choose sides." In orienting them to compatible religions, the therapist should listen to the ISH's advice and directly involve a clergyman, explaining the patient's spiritual needs and accepting the religious specialist as a "co-professional" (1978).

Allison also found that many other alter egos that emerged in MPD patients identified themselves as the obsessing spirits of persons who had been victimized in former lives. Such accounts included alleged memories of traumas that occurred during and even before birth, which some therapists hold lead to otherwise inexplicable mental problems. In a mythology similar to Koch's, L. Ron Hubbard argued that traumas occurring in the womb led to "engrams" that blocked spiritual development, treatment of which led to the formation of the alternative religion of Scientology. And a number of therapists even experimented with "past-life therapy," regressing patients past this stage to a "previous life" in which traumas occurred that affected their present mental health (Rogo 1985). The convincingly accurate "witchcraft" story discussed earlier in this chapter is typical of this tradition, except that in this case data existed to prove that the memories must have come from a media source. In most instances, these narratives are strong in mundane, real-sounding details but tantalizingly elusive when researchers seek proof of the past lives' historical accuracy.

In this regard, Allison's therapy follows others in the deliverance ministry who engaged in a form of "past-life therapy." Pat Brooks describes a case of a ten-year-old girl who assumed more than thirty-five personalities before being completely delivered. During the exorcism, three of the personalities identified themselves as participants in a gruesome murder-suicide that had occurred in Nova Scotia on December 14, 1934. Shocked by the graphic quality of the child's stories, her parents admitted that for a time they had belonged to a healing group that had expressed belief in reincarnation. They had in fact discussed the possibility that the child's precocious ability to speak French was proof that she had experienced a previous life in French Canada. Her father commented that the details of the exorcism "would probably convince a person who believed in reincarnation that he was right." Brooks firmly contradicted him: "Demons who have indwelt other people in other places and times get into a contemporary body and express themselves. In fact, this is why they desperately seek human bodies. Since they are disincarnate spirits, they must have human bodies in order to express their wretched personalities. Tonight I believe we have seen evidence of demons, converged in this child's body, from three separate people in Nova Scotia who were involved in a marital triangle in 1934"(1972:122).

Even psychic investigators seriously trying to find evidence for reincarnation have found it impossible to document the facts revealed under such circumstances. Similarly, Allison admitted that he could not confirm the truth of statements made by alters, and D. Scott Rogo commented:

It . . . strikes me that the entities Dr. Allison has seen in therapy behave suspiciously like the spirits contacted by amateur Ouija board operators. These personalities, too, are prone to telling fanciful stories about themselves; they claim to be spirits and demons but are really repressed aspects of the operator's psyche. Most Ouija board entities are also notorious for evading any questions regarding their earthly lives, especially if their information can be checked. Dr. Allison has confronted this same problem time and time again with the "spirits" he's contacted.... Dr. Allison is, of course, concerned about these important issues. He told me that some stories told by possession spirits are total and deliberate fabrications.

"I've been fooled," he admitted candidly. "You can never be sure." (Rogo 1987:264)

Still, Allison told Rogo in his 1982 interview, he felt that about twenty percent of the patients he had treated were possessed by some kind of external spirit, particularly those with large numbers of personalities. In addition, he said that most therapists working with such patients could cite similar experiences and "most of them secretly believe in spirit possession" (1987:266).

To be sure, Allison was hardly as credulous as some of the MPD therapists that followed in his path. After leaving his clinical practice, he worked for many years with criminals using multiple personalities as an excuse for committing violent crimes, and determined that many of them were faking. In 1991, he also delivered a sharp attack on the satanic ritual abuse theory, citing Robert Hicks among other skeptics in insisting that therapists should not represent their patients' "memories" as the truth. He also continued to develop his concept of the ISH, however, and most recently has given a workshop in a local church on getting in touch with one's "essence," or higher self, through techniques such as automatic writing (1998). Allison's experiences and their acceptance in a conduit of sympathetic therapists make it clear that the early stages of MPD therapy were influenced by ideas and techniques both from the deliverance ministry and from spiritualism. This is hardly surprising, as evangelists working in this area had practical experience in dealing with the dangerous situations that arose once alternate personalities were invoked.

But if deliverance was in practice difficult to distinguish from spiritualism, and if their form of exorcism called on the same mental processes as the Ouija ritual, then Rogo's insight is disturbingly suggestive. The Ouija board requires two users to construct messages, and the principles that make the planchette move create the tactile illusion that neither one is responsible for the messages that emerge. Also, the obscene, violent nature of Ouija "spirits'" messages further insulates the two users from responsibility for the messages' content.

In a similar way, the nature of MPD therapy creates a situation in which both patient and therapist cooperate in the creation of narratives for which neither one claims responsibility. Both may come to accept these narratives as objective reality truthfully remembered—and with good warrant, as alternate states of consciousness create the sensation of losing conscious volition and tapping some external source of information. Patients may see such narratives as genuine memories, and their expression may produce objective improvements in their mental health. Therapists may likewise see no specific ways in which they have coached or led their patients to tell such stories. Both may find the content too horrible to be a fiction in intent. But the same may be said of messages received from "spirit guides," either through mediums or through the Ouija board. Such message from the occult otherworld, as all involved have admitted, may be detailed, terrifyingly accurate in some details, but ultimately they are unreliable and potentially damaging.

What Michelle Remembered

In documenting a religious revival that occurred in the western provinces of Canada in 1971–1972, Kurt E. Koch noted that Canada seemed to have an unusually high rate of mental illness. He cited one psychiatrist as estimating that one out of every eight Canadians had some sort of psychological trouble. Another Vancouver teacher said that as many as 40 percent of schoolchildren needed psychotherapy. If such figures were found in the US, where Koch had already found widespread interest in the occult and new religions, he would find this rate "quite intelligible." But he was unable to discover the cause of this high incidence in Canada until a visit revealed that Christian counselors were also finding high levels of demonic oppression there (1973b:14). Whether or not Canadians are especially prone to mental problems or demon possession, Koch's comments show that deliverance had become popular in many denominations in Western Canada, and that secular therapists as well as Christian counselors were beginning to treat a wide range of mental problems as linked to occult activities.

During the summer of 1976, Michelle Smith came from Victoria, British Columbia, to visit psychiatrist Lawrence Pazder. Profoundly depressed by a miscarriage she had suffered six weeks before, she began by telling of an extraordinary dream she had recently had:

> "I dreamed that I had an itchy place on my hand . . ."
>
> "Yes?"
>
> "And when I scratched it, all these bugs came out of where I was scratching it! Little spiders, just pouring out of the skin on my hand. It was just—I can't even tell you how it was. It was terrible." (1981:9)

Folklorists recognize this scenario as a contemporary legend, "The Spider Bite." Well known in both European and American tradition during the 1970s, the story tells of a woman who visits a tropical resort and is bitten by a strange insect. Returning home, she develops a huge, ugly boil. In many versions, she is so tormented by the boil's itching that she scratches it open, "and dozens of tiny spiders rush out. . . . The young woman is so horrified that she either has a heart attack or must undergo psychiatric treatment" (Brunvand 1986:76–77).

Pazder felt that this dream was "blatantly symbolic" and "connected subconsciously to something very important" (1981:9). Hence, he invited her to return to regular therapy when she was released from the hospital. She did so, but with the recurring sense that she had something important to relate. "I don't know what I'm going to say," she told him while setting an appointment, "but I know I'll be able to tell you." The therapy became increasingly intense in October, after one session in which she uncharacteristically chose to lie on a couch, concentrating intently on the ceiling. She soon visibly changed, her face turning to a look of "frozen terror" and her breathing increasingly labored. Nevertheless, she said nothing, and after an hour Pazder gently helped her to "come back up out of it" (1981:16–17). In the subsequent session, she again stared at the ceiling, changed expressions and breathing patterns, and abruptly began to scream. After some twenty-five minutes of this violent outbreak, she began to speak in the persona of a five-year-old child responding to a horrific scene of child abuse being orchestrated by a man she called "Malachi."

He's hurting me all over, and something's really scaring me. His eyes are scaring me. I can't stand them. They look crazy. No! Take them away. He's hurting my arms. Ow. Ow. He's throwing me upside down fast.

. . . He said if . . . if I . . . if I want to stay alive . . . I better be a good girl . . . I was so afraid. He seemed so scary. He's bad. He told me . . . he said, "You listen, Michelle." He said, "You have to cooperate."

. . . I . . . when I found out I couldn't get away . . . and no one was going to hear me . . . when they didn't care . . . I . . . had to change. . . . I didn't want to get hit anymore. You see . . . the first thing I had to do was not to hurt. . . . I didn't want any more pain. . . . I had to put on a happy face. (1981:22–24)

In subsequent sessions, Pazder allowed Michelle to return to this scene and others like it, constructing them in much more detail. At first she described the abuse scene as one carried out in a roomful of "Mommies." But as therapy developed and the memories grew more detailed, it became clear that Malachi was the head of a coven of witches who had traumatized Michelle in many ways. She was physically and sexually assaulted, forced to witness animal and human sacrifices, and included in a complex ceremony in which Satan received homage, in the form of a heap of murdered babies, from a group of worshippers, each of whom had had their left middle fingers amputated.[10] Overall, Pazder concluded, Michelle "unearthed and relived fourteen months of her past in astonishing detail" (1981: xv). Unable to detect any sign that she was fabricating or attempting to do anything other than express a painful truth, he concluded that the stories must be at core truthful.

However, other researchers found no evidence to corroborate her story. This leads us back to the primary question: if Michelle's memories were not memories, where did the astonishing details come from? Some of them presumably were repressed memories of real events, though now reemerging in a new context. One prominent incident in the book describes how Malachi put the child in an automobile with the corpse of a woman, then smashed it into a rock embankment to make it appear that the woman had been killed in the wreck (1981:61 ff.) While a thorough search of newspaper records located no account of a fatal accident matching this account (Nathan and Snedeker 1995:45), Michelle's father recalls that while driving they had witnessed a crash in which a woman had been ejected from a car and lay disemboweled and bleeding to death on the pavement. "Michelle started to scream," he recalled, "and we could not stop her for ages" (Allen and Midwinter 1990).

But where did the pattern emerge that fit these images together? Folklorists can identify three basic sources: the therapist's background, the influence of the Charismatic movement on conservative Catholicism, and media attention to real ritual child abuse cases. First, we can infer that Pazder, a devoted old-style Catholic, explicated the material in these early sessions in terms of his own experience, bringing concepts both from his religious upbringing and his medical practice in West Africa. There, he admits, he "had become fascinated with African ceremonies and had taken countless photos of them. Many ceremonies involved the burning of juju, little dolls and amulets used in black magic, and replacing them with a cross—this as a way of trying to get rid of the animistic beliefs among West Africans in the spirits of the jungle. Dr. Pazder had built up a very extensive collection of photographs of such ceremonies, planning someday to use them in some sort of transcultural study" (1981:188).

A number of commentators on Michelle's story have noted this African connection in Pazder's practice. However, closer examination shows that the link is not to genuine African traditions but to a European missionary worldview that diabolized non-Christian religions as forms of black magic. The term "juju" is a genuine African word, originally a term used to refer to the priest-king of a Nigerian tribe. It also referred to the ancestral spirits of past kings, and hence to their power concentrated in a fetish kept by religious specialists (Jobes 1962:894). Europeans, used to seeing African religions as primitive, misunderstood and applied the term to amulets used for all sorts of social and religious purposes. Eventually "juju" became a catch-term for any sort of African religious concept, magical idea, equivalent to "mumbo-jumbo" or "voodoo." Pazder primarily saw "jujus" while they were being destroyed and replaced by Christian symbols, indicating that his information mainly derived from missionaries devoted to diabolizing traditional African folk culture and attempting to westernize their contacts.

A similar network of missionaries had made efforts to extirpate traditional African religions in Kenya, like Nigeria, a British colony. Jomo Kenyatta, the first ruler of Kenya after its independence, had previously studied anthropology under Bronislaw Malinowski in London. In 1938, Kenyatta sympathetically described the religious world of his tribe, the Kikuyu, and sharply criticized missionary efforts:

All "doctors" and "seers" of every type, even men who can do nothing but good, are liable to prosecution. Indeed, it is now the innocent who suffer. My grandfather was a "seer," *morathi*, or "wise man," whose duty it was to give general advice and foretell the future as far as he could. . . . He bequeathed his profession, together with some calabashes which were his insignia, to my father. . . .

But missionaries, aided by Government officials, searched the homesteads for the "works of the devil." My father's calabashes were taken as evidence of guilt, and he, with many others in the same position, served a period of imprisonment. Although they preserved these traditional symbols they had not taken part in any nefarious activities; it was simply the policy that everything to do with "magic" was to be stamped out, for the missionaries to get rid of "Satan's" influence, and to clear the ground for their proselytising work. (1965:294)

In 1952, after a long period of resentment over colonial policies, the Mau Mau rebellion erupted in Kenya. A largely nationalistic movement, the members took a public oath of loyalty to the cause of Kenyan independence. The British colonial government declared an emergency, arrested Kenyatta as the reputed Mau Mau leader, and insisted that influential tribe chiefs take a "cleansing oath" to prove their loyalty to Great Britain. This led to acts of violence against Europeans and pro-British Kenyans. In the context of this scare, horrific stories circulated among Europeans diabolizing the Mau Maus as no better than primitive devil-worshippers who forced their members to take blood oaths and practiced black magic. As late as 1969, well after Kenya had won its independence, such stories were still circulating in pulp publications like Charles Lefebure's *The Blood Cults*. He described the group's practices in terms that closely fit Pazder's description of how Michelle's cult had ensured the loyalty and silence of its members:

Having first ensured the new member's loyalty by binding oaths in a ceremony that was based on the tribe's traditional witchcraft practices, the stage was set for further enslavement. There were at least seven stages of oath-taking and the initiate proceeded from oath to oath, each more bestial than the last till he or she entered the final stage, a complete tool of the Mau Mau through total loss of self-dignity. . . .

To give some idea of the degradation inflicted, it will be sufficient to mention that the oathing ceremonies included forced cohabiting with animals, the drinking of menstrual blood, cannibalism, eating the brains of disinterred [*sic*] corpses and many other practices. In fact it was the declared policy of the Mau Mau that those responsible for administering oaths should try to think up ever more debased details, and pass them on to brother administrators.

As if these loathsome rituals were not enough to test a man's loyalty, every member was forced to begin the cycle again after reaching the seventh oath. No man, not even the "generals," was free of this. Small wonder that members of the Mau Mau, who felt themselves lower than animals, could behave worse than them. (Lefebure 1969:28–29)

Such images of the Mau Mau rebels, more recent historians show, were xenophobic propaganda intended to generate support for the British military counteroffensive, during which some eleven thousand Kenyans were killed and eighty thousand more confined to detention camps. Nevertheless, these ideas passed for literal truth among missionaries that returned from the British colonies to the United States. Fundamentalist Jess Pedigo, in his influential 1971 tract on the perils of Satanism, repeats much the same story about the Mau Mau's oaths (18).

As Michelle continued to relate stories of child abuse, Pazder reasoned that she had grown up in a circle of Satanists who had used the "sophisticated techniques of psychological manipulation" that European missionaries attributed to African black magic sorcerers. "Such mind-control techniques had unbelievable power," Pazder reasoned. "In Africa he had seen the influence of the juju dolls; if a person believed in juju, the dolls could be used to make that person roll over and die, on the spot, without any other intervention" (1981:194).

A second development was the somewhat tardy involvement of many Catholics in the Charismatic movement. This was partly a result of widespread dissatisfaction among conservatives with the reforms of Vatican II, which eliminated many of the ritual and formalistic elements of worship. A small but intense body of literature developed, linking these changes to satanic elements that had penetrated the Vatican. One dramatic reflection of this reaction was the increased interest in the rite of exorcism in the wake of *The Exorcist*'s success. In 1975, for instance,

Doubleday published *Possessed by Satan,* a translation of a German account of a successful exorcism by the Jesuit priest, Adolf Rodewyk.

In the following year, Reader's Digest Press published Malachi Martin's *Hostage to the Devil,* which generated even more attention. Martin was a former Jesuit and close associate of Pope John XXIII, but had left the priesthood in 1964 in the wake of the Vatican II reforms. Irish by birth, he emigrated to the United States and was active in conservative factions of Catholicism until his death in 1999. *Hostage to the Devil* gave a brief overview of the exorcism ritual and described five contemporary cases of demon possession that had occurred in North America. His subsequent book, *The Final Conclave* (1978), significantly described internal politics among the liberalized Vatican and suggested that factions were planning to elect a pope who would align himself with a communist-dominated one-world government. Many of the same fears that had been generated by the deliverance ministry among Protestants now were arising among disenfranchised conservative Catholics.

The same group contributed to the network of believers that developed around the so-called "Bayside Prophecies" of Veronica Lueken. Beginning in 1971, she began to have visions of the Virgin Mary, warning that great dangers were imminent for the Catholic Church and for the United States. She began to hold public prayer vigils, which were recorded on tape and distributed through an active media-enhanced conduit. From the beginning, Lueken's prophecies decried the liberalizing tendencies of Vatican II. "Satan has gone into the highest positions in My House," one 1971 prophecy warned, and another soon followed warning that "sins being committed in the disguise and name of HUMANISM—MODERNISM—all true Satanism!" (1991:2–3). A 1975 prophecy was even sharper: "All manner of novelty and experimentation must be removed from My Church now!" Lueken heard Jesus Christ say. "Restore My House NOW," the figure warned, or "Blood shall flow in the streets. Death shall become common-place. Is this what you want?" (1991:307). By 1976, her prophecies were attacking the liberalizing professors in American seminaries, "who call themselves My Son's chosen priests [but] are vile sons of satan. . . . No, My children, it is the minds poisoned by satan that spread this filthy and error, this distortion of doctrine, this distortion of Tradition, and this distortion of your Faith!" (1991:55).

Soon the prophecies also began to stress the threat of underground satanic organizations. "Satan has many agents now in your country and the world," a 1974 message said, adding, "He has placed them in the highest positions of power." Another prophecy from the same time stressed, "Your Government, your media have given themselves unto the agents of Satan" (1991:16–17). By 1977, the year of Michelle's testimony, her warnings of danger had become even more explicit: "Children shall disappear from the streets, never more to be seen, taken into covens and buried in their burial grounds. Know it now; don't cast it aside and say that this is a reign of terror. Do not cast it aside, for your child may be next! . . . The attacks shall become more frequent unless you pray. Pray, My children, a constant vigilance of prayer now. Keep it going throughout your country. Pray that those who are working shall remove this demon from among you" (1991:328–29). Such prophetic predictions of doom also provide the climax of Michelle's account, a lengthy rhyming "Master Plan," in which Satan (supposedly speaking in 1955) revealed his intentions for the next twenty-eight years. The prophetic verse proceeds year by year:

> Seventy-nine goes down to the fire;
> It's the time when the flames grow higher.
> Division and fight, death and hate;
> Seventy-nine is an open gate. . . .
> When the year is seven and nine,
> Most of the world will be mine.
> They don't even know what I'm about;
> By 1980 they won't even shout. (1981:288)

The entire prophecy is cryptic and reminiscent of previous versified predictions by psychics like Nostradamus and Mother Shipton. Nevertheless, it is similar to Veronica Lueken's doomsday visions, foretelling increasing violence and satanic control until the time of the next visitation of Satan, which Pazder reasoned would take place in 1982. Although it is actually spoken by the Devil, the content conforms to messages Lueken was receiving from her Jesus and Mary. Again, we recall Koch's testimony that demons repeatedly predicted the imminent end of the world, a sign that for him diabolical theology was superior to liberal Christianity.

A further link with the reactionary Catholic network is Pazder's use of photography to provide a miraculous proof of Michelle's testimony. While attending a service at a local church, she recognized a small wooden bench as containing the symbol of the "Horns of Death," used by Satanists in their rites. The priest agreed to burn the bench, and Pazder, feeling the ritual similar to those in which African amulets were destroyed, took photographs. Several turned out to have anomalous images in the background: three seemed to show a figure "dressed in a long, flowing gown" moving behind the fire to a place behind Michelle. Another showed about thirty smaller "fierce-looking" images. The priest looked at the photographs and made no comment, but his mother commented, "Yes . . . that's Mary with the child" (1981:190–91). Interestingly, the use of miraculous photographs such as these is one of the most distinctive practices of the Bayside group that formed around Veronica Lueken. During her vigils, while she was in trance speaking with Jesus and Mary, her followers took photographs of the sky and surroundings. Any unusual blurs or streaks of light were interpreted as divine figures or as symbolic messages. Daniel Wojcik (1997) has argued that this use of technology to create messages is, like automatic writing and the Ouija, a form of divination. This again connects Pazder's act of therapy itself with folk and alternative religious roots.

A final event that influenced Michelle's narrative, sadly, was one that reminds us that ritual child abuse is real. On September 19, 1976, a month before Michelle began to tell her story, police broke into the home of Leon Cunningham, leader of a splinter Pentecostal group in Yakima, Washington. There they found the decomposed corpse of three-year-old David Weilbacher. In a defiant statement given to police, Cunningham explained that the child had died during efforts to exorcise a "demon of rebelliousness" from him. Further investigation found that Cunningham had been in charge of a series of small Charismatic congregations after feeling a special conviction that he had been blessed with a gift of prophecy. In 1975 he became convinced that the last days were imminent, and began preparing to move the family to a place in Texas indicated in one of his visions. Debra Weilbacher, a single mother with a history of drug use, met Cunningham while "searching for God" and was invited to live with the Cunninghams. Soon after she arrived, Leon Cunningham discerned a demon in the child's personality, citing symptoms such as his "silly laugh" and bed-wetting. He explained to detectives:

> I said, "Something is wrong with the child. He has a spell about him". . . . I mean it was just like he wanted to possess somebody, you know, just total take over, the mind control and everything. You could feel it; you could see it. You could see him trying to possess his own mother. . . . She hadn't noticed it until I called her

attention to it. . . . I know when I feel the spirit of the devil and I know when I feel the spirit of God. I knew it was the wrong spirit.[11]

To drive it out, he devised a rite of exorcism that involved ceremonial beatings administered by himself, the child's mother, his wife, and his daughter-in-law and her mother. After each beating, Cunningham would ask the child, "Do you have love in your heart?" and the boy was expected to hug and kiss the minister. These ritual beatings continued twice daily for several months, with the exorcist convinced he could still see the demon in the child's eyes. "If you didn't whip him it would just continue; it would get more and more," he said. "His face would turn into the expression that was just the devil's imp." Dissatisfied with the results he was getting with a lathe board, Cunningham began to "humble" the child by pushing him down on the ground on his backside. "You could tell when he submitted or humbled himself, you know," he said. "Sometimes you could push him, you know, and he would just do it himself and would flop back and hit his head. . . . I would quit when I seen him do that."

Still, conflicts with the three-year-old continued until a final "major exorcism" took place on July 22, 1976. Cunningham explained:

> That day I had pushed him down . . . he was mean and got to where he would just snap at you like a dog. . . he was pushed down and brought back and whipped and then pushed down again . . . ten or fifteen times. . . . He was mean, really mean and he hadn't submitted, you see and that is why I pushed him down. . . . He would put on acts. Sometimes he would act like he was tired.
>
> [His mother] picked him up . . . I had given her the paddle, you know, and told her to whip him and make him get up and come back over here, you know . . . . She said when she picked him up . . . he had fell on his side, turned over on his back and he was . . . screaming like and pushing himself around on his back and feet, with his feet. He just rolled over and passed out. . . .
>
> I tell you what I felt like it was and God only knows. I feel like he finally submitted, finally gave up and that is all the life he had in him before. It was the mean, stubborn will of his. That is what I feel about him. I feel like he finally broke.

Feeling certain the child would reawaken in a dispossessed state, Cunningham ordered the child to be taken into a spare room to await God's sign. When it became clear that the boy was in fact dead and his body was decomposing, one of Cunningham's daughters defected, and police intervened. Cunningham, Debra Weilbacher, and three participating women were found guilty of manslaughter, although to the end the minister insisted, "I'm not guilty before God. He will judge me."

The case did not receive national publicity, but the trial provoked sensational coverage in the Washington State area, which reached across the border to adjacent Victoria, British Columbia. The details of the fatal Cunningham exorcism closely parallel Michelle's first recollections. In both, a child is abused ritualistically by a male in a room of females who choose not to intervene. Motivated by demonology, the abuser repeatedly hurts a child all over, throws the child upside down, and insists that he "be good" and "cooperate." The name Michelle gives her chief abuser—"Malachi"—at first seems incongruous for a Satanist, as it names both a minor prophet and a book of the Old Testament. But this too fits, if we recall that Malachi *Martin* was one of the strongest advocates for reviving exorcism in the United States.

It is impossible to tell if Leon Cunningham was influenced by his book *Hostage to the Devil*, but Cunningham's conception of exorcism owes more to the protracted process advocated by conservative Catholics like Martin than to the relatively streamlined process of deliverance in use among Protestant Charismatics. Martin, for instance, cautions that the exorcist must first fight through an extended process of breaking down the possessing spirit's "pretense" that there is nothing, after all, wrong with the person being exorcised. "It can be very disarming, even pitiful," Malachi Martin observed. "It can make everyone, including the priest, feel that it is the priest who is the villain, subjecting an innocent person to terrible rigors. Even the mannerisms and characteristics of the possessed are used by the spirit as its own camouflage." Nevertheless, in this tradition, the priest is urged to press onward, motivated by his own psychological conviction that he is in the presence of supernatural evil. Meantime his helpers, Martin stresses, "are to obey the exorcist's commands immediately and without question, no matter how absurd or unsympathetic those commands may appear to them to be" (1976:16–18). Such a process is, in short, a form of Christian ritual abuse, justified only by the exorcist's faith that he is punishing not the person in front of him but an evil spirit that has invaded the personality from outside. *Hos-*

tage to the Devil, we recall, was a best-seller in 1976, the year of David Weilbacher's death and the year Michelle began to recover her memories of ritual abuse.

The differences are significant, too. The cult members in Michelle's story maintain their secrecy, even after two decades, while shocked members the Cunningham family defected within days of the child's death and brought the abuse to official attention. In Michelle's case, the abuse ended when the cult realized that God was with the child, but in David Weilbacher's case, the worshipers remained steadfast in their belief that God did not wish them to relent until the child submitted. And, of course, Michelle survived to tell her story and find support in those who believed her, a satisfying ending to a well-constructed narrative. David died and was forgotten.

Conclusions: From Michelle to McMartin

Pazder's book about Michelle's experiences, *Michelle Remembers,* was essentially a popular work of psychological spiritualism. With its ties to Charismatic religion, spiritualism, and exorcism, it might well have enjoyed a vogue only among specialized conduits. However, the book became socially influential partly because it spoke out against many real-life influences that its readers could accept as credible. The satanic religion described is one that privileges males, allows the degradation of women and abuse of children, and seeks to use supernatural powers against religions that have in turn renounced their use of spiritual gifts. Sadly, groups like the Cunningham "family," in combating Satan, tended to become identical with the forces they allegedly opposed. Carolyn Cunningham, one of Leon's daughters, initially a supporter of her father in court, later reflected ruefully to E. Ann Neel (1990):

> Dad didn't really give us the free choice to decide what we
> thought about God or what we felt about God. We strictly had to
> have his faith and his feeling and his beliefs or we were wrong. . . .
> It was a dictatorship, total dictatorship. "This is what I say it is.
> This is what it is. And if you contradict it, you are out of here.
> You're not good enough to be and your soul is in hellfire danger!"
> . . . I thank God I had three years in prison, I really do. Because it
> gave me a chance with no family influence to decide, to look at

myself and decide what am I as a human being. Because I had no
identity, I was nothing but whatever the soldiers were supposed
to be.

We have seen that traditions such as "real" witchcraft in which women,
repressed by patriarchal religious ideas like these, created professions for
themselves based on the fear of evil magic. Modern demonological works,
like those produced in previous ages, were founded in fear (or recognition) that women might use a form of spirit possession to empower themselves. And indeed the inversion of this threat is itself a form of
empowering spirit possession, just as the Charismatic gifts of the spirit
appropriated the same ideas and principles of magical healing and divination.

Ironically, one way of empowering oneself in such situations is to
produce evidence *against* the demons afflicting this world and so gain
power by joining and partially directing a crusade against patriarchy.
Thus, folklorist Donna Wyckoff argues that ritual abuse narratives are
ways of focusing patients' ill-defined sense that the social order they inhabit is also "fragmented into multiple and competing 'personalities.'"
When they cannot express this malaise directly, they look for villains
either within their family circles or in the folk demons of the outside
world: "satanic forces, male hegemonies, contemporary social attitudes,
or past injustices." Hence, she argues, the construction of the ritual abuse
narrative effectively exorcises this poorly defined anxiety by projecting it
outward onto specific persons or agents (1996:374). It is no surprise that
Michelle's "memories" of her struggle to free herself from her family's
satanic beliefs parallel Carolyn's sad recognition that her faith in her
father's Christian ritual of exorcism was in fact a form of mind control
imposed by a child abuser.

Michelle's stories did not provoke a hunt for Satanists in British
Columbia, perhaps because the alleged crimes no longer fell within the
statute of limitations and might not be feasible for police to investigate.
However, as therapists working in the new field of repressed child abuse
memories began to see analogous memories emerging from their patients, *Michelle Remembers* created a pattern for many other women's
accounts of childhood torture and sexual abuse. During the 1980s, a conduit of information formed among therapists working with such patients, particularly those participating in the national and regional
conferences of the International Society for the Study of Multiple Per-

sonality and Dissociation. During such conferences, workshops and training sessions were held on how to detect satanic ritual abuse, and presentations were often circulated in cassette tapes and photocopies, reaching a broad audience within the conduit even when they were never submitted formally to journals for refereeing (Victor 1993:95). This conduit resembled the network set up a decade earlier by Don Basham and other Charismatics working within the deliverance movement.

More importantly, Michelle's testimony was crucial to the first criminal prosecutions based on stories of ritual abuse. In 1983, seven workers at the McMartin Preschool were indicted on charges of abusing 360 children, both through sexual assault and also by involving them in blood sacrifices. The case proved to be the longest and most expensive criminal trial in U.S. history, costing the public more than fifteen million dollars before it terminated in 1990 with no convictions. While based on allegations similar to those elicited by Pazder, this case was different in that the ritual abuse was said to be going on in the immediate past and present, and the stories were being told by children aged three to eight. The most dramatic stories came from a two-year-old, Matthew Johnson, as filtered through his mother Judy, a single mother with a mental condition that eventually would be diagnosed as paranoid schizophrenia.

Judy Johnson first made complaints about her fears that her child was being abused at the preschool, and police reports record increasingly bizarre stories that she had allegedly gotten from him. These included sessions at a church, where the preschool workers dressed as "witches," flew in the air, burned black candles, chopped up animals, and made the child drink baby's blood. Her stories might have been taken as delusions, except that soon many of the other children appeared to be presenting similar stories pointing to widespread ritual abuse. Police and social workers responded with increasing panic, and while only the workers at the McMartin Preschool were prosecuted, parents believed that their children's allegations proved that a large portion of the community, including prominent businessmen and politicians, were deeply involved in a child-abusing satanic cult. As the investigation developed, Lawrence Pazder came to Los Angeles to consult with therapists and parents. By this time, he was convinced that the cult that had abused Michelle was not only still active but was international in scope. According to police reports, he explained that "anybody could be involved in this plot, including teachers, doctors, movie stars, merchants, even . . . members of the Anaheim Angels baseball team" (Nathan and Snedeker 1995:89).

As in the case of most adult survivors, though, such testimony was often the result of extensive coaching and modeling by the investigators. Journalists Debbie Nathan and Michael Snedeker were able to gain access to several of these interviews and found that time and again children had denied being abused and agreed to discuss the topic only after being told that they were playing "pretend" with hand puppets. Even then, in one interview, the child cooperated only after being given hints about what to say and pointedly warned that her other friends had already told the questioner "all the bad secrets" (1995:80). This style of investigation became a pattern in a series of additional scandals that occurred in the U.S. and Canada throughout the 1980s and that briefly affected Great Britain in the early 1990s.

However, children's testimony in fact had been an integral part of witch-hunts for a long time. As early as 1969, historian Ronald Seth had described how prosecutors of witches successfully managed to overturn judicial common law, which had previously held that no witness under the age of fourteen could be sworn as a witness. But a person who had rejected God and worshipped the Devil, prosecutors successfully argued, was so evil that he or she would immediately be recognized by "innocent" children. These child witnesses did not need to provide *direct* testimony of specific acts they had witnessed. Since in their innocence they could unfailingly recognize evil, any information they might be able to give of acts of *maleficia* [black magic] could be, even *must* be, accepted as true. In other words, all the evidence offered by children concerning all or any of the defined acts of witchcraft *maleficia* was sufficient to prove the guilt of the accused because it was given by "innocent" children (1969:14).

In fact, Seth points out, in a number of instances English children later confessed that they had made up their torments in order to gain attention. On the continent, sociologist Hans Sebald (1995) notes, children exhibiting signs of demonic possession likewise played an active role in witchcraft accusations, often implicating close family members. Their motives may have ranged from a grudge that they held against members of the community to a generalized desire to rebel against a society that typically kept children's behavior in tight check. However, Sebald adds, modern psychological research has shown that children, especially those under eight years of age, can be extremely suggestible, mingling accurate recollections of events with other fantasy elements that had merely been suggested to them. It follows that many children may simply not have been able to tell when they were distorting information in line with what questioners wanted them to say (1995:215–33). Whatever the motives behind children's testimonies about blood sacrifices and evil witchcraft, the bottom line was, as the sixteenth-century French witch-hunter Jean Bodin admitted, children made good witnesses "because at a very young age they could without difficulty be persuaded or compelled to inform against the accused" (Seth 1969:13). Sadly, in early witch trials, many of the children who thus confessed to involvement in witchcraft were executed along with those they implicated.

Demonologies have always affected first the theological world, validating essentially magical rituals of summoning divine spirits and combating evil, then introducing such methods into the practical world of medicine. "Scientific" efforts to respond to mental illnesses already defined as occult in origin fostered the creation of a medicine whose agenda included both treatment of the patient and also punishment of the occultist responsible. As Leland L. Estes (1986) noted, a "diabolical medicine" was an essential first step in inciting police officers to define demon possession as a law enforcement problem. Hence, in the Salem panic of 1692, a physician was called in to diagnose the mysterious ailment that afflicted the children in the Parris household. When he confirmed the disease's magical cause, the community then sought out and arrested the usual suspects—non-Europeans, homeless transients, and women who had empowered themselves by taking over traditionally male roles. The "afflicted children," often functioning as a group in an alternate state of consciousness, produced the evidence needed to convict these people. And a conspiracy scenario emerged that explained why otherwise normal, prominent persons were in fact secretly in league with the Devil.

Much the same process took place in our generation, when therapists diagnosed patients' mental diseases as having been caused by evil people conducting occult ceremonies. Again, the target was not self-proclaimed witches or Satanists, but otherwise ordinary citizens in the wrong place and considered socially suspect for other reasons. But before such stories as Michelle's could motivate law enforcement agents to move against alleged ritual abusers, this element of *conspiracy* needed to be made credible. The final element was the invention and dissemination of conspiracy theories parallel to those of the witch trials. These theories, compelling in their own right, were given powerful social warrant by persons willing to empower themselves by "confessing" to their own satanic pasts.

5

The One-World Demonology

Projection and Conspiracy

*The reaction of the people is to disbelieve or discount the
stories.* Men cannot, or will not, recognize the dangers
that face them
—Dr. Jess Pedigo, *Satanism:
Diabolical Religion of Darkness*

Many contemporary mythologies present positive scenarios in which
individuals and groups are transformed by divine powers. The deliverance movement's key beliefs constitute one such myth, focusing a
believer's physical and mental ailments into demonic personalities, then
banishing them with the power of The Blood. Less formally, the Ouija
ritual enacts a similar optimistic myth in which teens summon, then
mock and dismiss their fears in the form of "demonic" personalities. But
if we accept that Holy Spirit baptism, exorcism, spiritualism, and many
forms of MPD therapy were in fact governed by the same kinds of psychological processes and are equivalent forms of magic, then those involved in these activities were left in an awkward position. Particularly
those in the Charismatic movement had to take pains not only to oppose
"Satan's counterfeits" in their own congregations, they had to deflect criticisms from other Christians. It was not difficult for members of the deliverance ministry itself to see even co-workers as trafficking with "the unholy
Jesus." It therefore became expedient to deflect such criticisms by finding
convenient scapegoats who were involved in even more unholy practices.

For this reason, such optimistic mythologies are often balanced by
another, closely related set of scenarios that describe the world transformed for the worse by the influence of otherworldly evil. These sce-

narios, or *subversion myths*, blame problems of contemporary culture on a small but influential group that intellectually or financially manipulates culture for its own good. Their plot may be to corrupt a culture morally, by encouraging self-indulgence, or it may be literal, showing the conspirators literally sucking the life substances out of children. As the next three chapters will describe, this strategy involved a psychological *projection* of uncertainty over one's own practices out onto a convenient scapegoat, whose magic was clearly not sanctioned by divine or secular law. This produced a set of conspiracy theories, which could then be used to pull together disparate events into an argument that Satanists were silently infiltrating into positions of social control.

To bring God's spirit fully into action, Charismatic communities sought to identify organizations of *human* devil-worshippers. Sadly, in doing so, they tapped into age-old subversion myths of blood sacrifice and financial conspiracy that had proved to be the cause of much more social evil in this century than occultism ever had.

Subversion Myths

Historian Norman Cohn (1967) and folklorist Alan Dundes (1991), using different methodologies, came to similar conclusions about the origins of Christian crusades against communities of Jews. Cohn studied the anti-Semitic ideologies used to justify official massacres of Jews, most notably the Nazi Holocaust. He suggested that these ideologies were grounded in "unconscious negative projections" in which one social group saw in another group's behavior "the anarchic tendencies which they fear to recognize in themselves" (1967:256). More particularly, Cohn argued, the Judaic religious tradition, being the source of Christianity, tended to be cast in the role of the "bad father" of many individuals' psychopathic fantasies. That is, children feeling ambivalent emotions about their parents tend to split their fantasies into two polarized images. One is an idealized parent, perfect and thus infinitely lovable; the other is a completely hateful parent who fully deserves to be attacked. Since this image cannot be applied to the children's real parents without guilt, it persists in the unconscious until it finds an object worthy of such hate. Cohn concludes, "The fantasied figure of the 'bad' parent becomes a persecutor, endowed with all the merciless hatred and destructive fury which the child feels, but dare[s] not fully recognize, in himself. So it comes about that the small child constructs (out of his own monstrous cruelty and murderousness) castrating, torturing, cannibalistic, all-powerful beings, beside whom even the harshest of real parents should appear harmless" (1967:258).

Cohn suggests that such fantasies often persist past childhood into adult life, predisposing some individuals to participate in groups that engage in crusades against other groups alleged to be involved in global conspiracies of this sort. Some support for Cohn's theory was found by psychologists who found that participants in Nazi activities often expressed "a quite abnormal degree of fear and hatred of parental figures, who are seen now as menacing and now as mutilated and killed" (1967:266). Interestingly, he notes, one of the most common libels against Jews was that they tortured, castrated, and drew blood from Christian children during ritual murders, a clear and visible image of negative projection.

Dundes calls this same psychological process "projective inversion." First described by Otto Rank in his analysis of Indo-European mythologies, this process allows one group to attribute a tabooed action to another group that the first group in fact has committed, or wishes to commit. This is particularly true, Dundes notes, in social situations in which a dominant culture finds it to their advantage to victimize a weaker one. In such instances, the victimized minority is paradoxically blamed for wishing to victimize the majority. For this reason, African American men are assumed by many Anglos to lust after white women, when in fact the exact reverse is historically true: at least 20 percent of slave children were fathered by white males.

In the case of the blood libel, Dundes continues, Jews are blamed for carrying out in life what Christians enact in ceremony: the murder and cannibalization of a ritually chosen victim. Whether one believes that the Eucharist literally becomes Jesus' body and blood or simply commemorates his crucifixion, he argues, it involves "at the very least symbolic cannibalization." The transformed Host was often visualized as a newborn child, so it was logical that unconscious anxiety over engaging in this ritual would emerge as a claim that evil Others were literally killing and eating babies. "By means of this projective inversion," Dundes feels anti-Semites are unconsciously saying, "it is not we Christians who are guilty of murdering an individual in order to use his blood for ritual religious purposes (the Eucharist), but rather it is you Jews who are guilty of murdering an individual in order to use his or her blood for ritual religious purposes" (1991:354).

Cohn comments that studying anti-Semitic mythologies has applications far beyond Jewish history; such research could help us recognize, limit, or even forestall similar delusions in the future (1967:268A). Jews, along with marginalized women, were one of the initial targets of the early modern witchcraft scare. Few of these targets actually practiced folk magic, but were simply convenient targets who for some social or economic reason were profitable to attack and unable to fight back. In short, projective inversion tells us more about the persecuting group's inner stresses than about folk witchcraft or Judaism.

So the threat of satanic cults functioned for Charismatics as a projection of elements *within* such groups that were causing intense internal debate. We might expect modern demonological works to project the internal problems of the deliverance ministry onto "the usual suspects": women and occultists. But women appropriated the crusade against Satanism for empowering agendas of their own. And the crusade against devil-worshippers did not primarily target openly operating occult groups like the Church of Satan, although its leader Anton LeVey showed up regularly in crusaders' literature as a conspicuous bad example. Rather, the agenda was to justify a *hidden* source of social evil that would explain the world's economic, social, and moral problems. Recognizing the existence of this evil would then encourage people to adopt Charismatic religion in spite of its internal problems.

In addition, launching a crusade allowed the differing parties to form a common front. The points on which Maxwell Whyte and Basham agreed with Koch were, after all, more influential than the ministries of any one of them, because the common points that they made could be combined into a demonology that justified action against Satan and his agents on earth. All were satisfied that Satan's agents were ubiquitous and silently active inside many human personalities. In many cases, they added, individuals had given themselves to the Devil, either overtly through blood pacts or witchcraft, or innocently, by dabbling in occult practices. And all three agreed that such dabbling could intentionally or unintentionally expose oneself or one's children to demonic influence. They also concurred that a morally bankrupt media was making occultism attractive and available to inexperienced youths. Such a process could be seen as a sign of satanic influence; that is, the Devil was manipulating the media to influence as many souls as possible. This image of the diabolical media, not surprisingly, was carefully balanced against the spirit-filled media-enhanced conduits that Charismatics were successfully using.

However, such a global electronic plot was still essentially theological in nature: Satan was the active adversary, and the media was no more than his naive pawn. Thus, the path that his movement took somehow had to project this theological myth outward onto the real world. The diabolical medicine of exorcism had identified scapegoats and brought spiritual warfare onto a literal, secular plane. But before these scapegoats could be arrested, or their social agendas frustrated, Charismatic communities had to convince influential secular institutions that a secret conspiracy existed. Such projections thus led to the formation and circulation of *subversion myths* that translate what is essentially a religious dispute into a secular one. Demons (and those who traffic with them) may weaken the faith of true believers, but devil-worshippers allegedly commit real crimes such as drug dealing, abduction, child abuse, and ritual murder. So when theological issues are projected into subversion myths, they effectively turn what is a matter for religious specialists into a law enforcement problem.

Subversion myths have been studied by sociologists, who see them as indications of cultural tension and change. But the way these traditions develop and function has not been widely studied by folklorists. Part of this is caused by the method in which subversion myths operate:

1. Like all myths, *subversion myths are cultural grammars* that link together bodies of information that are otherwise difficult to comprehend.
2. *They cannot be proved*: the individual facts may be verifiably true, but the pattern into which they are constructed ultimately rests on an act of faith.
3. *The power of subversion myths lies in the underlying pattern that they construct* out of the facts, not in the accuracy of the individual facts that they link together.
4. It follows that *disproof of any factual statement in the subversion myth does not discredit the perceived pattern*. Individuals promoting a subversion myth may be exposed as frauds or even admit that they have perpetrated a hoax. This does not, however, affect the perceived truth of the underlying myth. The number of facts linked by any subversion myth is open-ended and so will always be too great for even the most committed debunker to challenge. In any case, the pattern allows believers to revise and update the myth by adding facts from emerging events.

5. *Widespread belief in a subversion myth is assumed to be proof of its essential truth*. Expressed *dis*belief, conversely, is often taken as evidence for a hidden agenda. Such myths typically hold that subversive groups always try to hide their existence; hence, any overt attempt to show that a subversion myth is *not* true paradoxically demonstrates that it *is* true.

6. Therefore, *subversion myths can never be disproved*. Attempts to debunk them only transmit them to broader audiences. Once facts are constructed into a pattern, people will continue to see that pattern. "It is *not* true that . . ." easily mutates to "It *is* true that. . . ."

7. *Subversion myths change targets*, however, as soon as one scapegoat is no longer seen as a cultural threat. But a myth attached to one scapegoat will easily attach itself to another, even if the two scapegoated groups have little in common. Similarly, a group that has been persecuted with the help of a subversion myth may appropriate that myth to scapegoat other groups.

I recognize that this section of this study may help disseminate the subversion myths that it discusses. It is impossible to warn readers to disregard the patterns that such scenarios form out of historical events and phenomena, just as it would be futile to caution people *not* to think of a blue monkey. But such myths are already pervasive in western culture, and the development of the modern "Satanism Scare" would be impossible to explain without showing how these myths helped organize concerns and beliefs. What is not widely understood is the long-range history of specific myths and the variety of uses to which they have been put. Even if it is impossible to disprove any given subversion myth, it is possible to show that such traditions in the past have repeatedly justified sociopathic episodes of persecution and violence. I hope that readers will look at contemporary and future conspiracy scenarios with more caution and objectivity.

The Illuminati

Basham was one of the first Charismatics to describe satanic networks: by 1973 he was receiving letters from his contacts that describe a "surge of Satanism," even in seminaries, where witchcraft books were being circulated and used (Basham and Leggatt 1974:103–4). But Basham viewed Satanism as a mirror image of his own Charismatic work. In *The Most Dangerous Game* (1974), he gave a detailed set of parallels, setting up "God's Reality" (the deliverance ministry) against "Satan's Mockery" (individual religious practices that mimic Charismatic beliefs but in a non-Christian setting). Hence, Basham defines a whole range of New Age ideas as "Satanism" because they rely on supernatural powers not firmly grounded in institutional Christianity. "Satanists," moreover, work malefic magic, using spellbooks to cause illness instead of using scripture-based magic to produce healing and spiritual renewal. "Demonic mutterings" take the place of speaking in tongues. Thus far, this image of Satanism relies on ideas familiar from Koch, who assumed that Satan would combat spirit-filled ministry with equal and opposite spiritualistic powers.

A more literal enemy emerges when Basham describes the religious services Satanists allegedly hold. Rather than honoring the spiritual Blood of Christ, Satanists honor literal blood: they commit themselves to the Devil by blood subscription, drink animal blood, and use a satanic altar "where blood sacrifices, even human sacrifices are made." Rather than casting out demons that lead people into sin, demons are invited into worshippers, and all sins of the flesh are overindulged, with "numerous sexual participations with members of the satanic group" (Basham and Leggatt 1974:64–72). Such a description assumed not only a diabolical supernatural force opposing charisma, but also a flesh-and-blood institution. If such an institution existed and did things so obviously repugnant to society, then why were Satanists not being arrested and their blood sacrifices prevented? The answer, as it developed in the early 1970s, was that Satanism had penetrated to the most influential parts of English and American cultures, so powerful secular forces were protecting the devil cults.

The primary conspiracy myth that most directly explained how this was allegedly done was based on a genuinely subversive secret society called the Order of the Illuminati.[1] Born of the 1770s European intellectual reaction against religion, this society's distrust of institutional Christianity had much in common with the agendas of American revolutionaries such as Thomas Jefferson, who argued for universal religious tolerance and separation of church and state. The founder of the Illuminati, Adam Weishaupt (1748–1830), found little support for overt revolution in his native Bavaria, so he maintained that such reforms were best accomplished through stealth rather than open protest. The order, founded in 1776, was devoted to educating members in enlightenment ideas, so that when they advanced into the upper circles of government and society, they could accomplish reforms from the top down. His sect did not gain many followers, though, until he decided to form an alliance with the existing fraternal organization of Freemasonry. His followers were encouraged to join Masonic lodges, introduce more radical ideas into them, and so convert them into branches of the Illuminati.

Weishaupt's followers exchanged anticlerical and antimonarchical tracts, so when they were denounced to the Bavarian government in 1785, vast numbers of incriminating documents were seized and made public. Freemasons were especially hard put to prove that their lodges had not been infiltrated by Illuminist members or ideas. English Masons, fearing that their organization might be suppressed as disloyal to the monarchy, took an especially solid stand against allegedly subversive elements, and John Robison, a Scottish Mason, translated many of the tracts of the Illuminati in a warning titled *Proofs of a Conspiracy Against all the Religions and Governments of Europe* (1797). When this work was brought to the United States, a brief panic broke out in which Illuminati-influenced Masonic lodges were said to be operating in many parts of America (Stauffer 1918).

This scare soon died down, only to reawaken periodically in different parts of Europe. In the 1890s, journalist Leo Taxil (Gabriel Jogand-Pages) excited France with a series of disclosures that claimed that a renegade group of "Palladian Masons" were openly worshipping "Lucifer" and making secret plans to overthrow world governments. Taxil later admitted that his disclosures were hoaxes intended to embarrass prominent Catholics (he had previously edited an anticlerical publication that had been shut down by legal action). However, his claims lived on among those who felt that he had been intimidated or bribed into recanting by prominent Freemasons (Rhodes 1954). In particular, many of his ideas were recycled into contemporary anti-Semitism. *The Protocols of the Elders of Zion*, a forged document circulated by the Russian secret police to justify pogroms, held that Freemasonry was secretly controlled by Jewish financial interest, and that political movements such as Communism were part of a Zionist plot to take over the world (Cohn 1967).

This document, and the many rumors that went with it, were combined with the older Illuminati and Palladian Freemasonry scenarios by the British Fascisti, a group openly supportive of Hitler and Mussolini and opposed to the Allies' efforts to contain their aggression. Among the Fascisti's propagandists was Nesta Webster, who produced influential works portraying a wide range of movements ranging from feminism to modern art as Jewish/Masonic/Illuminati plots to destroy civilization. Further, Webster warned that the battle was not simply a political one. So pervasive was the conspiracy, she reasoned, that no less than Satan could be coordinating it, lending occult powers of black magic and hypnotism to his followers (1921:325).

Anti-Semitism did not strike as deeply into American culture as it did in Europe. Likewise, anti-Masonic rumors were not especially prevalent or influential during the early part of the twentieth century. Nevertheless, scattered allusions to the Illuminati myth appeared, by now associated with the American Communist Scare. In 1953, at the depth of the McCarthy investigations, government agencies such as the California State Senate Committee on Education were learning that "So-called modern communism is apparently the same hypocritical and deadly world conspiracy to destroy civilization that was founded by the secret order of the Illuminati in Bavaria on May 1, 1776" (Pedigo 1971:22).

The most influential source in creating the American Illuminati demonology was Canadian William Guy Carr, founder and leading propagandist for the Federation of Christian Laymen, a Catholic auxiliary based in Willowdale, Ontario. Carr, a career military person in the Canadian Navy, capped a lifetime of minor conspiracy theorizing with his 1958 book *Pawns in the Game.* This book relies heavily on the arguments of the British Fascisti in arguing that the world's troubles were being secretly orchestrated by a small group of "International Bankers" led by the Rothschild family. Carr follows Webster in combining information about Weishaupt's lodge, Taxil's revelations, and the anti-Semitism of *The Protocols of the Elders of Zion.* But Carr argued that the Jewish-controlled world conspiracy was, if anything, even more ancient and pervasive than previous authors had stated.

Like his predecessors, Carr argued that the Illuminati were only the most recent agents in a cosmic struggle originating with Satan's rebellion. The Old Testament serves only to describe "how Satan became prince of the world . . . [and] how the synagogue of Satan was established on this earth" to thwart God's will. Jesus Christ was incarnated, according to Carr's theological vision, to denounce the money-lenders and false priests as the Illuminati of their day (ix-x). In a remarkable argumentative twist, he argues that the Illuminati managed Jesus' execution so that the Jewish people would appear to have been responsible for His death. This led to Christian persecution, which in turn allowed the Illuminati to "use the hate, engendered amongst the Jewish people as the result of persecution, to serve their vile purposes, and further their secret totalitarian ambitions" (1958:12–13).

In fact, most of the wars and massacres in succeeding history, Carr suggests, were the result of Jewish efforts to seek revenge against Christian attempts to restrict their control over finance. In the meantime, he said, the Illuminati fostered an atmosphere of hatred and thirst for revenge within the Jewish ghettos, which eventually emerged as a "World Revolutionary Movement" aimed at all monarchs and Christian churches, particularly Catholicism (1958:16–18). Carr blamed the Jewish Illuminati for virtually every world event that followed. The Protestant schism was, for example, a Jewish plot: "Calvinism is of Jewish origin. It was deliberately conceived to split the adherents of the Christian religions, and divide the people. Calvin's real name was Cohen! . . . there is hardly a Jewish revolutionary leader who hasn't changed his name" (1958:20). Oliver Cromwell's rebellion against the Catholic monarch Charles II was also financed by Jewish synagogues, Carr claims, and the resulting separation of church and state was a further part of their plot to encourage atheism.

Carr claimed to have located "original documents" that show that *The Protocols of the Elders of Zion* were composed in 1773 by Mayer Rothschild, founder of the influential banking family. It was supposedly presented to a small group of Jewish conspirators meeting in the "Jundenstrasse"[2] in Frankfurt, Germany (1958:26 ff.). These conspirators, who "had literally 'Sold their souls to the devil,'" made up the group that originally laid out the grand plan for world domination. The Russian authorities' discovery of another version of this document "confirms the existence of the earlier one" (which, up to now, not even the British Fascisti had detected). The Russian version, Carr adds, is "an enlargement of the original plot . . . probably due to the rapid development of the international conspiracy" (31).

According to Carr's scenario, the Illuminati were founded not by Weishaupt but by a group of Jewish rabbis and high priests according to "inspirations given to [them] by Lucifer during the performance of their Cabalistic Rites. Thus Christ is proved justified when he named them *Of the Synagogue of Satan.*" The conspiracy thus founded was controlled by a "Supreme Council" of specialists in Jewish doctrine, rites, and ceremonies. There were thirteen of them "to remind the members that their one and only duty was to destroy the religion founded by Christ and his twelve Apostles" (32–33). This Supreme Council used Weishaupt's organization to infiltrate Freemasonry, instigate the French Revolution, use the Napoleonic Wars to enrich the Rothschilds, and eventually create "the Atheistic-materialistic ideology" of Communism.

Asked how he came to know such secrets, Carr explained that much of this information was included in documents being carried by an Illuminati courier from Frankfurt to Paris in 1785. A bolt of lightning, directed by God Himself, struck the courier dead, and the documents he carried fell into the hands of the Bavarian government. The influence of the Illuminati was by that time already so strong, Carr implies, that the contents of these documents were only partially shared with crusaders like Robison. Only Divine Providence allowed William Guy Carr to uncover them through research, revealing them to the world for the first time in 1958. A simpler explanation is that Carr or one of his military associates[3] simply made up these stories, which are not paralleled even in the most virulent of anti-Semitic documents from the first part of the century.

This scenario allowed him to account for a wide range of world events. Many of these developed Carr's Anglophile distrust of United States politics, which he saw as irretrievably contaminated by Jewish/Illuminati influences. Abraham Lincoln was assassinated to prevent financial reforms he had planned. John Wilkes Booth, who was (like all Carr's historical villains) secretly a Jew, pulled the trigger, but the Rothschilds had given the orders (1958:57). More recently, the creation of the Federal Reserve System and Roosevelt's New Deal were likewise an International Bankers' plot. In fact, Carr includes a page explicating the reverse of the U.S. Seal in terms of Illuminati symbols. The triangle was itself a sinister symbol that "represents the conspiracy for destruction of the Catholic (Universal Christian) Church," and the date 1776 represents not the Declaration of Independence but the founding of Weishaupt's lodge the same year. One Latin motto, "Novus Ordo Seclorum," is a reference to the Illuminati plot, meaning "New Social Order," or more plainly "New Deal," while the other, "Annuit Coeptis," says "our enterprise (conspiracy) has been crowned with success." The symbol, Carr notes, was first printed on the U.S. one dollar bill in 1933, just as Roosevelt's New Deal was set up.

In effect [Carr sums up] this seal proclaims to the One Worlders that the entire power of the U.S. Government is now controlled by the Illuminati's agentur and is persuaded or forced to adopt policies which further the secret plans of the conspirators to undermine and destroy it together with the remaining governments of the so-called 'Free World,' ALL existing religions, etc., etc., so that the Synagogue of Satan will be able to usurp the powers of the first world government to be established and then impose a Luciferian totalitarian dictatorship upon what remains of the Human Race. (1958:xiii)

As part of this dictatorship, the government will be made up of the Luciferians, while the great mass of humanity, the "pawns" in the Illuminati's chess game, will simply be "integrated into a vast conglomeration of mongrelized humanity, by artificial insemination practiced on an international scale." Under this scheme no more than 5 percent of males would be used for breeding purposes (1958:xix). This idea, which has its origins in Nazi theories of Jewish "blood" contaminating the purer German stock (see Cohn 1967:184 ff.) also contains implications of castration. These notions, combined with panicky speculations about gun control, would later reemerge as part of the more developed versions of the American Satanism Scare.

For all the political discussions, however, Carr's historical view is, like Webster's, essentially theological. Asked how the Illuminati are able to succeed in convincing people to follow their lead, Carr develops a theory of demonic obsession that is clearly linked to the early Charismatics like H.A. Maxwell Whyte. "If human BEINGS can establish radio, and television stations," he argues, "from which one individual can influence millions of others by broadcasting his opinions on any given subject over the invisible air-waves then why shouldn't it be possible for CELESTIAL beings to broadcast their messages to us? No brain specialist has dared to deny that in the brain of each individual there is some kind of mysterious receiving set" (1958:7). Those who attend religious services, receive the Sacraments, and pray, receive divine messages through the Grace of God. But Carr warns, "the Devil does inoculate his evil influence and powers into the hearts and souls of the men and women who accept, as their religion, Satanism and atheism." Indoctrinated "through the ceremonies and Rites of the Illuminati," such as those of "the Semitic Cabala" and Freemasonry, they "put the theories of their High Priests into practice" (1958:36).

Carr's theological links to the Charismatic movement are also clear. If one is in doubt about the essential truth of his conspiracy theory, Carr advises his reader, "all he or she needs to do to solve his or her uncertainty is recite the first half of the Lord's Prayer SLOWLY. ..." The result will be a miraculous confirmation from the Holy Spirit. Carr concludes, "It doesn't require more than a few minutes to decide if any act to be performed individually, or collectively is in accordance with the Will of God, or furthering the machinations of the Devil" (1958:178). Likewise, Carr's immediate agenda was primarily religious rather than political in nature. He called for a "Christian Crusade" in the evangelical style, focusing on mass evangelical meetings: "A religious revival amongst the members of all Christian denominations is essential in order to change men's thinking in regard to the values and importance they place on worldly possessions. The hearts of men must be turned towards love of Almighty God. We must learn once again to take a real delight in rendering Him service and in performing His Holy Will. The National Federation of Christian Laymen has been organized to put this idea into action" (1958:180).

Despite Carr's distaste for U.S. politics, his book had a huge influence among the extreme right wing of American anti-Communists, particularly Robert Welch of the John Birch Society. By 1966, Welch had paraphrased the Illuminati theme in *American Opinion*, his Society's widely distributed magazine. Conscious of his audience, Welch eliminated Carr's references to "the Synagogue of Satan." And while claiming that the Federal Reserve System was the product of "highly placed Marxian influences in the Woodrow Wilson administration" (1966:148), he pointedly did not refer to "Jewish influence" or "International Bankers."[4] Nevertheless, Welch prefaced his description of the Bavarian Illuminati (drawn mainly from Robison by way of Nesta Webster) with a telling allusion to the "cult of Satanism, which incorporated into its beliefs, methods, and purposes practically all of the foulness now associated with our contemporary tyranny, Communism" (1966:124). He left open to question whether Satanism was extensively practiced, or whether Communism is a *direct* descendent of such cults. But he implied as much, saying "hundreds of small leaks" show that by the eighteenth century, a multitude of small secret organizations "had pretty much coalesced into a uniformly Satanic creed and program." Their agenda "was to establish the power of the sect through the destruction of all governments, all religion, all morality, [and] all economic systems" (1966:125).

Welch's exposé of the Illuminati, though, called American right-wingers' attention to Webster and Carr, and he later encouraged the Reverend Clarence Kelly to compose his own version of the Illuminati myth as *Conspiracy Against God and Man* (1974). Published by the John Birch Society's press, Western Islands, this book references Webster and other anti-Jewish authors, but softens many of the explicitly anti-Semitic materials in these sources. Nevertheless, any reader following up Kelly's extensive footnotes found the Jewish Banker plots abundantly referenced. And other works that drew on Carr included anti-Jewish elements, though sometimes suggesting that the *real* Illuminati had deliberately fingered the Jews as convenient targets, allowing them to exploit the turmoil that followed for their own purposes. *The Missing Dimension in World Affairs* (1976), by "Michael J. Goy" (a pseudonym based on the Yiddish term for "non-Jew") was one work that gave this explanation. Nevertheless, "Goy" added, "to deny that many Jews have been involved in the Plot would be ridiculous: Weishaupt, Marx, the Warburgs, the Rothschilds, Jacob Schiff, etc. were all Jews!" (197). A flood of other Illuminati exposés soon circulated in right-wing and evangelical media-enhanced conduits, mainly drawing on Carr and other anti-Semitic sources.[5]

One especially popular item was a sound recording, initially released on two long-playing phonograph discs, and allegedly made ca. 1967–1968 by a certain "Myron Fagan." Fagan claimed to have been a well-known Jewish playwright and producer in both Hollywood and New York City. Intimate with the Jews and "Reds" who controlled the entertainment industry, he broke with them when they refused to allow him to produce a play that exposed the influence of Communists. He then allegedly spent thousands of dollars privately researching the Illuminati and released this recording documenting their secret role in American political and social life. In fact, like "Goy," "Fagan" is probably a pseudonym intended to recall the villainous Jew, Fagin, who secretly manipulates a gang of child thieves in Charles Dickens's *Oliver Twist*. Much of his recording is plagiarized directly from Carr's *Pawns in the Game*, with names of contemporary politicians like Senator William Fulbright and Secretary of State Dean Rusk added to connect the theories to current events.

"Fagan's" main contribution was to pass Carr's anti-Semitic ideas into the Pentecostal conduit of sound recordings. He also extended Carr's intolerance an extra step by arguing that the race riots of the mid-1960s had in fact been fomented by chapters of the Jewish Anti-Defamation

League. He characterized this organization as "the Gestapo and hatchet-men operation" of the Illuminati, who enlisted "Negroes who would do the demonstrating and commit the rioting, looting, and lawlessness." The ADL, Fagan said, secretly advised and controlled every major African American civil rights organization, including such leaders as "Martin Lucifer King." Fagan's LP's were subsequently dubbed onto cassette tapes by the Louisiana-based neo-Nazi organization, the Sons of Liberty.

Jess Pedigo and *The Two Babylons*

It is no surprise to find the Modern Illuminati theme being used early on by the deliverance ministry to construct the social threat of Satanism. An early example of this merging of traditions is Dr. Jess Pedigo's 1971 tract, *Satanism: Diabolical Religion of Darkness*. Pedigo was a journalist associated with Dr. Billy James Hargis, a Tulsa, Oklahoma, Charismatic evangelist with a strong campaign directed against "the forces of antichrist communism and satanic immorality." Pedigo's other titles included *X-Rated Movies: Hollywood's Scheme to Corrupt America*, and *Yes, Ginger, Communism Is Your Enemy*.

On the one side, Pedigo's message was an orthodox form of the deliverance mythology as we have seen it. He denounces "spiritism" in all its forms, from the Ouija board to wart-charming, and he warns readers that they can open themselves to "satanic infestation by following—and believing—the daily horoscope columns in the newspapers" (58). Pedigo accepts Koch's theory that parents and grandparents can demonize their children and adds guilt by association to the scene by adding that one can also contract demons through "fellowshipping with one who dabbles in the occult" (62).

Pedigo also adopts some of the antifeminist rhetoric that we have seen in the deliverance literature. He finds "Mrs. Suburban Housewife" especially susceptible to pastimes that open doors and lead to "the intrusion of demonic spirits" (47). He particularly decries the popularity of the television sitcom *Bewitched*, which showed the comic results when Samantha, a witch with supernatural powers, marries a klutzy advertising executive and moves into suburbia. Even though a fantasy, Pedigo says, it portrays witchcraft as a way to "put *hexes* on people [emphasis his], and . . . get what you want, so you are revenged of your enemies and rewarded, too." He concludes severely that the modern housewife "would give much to be a witch" (7–8).

If Pedigo's argument had been limited to this side of demonology, it would have been no different from the warnings of the evangelists already surveyed: otherworldly demons will interfere with the religious experiences of individuals dabbling with the occult. But Pedigo finds a *social* threat behind Satanism, and to prove this he puts together elements from all the conspiracy scenarios available to him. He asserts that the confessions given in historical witch trials were based on a substantial base of truth:

> Could a mere figment of the imagination prompt a lovely young girl of 16 to stand proud, boastfully, before a court and calmly state that the devil had indeed seduced her and that he had copulated with her every night for months? No! This lass knew fully well that her confession must certainly result in a death of barbaric cruelty. Is it at all possible that the multitudinous covens of witches and adherents to the satanic churches presently scattered across America are bearing the stigma, the ostracism from society, the persecution of their peers, for nothing at all; no power, no experience, no sensation or reward above the ordinary? (4)

Pedigo joins Webster, Carr, and Welch in saying that modern witchcraft is part of an ancient secret society that predates Christianity. However, rather than targeting the Jews, Pedigo here followed the argument of a nineteenth-century Scottish anti-Catholic propagandist, Alexander Hislop, whose book *The Two Babylons* mingled sketchy knowledge of Middle Eastern antiquity with a vivid imagination. Hislop argued that Nimrod, the Biblical "mighty hunter" of Genesis 10:8–12, was the same as the legendary Ninus of Babylon. His wife, Semiramis, founded "the Babylonian Cult," which promised "illumination" to all who obeyed the cult's leaders. Ninus's goal was to create a one-world government and a one-world religion, which would be Satanism. On the female side, Semiramis developed her "unbridled lust" into a satanic witchcraft ritual called "The Babylonian Mysteries." This was the first Babylon, Hislop argued, which Jesus Christ came to destroy.

Hislop's original argument continues on to a "second Babylon," in which Satan secretly replaced the apostle Simon Peter with the occultist

Simon Magus as Bishop of Rome, thus creating the "satanic religion" of Roman Catholicism. Pedigo, however, did not follow this link and instead developed a version of the "world government" theme. Pedigo stresses, "*From Nimrod's day, each succeeding Satanist sect has operated with a single eye toward world rule . . . world government . . . as its ultimate goal.*" These cults invariably are composed of men and women who have gained influence in their countries: diplomats, scholars, scientists, men of letters. Most Satanists are not ignorant but rather "the most intellectual members of a decadent society" (1971:19; emphasis and ellipses his). The nature of Nimrod's cult is difficult to document because new members have to be indoctrinated to put aside all ties to country and family and obey without question the mystical brotherhood.

The nature of the initiation ceremony, he argues, successfully prevents new members from defecting. He cites documents from earlier anti-Masonic scares that claimed that initiates had to perform sexual intercourse with goats and other "unspeakable perversions" (presumably homosexual acts). Initiations featured "blood-smeared crucifixes, black candles and an altar made of human skeletons." An infant was killed and its blood drunk on the spot, while "grisly oaths" were followed by invocations of demons (1971:21–22). Such oaths were taken "under such disgusting, mind-breaking, manhood dispelling circumstances" in order to ensure the silence of initiates, Pedigo said, since the initiate would then feel "himself to be less than human, bestial in conduct, bestial in nature" (1971:17–18). Pedigo derived this argument from 1950s British anti-African propaganda, justifying the brutal military response to the Kenyan war for independence.

Moving on to older antiwitchcraft traditions, Pedigo explains what allegedly went on in sabbats. After magically traveling to the site of the ceremony, they first devoured the corpse of a murdered or disinterred child, then engaged in an orgy in which the Devil and demons freely copulated with the witches. "Brothers joined themselves with sisters," Pedigo says, "fathers with daughters, mothers with sons and any witch, regardless of family relationship, was free to exercise his desire upon the person of his or her choice" (1971:30–31). One recalls the rumor that plagued Don Basham in seminary: that his prayer meetings to practice tongue-speaking were really "séances" during which he turned off the lights to carry out an orgy. Patently false when applied to Charismatics, such rumors were eminently credible when used to describe black magic cults.

The same rites are still practiced today, Pedigo argues, with new witches constantly being initiated in ceremonies involving sexual intercourse between the initiate and the coven. "There is no little amount of proof," he adds "that some of England's governmental leaders are active or passive participants in the rituals of Satanism" (1971:24–25). Pedigo specifically mentions the Illuminati as a case in point: its schemes carried out with "such diabolical cunning that the name and principal leaders of the orders seldom are known." And for cults, Pedigo says, such initiations and orgies are only the beginning. In time participants turn to the shedding of blood for sacrifices— first animal and then human. Then, as the cults increase in scope and power, they drift into the realm of politics and prepare for a power grab. This is possible because, as proven through history, wealthy and influential men and women are drawn as if by a magnet into the societies as initiates (35–36).

The reason such horrors are not public knowledge, he concludes, is simple: even when such diabolical rites are uncovered and the leaders executed or overthrown, *the reaction of the people is to disbelieve or discount the stories. Men cannot, or will not, recognize the dangers that face them*" (1971:21; emphasis his). In other words, the sheer unbelievability of the stories was in itself proof that they were true; otherwise why would anyone ask people to believe them?

Mainstreaming the Illuminati

In the early anti-Satanism literature, however, Pedigo was an exception in emphasizing perverse sex and baby-eating, and even he was vague on when and where such ritual murders occurred. Besides his tract, references to infant sacrifice in early anti-Satanism literature are brief and sketchy. An "ex-Satanist's" testimony, published in the Summer 1970 issue of *Focus on Youth*, a college religious magazine, briefly described a Black Mass in which "A girl named Jan sacrificed her baby, burning it alive" (15; also Wilburn 1972:156). And in 1973, popular author Roger Elwood quotes a New Jersey minister as telling him, "I had to talk to a mother the other day whose baby was found dead. . . . The poor child didn't have one inch of skin left on its little body" (41). Nevertheless, even anti-occult crusader Gary Wilburn admitted that claims that stories about babies being sacrificed in recent times were no more than "rumors" and added "the probability of this being a common practice is rare (and its documentation ever [*sic*] more rare)" (1972:147).

Even though explicit anti-Semitism did not find a place in much of the deliverance ministry's literature, both the baby-murder story and the "one-world government" theme of the *Protocols* proved useful to many fringe groups within the Charismatic movement. We have noted the influence of Veronica Lueken on Lawrence Pazder's investigation of Michelle Smith's ritual abuse stories. From the early 1970s, Lueken had developed a strong conduit of followers, who circulated the prophecies and revelations she allegedly received from the Virgin Mary, Jesus, and other divine figures. In 1975, however, she began to circulate warnings based on Carr's anti-Semitic "One-World Government" myth. One prayer vigil produced the following dramatic revelation:

> *St. Michael* - "There is a man who hides behind the mask ruling your country! He will soon approach and reveal himself. He is the man who compromises your country for the love of power.
> "He has affiliated A-L-L of the money powers of the world, joined them for unity of a one-world government.
> "Step down and reveal yourself, the leader . . ."
> *Veronica* - Oh, my goodness! Oh my goodness! The man behind the mask, Mr. Rockefeller.[6] The man behind the mask!
> *Our Lady* - "There sets in your country masters of great magnitude! Recognize the Grand Masters in control! As it was in the time of My Son, they now control your country. A synagogue of Satan is covering your land!" (*Incredible Bayside Prophecies* 1991:276–77)

By 1977 Lueken had dropped the anti-Semitic elements and, like Pedigo, was describing the Illuminati as essentially an occult organization. "It has now been interwoven with the churches of satan and the massive international organization of Wicca," she explained (1991:55). A lengthy prophecy received on November 25, 1978, detailed this Wicca/Illuminati plot. The Virgin Mary told Lueken to warn parents that because they were discarding the old Catholic ways, "your children are being brainwashed by Lucifer. He sends into your homes music. You accept these to make your children happy, but there is a power called witchcraft." In fact, the followers of the Devil have infiltrated the United States and Canada, developing a complex plan "to destroy your children with drugs, using your school systems, your medias of communication[;] your newspapers, your televisions, your radios, every means of communication has been infiltrated by the member and sub-members [*sic*] of the Illuminati." In the end, the prophecy warned, "Lucifer plans to turn father against son, mother against daughter, and shall direct them to kill ... within the home. ... rivers of blood shall flow in your streets as children will rise against their parents." In a somewhat obscure statement, the message cautioned parents to investigate "what your children are wearing upon the temples of satan," presumably an allusion to the alleged occult properties of the "peace sign" and other popular adolescent amulets, and concluded that hundreds of Satanists were actively at work "to destroy your country, to destroy your children. ... You must act upon this" (1991:83–84, 265–67).

Simultaneously, Lueken was indeed acting upon this and similar revelations. Maury Terry, an investigative reporter working with the Queens police force on the notorious "Son of Sam" murders committed by David Berkowitz in 1976–1977, records that one of the detectives was regularly receiving anonymous phone calls giving "lurid tales of a satanic cult" to which the murderer had belonged. In fact, the woman claimed, Berkowitz was only one of the soldiers of this cult, which had a "safe house" on Staten Island where Black Masses involving infant sacrifices were being performed. The leader, a local accountant, was a drug dealer as well, and the woman also claimed that a former NYPD detective was one of the cult's dope suppliers. Although she refused to give her identity or the source of her information over the phone, her information was so detailed that Queens police placed the cult's "safe house" under surveillance and traced the license plate numbers of cars that visited.

The story came to an anticlimactic end when the officers learned that the bartender at their regular hangout knew the people who lived at the "safe house" address. He agreed to accompany detectives to the house and get them inside. The couple living there was just a normal, middle-aged couple, and when the officers circumspectly asked if they had ever had difficulties with neighbors, the husband responded that a "strange woman" in a long robe had regularly come by to stare at the house. At one point she had stopped their son, saying, "I know who you are and what you're involved with. Don't think you're going to get away with it." A visit to the landlady of the house where the woman lived turned up a letter from Lueken, repeating the claim about the satanic "safe house" and claiming that she was on a "secret mission." When detectives in turn went to Lueken to make further inquiries, she refused to talk to them, and police found the rest of the story impossible to confirm. "The whole thing is Lueken's hallucination," the detective finally realized, adding, "She sounded believable; she really did." "To her, it probably *seems* real," Terry responded. "That's why she was so convincing. I'd love for us to write something about all this, but it would only hurt the investigation. But can you see the headline? 'FAMOUS SEER OF BAYSIDE EXPOSED'" (1987:191–99). Nevertheless, Terry did follow up some of Lueken's other "secret" information, and his book, *The Ultimate Evil* (1987) became an influential argument that shadowy blood cults such as she had described did in fact exist.

Another influential figure in the mainstreaming of the Illuminati myth into religious conduits was Pat Brooks, an associate of Basham and author of a series of anti-occult books. An explicit conspiracy theory appeared in her writings as early as 1972, when she told of an alleged secret government meeting called to investigate a supernatural danger to U.S. security: "Sweeping into our country, across various points of its territorial borders, hordes of dark, shadowy figures have been observed on our radar screens. Soon after such an invasion, the area entered had erupted in chaos. Ghetto and campus violence, large concentrations of drug addicts and hippie pads, as well as corruption and excessive Mafia activity were noted in these areas. Yet these dark invaders cannot be photographed or observed with the natural eyes" (1972:221–22). In her influential book, *The Return of the Puritans* (1976, 3rd. ed., 1981b), Brooks cites Nesta Webster at length in connecting Judaism with the Illuminati. By 1978, she had imitated Basham in composing a list of activities that her followers were supposed to renounce by name before receiving the Holy Spirit. But her list came close to all-encompassing: it also included rock music and "senseless, immoral, subversive, or even occultic television." Tabooed as well were participation in martial arts, yoga, acupuncture or any other activity associated with eastern religions. Most importantly, she included Masonry and its female auxiliary, the Order of the Eastern Star. Finally, believers were to combat "liberal theology," and all other "Luciferian scheme[s] designed to bring in an antichrist-inspired world government," among them "humanism, socialism, communism, [and] Zionism" (1978:83).

Soon after, Brooks openly cited the *Protocols* as the basis of her own *Hear, O Israel* (1981a), a passionate attack on Judaism as the satanic source of all social evil in the world today. By this time she had adopted a mythology drawn from the Christian Identity movement,[7] which held that the English were in fact the true descendents of God's chosen people in the Old Testament. The real descendants of Abraham, according to this myth, emigrated to northern Germany and eventually became the founders of the English empire. In a providential turn of history, the most inspired of these Israelite descendants in turn emigrated to New England as the Puritans. By contrast, the politically dominant Ashkenazic Jews actually descended from Gentiles in the Middle East. These bogus Jews gave rise to "the self-assertive people who throng the theaters (and subways) of New York. . . . With a constant drive to make money, to come out on top, they consummate endless business deals at the synagogue" (1981a:54). Brooks concludes, "If our Puritan forbears were not only like the Hebrews, but were Israelites themselves, the very propensity for theocracy may well lie in our genes, placed there by our Creator, the Holy One of Israel. . . . The research . . . has convinced this author that the nation born at Sinai has been reborn here."

Brooks prophecied that the United States would be reborn as a benign theocracy, an American "promised land," ruled by God's spiritual power, (1981a:150–53). This is why Satan had developed a complex conspiracy, put into operation by Jewish folk magic, "to turn it into a humanistic, socialist state." She argues:

> It is only when we face the common origins of socialism, communism, Freemasonry, humanism and Zionism that we have any hope of understanding what is going on in the world today. All come from ancient Hebrew Cabalism, a system of sorcery which uses the Old Testament Scriptures to find magic rites in the numerical values of the Hebrew letters. . . .
>
> It is high time Christians understand that the Talmud, on which most modern Jewish religion is based, is not Biblical at all. It is cabalistic. . . . Basically, it is a system of ancient Hebrew sorcery. (1981a:71, 112)

As evidence for the essentially satanic nature of Judaism, Brooks presents an anecdote in which a "Christian patriot" babysitting a Jewish ten-year-old tried to say a good-night prayer with her. The child refused, saying, "We pray differently from you." When the Christian persisted, saying that they did not have to mention the name of Jesus in their prayers, the child elaborated: "We pray *differently* from you. I mean, we pray to Lucifer" (1981a:112). That such explicit anti-Semitism would emerge in the anti-occult crusade is not surprising; the traditional image of black magic is founded in early modern distortions of Jewish traditions (Trachtenburg 1943). But Brooks moves beyond the notion that dabbling in Jewish cabalism is a dangerous form of occultism: here the entire religious tradition of Judaism is a "Synagogue of Satan."

Conclusions

True, anti-Semitism made up only a small proportion of the deliverance ministry's attacks on Satanism. Nevertheless, the image of financially powerful, invisible, utterly malign conspirators, tightly organized by family and religion, clearly was one base on which images of the satanic underground was founded. Once Israel had been established as an independent state, thereby clearing the way in many millenarian scenarios of the Apocalypse, anti-Semitic ideas became an even more attractive model for constructing satanic cults. Jews and their shadowy co-workers, the international bankers and the media, were to emerge more than once later on as the terrestrial side of Satan's plot to thwart Christianity and democracy.

The Illuminati crusaders continue to influence the religious scene. In his 1991 best seller, *The New World Order*, Pat Robertson claims that the Illuminati, "atheists and Satanists," were behind the United Nations and other liberal causes he decried. Echoing the all-inclusiveness of this subversion myth, Robertson concluded, "The New Age religions, the beliefs of the Illuminati, and Illuminated Freemasonry all seem to move along parallel tracks with world communism and world finance."

Witches, New Agers, Masons, Catholics, Jews, Liberals, Calvinists, Communists, the media, the Mafia, the occult, the Illuminati—all of these enemies tended to blend into each other as each theorist selected the details they chose to emphasize. What they all agreed upon was that there was a plot to control the world and oppose spirit-filled religion. Most useful was the notion that the "rich and influential" somehow had gained the upper hand in ruling the social and religious world. Widely available and easily adaptable to fit virtually any controversial topic, the Illuminati scenario formed a matrix for just about every conspiracy theory that emerged during the 1960s and 1970s. As we shall see, the first generation of "confessing Satanists" all in some way grounded their revelations in this body of pseudohistory.

Brits and the Black Mass

The First "Confessing Witches"

There was no prosecution,
because there was no evidence.
—Robert Fabian,
Fabian of the Yard

Thus far we have found a number of elements that fit together to provide grounds for believing that underground satanic cults were operating in Anglo-American culture. Among Charismatics, we have found the pervasive belief that Satan is actively recruiting and maintaining a *civitas diaboli* made up of demon-possessed people, saints and sinners alike, who resist revivals and the gifts of the spirit. And subversion myths identified devil-worshipping scapegoats for diffuse social threats ranging from plagues to economic depressions. The Satanism Scare was born from the fusion of these elements into a vision of a flesh-and-blood subversive institution, targeting adolescents, directed by the Devil, and carrying out an Illuminati-style agenda of world domination.

As with the early modern witch-hunts, however, such a scare could not gain momentum without a firsthand "insider's" view of what was going on inside such groups of devil-worshippers. The most important of these participants were England's Doreen Irvine and the United States' Mike Warnke and John Todd, who in the early 1970s published detailed accounts of their careers as Satanists. These confessions all originally emerged and were circulated within the deliverance ministry, and all three people attributed their salvation to the gifts of the spirit practiced by Charismatics, though Todd later adopted Koch's point of view and denounced many Pentecostals as demon-possessed. But the stories they told were far more complex than those told by ex-spiritualists. All of them described elaborate cults, made up of intelligent, politically powerful people who communicated their subversive agenda through a secret worldwide network. On the ground level, such cults were said to entice curious youngsters, then involve them in occult ceremonies invoking demonic powers. On the global level, these groups allegedly planned to infiltrate and take over western society.

However, none of these confessions emerged in a vacuum. They emerged and found audiences in cultures well prepared to hear them. In Great Britain, the emergence of Gardnerian Wicca was certainly the catalyst for the first "confessing Satanists," the more so because the first generation of Wiccans frequently justified their activities by contrast with shadowy "black magicians" whom they promised to help society resist. To see how Doreen Irvine became "Queen of all Black Witches," we need to examine how interest in ceremonial magick developed from a fringe intellectual tradition to an adolescent fad.

Aleister Crowley and Dennis Wheatley

Much of the immediate context of the first "confessing Satanists" was provided by the lengthy and wide-ranging legacy of the 1890s Order of the Golden Dawn. This organization combined existing Masonic and Rosicrucian concepts with ceremonial magick practices drawn from earlier occult traditions. To call it a "secret" society would be misleading, however, as its internal correspondence and publications were legion. A young Aleister Crowley, then an undergraduate at Cambridge, found himself drawn to the group by one of A.E. Waite's books[1] and was introduced to the London Golden Dawn lodge in 1898. Crowley went on to a lengthy and influential career in occultism. Most of his work involves his efforts to reconstruct "Gnostic" and pagan rituals and does not address demonology except in a highly philosophical way. But Crowley enjoyed the notoriety he gained in the popular press and openly associated the Biblical "666" and "Great Beast" titles with himself. Hence, to some extent he was responsible for the popular belief that he was genuinely involved in devil worship. By 1931, Nash's *Pall Mall Magazine* could publish an article "I know that Black Masses are being celebrated to-day" and head it with a portrait of Crowley. The article repeated some of the rumors that Crowley inspired and at times encouraged about his own esoteric society: "On Friday nights there were special invocations to Pan and, on one occasion, a cat, which was considered to be an evil spirit, was sacrificed. It is even said that the blood of the cat was drunk" (Price and Coster 1931).

Although Crowley promoted his own image as a self-proclaimed Antichrist in some of his own writings, these were, however, less influential than the caricature of him used in a series of British popular novels by Dennis Wheatley (1897–1977). Best known for novels of espionage and historical adventure, Wheatley occasionally included Satanism as a plot device. In such fictions, circles of wealthy, intelligent devil-worshippers were shown permeating British society. Highly organized and often in league with Nazis or Communists, they met regularly to hold occult ceremonies and invoke Satan. The novels include a wealth of detail about contemporary devil worship, leading Wheatley to include a disclaimer to each of his occult novels stating that he, personally, had never participated in any actual ceremony but had derived his material from books and from conversations with "actual practitioners of the Art." Wheatley in fact was acquainted with both Crowley and demonologist Montague Summers and derived most of these authenticating details from their works.

The first of Wheatley's "black magic" novels, *The Devil Rides Out* (1934), for instance, includes a detailed account of a "sabbat" held out in the English countryside by a group of wealthy, upper-class Satanists, who arrive in a fleet of expensive automobiles, bearing out the hero's suspicion "that the practitioners of the Black Art in modern times were almost exclusively people of great wealth" (1954:84). A detailed account of the ceremony follows, which is conducted by the Devil himself, appearing as a goat-headed creature. Complete with ritual desecration of crucifixes and cannibalism, the story's details were drawn not from contemporary rumors about cults but from a work by the Basque witchhunter Pierre de Lancre (1553–1631), as reported in Summers's 1925 *History of Witchcraft*. The main villain of Wheatley's novel, the "Ipsissimus" Mocata, head of the British Satanists, is openly based on Crowley, and Wheatley derives much of his occult terminology from Crowley's *Magick in Theory and Practice* (1929), an inscribed copy of which the occultist gave to Wheatley (1971:275). Wheatley, for instance, incorporates Crowley's famous definition of magick as "the Science and Art of Causing Change to occur in conformity with Will" (1954:41) and his description of the grades through which his band of Satanists proceed is that of Crowley's own occult organization, the OTO.

Mocata, however, incorporates most of the malicious rumors lodged against Crowley: visiting the wife of one of his opponents, he tries to get her into his power by hypnotizing her with his penetrating gaze. Failing in this and other psychic attacks, he abducts her young child. The climactic scene of the novel takes place in a ruined monastery on the island of Corfu, where Mocata attempts to sacrifice the child during a Black Mass. This scene is a thinly disguised version of the rumors that circulated around Crowley's commune at the Abbey of Thelema, on the island of Sicily. Wheatley later said, "Black masses were said there and animals offered up to Satan. It was then rumoured that human infants were also being sacrificed, upon which the authorities expelled Crowley from Italy" (1971:273).

Wheatley followed up the success of *The Devil Rides Out* with several sequels that feature Crowleyesque villains: *Strange Conflict* (1941) and *The Haunting of Toby Jugg* (1948). Most influential was *To the Devil—a Daughter* (1953), the story of an ambitious father who promises his infant daughter to Satan in return for success in the business world. She grows up with a dual personality, a "normal" innocent self that dominates during the daytime, and a more sexually alluring and daring "alter" that takes over during the night. The plot describes how her lover uncovers her secret, burns the blood pact her father had made, and saves her just as the Crowleyian head Satanist is about to sacrifice her. The story even includes a legend about Crowley that Wheatley recounted as true. Aleister Crowley had a disciple named MacAleister ("Aleister's son"), the story goes, who performed a ceremony to summon the god Pan. Their rite was all too successful: in the morning the disciple was found dead and Crowley was temporarily driven insane (1956:211–15; 1971:276).[2]

In 1954, criminologist Henry T.F. Rhodes produced a history of the Black Mass, sympathetically citing witch-hunt evidence as proof that underground satanic movements had abducted and sacrificed children at least through the 1700s. Today, however, he believed that Satanism was no longer a widespread practice (1954:210–11). Yet simultaneously, Chief Inspector Robert Fabian, ex-superintendent of Scotland Yard and formerly head of their vice squad, was writing that "There is more active Satan-worship today than ever since the Dark Ages" (1954:74). Describing a 1945 Warwickshire murder, in which a villager had been slashed with a sickle and then pinned to the ground with a hayfork, Fabian explained how he became convinced that the killing was a witchcraft murder (1953:105–11). In the wake of Fabian's popular account, an elderly woman from Birmingham came forward to confess that she had been a member of the "black magic society" who had committed the murder as part of a midnight Black Mass. Police evidently were not impressed by her testimony, and the case was closed as unsolved.

In a follow-up volume, Fabian presented a brief but hair-raising account of urban Satanism. "When a Sunday in December falls on the 13th day of the month (as it did in 1953) and is, therefore, the 13th day before Christmas," he claimed, Satanists gathered all over London in "secret temples" to perform rites "that would shame an African savage!" (1954:74). He described one Wheatleyesque "Temple of Satanism" in loving detail, including black candles, inverted crucifixes, and "symbols of wizardry" including pentagrams daubed on the walls and ceilings. During rituals, communion wafers were blasphemed and ritually soiled, and an orgy followed, including one "witchcraft ritual in which young girls or susceptible boys are dedicated to Pan, that is indescribable" (1954:76).

Fabian admitted that police had never made any arrests, but he countered that such cults were difficult to infiltrate: in order to witness the positively vile ceremonies, initiates had to cooperate wholeheartedly in "the early, trivial obscenities." And, he concludes, "There is also a very real danger of police witnesses being hypnotised" (1954:77). Still, Fabian says, there are notes in Scotland Yard on one cult "survivor," a twenty-one-year-old girl who had been taken by her mother to a lecture on Satanism. "She was invited to a garden party at the house of a woman calling herself a 'High Priestess,' who persuaded the girl to sing a 'magical invocation,' in the process of which the girl was successfully hypnotised. She did not return home for months. When, with the help of the Yard, her parents finally recovered her, the girl had been hypnotised and exposed to occult obscenities so persistently that she was almost insane. Her own pet dog ran howling in fear from her. It took two years to restore her mind." Fabian concludes, "There was no prosecution, because there was no evidence. The girl had been 'willed' to forget how it had happened" (1954:75). Fabian blamed "psychic circles" that draw in curiosity-seekers with "harmless spiritualism" and then gradually seduce them through hypnosis and drugs into Satanism (1954:77). Although Fabian's concerns were by no means universal, they show that by the early 1950s at least some police accepted the reality of Wheatley-style Black Lodges in London.

"Confessing" to the Witch-Cult

The year 1954 also saw the publication of Gerald Gardner's *Witchcraft Today*, an instrumental book in what later became the neo-pagan movement. Gardner (1884–1964) claimed to have contacted an underground coven of witches in the New Forest region that had survived directly from one of the medieval "witch-cults" that Margaret Murray (1921) had claimed were driven underground by Christianity. Knowledge of the Gardnerian movement began to come to public perception as early as 1952, when the popular British magazine *Illustrated* published an account of the New Forest coven, quoting Gardner at some length. The resulting interest spurred Gardner to write his book, which printed excerpts from a "Book of Shadows" used by practitioners of "the Old Religion." Initiates were instructed to copy these rites by hand from their mentors' copies, Gardner explained, and each copy was burned at the witch's death, which accounted for the lack of any earlier manuscripts to substantiate his circle's antiquity. Gardner's claim was received with incredulity by many scholars, but Murray contributed an approving foreword to *Witchcraft Today*.

In fact, the primary source was published material, primarily from the Golden Dawn movement and the OTO. Gardner's "Book of Shadows" (titled "Ye Bok of ye Art Magical") was largely a collage of passages from Macgregor Mathers's translation of the medieval spellbook *The Greater Key of Solomon* with additions from Crowley's *Magick in Theory and Practice*. The rites focused on repetitive chanting and dancing, with nudity and ritual flagellation prescribed as part of the rites. There are indications that such elements were added because Gardner, like many products of the British private school system, found physical punishment sexually arousing (Kelly 1991). The early Book of Shadows also includes many elements from standard Masonic rituals, most notably the use of "the Craft" to describe the movement and the regular use of "so mote it be" to conclude prayers and incantation. None of this is surprising: Gardner was an initiated member of Crowley's OTO (King 1989:179–80) and one of his close friends was J.S.M. Ward, an eminent historian of Freemasonry (Kelly 1991:32).

Nevertheless, the issue of whether these secret witchcraft groups really existed is moot, as Gardner's rituals were enormously influential, and since then neo-pagan or "Wiccan" groups have proliferated in Europe and North America. The claim that they existed seems to have brought the witch-cults into existence. And even if the original rites focused on Gardner's sexual fantasies, within ten years of his death the most sensational elements—the nudity and whipping—were being quietly toned down or edited out of most covens' practice. Frank Smyth notes that the rumored sex orgies that occurred during Wiccan meetings were nonexistent because most members were in fact sedentary workers in their late thirties and up, and they were usually winded by the physical activities of the rite. "I have scarcely ever seen a male witch with an erection after such a communal dance," one early coven member admitted to an investigator (1973:22).

Gardner's movement had to contend, however, with a fresh series of "black magic" panics. The *Sunday Empire News*, which had previously serialized Fabian's memoirs, announced on March 16, 1958, that a priest in one of London's most famous churches had asked for special police protection from a satanic cult centered in the Chelsea district. Composed of "highly intelligent men and women," the group held rites in a different house each week, culminating in "A Black Mass which finally perverts men and girls from God to devil-worship . . . based on the defamation of symbols and regalia." And on April 28 of that year, the *Empire News* published the alleged confession of a former cult "leader" who admitted to indulging in blood-drinking and orgies, during which "leaders photograph members in compromising settings . . . to ensure that no one can return to decent life." Faced with such blackmail, lesser members were often driven to suicide if they chose to leave the cult.

This "blackmail" theme actually derives from a lively British contemporary legend tradition. One version of it had been passed on in 1917 to William Guy Carr, who recorded it in detail in *Pawns in the Game*. In his version, officers in the British Armed Forces were invited to a private mansion, called "The Glass Club," that was funded by a group of nominally patriotic financiers. The officers arrived to find every luxury abundantly provided by their hosts, who also provided them with a female consort, discreetly masked. In the midst of "luxurious drapes, subdued lighting, beautiful women gorgeously dressed, soft dreamy music, [and] the smell of rare perfumes," the entertainment regularly featured a dance depicting "a scene in a Sultan's Harem." Five voluptuous girls performed a dance during which they stripped entirely naked, after which the officers and their masked consorts were encouraged to retire to their private rooms.

This went on without any official notice until "a very high personage" was lured to the club. He went to his private room to await his assigned consort, and, Carr says, the following scene ensued:

> A lady joined him. When she saw him she nearly fainted. It was his own wife. She was much younger than her husband. She had been acting as hostess to lonely officers on leave for a considerable time. It was a most embarrassing situation.
>
> The wife knew nothing of the plot. She had no secret information to give. She was convinced that both she and her husband were philandering. She thought it was only this unfortunate chance meeting which had brought them face to face. There was a scene. The husband was informed regarding the part hostesses played at the Club. But his lips were sealed as if in death. He was a member of the Government. He couldn't afford to figure in a scandal. (1958:82–84)

In Carr's version, it soon became public knowledge that the Glass Club was actually run by Illuminati spies who recorded their guests' moral weaknesses in what was called "The Black Book." These records then were used to blackmail officers into revealing military information. In fact, the key incident quoted above is a well-traveled contemporary legend motif, in fact still current today.[3] And the general belief—that secret organizations like Satanists use compromising records such as photographs and films to ensnare dabblers—was soon a staple explanation of why police could find so little tangible evidence of such rings.

In October of that year, churches in Lancashire and Manchester were robbed of religious objects including robes and communion vessels. One vicar blamed the string of thefts on a "religious crank who wants to set up his own chapel.... Whoever it was has been very selective in choosing what to take indicating a knowledge of Catholic ceremonies." Another agreed that this was possible, but added, "the vestments could be used in ceremonies by 'black mass' fanatics—Devil worshipers."[4] These stories were followed in December by a still more sensational account of a "satanic" infant sacrifice in the seaside town of Rottingdean, near Brighton.

In this case, the source was Leslie Roberts, a self-styled investigator of witchcraft and the occult, who had for some time been investigating black magic claims in the area. Brighton, the site of Crowley's 1947 death and cremation, had for some time had a reputation for harboring strange cults, and in his inquiries Roberts had contacted Doreen Valiente, formerly a leading member of Gardner's coven. Valiente had been attracted to Gardner by the 1952 magazine publicity and was initiated in 1953. She proved influential in rewriting the clumsy prose of his rituals into useable poetic chants, several of which Gardner quoted as traditional in his *Witchcraft Today* (Kelly 1991). Valiente continued to work up original rituals to replace Gardner's borrowings from Crowley, and Gardner's coven gradually built up a discreet conduit of their own, although the group often disagreed among themselves about the degree to which the movement should be publicized. By 1957, Doreen Valiente had split off a group who had disagreed with Gardner's increasing willingness to court media attention.

It was this group that Roberts had contacted, and Valiente offered to loan him some of her magickal instruments for a lecture on witchcraft to the Brighton Forum Society. The talk, however, did not go as well as she had hoped: Roberts told the society that there were numerous witchcraft covens in the area. One, led by a professional nurse in a local hospital, had "access to blood which is required at certain rites," and another was led by the rector of a local church. He offered to direct police to the private house in nearby Rottingdean where a "colored" [i.e., non-Anglo] baby had been sacrificed during a Black Mass, and he asserted that human sacrifices were held frequently at Eastbourne, too. A furor ensued during which Roberts was summoned to the local police station to tell what he knew, while reporters from London swarmed outside. "I have probed the truth for a long time and I know my facts are correct," he told the news, but said little more about the sacrifice. When police later found "no substance whatever in this matter," Roberts implied that they were deliberately shielding the cults.[5]

After 1960 Gerald Gardner, now increasingly fragile, was initiating considerably more members than the small-scale movement had contained before, and his ideas, now elaborated in a second book, *The Meaning of Witchcraft* (1959), were being imitated outside his group. Curious youngsters in Great Britain and, eventually, in North America, were finding their way into "Wica,"[6] as Gardner preferred to term his modern witchcraft. Evangelicals soon reacted with concern that such dabbling with the occult was apt to draw teens into satanic practices. However, a packet of letters now held at the Wayne State University Folklore Archive illustrates the way in which the Gardnerian movement actually did fit into adolescent interest in the occult.[7]

Written by a Canadian teenager to his American pen pal during the period 1962–1965, the letters record the activities of "Puck," (the author's Craft name) an otherwise typical North American adolescent in a small-town or rural setting. He described his hometown in northern Ontario as "the last outpost on Earth," dominated by a huge pulp and paper mill, providing teens only TV, radio, and "hanging out" for entertainment. Like many teens, Puck got brief thrills out of experimenting with a Ouija board: in one letter he describes how he contacted the spirit of a recent suicide victim in his neighborhood. But like most adolescents' involvement, Puck did little more than ask for signs and trivial predictions. Suspicious that one of his friends was occasionally manipulating the indicator to try to scare the group, he sums up his reaction to it as uncertain: "not morbid or macabre but . . ." [ellipses *sic*].

From the first letters, though, Puck emphasizes that he is "inwardly a believer in the Wica." Asked for more details, he explains that Wica is witchcraft, and not "imaginary 'hooey' . . . It is a very secret order, the name is not even supposed to be known." Over the next three months, Puck gradually let out details to his fascinated correspondent, though he emphasized that he himself was not an initiated member and therefore either would not or could not give out some of the details the movement held secret. The details he does provide, though, correspond with those of the movement's history as reconstructed by Aidan A. Kelly and others.

Wica practiced real magic, Puck claimed, a power that like electricity was used primarily for good, but could be misused. Repeatedly, he stressed that it was not a "hell-fire club" or associated with the black arts, and in fact he resented "the bad name they have gained because of the Satanist cult." The only sacrifice needed, he explained, was the dedication of its members' lives, and if blood is used in its rites, it is drawn from the body of the celebrant him- or herself: never from a freshly killed animal. Sex is a part of the movement—"I suppose a great part"—but he believed that this referred more to a spiritual "Power of Love" than to any ritual sex act.

Initially, Puck declined to gives names and addresses of his contacts, and even declined to give the high priestess's name. For more details, he referred to Gardner's and Margaret Murray's publications, all of which, he adds, were written "by permission of _____, the high priestess." (After a few months he replaced this mysterious blank with "Lady Olwen," the Craft name of Monique Wilson, Gardner's handpicked successor.) Initially, he estimated the movement's size at about 300–1,000 members, then, citing British press releases, he revised this upward to about 6,000 initiates. In October 1962 he commented sadly that, from what he had heard, there was no coven active in North America. This changed the following May, when Puck wrote, "Here is something very few people know, and very few are likely to know. I think Lady Olwen would prefer you and I not to mention it (you and I because not many outside the Craft know) but there is now a coven in the United States. It is the first coven in the American Continent in history to my knowledge. It seems sort of 'hush-hush' when she talks about it therefore my remark about being discreet." Despite this show of secrecy, he continues, "However Wica policy seems liable to constant change; a few years ago the Wica was totally secret and now they are talking about writing an even more informative book than 'The Meaning of Witchcraft.'"

This ambivalence accurately reflects the splits that had developed in Gardner's group, and Puck's details correspond with the movement's history as reconstructed from scattered documents and oral history. When Gardner died in 1964, various members sought to take over his leadership role and the disputes brought still more media attention to the movement. "Lady Olwen" and her husband had in fact not taken a major role in the covens but had mainly cared for the ailing Gardner and helped run his museum of witchcraft paraphernalia. Into this leadership vacuum entered a number of contestants for "King" or "Queen" of witches. Within Gardner's movement, the main figures, besides Wilson, were Eleanor "Ray" Bone, and New Yorkers Raymond and Rosemary Buckland, founders of the first American Gardnerian coven mentioned by Puck.

Challenging them from outside was Sybil Leek, who claimed to have been initiated by a different multigenerational coven. Leek was another discovery of Leslie Roberts, who had continued his research into real witchcraft after the Rottingdean "baby sacrifice" affair. Leek, a writer and telejournalist who also ran an antique store, came to Roberts's attention in 1962. She claimed that there were actually four traditional covens in the New Forest, and she belonged to one different from Gardner's. She soon became an articulate promoter of the neo-pagan movement, and by September 1963 she and her tame jackdaw, Hotfoot Jackson, were already appearing in press releases titled "Yes, I Am The Forest Witch" (Valiente 1989:144–46)

A proliferation of press releases followed, moving now from the British tabloids to television features to respectable American publications such as *Life* (Real Witches 1964) and *The Saturday Evening Post*

(Kobler 1966). Puck, like Buckland and the early American neo-pagans, remained loyal to Wilson despite her ineffectuality: he accepted Ray Bone as "Queen of London" but disputed her claim to lead the movement, concluding "I'd call her a heretic." As for Leek, he absolutely refused to accept her as Queen of anything, as "She recognizes black magick—the others don't." Leek readily admitted this in her autobiography. "It is better to know the degradation to which Black Magic sinks from a personal observation of it, than only to have information from books" (1968:20).

Not to be outdone, Alex Sanders came forward in 1965 with a story that in 1933 he had been independently initiated into Wicca by his grandmother in the Manchester area. He claimed to have been elected "King of the Witches" at a meeting of covens. Other neo-pagans expressed skepticism about his story, noting that he had in truth been initiated into a Gardnerian coven in 1963 and derived his allegedly independent "Book of Shadows" from Gardner's (Kelly 1991:178–79). But Sanders too had stories about his brushes with black magic; in fact, during the trying years after World War II, he had given way to temptation and practiced black magic to gain "wealth, riches, power." Later, though, he recognized his error and purged his guilt through white magic ceremonies (Johns 1969:36–68; Smyth 1973:115–20).

Like Leek, Sanders also claimed that British covens of white witches were helping to protect society against evil black magic rings, and, appropriating the Blood Libel myth, he told a story even more sensational than any of hers. A few years ago, a London Wiccan using a crystal ball to predict the future saw that a child was about to be ritually sacrificed in a church. With the help of the coven, the Wiccan magically learned where and when the sacrifice was scheduled, and three witches were sent to prevent it, "It was scheduled to be in a Roman Catholic church outside Rome two or three days hence. . . . [The white witches] arrived at the church to which they had been directed in time to see one of four priests take up a knife and approach the altar where a newly born baby was lying. Two nuns were standing by. The London witch snatched the knife from the priest and stabbed him in the throat, killing him. . . . Enquiries showed that the ritual about to have been done was black witchcraft" (Johns 1969:147).

An avid publicist, Sanders later initiated *Daily Mirror* reporter Stewart Farrar into his coven, ensuring an immediate and sympathetic link to the popular movement. Farrar's 1971 book *What Witches Do* incorporated much of Sanders's apology for Wicca, and he also assisted popular author June Johns compile a book detailing the sexual and psychological dangers of alleged black magic cults (1971). The more curious could come to Sanders's stage shows, during which he would handcuff and chain his wife before hypnotizing her to summon a demon to possess her, a clear appropriation of deliverance ministry tactics. For much of the early 1970s, photographs of his prominently balding head and his young wife's naked breasts embodied Wiccan rituals for the British popular press (e.g. Maple 1973:130 ff.).

Overall, the early sixties were a heady time for those wanting to participate in witchcraft revival movements. Puck's correspondence shows that Gardnerian Wicca (as it was now becoming known) was the best organized of these groups despite its internal fissions. It also confirms what its apologists said in public statements: that it had no interest in attracting and initiating large numbers of adolescents whose interests in sex and sorcery might bring disrepute to the new movement. In fact, an extensive survey conducted by Smyth (1973) found that Gardnerian Wicca at this time was dominated by middle-aged blue-collar workers with a strong conservative political bias. Most of them admired the xenophobic British politician Enoch Powell, and at this time covens tended to exclude non-Europeans. One early member of the movement was concerned that teaching magick to "an inferior race" could result in "untold harm," a point reinforced by Wheatley, who in several of his books portrays Africans or African Americans as especially dangerous occult villains.[8] Another said, more perceptively, "I wouldn't admit coloured people to our meetings ... [because] they wouldn't harmonise with us. I'm not biased of course, but that is the way it is" (Smyth 1973:18–20).

But in the American adolescent world, Wicca fed into a growing fantasy that fed on the country's growing sexual and cultural freedom. Briefly, Puck alludes to being "in the Druid Order," evidently yet another brotherhood that members were supposed to keep "secret in theory" though they could publicize it at discretion. He says rather little about it, other than saying that participants sent some kind of mental impulses through a time barrier to affect a future life. In return, Puck's correspondent referred to a "Whician" movement that he evidently practiced, or at least fantasized. In any case, Puck found it difficult to believe in its tenets, finding its god too close to the conventional Christian deity and adding, "You believe sex is sacred but we believe that our lives are sacred."

Whatever "Whicia" was is now impossible to determine: from the context it seems likely to have mined the same media interests in sexual freedom and occultism that the Gardnerian movement drew on. Eventually the witchcraft revival begun by the British neo-pagans did come to North America, but, as we can see from Puck's letters, less on its secrecy than on its media image. The publication of "secrets" turned into a flood of popular books in the late sixties, then a modest industry that established publishers like Llewellyn Publications and Samuel Weiser, Inc. This trade succeeded not because there was a proliferation of multi-generational pagans seeking converts but because it drew on the same adolescent urge for role-playing that the Ouija ritual attracted. Such links were aggressively exploited by the British mass media and hence impossible for the evangelical community to ignore.

Black Magic Mainstreamed: the Hammer Studio Films

None of the Gardnerian groups or their imitators denied the existence of black magic rings: they only denied that they were part of this evil tradition. To that extent, the neo-pagans themselves provided a conduit for information about Satanists. Patricia and Arnold Crowther, leaders of a Sheffield Gardnerian coven, offered fifty pounds in vain to anyone who could direct them to a real Black Mass. Nevertheless, they continued,

> Anyone who . . . was able to celebrate the Black Mass throughout the country, would have lots of followers and, no doubt, become a wealthy man. His followers would not be teenagers either, but so-called respectable people. You would be surprised if you saw the type of man who approaches witches to join the craft, hoping that it is connected with Black Magic and sex orgies. They are all too ready to become members, providing their names are kept secret and their wives and business associates know nothing about it. Their absence from home, to attend meetings, could always be blamed upon business appointments. (1976:95–96)

Sybil Leek, characteristically, added more detail: she had personally witnessed *three* Black Masses, one conducted by Aleister Crowley himself, and "every Black Magic group" had at one time or another offered to make her a "Queen of Darkness" in their festivities (1968:92). She was well acquainted with the Satanist who was responsible for church desecrations in the London area, she told a reporter, but added, "I dare not disclose his identity" (Kobler 1966:78). Later she explained that he was "A mathematician [and] a man of high intellect," whom she had magically healed in exchange for his promise to spare the New Forest area any more black magic operations. "He remains a still-powerful force in the world of Black Magic," she concluded (1968:91–94). At the same time, the Witchcraft Research Association, a network of London Wiccans, circulated several attacks on renegade covens, warning, "It is known that one such group is organized by thoroughly undesirable people practicing the most horrible sexual and other deviations. Please be extremely careful" (qtd. in Kobler 1966:77).

Those who wished to see what a Black Mass was like, however, needed only to head to the nearest cinema, where a number of British studios were producing sensational B films on satanic themes. Among the first of these was a film variously titled *13* or *Eye of the Devil* (1965), a Wheatleyesque story of an evil black magic ring. To ensure an accurate portrayal of satanic activities, ex-black-magician Alex Sanders was called in as a consultant on the film, and gossip held that he had used the opportunity to introduce the lead actress, Sharon Tate, to the occult. Indeed, some went so far as to allege that he had initiated her into Wicca, after which she visited "some of those English shops that specialized in old occult books. She purchased several volumes" (Sanders 1971:73).

A more influential role, however, was played by Hammer Film Productions, Ltd., a company that had been making B horror films for a British audience since 1934. Starting in 1958, Hammer began updating popular American horror themes, including Frankenstein, the Mummy, the Werewolf, and the Phantom of the Opera. Made in frequently gaudy color rather than the traditional black-and-white, these features soon gained a reputation for explicit bloodshed and Grand Guignol horror motifs including torture, cannibalism, and dismemberment. These movies frequently incorporated motifs from folklore, as in *The Revenge of Frankenstein* (1958), which is based on a long-lived contemporary legend in which an amoral doctor uses poor people at a clinic as a source for experimental organ transplants (see Campion-Vincent 1991). Film historians such as John McCarty (1984) credit this series as having influenced the tradition of "splatter movies," horror films often incorporating elements from occult or horror traditions and enormously popular among adolescents from the 1960s on.

Hence, when Hammer Studios released a film version of Wheatley's *The Devil Rides Out* [U.S.: *The Devil's Bride*] in 1967, it was ideally placed to introduce Wheatley's vision of "black magic lodges" to British teenagers. Adapted closely from the novel by the veteran B movie scriptwriter Richard Matheson, the movie featured well-known British character actors Charles Gray as the Crowleyesque villain Mocata and Christopher Lee as the white magician de Richleau. The British cinema censors demanded a number of changes to the screenplay, Lee recalled, "because rather than fantasy, these books dealt with the absolute reality of Black Magic. There are such cults and such people even today, at every level of society." Perhaps for this reason, the characters throughout the plot are visibly careful never to say the words "Satan" or even "cult," and the black sabbat on the moors is cautiously realized, participants never removing their long *white* robes. Nevertheless, Wheatley was delighted that the movie included most of his key episodes and sent Matheson a cordial thank-you letter (*Devil Rides Out* 1996).

Hammer film aficionados soon learned that the action included a number of authentic incantations, symbols, and allusions to the Golden Dawn rituals (Chapman 1991:8). Practically unnoticed in its American release, it became a huge success among British adolescents, and popular publishers were quick to follow with a series of cheap reprints of Wheatley's "Black Magic Novels." Wheatley himself had already responded to increasing interest in the occult with his 1960 novel *The Satanist,* a portrayal of a London "black lodge" that turns out to be controlled by an Illuminati-style cadre of international Communists. He was encouraged to produce a number of new works in this vein, including *They Used Dark Forces* (1964), *Gateway to Hell* (1970), and *The Irish Witch* (1972). His publisher also initiated a "Dennis Wheatley Library of the Occult" to repeat older fiction and non-fiction titles that could be packaged to fit the new interest. These included works ranging from popular handlings of psychic phenomenon to demonologist Montague Summers's *History of Witchcraft.*

Soon it was unnecessary to visit arcane bookstores to get detailed information on magical practices: Richard Cavendish's *The Black Arts* (1967; paper 1969) filled that need. Despite its lurid title (and paperback cover, with a candle burning eerily by a skull and an ancient tome of presumably occult lore), it mainly gave a popular summary of ancient and medieval sources on numerology, alchemy, astrology, and witch-trial confessions. While the book gives some information on the Golden

Dawn's version of the Cabala and ceremonial magick, its most influential sections dealt with lore on summoning demonic spirits, whose symbols are helpfully given, and using them for purposes such as necromancy and psychic attack. Cavendish's book owes more to this older tradition than to Wicca, but it became the underground classic among British adolescents and one of the standard sources for occult-focused movies.

Hammer continued to mine this popular vein until 1976, when the studio made a version of Wheatley's *To the Devil—a Daughter*. Despite the talents of Richard Widmark and Nastassja Kinski in her first leading role, this movie did not make as much of an impression as the earlier Wheatley adaptation. One reason might have been that Wheatley's basic plot had already been used in 1967 by Ira Levin in his popular novel *Rosemary's Baby*. As in Wheatley, a girl is secretly promised to the Devil by an ambitious male, in this case her husband, a New York City actor. The plot ends more cynically and ambiguously: the woman is in fact impregnated by Satan and bears a baby with devil's horns (yet another contemporary legend motif), which she accepts and promises to raise with maternal love.[9]

Director Roman Polanski, whose first Hollywood B movie *The Fearless Vampire Killers* (1967) made him an emerging figure in the "splatter film" tradition, adapted the novel into a hit movie. *Rosemary's Baby* premiered in London in January 1968, underlining its connection to the Hammer Studio's occult movie tradition. In a publicity appearance on Johnny Carson's *Tonight Show*, Polanski complained that British censors had given him unusual trouble before passing the film, telling him that "there is quite a lot of this particular kind of Witchcraft going on in Britain today." In fact, Polanski insisted, he had done "absolutely no research" into occultism before making the movie, with one exception: designs for some of the amulets and symbols used as props had been drawn from a picture book (Steiger 1969:176–77).

Very little of this popular outpouring had anything to do with the Golden Dawn/Gardnerian tradition of ceremonial magick. But what it did mainstream is the idea that there was such an allegedly "secret" ritual tradition, and if that existed, then it must be accompanied by other such secret magickal traditions. Wicca's emergence into the public eye was accompanied by assurances that despite its emphasis on nudity, it really had no scandalous content to hide. It followed that the other traditions remained secret because they *did* have something to hide: something far more evil and hence far more interesting to the general public.

From Witchcraft to Christ: Doreen Irvine

With so many Gardnerian witches admitting belief in or even direct knowledge of black magic cults, it is hardly surprising to find such information surfacing in Pentecostal "confessions" that illustrate the dangers of Satanism. Confessions from repentant occultists were not new among Pentecostals: indeed, both Basham and Maxwell Whyte included accounts of their early involvement with the occult. But up to this point most of the firsthand material had come from former spiritualists rather than ex-Satanists. One important example was Raphael Gasson, whose anti-occult book *The Challenging Counterfeit* (1966) opened with an autobiographical testimony titled "From Satan to Christ." Born in England of a Jewish family, Gasson experimented for years with various forms of spiritualism, often going into trance and allowing spirit guides to speak through him. He became troubled with his craft after his encounter with a "master in black magic" who promised to raise a group of evil spirits to confront Gasson's "good" spirit guides. The two went into trance together, and when he came to, Gasson was astonished to find that his spirit guides had conversed amiably with the black magicians', "and apparently they were all friends together" (1966:21–22).

Puzzled, he contacted several Christian churches until he joined a Pentecostal Assembly. He formally renounced his spiritualism in 1947 and soon after received the gift of tongues. He entered a career of ministry opposing spiritualism, despite dizzy spells and unintended trances, including episodes in which he attempted to strangle himself with his own hands. By pleading the Blood, however, he eventually gained complete deliverance (1966:24–29).

Gasson's life story was paralleled by American Victor H. Ernest, raised in a spiritualist family in Minnesota. Ernest's autobiography, *I Talked with Spirits* (1970), describes his early involvement in trance mediumship, giving accounts of séances held by his family and his neighbors, along with samples of automatic writing. Ernest renounced spiritualism in 1929 and began an anti-occult ministry. Like Gasson, he suffered baffling psychic attacks: "Sometimes my memory would go blank; other times my throat would constrict and I couldn't speak." As with Gasson, prayer through "the power of Jesus' blood" usually ended the attack.

Ernest also gives a brief account of a Minnesota woman who came to him in 1948 to confess that she and a friend were overt Satan-wor-shippers who held services intended to allow one of them to conceive the Antichrist. Yet even this confession (discussed in Chapter One) described no organized cult, and the woman admitted doing nothing more hei-nous than shoplift and disrupt religious services "for entertainment" (1970:60). And the séance messages Ernest reports all express a conven-tionally Victorian Christian faith in Jesus and the afterlife. Both books were influential among anti-occult crusaders, as they created patterns that were used by later "confessing Satanists." But such testimonials spoke more to the broad popular tradition of spiritualism, not to any genu-inely sinister cult devoted to evil.

Doreen Irvine was the first of the evangelical ex-Satanists who de-scribed an explicitly diabolical cult in the image of the Golden Dawn/ Wiccan tradition. The account she gives about her early years is vague, but she apparently ran away from an abusive Uxbridge family sometime after the end of the Second World War, to become an exotic dancer and prostitute. After years of street life, including at least one term in prison for shoplifting to support a drug habit, Irvine responded to an altar call during a crusade conducted by British evangelist Eric Hutchings. Re-ferred to local churches by counselors, she found herself losing control whenever the Blood of Christ was mentioned, tearing up Bibles, knock-ing communion plates to the ground, and falling to the ground hissing like a snake.

In 1964 sympathetic ministers referred her to the Reverend Arthur Neil of Bristol, who had some experience in the deliverance ministry. On their first meeting, Rev. Neil used "a strange tongue that the demons understood"—i.e., glossolalia—which the minister explained was "the authoritative tongue the Lord had given him in dealing with demons" (1973:124). In this way he confirmed that Irvine was demon-possessed. At a second meeting, Irvine began expressing alternate personalities and proved an apt subject for deliverance. Rev. Neil commented, "The New Testament came alive in terms of encounters with demons of different character. . . . With extraordinary intelligence, utterly beyond the hu-man, they acted and spoke *through* [emphasis his] her and yet certainly not from her mind" (1973:7). Six demons came out in turn, identifying themselves in terms of their individual nature: Doubt and Unbelief, De-ceit, Lust, Lies, Pride, and finally Witchcraft, an unusually noisy one that tried to hex Rev. Neil with "certain enchanted wailings." A second exor-cism cast out Solicit, Dark Enticer, Seducer, Stripper, Corruption, and

Lesbian, the last speaking in "a refined society voice" quite unlike Irvine's own (1973:127–32).

Although the exorcisms were apparently successful, Irvine showed up five months later in a mental hospital, suffering from the effects of drug addiction and what was then diagnosed as "religious mania." Given a weekend pass, Irvine again sought out Rev. Neil and insisted that he cast out the rest of the demons. During a dramatic all-night session in February 1965, he successfully cleared Irvine of her demons, the last being Dementia. Irvine then joined Eric Hutchings's crusades, warning youths against "an unhealthy interest in witchcraft and other forms of the occult" (1973:7, 112–61).

In 1973 she collected her testimony into a book titled *From Witchcraft to Christ*, the title clearly echoing Gasson's antispiritualist confession "From Satan to Christ." Her accounts of Satanism and witchcraft also show a strong and constant debt to the Dennis Wheatley tradition of "black lodges." Her first contact with devil worship came, she said, as she was working as a stripper under the name "Daring Diana." When she overheard two fellow dancers whispering about "the Satanists' temple," she expressed curiosity. Sworn to secrecy, she was blindfolded and taken to a large hall in London where about five hundred people gathered to worship "Lucifer." A two-hour "Black Mass" ceremony followed, conducted with much chanting and manipulation of magical vessels, knives, and emblems by a "chief Satanist" and thirteen black-robed assistants. It climaxed in the sudden extinguishing of lights and the sacrifice of a white cockerel.

The mysterious large hall, scene of a complex quasi-religious ceremony with instruments and occult symbols, and both the Crowleyesque "chief Satanist" and the sacrificed cockerel are all clichés in Wheatley's novels. The obvious scope of the conspiracy is made clear when the chief Satanist took Irvine under his special care, explaining, "All kinds of people are Satanists. From the high to the low—bankers, shopkeepers, teachers, nurses, prostitutes, drug addicts. . . . We are here to promote Satan on the earth whenever and however we can" (1973:89). Making Irvine his mistress, he gave her free drugs, indoctrinating her to mock all Christian literature and to pray to and obey only Lucifer. "Lying, cheating, swearing, free lust—even murder—are condoned," he explains, adding that he believed that when he died, "he would be in charge of legions of devils" (1973:91).

And the extinguishing of lights recalls the Blood Libel scenario, with the implicit orgy that follows being implied more and more clearly as Irvine's narrative continues. Taken to a second meeting, Irvine discreetly says that she saw "all manner of evil scenes, far worse than the last." When she was ready to be a "sworn-in child of Lucifer," Satanists from all over England were invited to an especially complex ceremony. She drank a mixture of her own blood with that of a sacrificed white cockerel and signed a parchment with her name, selling her soul to Satan forever. At this point, she says with her typical discretion, "The people went crazy, and all kinds of evil scenes followed." At the end, she found to her surprise that she was "the great priestess Diana," a high honor given by "the great Lucifer himself" (1973:91–92).[10]

Irvine describes several occasions during temple ceremonies when she heard a mystical demonic voice or even a dark shape that identified itself as "Lucifer, your master," and urged the worshippers to "Do all the evil you wish . . . Revel in your freedom of lust this night." With her usual indirection, Irvine simply adds, "we all obeyed without question." She also recalls that the leading Satanists could perform magical operations on themselves or others without using drugs or leaving scars: she found that she could also read minds and travel to "the demon sphere" to see activities there, the last a theme characteristic of Wheatley's novels (1973:91–93).

Once she had become a high priestess of Lucifer, the chief Satanist encouraged Irvine to move on to "black witchcraft." The two, he explained, are not very different: while Satanists worshipped in a temple en masse, witches operated in the open air in covens of thirteen each. Here we meet some of the details entering the popular media from the Gardnerian movement, which did indeed operate in the open countryside in small groups. However, Irvine holds that their ceremonies were in fact orgiastic blood rites in nature. She was initiated by being smeared in goat's blood and witnessing scenes "far worse" than those she had seen in the London temples. These involved things that, with her usual reticence, she simply says are "too evil to be brought to mind." This time, however, she does add that all coven meetings included lesbian or homosexual acts accompanied by sadism. "Imagine one hundred black witches all taking part in such perversions at the same time," she exclaims, adding, "And this still goes on today."[11]

Included in their activities were desecrating churches and exhuming dead bodies to offer as sacrifices to Satan. Holy books were burned and goat's blood was splashed on gravestones and church walls, with "an emblem of witchcraft" left behind. Irvine gained the ability to levitate as well as the more unique power to kill birds in flight after they were released from a cage. After practicing for some time, she was encouraged to compete for the title of "Queen of Black Witches" at a Halloween "test of power" held at Dartmoor. Witches from all over England, as well as from Holland, Germany, and France, attended this meet. Participants (as in *The Devil Rides Out*) "arrived in smart cars, not on broomsticks, and booked in at hotels looking for all the world like successful businessmen and women—which some were. This was the new face of witchcraft—prosperous, almost respectable—a veneer that concealed tremendous forces of evil." Irvine showed off her bird-killing spell and other occult skills, then in the final test, she walked confidently into the middle of a great bonfire.

> Suddenly I saw him materialize before me—a great black figure. I took his hand and walked with him to the center of the great blaze. There I paused, the great flames leaping around me.
> Only when I emerged at the other side of the blaze did my master Diablos disappear. Not even the smell of burning was upon my loose witch's robe or my long flowing hair.
> Everyone was prostrated on the ground.
> "Hail, Diana, queen of black witches!" rose the loud cry of over a thousand witches. (1973:97–99)

Irvine describes a year of luxurious living, traveling at the movement's expense from one continental grand hotel or country home to another. In a diabolical parody of Pentecostal beliefs, she found herself able to understand and speak the languages of all the countries she visited. She visited covens, traded magical techniques, and discussed at length how to make evil witchcraft more appealing to young people, making it seem like a "natural, innocent adventure." Once young people were involved, she learned, "There would be no way out," and fear would hold them back from defecting.

Then came a fall from grace: at the end of the year, Irvine found she had to turn over her position to another witch, and her satanic mentor also took up with a new woman. She turned to her earlier career of prostitution and drug dealing, maintaining her contacts with her old coven. Then came her conversion and deliverance, after which, she says, she went back to her old associates to tell them she was quitting Satanism.

They attacked her physically and left her battered body in a lonely spot, where she was found and taken to hospital. After her deliverance, however, they did not molest her further when she appeared at Dr. Hutchins' evangelistic meetings and on British television.

Asked during a TV interview how a prostitute, drug addict, and witch could act as an evangelist, she replied, "I'm no longer any of those things, for my life has been changed by Jesus. I am now a new creature in Christ" (1973:162). Rev. Neil agreed that she was "a trophy of God's Grace" and adds that her actions since her deliverance "confirm the reality and validity of the work of God" in her. Her story gives a valid warning to those who dabble in the occult, he concluded, but the rest of his endorsement of her testimony is equivocal, "There can be no doubt about the blatant way in which the forces of darkness are at work in the world today. The rapidly increasing interest in and practice of magic, its sinister association with occultism, witchcraft, and Satanism, are grim factors of awful import. That there are strange and malevolent powers at work in supernatural reality behind the scenes is both a scriptural truth and a fact of experience" (Irvine 1973:8). His comment, that is, stops short of explicitly endorsing Irvine's main claim. Most evangelical Christians would agree that "forces of darkness" and "strange and malevolent powers" lie behind the occult. Rev. Neil does not *insist* that hundreds, perhaps thousands of well-financed and influential witches and Satanists are conspiring to promote this interest. But he does not explicitly deny Irvine's claim.

Conclusions

Irvine did resurface in 1988 as a member of a British Evangelical Alliance committee devoted to investigating and publicizing claims of satanic ritual abuse of children. But she seems not to have taken a central role in this group's efforts, which relied more on North American theories deriving from MPD therapists' work. The scenarios that emerged at this time are distantly related to the "Black Lodge" lore that Irvine related, but Irvine's presence does not seem to have incited crusades against Wiccans or Masons.

If Irvine's story included fantasy elements worked up out of anti-Masonic, anti-Semitic, and popular fiction lore, it was nevertheless a *safe* story for Pentecostals to believe. Both Maxwell Whyte and Koch, for all their mutual animosity over the validity of glossolalia, joined in adopting Irvine's testimony in their crusades against Satanism because Irvine's testimony had the dual advantage of being both vague and supernatural. (Whyte 1973c:39–40; Koch 1978:175 ff.). Her experiences as Satanist and as Queen of Black Witches occurred at an indeterminate date, sometime after the end of World War II and before her public conversion in 1964. Even the most recent of her encounters with Satanists, her near-fatal beating, occurred five months before she was institutionalized for drug addiction, so it is unclear whether even this attack could be documented.

Unlike her American counterparts, Irvine's story adds no political scapegoats to the world of Satanism, so police showed no particular interest in attempting to verify details in her story. Indeed, the frank supernaturalism of her story makes it clear that the battle takes place in the realm of the soul, not in a terrestrial venue. In any case, neither Irvine nor her followers showed interest in leading a hunt for the cult leaders they had known. Her testimony was valuable not as legal evidence but rather as a symbolic example of the strength of Christian magic. To receive the transforming power of the Holy Spirit, she needed to recall and confess her occult sins, and the more stubborn and extreme the problem, the Pentecostal mythology would infer, the more dramatic her occult sin would have had to be. And once the saving gifts were received, and with them transforming social power, the important thing was to win souls for Christ, not hunt for witches. Only when such confessions were tied to a political agenda did they become useful in more than an evangelical sense, as Irvine's American counterparts soon learned.

7

ℌippie Commune Ⓦitchcraft Ɓlood Ɍites

Satanic "Confessions" in North America

> I had developed a way to use my slick tongue along
> with a hypnotic tone to my voice, and I found I had
> my group eating out of my hand. It helped for them to
> know that I was a big shot with the higher-ups. . . .
> —Michael Warnke, *The Satan-Seller*

As constructed in the late 1960s and early 1970s, the American Satanism Scare was somewhat different from the British concern over "black magic rings." While the British scare focused on church desecrations and perverse sex orgies, the American threat mainly drew from anxieties caused by the radical counterculture. Drug use, casual sex, and the threat of random violence were its main constituents. And while adults with culture and influence were said to be the main participants in British-style Satanism, rebellious and rootless adolescents and young adults were described as the mainstream of the California-style cults. Ultimately, "Communism" (which for the right wing at this time could include any political philosophy not wholly loyal to Americanism) was the source of the agenda attributed to cults. Thus, the British scare focused mainly on a moral and supernatural threat—and was exemplified by Doreen Irvine's mainly otherworldly experiences punctuated by wild orgies. The American threat, by contrast, was to a large extent secular, with sex and magic being only an introductory stage toward cultural domination.

Initially, Satanism rumors were slow to enter North American culture. Dennis Wheatley's books were not reprinted by American publishers until 1972 and even then did not achieve much success. Without Wheatley's influence, Aleister Crowley's own works, though available from specialty houses, likewise had little impact on American culture, though there were a few chapters of the OTO in the U.S., mainly on the west coast. One of these chapters was headed by scientist Jack Parsons, who in 1946 attempted to father a "moonchild" through Crowley's sex magick with the help of an unnamed woman and his assistant, L. Ron Hubbard (later the founder of Scientology). The effort failed, and when Crowley was apprised of their work, he commented to an OTO associate, "I get fairly frantic when I contemplate the idiocy of those louts" (King 1989:162–65). Hubbard eventually broke with Parsons, explaining afterwards that he had been helping the U.S. military break up a dangerous satanic plot. Parsons, who helped invent the solid fuel rockets used by aircraft in jet-assisted take-off (JATO), died in 1952 when a project he was working on at home detonated. Rumor had it, however, that he had been dabbling in alchemy and the explosion resulted from a dangerous black magick operation (Freedland 1972:163–64).

Crowley's niche was eventually filled by San Franciscan Anton LaVey, though he and his followers were, like the first British neo-pagans, strongly right-wing in their politics; hence, his influence on the left-leaning youth counterculture was more symbolic than real. More representative of the emerging threat of teen rebellion was Isaac Bonewits, who had a brief career in LaVey's Church of Satan, but moved beyond that into an influential career in the developing neo-pagan scene in the United States. A look at the experiences of both men shows that the occult, however useful it was as a sign of the counterculture, was hardly an organized plot.

The conspiracy elements remained to be added by the prominent "confessing ex-Satanists" of the 1970s. While undefined rumors of "hippie" cults began to emerge in the late 1960s, the public image of Satanism was largely created by three influential people: counterculture author Ed Sanders and evangelists Michael Warnke and John Todd. Sanders took a complex of rumors generated in the wake of the Manson Family murders and codified them in terms of existing legends about sex-and-black-magic rings. Warnke and Todd took this scenario and linked it to right-wing conspiracy myths featuring Jews, Masons, and the Illuminati. All three stories were exposed as fallible or even fraudulent, but the image they created of Satanism as a massive secular threat to American politics survived their downfall.

La Vey and Bonewits:
The Devil's Advocates

Anton LaVey came to public attention in 1966, when he ceremonially shaved his head on the traditional pagan holiday of Walpurgisnacht, or May Eve, and announced that he was forming a "Church of Satan." His philosophy drew heavily on nineteenth-century American freethinking (most notably Emerson's "Self-Reliance") and the German philosopher Nietzsche, while his rituals picked up elements from earlier anti-Masonic sources. For instance, he chose as the symbol of his movement a Solomon's seal, or inverted pentagram with a goat's head and Hebrew letters superimposed, drawing from the turn-of-the-century belief that Masons were dominated by Lucifer-worshipping Jews. Despite his right-leaning politics, however, LaVey's activities drew considerable attention from the counterculture. On January 31, 1967, he held a "satanic wedding," dressed in a red devil suit with horns, in which he intoned, "By the power of Satan, I now confer the possession of each other upon you. Take the woman." The street outside was mobbed by reporters, television cameras, and teenagers who clamored, "We want to get in," and, later, "There's a nude in there." The marriage was not official, the groom later conceded, but still "as valid as the war in Vietnam. . . . The state doesn't recognize the Satanic church and until it does, I don't recognize the state."[1]

Wheatley's niche, in turn, was occupied in 1967 by Ira Levin's popular novel *Rosemary's Baby*, in which an ambitious New York actor joins a coven and allows his wife to bear the Devil's child. When director Roman Polanski made a hit movie from Levin's novel, he used LaVey as a technical advisor on scenes involving occult rites and allowed him to appear as the Devil in a surreal impregnation scene. While Polanski himself disclaimed any occult knowledge, numerous Hollywood rumors circulated about bizarre things that had happened at Polanski's parties that linked him to the developing California Satanism scene. His wife Sharon Tate, like many legendary hippies, was also said to have served "marijuana brownies," or, alternatively, to have sprinkled "powdered marijuana" on salads to give guests unintended drug trips. Someone knew someone who had gone to the Polanski's house while *Rosemary's Baby* was being made and found a "black magic ritual" underway. According to one account, the visitor "was blindfolded and led into a dark parlor. The room was filled with people dressed in white robes. They wore grotesque animal masks over their faces. Two black candles burned on a wood altar" (Steiger and Smith 1971:139–40; cf. Sanders 1971a:77).

The success of the movie brought forth a flood of attention to occultism in the American popular press. A series of pulp paperbacks appeared, such as Charles Lefebure's *The Blood Cults* (1969) and *Witness to Witchcraft* (1970), which combined modern British "Black Mass" rumors and information from historical witch trials, mixing them together in a sensationalized format. This genre of popular paperbacks included Brad Steiger's *Sex and Satanism* (1969), one of several books that promised to inform readers about the extent of devil worship in Anglo-American circles. In fact, most of the documentable incidents mentioned in his book occurred in Europe or involved foreigners, but Steiger did present several alleged eyewitness accounts of occult sex rings in middle America. These often come close to pornography in style and structure: one such episode, spanning some ten pages, gives the account of "Peter B.," a New York City businessman, whose encounter with Satanism began when he picked up a call girl who took him to an occult ceremony in the hippie enclave of Greenwich Village. There he partook of drug-laced wine while a group of "witches" watched their high priest deflower a teenaged initiate.

The call girl then told Peter B. of a nearby coven that was mainly a wife-swapping circle, whose initiation rites required the new male members to have sex with all female members or vice versa. Steiger's source allegedly attended several of these ceremonies (taking his secretary rather than his wife, however) until he witnessed an unusually lurid initiation. When the coven leader discovered "that rarest of rare commodities, a virgin" interested in reading occult books, he used the promise of lending her his private magic library to entice her to a coven meeting. On April 30 (or Walpurgisnacht, the birthday of LaVey's Church of Satan), they broke into a church and held a mock mass, using a black turnip as the host and ripping a living toad in half. Then the coven leader brushed the cross and Bible from the church's altar, put on a devil mask, and penetrated the virgin, wiping the blood from his penis on the altar cloth. The male coven members then lined up to have sex with the new initiate, while the female members gratified themselves with dildoes.

Peter B., like many of Steiger's informants, politely excused himself at this point before being asked to participate in the following orgy. He commented (a la Wheatley) that what he witnessed was not religion nor uninhibited sex, but "pure and simply obscene bestiality." Later, he allegedly learned that the cult had continued to trash the church inside and out, tipping over grave markers, breaking stained glass, and burning hymnals. The newspapers, as usual, attributed these actions to vandals, not cults, while the initiate's silence was purchased with a salary raise and the position of High Priestess (1969:53–63). Nevertheless, Steiger gives no place names or dates for this or other "eyewitness" stories, and they are otherwise not mentioned in accounts of occultism in the United States, even those by cult-hunters. This suggests that he or his sources frankly had made them up to provide spice for the book.

But having gained an avid readership through such lurid accounts, Steiger gave the names and addresses of a number of "white witchcraft" groups, all of whom passionately deplored such activities. A strong early booster of the neo-pagan movement, Steiger argued that Satanism was actually a Christian invention intended to discredit the Craft. Wicca, he maintained, was created to complement society, while Satanism was the enemy of the Establishment and thus the antithesis of white magic (1969:10). But in passing on the gist of the British "black magic" rumors, Steiger communicated precedents for believing that unwary dabblers were being initiated into dangerous sex-and-magic cults. Indeed, the anti-occult theologian Merrill F.Unger, author of the influential *Demons in the World Today*, cited Steiger's book with horror as evidence of "the moral degeneracy such initiation into devil cults leads to" (1971:97).

Already evangelists had been addressing this threat by aggressively targeting college-age youth for revivals and crusades. As British black magic rumors were beginning to enter American consciousness, papers were simultaneously publicizing the efforts of California evangelists such as Hal Lindsey, a student of Unger's at Dallas Theological Seminary. Their crusades often used hippie-style language and activities to involve youngsters in Christian communities. Portraying religion as "the ultimate trip," flyers for teen revivals encouraged participants to "groove on God . . . the more we groove on God and His words, the more His Spirit and ours experience each other."[2] And ministers regularly used areas on college campuses to attract and try to convert students. One such scene near the UC-Berkeley Student Union attracted a youthful Isaac Bonewits, then a seventeen-year-old undergraduate with strong interests in magic and comparative religion. He and other freethinking students began by heckling these preachers but soon noticed that they were not especially bothered or affected by their objections.

So, in spring 1968, Bonewits joined the group of soapbox evangelists, dressed in a black robe and presenting sermons through a small loudspeaker on behalf of Satan. "I had a 'Hell' of a good time flaying my audiences for not being sinful enough," Bonewits later recalled, adding, "Inside of five minutes there was an audience around my platform larger than any [that] the evangelists had ever raised." His act was then, by his own admission, "improvisational street theater" rather than serious "recruiting for Satan," but his notoriety brought him to LaVey's attention. Within a week, he was accosted by a woman with a "deliberately erotic voice" who said, "Hi. I'm a Witch. Would you like to join the Church of Satan?" He was given an audience with the leader, who offered Bonewits support and gave him flyers to hand out. Eventually, with help from LaVey's followers, Bonewits constructed a "Sinmobile" with a more powerful loudspeaker that he could wheel over to the evangelical corner.

Bonewits also became a regular at rituals at LaVey's Church of Satan, even being filmed as one of LaVey's assistants. During one ceremony, he decided to improvise an invocation in the supernatural "Enochian" language that LaVey was then including. "I dramatically intoned a lot of gibberish, using the same guttural tones that Anton always used, and everyone in the ritual acted very impressed," Bonewits remembered (1997). LaVey was not amused at this parody, which was itself already a parody of the use of "heavenly languages" in Pentecostal rites. After a spring and summer of involvement with the Church of Satan the seventeen-year-old Bonewits became less and less comfortable with the conservative political climate of the movement. While he and his Berkeley classmates were moving toward the left in response to the Vietnam protests, LaVey's movement tended to cite conservative author Ayn Rand and even Adolf Hitler as their models. "Some were bringing authentic Ku Klux Klan robes and Nazi uniforms for the ceremonies," he later recalled. "I was assured that the clothes were merely for 'Satanic shock value' to jar people from their usual staid patterns of thinking. Then I would talk to the men wearing these clothes and realize that they were not pretending anything. I noticed that there were no black members of the Church and only one Asian, and began to ask why." In October 1968, Bonewits was asked to leave the Church of Satan, ostensibly because his radical politics were seen as "deviationalist" by LaVey and his inner circle of followers. Bonewits, however, suspected that LaVey was becoming increasingly jealous of the way Church members were coming to the newcomer for advice on magickal rituals (1997). Nevertheless, Bonewits continued his evangelist-baiting "devil's advocate" act for the next two years. At this time he took a degree in magic from UC-Berkeley, the result of a self-designed course of study in a variety of disciplines including anthropology, biology, and psychology. Among associations with several other alternative religious groups, he joined the Reformed Druids of North America, a neo-pagan group, and eventually became one of the leading theorists and advocates for this movement.

Bonewits' first book, *Real Magic* (1971, rev.ed. 1989), was influential in moving the American neo-pagan philosophy away from the "white vs. black magic" that characterized British Wiccans like Sybil Leek. Bonewits was highly critical of Leek, whom he paired with LaVey, and he concluded that there were indeed few differences between the two philosophies, even though each portrayed the other as the enemy. Both derived their lore from the same sources—Masonry and the Golden Dawn—and both performed activities that they claimed were characteristic of "the Other." He argued for a pluralistic conception of magickal systems, in which one could opt for red, orange, yellow, green, or even ultraviolet magic. (*Real Magic* claimed to be "yellow" in hue, the color of the mind and nervous system and focusing on logic and philosophy).

In short, Bonewits observed, the early neo-pagan movement suffered from the same "internecine warfare" as had the Pentecostal movement, and reacted by projecting the same kinds of evil Others into the world that surrounded them. Like the more realistic British neo-pagans, Bonewits found that he could not find any hard evidence for the existence of genuinely evil "Black Lodges," though he noted that "many White Lodges are labeled as such by their competitors." In a cautious footnote, however, he conceded that "there is bound to be at least one genuine Black Lodge, and since there are always 'sickies' in any field of study, there are probably many such groups" (1989:115).

Ed Sanders, Charles Manson, and Snuff Films

Bonewits was hardly the only person who found the occult a convenient vehicle for expressing protest against the Silent Majority. Another such was Ed Sanders, who had become a central figure in New York City's "beat generation" culture. Jailed in 1961 for protesting the commissioning of the *Ethan Allen,* a submarine built to launch nuclear missiles, Sanders began publishing poems protesting militarism and puritanical canons of censorship. His poetry magazine, *Fuck You! A Magazine of the Arts* (founded 1962), published work by himself and other "beat" poets that frequently went well beyond the current community definitions of vulgarity and pornography, particularly in describing homosexual acts. Similarly, his rock group, The Fugs, gained considerable following in the counterculture by writing and performing songs with explicit references to sex and drug use.

From the start fascinated by themes from Greek and Egyptian mythology, Sanders frequently introduced occult symbols and references into his poetry. In 1961, shortly after his term in jail, he passed a New York City meat market and was struck by the image he saw: "There, resting upon white paper in a flat tray was half of a cow's head, stripped of skin, with a huge eye staring up. It had the effect of a religious revelation. The phrase *Peace Eye* came into my mind" (Sanders 1987:240). At the time intensely interested in Egyptian hieroglyphics, Sanders began to introduce the image of the "Eye of Horus" into his work as the center of a transcendental vision of humanity uniting with primal forces of nature, which often was symbolized through description of an act of "earth fuck." Simultaneously, forces that endangered peace and the environment were more and more directly challenged in his work. In 1967, Sanders extended this confrontational approach to conventional religion with his collection *Fuck God in the Ass.*[3] The volume featured the poet's notorious "Elm Fuck Poem," which expressed his fascination with nature in the form of a frankly sexual encounter with a nature spirit.[4] In addition to a trade edition, Sanders advertised a special "Tree Frig Edition," four "signed & spewed-on volumes, each containing an actual photograph of Ed Sanders coming into the oily summer crotch of an Elm tree." Other poems expressed his impatience with the sanitized proprieties of institutional religion:

> I don't give
> a pound of
> mule mucous
> for any fucking
> "Transformation Symbolism
> in the Eucharist"
>
> if you can't dance to it
> or if it isn't dope
> or possessed of a dick-sized
> aperture
>
> then shit on it (1967:4)

Sanders's rage over the Vietnam Conflict came most dramatically to the public eye in October 1967, during a protest demonstration in Washington, D.C. The focus of this event was a series of speeches at the Lincoln Memorial, a conventional locus for such events. But during the planning of the event, the organizers were inspired by a passage in a Lewis Mumford book suggesting that peace could not be attained until the evil embodied in the Pentagon could be destroyed. This was a logical connection, as the *pentagon* shape of the U.S. military headquarters embodied the border of the Church of Satan's inverted *pentagram*. The leaders suggested that the demonstration be capped with a march on the Pentagon to hold a magic ceremony exorcising the evil from the building. Typical of the syncretism of the time, the idea quickly merged with an idea of using magickal chants to *levitate* the structure. Sanders recalled: "Someone came up with their idea for exorcism and levitation modeled on the Catholic or Episcopalian exorcism, so we said, 'Let's do it,' [and] had meetings at my bookstore where I consulted a Hittite book. I studied linguistics at college, so I dug up some phrases, and some Graeco-Roman magic formulae I knew, and cobbled together all this stuff" (Taylor 1987:225–26). The idea was enthusiastically received among the counterculture, who speculated wildly over possible results: Would the exorcism detonate nuclear devices stored there? Would the building actually rise into the air? Would powerful demons be released into the world at large?[5] Agitator Abbie Hoffmann generated publicity for the event by getting himself arrested by measuring the sides of the Pentagon and explaining to the media that he was "finding out how many witches we would need" (Taylor 1987:228).

None of the interviewers specifically mentioned the emerging neopagan movement; it could hardly have missed influencing the syncretistic event that occurred. In any case, the leaflet distributed by Sanders (reproduced in Taylor 1987:232) places his Hittite chant and Egyptian symbols into the standard format of Wiccan ceremonies: consecration of the four directions, followed by the casting of a magick circle and invocation of "Powers and Spirits" to aid in the exorcism. The exorcism itself was planned to employ the four elements—earth, air, water, and fire—and conclude with an "Exorgasm" during which the evil spirits would be banished with singing and shrieking. Even the "rising of the pentagon" mentioned in Sanders's leaflet suggests the raising of the "cone of power" that was the usual aim of the Gardnerian rite.

The event itself was not as organized as this agenda implied. Gathering a crowd variously estimated from 25,000 to 250,000, the march was not permitted to actually enclose the Pentagon in a circle, and in fact the marchers were directed to a huge parking lot adjacent to the building but separated from it by a four-lane highway. Although a stage was set up there for more addresses, Sanders and the rest of the Fugs performed on the rear bed of a truck driven in at another end. Sanders later said only that, given the conditions, they "jibberished this thing out" (Taylor 1987:231), But according to Norman Mailer, who made the march the subject of his experimental "history as a novel," *The Armies of the Night* (1968), the event was in its own way impressive. Sanders and his group made a series of invocations from the truck bed, accompanied by exotic music, before crying out, "Out, demons, out—back to darkness, ye servants of Satan—out, demons, out! Out, demons, out!" Sanders then announced that there would be an act of "Seminal culmination in the spirit of peace and brotherhood, a real grope for peace," and asked participants to form "a circle of protection around the lovers."

It is unclear whether the grope for peace actually took place (Mailer notes that increasing confrontations between the marchers and military police soon made the event chaotic) but this presumably was an attempt at performing a literal Gardnerian "Great Rite" of magickal intercourse. In any case, Mailer recalls that the crowd took up the chant of "Out, demons, out" in a way that eventually caught him up as well. In *Armies of the Night* he muses:

> On which acidic journeys had the hippies met the witches and the devils and the cutting edge of all primitive awe, the savage's sense of explosion—the fuse of blasphemy, the cap of taboo now struck, the answering roar of the Gods. ... now suddenly an entire generation of acid-heads seemed to have said good-bye to easy visions of heaven, no, now the witches were here, and rites of exorcism, and black terrors of the night. ... Yes, the hippies had gone from Tibet to Christ to the Middle Ages, now they were Revolutionary Alchemists. Well, thought Mailer, that was all right, he was a Left Conservative himself.[6] "Out demons, out! Out, demons, out!" (1968:123–24)

The exorcism of the Pentagon entered the mythology of the Peace Movement. Although the Vietnam War continued for more than six years, the march marked a turning point in public support for the military action.

Allen Ginsberg commented, "I think it demystified the authority of the Pentagon, and in that sense we *did* levitate it. . . . Afterwards the public decided that the Pentagon was wrong. It was as simple as that. So the levitation of the Pentagon was a success. It must be understood for what it was—a poetic metaphor; basically a triumph of the human imagination over heavy metal materialism" (Taylor 1987:235). Certainly the event and the publicity it received transformed Sanders from an underground influence in Greenwich Village to a national media figure. The Fugs toured nationally and internationally, and mainstream publishers became interested in marketing Sanders's writing talents more broadly.

He soon had a subject. On August 9, 1969, Roman Polanski's wife Sharon Tate and four others were found brutally murdered in Polanski's Los Angeles home. Police called the slashes on Tate's body "ritualistic" and the bodies left "in weird positions, suggestive of perverted sex practices" (Steiger and Smith 1971:135). Tate's close friend and hair stylist Jay Sebring was found nearby, his face covered by what journalists variously termed a "black hood" or "a dark, grotesque mummer's mask."[7] Rumor held that Tate and the other victims had been killed as part of a *Rosemary's-Baby*-style "Black Mass."

The truth was nearly as bizarre: in December, Charles Manson and a group of his followers were charged for this murder and two others. Manson, a lifetime criminal, had briefly contacted a number of occult and alternative religious organizations, including the Church of Scientology and the Esalen Institute. After a series of drug-induced visions, he became convinced that he was an incarnation of Jesus Christ and had been sent on a mission to save the United States from a variety of cultural threats by African Americans. Despite his right-wing political leanings, he had circulated in the counterculture world of the West Coast and gathered around him a group of followers, mainly female, whom he manipulated through a mixture of drugs, sex, and threats. His ability to hold this loose assemblage of dropouts together gained him a reputation for hypnotic powers, and stories soon circulated that while in prison he had learned how to implant "subliminal motivations" into the minds of his fellow inmates.

Despite his nominal link with Christianity, Manson was quickly interpreted by the media as the leader of a satanic cult, and indeed it was not difficult to find occult groups that he *might* have encountered through the various stages of his drifting. One member of Manson's "Family," Susan Atkins, had been part of LaVey's Church of Satan; in fact, she had appeared in a topless "Witches' Sabbath" show and shows up in erotic photographs with LaVey in his devil suit amid other scantily-clothed women underneath an inverted pentagram (Lyons 1988:88). Another Manson Family member, Bobby Beausoleil, had performed background music and played the role of Lucifer in the film *Lucifer Rising,* one of a series of art movies based on Crowleyian themes by counterculture artist Kenneth Anger.[8] Occultism, LaVey's Church of Satan, and the counterculture, inevitably, had become linked to pop Satanism and blood crimes.

Within a month of Manson's arrest, rumors about satanic cults were rampant. The *Los Angeles Herald Examiner* ran a front-page article titled "HIPPIE COMMUNE WITCHCRAFT BLOOD RITES TOLD." The article revealed fears expressed by police in Santa Cruz, a counterculture haven, that "witchcraft cults that sacrifice animals and turn humans into 'slaves of Satan'" were becoming common there. The piece was a collage of rumors and unconfirmed stories from convicted drug users and adolescents: Another article told of an alleged initiation rite in which new members "must eat the entrails of an animal while its heart is still beating." The leading investigator said that police had suspected some sort of cult even before the Tate murders "because of the number of skinned dogs that have been found in the last 18 months." The head of the Santa Cruz animal shelter confirmed this epidemic, adding: "Whoever is doing this is a real expert with a knife. The skin is cut away without even marking the flesh. The really strange thing is that these dogs have been drained of blood." One implication is that the animal blood was mixed with drugs in order to induce a more profound "high." Certainly by 1971, Los Angeles-area police were convinced that "hippie types" were mixing LSD with the blood of sacrificed animals "to heighten their trances" (Cerullo 1973:92).[9] One teen told police how he'd seen "hippies . . . engaged in a weird dance around a parked auto that had five skinned animals, apparently dogs, on its hood." Police were looking for a man with a weird "hypnotic stare" who, drug dealers assured them, was the "head witch."

This mysterious man eluded authorities, as did the dog-skinners[10] but the same summer brought LaVey back into the headlines in the context of two more gruesome satanic murders . On June 3, 1970, a schoolteacher, Florence Nancy Brown, was found murdered and partially dismembered. On June 28, Stephen C. Hurd, the leader of a loosely organized group of drug users, was arrested and charged with this and an earlier robbery-murder. Police did not suspect any ritual connection, but after he was charged, Hurd's attorney told a lurid story to the media. Announcing his intentions to seek a verdict of "not guilty by reason of insanity," he declared that Hurd had been "an avowed worshiper of Satan." In fact, the attorney said, he belonged to a cult which preached that "it is all right to 'snuff people out' providing a part of the body is used in a sacrifice." Accordingly, Hurd said, one of Brown's arms had been cut off and later used as a "sacrifice to Satan." In this he had been counseled by a San Francisco man "known as the Devil, or chief Devil, who advises on problems."[11]

By a grim coincidence, the same week that this story was making its way through the California papers, another satanic case emerged. After stopping a car trying to leave the scene of an accident on the Pacific Coast Highway south of Big Sur, police arrested Stanley D. Baker and Harry A. Stroup, two "hippie types, with beards and long hair." The car they were driving belonged to a Billings man who had been found shot and dismembered a few days earlier in Yellowstone National Park. Shortly after the arrest, Baker told one of the officers, "I have a problem—I am a cannibal," and showed the officer one of the victim's fingers that he had severed and carried with him. A University of California anthropologist, noting that the victim's heart had been cut out during the dismemberment, suggested that the killing "could have been an imitation of some religious rite." No information ever emerged to link either man with any organized cult, but the media soon assumed them to be "Satan-worshippers" as well and their escape to California an attempt to link up with organized cults.[12]

Exasperated by this unwanted notoriety, Anton LaVey held an interview with a *Los Angeles Times* reporter, who described the head of the Church of Satan as being "as American as crabapple pie." The cases of the past year were "damned sickening," LaVey said, and called Manson a "mad-dog killer" who should be drawn and quartered on Pershing Square. He continued:

> I'd like to set the record straight. . . . If someone waltzes up to our front door and says "Lucifer told me to come," he gets the bum's rush, you'd better believe it. This is really an elitist movement and we're very fussy who is coming in and whom we traffic with. We have to guard ourselves against the creeps, and we've screened out a lot of people who turned out to be bad apples. Mostly they turned out to be people who were disappointed when they didn't

get the orgies and all the nefarious activities they'd been looking forward to.

In fact, LaVey called his operation mainly "showmanship . . . nine parts outrage and one part social respectability" that allowed participants to channel their "demons" into "a ritualized hatred that finally absorbs the hate itself, rather than turning it loose in such meaningless, antisocial outbursts as the Tate massacre." As for his "religion," he called it "just Ayn Rand's philosophy, with ceremony and ritual added," and he actually looked forward to the arrival of a "benign police state."[13]

But the sex-and-ritual-murder pattern had now been set in the California media, and it would henceforth be difficult for any non-standard religion to detach itself from that connection. Other conspiracy elements were quickly added on. The September 1970 issue of *American Opinion*, the publication of the right-wing John Birch Society, featured a lengthy article by David Emerson Gumaer, referencing Crowley, Manson, LaVey, Roman Polanski, and the Santa Cruz dog-skinners. All of these, Gumaer said, demonstrated that Satanism, "next to Communism, has become the fastest growing criminal menace of our time" (1970:47). The article, using a variety of popular sources, traces occult movements through Weishaupt's Bavarian Illuminati, the members of which, he claims on the strength of 1790s pamphlets, drank human blood, worshipped Satan, and conducted the Black Mass on an altar of human skeletons. They also developed a *Protocol*-like agenda, i.e., they "worked to destroy patriotism and nationalism through infiltration of education, administration, and the press; and, had plans to infiltrate both national and international organizations through which they would maintain secret cells—all while posing as promoters of peace and brotherhood" (1970:58).

The article concluded with an interview with an unusually cooperative "radical socialist" LaVey, who was happy to inscribe a copy of *The Satanic Bible* for a member of the John Birch Society and show him his extensive library of books (mostly unread, Bonewits cynically recalled) from presses whose lists included dozens of titles by "identified Communists." Yes, Weishaupt was indeed "a practicing Satanist," LaVey proudly confirmed, and the Illuminati were "quite a powerful force for evil." (1970:67).

The adventurous Sanders was drawn to this complex of rumors for reasons of his own. He had ample reason to demonize Manson: satanic filmmaker Kenneth Anger had been with him during the Pentagon Exorcism. Indeed, Sanders recalls him crouching underneath the Fugs' flatbed truck during the ceremony to burn an image of the Devil inside a consecrated pentagram while curious reporters observed (1971a:48). Sanders traveled to the Los Angeles area and spent a year collecting and organizing "literally everything [he] heard or saw" about the Manson Family. Visiting all the areas where the Family was alleged to have been active, Sanders posed variously as a pornographer, occultist, or "drooling maniac." He also employed a private investigator and advertised for information in California underground papers.

The resulting book, *The Family: The Story of Charles Manson's Dune Buggy Attack Battalion*, tells less about Manson and his followers than about the wealth of rumors and beliefs about Satanism that were then current in the California subculture. According to police reconstructions of Manson's activities, the groups he associated with were not religious or occult in nature but rather violent motorcycle gangs who took names such as "The Gypsy Jokers" or even "The Straight Satans," "Satan's Slaves," or "Sons of Satan." Nevertheless, Sanders made the most of suggestions that Manson had contacted, even received instruction from, organized groups who practiced ritual mutilations and even human sacrifices. Sanders referred to the California chapter of the Crowleyian OTO as "a loony-tune magical cult specializing in blood-drinking" (1971a:69). He implied that the group's rituals were intended to induce mind control and suggested devious ways in which Manson might have be in contact with the Crowleyans (1971a:159–60).

But the most obvious suspect for turning Manson on to Satanism was a group called variously "The Church of the Final Judgment" or simply "The Process." Led by Briton Robert DeGrimston, the movement was another offshoot of Scientology's "engram therapy" with Masonic overtones.[14] Essentially, the Processean point of view described the world in terms of three equally valid ways of life, each overseen by a divinity. "Jehovah" governed a "stringent road of purity" and self-denial; "Satan," a path of "lust and licentiousness," and "Lucifer," a mystical third way, "pursuing the ideal of perfect human love." Anyone willing to commit totally to any of these paths, the Process held, would find salvation; the rest would find themselves on "a path to nowhere, half-in, half-out, half-up, half-down, your instincts and ideals buried in a deep morass of hypocritical compromise and respectable mediocrity" (Lyons 1988:89–90).

After unsuccessful efforts to set up a religious commune in Mexico, DeGrimston and his followers came to the United States, briefly visiting

New Orleans, San Francisco, Los Angeles, and New York (Bainbridge 1978:83–87). Seeing motorcycle gangs as a source of potential converts, the Process put out a series of slick publications filled with Nazi-oriented, violent graphics and calling on followers to breach all social boundaries. These publications, notably the infamous "Sex" issue, ironically, failed to gain them more than token support from the bikers, but fell into the hands of horrified evangelicals, who used them to portray the generally peaceful DeGrimston as a Satanist recommending grave-robbing, rape, and "Black Masses."[15]

During its 1967 travels, The Process briefly opened a recruiting headquarters in the Haight-Ashbury district of San Francisco; Manson was then living about two blocks away. Although no Processean could recall meeting him (and Manson was uncooperative on the subject), he could conceivably have contacted one of the black-caped members who were passing out their literature on street corners. Even Sanders concedes that in the following year, when rumors began about the Santa Cruz dog-skinners, he could find no solid evidence that Processeans were operating in California. Nonetheless, his anonymous sources told him, there was a secret "closed chapter" of The Process in Santa Cruz called the "Four Pi movement . . . dedicated to the 'worship of evil.'" One person told Sanders that he had been present when Processeans held "ritual executions":

> The ceremonies involved use of a portable crematorium to dispose of the bodies, a wooden altar adorned with dragons and a wooden morgue table. There were as many as forty people in attendance at these sacrifices. The instrument of sacrifice was a set of 6 knives welded into a football shaped holder. The heart was eaten. . . . The leader of this human sacrifice group, a large man, held the cult title Grand Chingon. It was not Manson. However, at least five times in this writer's presence Manson has been called the Grand Chingon or the Head Chingon by members of his family. (1971a:132–33)

Sanders heard similar stories from motorcycle gang members about a group called "the Kirké [or Circe] Order of Dog Blood." This group allegedly met on the full and new moons on secluded beaches outside of Los Angeles to sacrifice black animals of all sorts, cats and dogs included. Sanders could link this group to Manson only through his contacts with motorcycle gangs and some of his followers' confessions that the Family killed animals and drank their blood. But one source claimed that The Process, the dog-blood-drinkers, and the Manson Family were all connected and in fact had participated together in the making of "snuff movies"—films of actual ritual murders—that were then shown at the Family's compound and circulated among cult members. Sanders had heard repeated rumors of such films: while posing as a pornographer, he had heard that a Family associate had footage of "Malibu and San Francisco ax murders" and that an unnamed New York artist had purchased a film "depicting the ritual murder of a woman" (1971a:228).

Such claims were not outrageous at the time: among the horrific evidence presented at the 1965 trial of British serial killers Esther Myra Hindley and Ian Brady was an audiotape that they had made while torturing a ten-year-old girl. Nevertheless, neither Sanders nor any other investigator was able to trace any actual footage of such films. *The Family* does quote one of Sanders's sources at length about some apparently homemade films that he claimed to have seen. One showed the ritual killing of an animal: "They cut up a dog. Then they brought a girl in there—two girls. They took their clothes off and poured the blood off the dog on top of the girls. They just held the dog. And they took the girls and they put the blood—and the bodies—all over both of them. And everyone balled the two girls ... it was a couple, two couples—they were being, uh—but I'm not, you know, this was a while ago. But I remember they were all taking hits of blood. It was really weird." A second film supposedly showed a cat being blown up with firecrackers, a scene that the source termed "the stupidest one I've seen." Another five-minute clip showed five black-robed people circling around what appeared to be a decapitated female body (1971:230–34). If these films actually existed (and no proof later emerged that they did exist) they still do not demonstrate the existence of cults or snuff films, as even Sanders's source did not claim to have seen footage of the girl's murder or dismemberment. Nevertheless, Sanders took such stories as authentic and ended his book with a solemn call for police intervention: "only when all these evil affairs are known and exposed can the curse of ritual sacrifice, Helter Skelter and Satanism be removed from the coasts and mountains and deserts of California" (1971a:412). Sanders also highlighted the cult and snuff film rumors for a broad popular audience in a contemporaneous *Esquire* article, "Charlie and the Devil," (1971b:109, 111).

The reception of *The Family* was mixed: mainstream reviewers generally gave it favorable reviews, but Sanders and his publishers were at once sued for libel by The Process and the OTO. Dutton and *Esquire* were quick to settle out of court, conceding that Sanders's allegations against the two groups "have not been substantiated" and promising to remove all references to them from future editions (Bainbridge 1978:123). The original edition, however, remained available in libraries for the next generation of conspiracy-hunters and was extensively used by Maury Terry in his 1987 book *The Ultimate Evil* to portray The Process and the OTO as dangerous satanic cults (see Terry 1987:172 ff. and Lyons 1988:92–94).

Sanders intended *The Family* to rehabilitate the hippie image, showing Manson as a right-wing authoritarian warped by satanic organizations in much the same way that Vietnam War generals were warped by the stultifying influence of Establishment Christianity. "The only claim [the book] makes," he insisted, "is to encourage people to be anarchists. For people not to follow leaders, to challenge every directive" (Wiloch 1984:449). Yet the book did more than any other early source to create the image of secretive counterculture satanic cults, seducing teenagers with sex and drugs and then programming them to commit blood crimes. In so doing, Sanders reintroduced the blood libel into popular images of Satanism and certainly mainstreamed the long-lived urban legend of "snuff films." One side effect of the story was the explosive popularity of "splatter films," or low-budget movies containing realistic images of murder and dismemberment.

Among these was a 1971 Argentinean zombie film originally titled *Slaughter*, which an American pornographic filmmaker dubbed and augmented with a scene depicting a young girl being dismembered by the film's crew. Rereleased in 1975 as *Snuff*, the movie gave additional credibility to the legend, primarily because its publicity poster (which showed a photograph of a nude woman cut into pieces with scissors) included phrases such as "The *Bloodiest* thing that *ever* happened in front of a camera!!" and "The film that could only be made in South America . . . where Life is *CHEAP!*" (McCarty 1984:128–29). By October 1975, Christian groups crusading against pornography were promoting this legend and forcing police investigations. One New York based investigation claimed that there were as many as eight snuff films circulating, with patrons paying as much as two thousand dollars per viewing to see them. Like Sanders, however, police were unable to locate any actual copies of these films, and eventually authorities discounted the "snuff film" story as no more than an urban legend. Nevertheless, the belief that Satanists made film records of their human sacrifices became a standard feature of cult lore and even of the early "satanic ritual abuse" cases (Stine 1999).

As one reviewer noted, Sanders's interests in sex, drugs, the occult, and revolt against conventions made him quite similar to Manson (Wiloch 1984:449). Similarly, LaVey's gospel of self-indulgence combined with white xenophobia was a close match for Manson's white supremacist ideals. Both profited by endorsing and helping publicize rumors of other movements, more organized and more depraved than the Peace Movement or the Church of Satan. In so doing, they unwittingly provided the first generation of Pentecostal cult-hunters with the raw materials to bring forward the first American "confessing witch."

Mike Warnke: The Satan-Seller

Michael Warnke, like Isaac Bonewits, was a college student who knew both sides of the California religious scene. Confirmed as a Catholic in 1965, Warnke attended San Bernardino Valley College for a year. College friends of Michael Warnke freely admitted that during 1965–1966 he had participated in typical adolescent occult-oriented folklore, including table-tipping and the Ouija ritual. Some were drinking parties that included séances; in one, Warnke put a girlfriend "into some kind of hypnotic state or whatever." Another friend described parties in which "spells" were read: "We would dress in black," he admitted, "maybe burn a black candle. That kind of thing. . . . We were into it because it attracted the girls. We were college kids, having a good time. . . . It's amazing to me that this is of any importance to anyone" (Hertenstein and Trott 1993:70–75). Another recalled that Warnke was also involved in the college's Campus Crusade and was beginning to talk to other students about "the born-again thing." At the end of his first year in college, he enlisted in the U.S. Navy.

In 1970, Mike Warnke appeared at Hotline, a drug rehabilitation center sponsored by Melodyland, a revival center in San Diego, California, where he now claimed to have been converted from Satanism to Pentecostal religion. Hotline was then a forum for many California hippie drug-and-sex confessions, and one participant recalled that the Charismatics were anxious to hear about his alleged cult experiences: "The times were right for that kind of testimony. People wanted to hear that their worst fears were true" (Hertenstein and Trott 1993:138–41). Warnke's conversion itself, like Irvine's, occurred in a typical Pentecostal way. He complained of demonic attacks, a result of his earlier occult dabblings. Diane Speakman ("Mrs. Hrera" in his book), a member of a charismatic prayer group, advised him to claim the power of The Blood in prayer, explaining: "In the Old Testament, people made blood sacrifices to God for their sins because they were under the law. Christ became for us the final sacrifice, and it was by His blood our sins were washed away, we were saved, and we became victorious over Satan. . . . But why use it only once? You have the power in you; you can apply it to any and all occurrences in your life. If the Blood can save you and wash away sins, it can surely take care of daily matters—even demon oppression" (1972:154–55). A few nights later, Warnke says, he woke to find a "tall, black, humanlike figure . . . standing in the doorway of our bedroom." As Mike fell to the floor in convulsions, his wife claimed the power of The Blood, and the demon left them (1972:156). From this point on, according to Warnke's story, his demonic oppression lessened, and a few months later, with the help of Charismatics, he began to speak in tongues (1972:181).[16] To this point, his development was typical of many people who came to the Pentecostal movement, confessing and renouncing earlier involvement with the occult as they did so.

But Warnke soon went far beyond the typical confession. Working with evangelist Morris Cerullo, he helped develop a San Diego ministry aimed at teens who dabbled with fortune-telling and other forms of the occult. They joined forces with journalist Dave Balsiger, previously a public relations consultant for Melodyland, to research and write Cerullo's book, *The Back Side of Satan* (1973). This book swept together many of the social issues then emerging around the evangelical anti-occult crusade. Like Gumaer's *American Opinion* article, it decried the public attention that the witchcraft revival was receiving and implied that one effect of this tolerance was "satanic" crimes like Manson's and Peter Hurd's. Cerullo also devoted a separate chapter to Bonewits, whose degree "with a major in magic" he considered both a waste of taxpayers' money and a direct affront to Christianity. Incorrectly noting that UC-Berkeley "now has an entire department in witchcraft" (perhaps an allusion to its program in folklore, recently established by Alan Dundes), Cerullo concluded that this degree "is a clear indication of the set of the sail in today's world" (1973:54).

Probably inspired by Bonewits's "Sinmobile," Warnke and Balsiger developed Cerullo's "Witchmobile," an early traveling display of occult paraphernalia. These included articles from California occult shops: a Ouija board, a crystal ball, magickal knives, a black robe and candle, and "voodoo" charms like "graveyard dust" and a jinx-removing "bag." Traveling with the Witchmobile in the first months of 1972, Warnke testified to his deliverance from the occult before youth organizations and church groups in California and other states (Hertenstein and Trott 1993:142–48). By June 1972, Warnke and Balsiger decided to form an independent, nationally based anti-occult crusade.

Now that Warnke had become something of a celebrity among the young Pentecostals, his detailed confessions soon emerged. Cerullo's *Back Side of Satan* included a version of Warnke's testimony, and Warnke's own book, *The Satan-Seller* (1972) appeared the same year.[17] According to Warnke's story, a satanic "recruiter" had approached him in September 1965, during his first weeks at college, and offered him free sex and drugs. After becoming involved in this self-indulgent "first stage" of involvement, Warnke became aware that there was a "second stage" of occultism, much larger than any journalist imagined, with several hundred practicing witches in the San Bernardino area alone. He says little about their meetings, though, other than that they, like LaVey's services, contained "calculated blasphemy" and "phony rituals that seemed pretty tame and hardly resulted in anyone getting hurt or attacked or anything" (1972:31).

But he learned by attending these meetings that one could "specialize, like picking a major in college" in such areas as necromancy, vampirism, lycanthropy—or Satanism (1972:32). Such an idea probably was an outgrowth from Bonewits's "major in magic" at UC-Berkeley (which Warnke's co-author Dave Balsiger had researched for Morris Cerullo). In fact, Warnke confessed later, all forms of occultism amounted to Satanism, even supposedly "white" witchcraft. In words echoing the standard Pentecostal line, he explains, "They all call on the same spirit force— which is *not* God! And any supernatural power which is not of God is of Satan. It *is* that simple" (1972:185; emphasis his).

After he chose Satanism as his "major," Warnke was taken to a Black Mass to see if he was ready for the "third level." The ceremony was held in a barn located out in the countryside, with a small group of participants sitting in a circle around a nude woman lying on an altar, a traditional continental witch trial detail that LaVey had occasionally included in publicity photographs for the Church of Satan. "All the traditional rituals were reversed and deliberately profaned," Warnke says. "The sacraments were desecrated. Blasphemies took the place of prayers." And in a telling detail that reflects the persistent friction caused by the feminist movement, he adds, "Words attributed to Satan were read from the book, *The Great Mother*."[18] After this, the head Satanist drew a pentagram on the woman's stomach, and the participants invoked a demon to afflict a troublesome right-winger who was agitating for a congressional investigation of the occult (1972:33–34).

Fascinated, Warnke asked to be initiated at the next Black Mass, during which he was invested with ornate jewelry and a black robe and hood "similar to the headgear of the Eastern Orthodox religion." At the conclusion, Warnke says, the recruiter slashed him on the wrist, caught the blood in a cup, and had him sign his name in what was described as "the devil's book." This he says, was "a large, black, leather-bound book two-feet square and almost a foot thick. . . . The yellow-edged pages showed three columns each, the left side full of names and the right about half-used. All the names were written in blood." Some signatures, Warnke says, had faded from red to green, and the recruiter explained that that was a sign that the person who had signed had "copped out." When that happened, he added, Satan knows he has lost that soul, "And when he gets mad, you've had it. It's not too healthy to have your name turn green" (1972:43–44).

Warnke quickly moved upward in the cult hierarchy, eventually being provided two rent-free apartments, an unlimited supply of drugs and money, and a silver-colored Lincoln Continental automobile. Such resources were readily available to the cult, since they also controlled the drug racket in Los Angeles. Higher-up cult members circulated in and out of the scene, invariably in fancy cars and carrying huge amounts of cash. Although these dealers, like his recruiter, were always male, Warnke found the most active participants were sensuous, nymphomaniac women. One, an otherwise "sophisticated, suburban-type American woman," showed Warnke how to mix up a magickal wishing potion from a melange of ingredients. Cautioning that any mistake could cause an enraged demon to attack, she "recited something . . . in Hebrew," at the spell's climax in the best pseudo-cabalistic way (1972:46–47).

When Warnke proved successful at luring adolescents into the lower levels of the operation, he became one of three "Master Counselors" of the California Brotherhood. At this point he began to attend cult-sponsored "training sessions" held all over the United States, some in California, others in New York City. Using ideas he got from these workshops, he began "improving" the third-level satanic rituals, introducing a part in which he and other volunteers trampled communion wafers and slashed themselves to draw blood to drink (86). Other "improvements" he claimed were "hypnotic rock music" and using the blood of a freshly sacrificed cat to draw an inverted pentagram on the nude female "altar." The success of this last effort was demonstrated when the "altar" then began to speak in a diabolical language. In a scene equally indebted to Pentecostal "blood-pleading" and Bonewits's mock-Enochian incantations, Warnke says, "From the weird utterances that now came from her mouth, I knew we were being graced by the presence of one of the denizens of hell" (1972:101)

At this point in the ritual, Warnke asked for volunteers to show higher dedication to the Devil, and one agreed to have one of his fingers amputated and passed around to be nibbled by cult members in an act of ritual cannibalism (1972:100–101). In his book, this act occurs only once more, at the beginning of Warnke's defection from the cult. But in Cerullo's book, Warnke implies that the practice was common, and that "it was an honor among Satanists to have one or more fingers missing" (1973:170).[19] Although one would think that a missing finger would make cult members easy to detect, this gruesome detail passed into cult lore tradition and reemerged in Michelle Smith's recollections of her ritual abuse.

Warnke's story, as it developed, found places for most of the details included in the West Coast media construction of Satanism. Yes, he had met LaVey in January 1966, at a conference his higher-ups paid for him to attend, but he was disappointed with the "Black Pope," finding him slightly phony, and the whole meeting, which was *not* secret but open to the public, was "like going back to kindergarten" (1972:102). In Cerullo's book, Warnke adds that he had seem him at other cult events, "panhandling around the edges" (1973:171). Yes, he had met Charles Manson twice, once at a satanic workshop sponsored by LaVey and again at a third-level satanic cult ritual during which a chicken was beheaded and its blood poured over the stomach of a nude woman. Manson, Warnke recalled, "thought he was being shortchanged. He favored actually sacrificing the person" (Cerullo 1973:170).[20]

Yes, Warnke even was the mysterious "head witch" responsible for at least some of the Santa Cruz dog-skinnings. A police officer in the pay of the Satanists came to him to complain that reports of blood-drained dogs had "increased by 500 percent over the past three months" and was causing a "litter problem." Warnke admitted that he had suggested that cults having trouble getting their members to donate blood for their rituals could use stray dogs instead. "In some cases," he added, "the incisions were made as expertly as any surgeon's—a 'tribute' to our movement's students of this art" (1972:104–5).

But Warnke confessed that he soon repented his involvement with Satanism; cult members expelled him from the coven and later tried to murder him with a drug overdose. Recovered, he joined the navy (as records show, in early June 1966) and soon after experienced conversion. Although Warnke describes various ways in which cult members threatened or injured defectors to keep them from revealing secrets, after his expulsion he seems not to have been molested further by the cult, except through spiritual attacks. At a Dallas press conference announcing his independent anti-occult crusade, Warnke was asked how someone with his past could help people. His answer echoes Doreen Irvine's description of how her confession had transformed her old ex-prostitute self into an instrument of God: "Well, I've been the whole route. I've been a Satanist, a Satanic high priest. I've had control over a lot of people. A bunch! And I've eaten human flesh and drunk human blood. . . . I was instrumental in leading a thousand people into Satan's kingdom. Now I pray to God that He will allow our ministry to influence a thousand souls for good for every one I led into the darkness" (1972:203–4).

Warnke's description of Satanism, like Irvine's, relies heavily on sex and desecration of religious symbols, both standard elements in the existing media construction of "black magic." Beyond that, there are few similarities that could not be explained by independent reliance on the earlier anti-occult mythologies. In particular, Warnke's Black Mass is not at all like the elaborate ceremony conducted in Irvine's "Black Lodge" ceremony but follows the Pentecostal tradition as a "counterfeit" of orthodox tradition: But Warnke's Satanists, like Masons and Wiccans, still say "so mote it be" at the end of their petitions. Warnke even gets "Lucifer" and "Pan" into one of his satanic sermons to a group of stoned "flower children": "Heard of the magic dragon?[21] That's Lucifer, man! Ever hear of Pan? He's love, man. Free and easy love. Satan's cloven hoofs are from Pan, and Pan was the god of natural love and fertility. Satan's the pusher of all your heart's desires and pushes up the flowers of the earth. Well, all I can say, man, is: get with it. You know" (1972:90). Probably, however, Warnke was not directly reflecting the lore about cabalistic Jews or Aleister

Crowley, but rather the pitch Isaac Bonewits had given for Satan in his Berkeley soap-box lectures: "What I was preaching that afternoon was what I have since come to call 'Liberal Heterodox' Satanism. I preached the Devil as Lucifer, the 'Light Bearer,' champion of the intellect against repressive tyrannies on the one hand, and the original 'party animal' on the other — sort of a combination of Prometheus, Bacchus and Pan" (1997).

Most tellingly, the hierarchical structure described by Warnke finds no parallel in Irvine's story, where she, like Diana Vaughan, finds herself suddenly elevated to positions of status. The structure of Warnke's cult seems to be a hybrid of the Masonic/Golden Dawn/OTO ladder of degrees and the American corporate world. At a training session held in the countryside near Salem, Massachusetts, by Bridget Bishop, a direct descendent of the executed witch, Warnke learned that there was above him a fourth level of American-style executives who were concerned about recruitment rates and the efficiency of the lower stages. This top level reminded Warnke of "a meeting of General Motors' board of directors."

During this conversation, Warnke became aware of yet a still more powerful and secretive fifth level. This was the dreaded Illuminati (1972:91–92). This conspiracy scenario was already part of the Pentecostal construction of Satanism worldview, so it is no surprise that a San Diego evangelist had introduced Carr's *Pawns in the Game* to Warnke in 1971 (Hertenstein and Trott 1993:101–4). While he is not explicitly anti-Semitic, Warnke clearly adapts elements from Carr's account of *The Protocols of the Elders of Zion* to describe this international threat: "A worldwide, super-secret control group with perhaps as few as a dozen at the very top ... with key men controlling governments, economies, armies, food supplies ... pulling the strings on every major international event ... and not just now, but for generations, centuries, since the beginning of civilization ... manipulating men by their egos and their appetites, rewarding and depriving, enraging and pacifying, raising up first one side and then the other, maintaining a balance of frustration, bitterness, and despair..." (1972:93; all ellipses *sic* in the original text). Warnke marvels at the "unbelievable co-ordination" that this scenario required and concludes that only Satan, using demons as his emissaries, had the power to mastermind this international plot. All the occultists and political assassins "*were* the pawns of a much bigger plot," in which "financiers could work in tandem with politicians and industrialists, often without direct contact or even conscious collusion" (1972:94; emphasis his).

For the next twenty years Warnke was a central and much-cited figure in the American anti-Satanism movement. His stories put dramatic flesh on the rumors and inferences about devil worship being circulated in the media and through Pentecostal conduits. His confession, like Irvine's, reflects what we have seen thus far as definitive factors of the Pentecostal mythology: the contagious danger of non-Christian magic, the necessity of blood, tongues as a spiritual counterpart to demon possession, mental illness cleared as occult dabbling is remembered and confessed. Warnke also successfully integrated the Illuminati scenario into the hippie blood cult threat, thus providing a broader framework for fitting still more elaborate elements into the developing Satanism Scare.

John Todd: Ex-Grand Druid

Once, while Warnke was presenting his stories of the Illuminati, there was a backstage confrontation with a second born-again ex-Satanist, John Todd. A former associate of Warnke's recalled that Todd was especially angry that Warnke was "stealing his material." In fact, Todd had come to the attention of fundamentalist pastors in the Phoenix area in 1968.[22] At that time, he claimed that he had received Holy Spirit baptism at a storefront church specializing in deliverance and had been traveling with a deliverance revival group. He enlisted in the U.S. Army in May 1969 and was discharged in July 1970 because of psychiatric disorders. "Todd finds it difficult to tell reality from fantasy," a military medical report concluded. By 1972, he had drifted to the San Antonio area, where he came to the attention of the Reverend Jack Taylor, who was then holding a revival featuring deliverance. He told Taylor and his helpers then that he "had been in the occult" and was acquainted with Anton LaVey.

Interested, Rev. Taylor allowed Todd to give testimony about his occult experiences to small groups associated with the revival, which generated enough attention to get him an interview in the *San Antonio News*. The story he gave then was a rather general one: he had become interested in Satanism while in the army, then, after his release, he had run "a little head shop down by the river [in San Antonio] that was funded, organized, and run by one of the occults" [*sic*]. Later Todd claimed to have been "born again" during this revival, but those who were involved recalled that he never really "got saved." Rev. Taylor said, "He left earlier than I felt he should. He launched out—a ministry. He needed time to mature and be sure that he was free from demon oppression" (Hicks and Lewis 1979:67–69).

Todd left in March 1973 to assist in a teen ministry in Phoenix, and soon was appearing on religious telethons. By November, he had attracted enough publicity that he was invited to California to confer with evangelists, among them Jack T. Chick, publisher of a popular series of religious tracts in comic book style. He still claimed to be an ex-Satanist, but his picture of the occult scene now reflected more details from the neopagan movement. He claimed to be the son of Louise Huebner (a California astrologer named "Official Witch of Los Angeles County" during the late 1960s), and that he had learned about "white witchcraft," during his childhood years. But his confessions resembled those of earlier Charismatics, who admitted mainly to participating in séances and fortune-telling. Todd now contrasted this tradition to "the Satan-type church," which he said he had joined while in the military. "Most of your military bases have groups practicing some type of cult arts," he explained, "—sometimes two or three of 'em" (Hicks and Lewis 1979:49). He began to associate "black witchcraft" with "Druids," probably reflecting Pentecostals' antipathy to Bonewits, who was now a leading figure in the neopagan Reformed Druids of North America.

By this time, too, he had been introduced to the Illuminati mythology, apparently through Myron Fagan's LPs, though he characteristically pronounced the name of the organization "IllumiNETi." Surviving tapes of his 1972–1973 talks show increasing knowledge of anti-Semitic and apocalyptic lore. He claimed to have been promoted to a "Grand Druid Council" that passed on instructions and bribe money from the Rothschild family to all the politicians in America. Like many end-time prophets, he identified Nixon's Jewish Secretary of State Henry Kissinger as the Antichrist: "Well, never has a name come out to 666 from that code except Kissinger's.... I believe it's him (Kissinger) because I believe if he's going to be the Antichrist, the Jews are going to take him to be their Messiah and they're not going to [take] a Gentile as a Messiah. I am just waiting to hear that he made a seven-year pact with the Jews—I'm getting out of here!" (Hicks and Lewis 1979:62–63). Prominent liberal Democrats were equally part of the plot: Todd claimed to have been present at a satanic ritual during which presidential candidate George McGovern plunged a knife into a young girl's chest (Hicks and Lewis 1979:73).

Todd's stories proved as popular among the Melodyland Jesus People crowd as Warnke's had, and he held a series of meetings at the Anaheim Disneyland Hotel on the perils of witchcraft. His sponsoring evangelist "kept John on the gory, grisly details," his ex-wife recalled, "and the kids especially really liked it." About thirty youngsters formed a Bible study group to learn more from him at his apartment, but this created a scandal when allegations arose that he had been trying to seduce the female members. Todd denied the allegations, but a group of Melodyland teachers asked him to leave the area. He reluctantly gave up his crusade and largely dropped out of sight for the next four years.

By June 1977, Todd was back in contact with Jack T. Chick, who introduced him to the Reverend Roland Rasmussen, one of the West Coast's most respected fundamentalist pastors. Rasmussen was impressed by Todd's knowledge of the occult and of "masonic symbolism," so he made arrangements for him to speak to youth and adult groups in California. When these went well, Todd was scheduled for an East Coast lecture tour (January–March 1978) during which he told his story to many large fundamentalist congregations. Often these talks were taped, and copies were distributed through anti-occult conduits. Suddenly Todd was a celebrity, and "those cassettes" (with or without his name attached) appeared all over the country. "We've had many great preachers in our pulpit," a Pennsylvania pastor commented, "but there was more talk around town after he left than with any other preacher we've had" (Plowman 1979:38).

Todd's story had become more elaborate since his first 1973–1974 popularity. Now he claimed to have come from a multigenerational family of witches whose family tree went back to Massachusetts. Witchcraft, he still said, was not the same as Satanism, but the distinction was now much harder to discern, since he explained, "Witchcraft is just the old pagan religion that used to go on in the temples.... There are covens that will go so far as to sacrifice a human being, they believe it is part of their worship to the gods." He was initiated as a witchcraft priest at the age of fourteen, and later, he said, he discovered that his cult's initiation ritual was "identical" to that practiced by Freemasons (Hicks and Lewis 1979:37).

Todd now claimed to have joined the military "so that he could establish witch covens at military bases." When he was discharged in 1970, his mother gave him a plane ticket to New York City. There he met Dr. Raymond Buckland, the leading U.S. representative of Gardnerian Wicca, who turned out to be the "chairman of the Druid Council of Thirteen," the occult group that secretly controlled American politics. (Buckland evidently objected to this libelous charge, and when Todd's story became the basis of a Christian comic book published by Chick Publications, his place was taken by a mysterious "Isaac," presumably meant to suggest the Druid Isaac Bonewits, who is seen only in silhouette.)

He underwent an apprenticeship under Buckland and Louise Huebner, Todd alleged, and in May 1971 he became a "Grand Druid high priest." From this perspective he was able to learn how the Illuminati worked and what their agenda was. His main task was to use rock music to demonize adolescents. Todd claimed to have been personal friends with most of the influential figures of rock 'n' roll, many of whom he personally initiated into witchcraft. Most rock music, he said, is written by witches: the words contain "coded spells or incantations," while the melodies are found in "an old druid manuscript." When recorded, the master tapes are the focus of an occult ceremony, during which some of the country's most powerful witches conjure up "Regé," a principal devil. The witches then ask this being to command his demonic servants to follow the recordings of this song into the homes of those who buy them (Chick 1978:20–25).

Todd also provided his audiences with handouts of common "occult signs" derived from earlier sources. He adopted a long-standing anti-Masonic tradition of interpreting the five-pointed star or pentagram as a witchcraft symbol for "Lucifer" with one point up and for the horned devil with two points up. But he also viewed the six-pointed Star of David as a "hexagram used to summon up demons" (Hicks and Lewis 1979:46). "In witchcraft this is the most evil sign in the occult world," Todd explained, adding that "The word hex, meaning to place a curse on someone, comes from this emblem" (Chick 1978:7). Another handout showed the financial power of the Illuminati based on money taken in by major oil and retail corporations (Hicks and Lewis 1979:34), and yet another showed that organizations as diverse as Rosecrucians, Wiccans, Scientologists, Communists, Masons, Jaycees, B'nai Brith, ACLU, and the John Birch Society were all part of a single complex conspiracy.

Todd learned that the head of the Illuminati was one Philip Rothschild, whose mansion in Great Britain Todd said he had visited. This mysterious man, the satanic head of the Jewish world bankers, had a plan to take over America as the first stage in world conquest. Abandoning his earlier belief that Nixon's aide Kissinger was destined to be the Antichrist, Todd now remembered seeing an Illuminati memo that designated Jimmy Carter as the person who was "willing to become world ruler and remain obedient to the Illuminati" (Hicks and Lewis 1979:45). Now that Carter was president, Todd predicted, he would soon declare martial law and impose gun control laws allowing the government to confiscate weapons from private citizens. The state of Israel would provoke World War III over a bogus fuel crisis, and, in 1979, a "helter-skelter" situation would ensue during which Christians would be massacred by military police at Carter's orders, and all currency, food, and medical supplies would fall under the control of a one-world government, with its capital in Jerusalem.

In a pamphlet handed out at his meetings, Todd advised Christians to prepare a retreat in an isolated place away from major cities, and stock it with at least a five-year reserve of dehydrated food, water, and other essential supplies. Since the Illuminati would eventually come to kill the people in these retreats, Todd also provided a detailed list of guns that believers should obtain and horde away, amounting to at least five rifles, one shotgun, and two pistols per family. "Killing to protect loved ones and even yourself when life is threatened," he reassured his followers, "is the moral thing to do on behalf of your loved ones and on behalf of innocent society whose lives are endangered by the person or people who would destroy them" (Hicks and Lewis 1979:133).

Reactions were mixed: some congregations dismissed such warnings as another in a series of unfulfilled end-time prophecies. Others responded with shock and concern. In January 1978, an Indianapolis Baptist church arranged through its pastor to purchase truckloads of storable food, while individuals purchased weapons (Hicks and Lewis 1979:13). In Somerset, Pennsylvania, one church member told the pastor, "we will not allow [the Illuminati] to torture our families; we have decided that we will kill our children before than happens" (Plowman 1979:42).

Todd's career, however, came to an abrupt end. Rev. Rasmussen had received "good reports" on Todd's East Coast lectures, but after his return he became suspicious of his truthfulness. He "began to earnestly pray to the Lord to show me whether or not John Todd was genuine and trustworthy." Almost as an answer to these prayers, one of his parishioners came to him with a cassette tape that Todd had loaned him. It contained a recent newscast on his crusade, but Todd had taped this program on an older cassette, on which he could be heard teaching a workshop on how to cast spells and use witchcraft. "One reason witchcraft, I feel is more powerful than Christianity," Todd could be heard explaining, "is it's got about 8,000 years up on it. It's got billions of people believing in it over that period of time. Christianity is a very new religion." The tape concluded by inviting two of the participants to stay afterward with himself and his wife (whose witch name was—of course—"Diana") to discuss joining a coven (Hicks and Lewis 1979:86–87).

Simultaneously, Todd had included in his talks a series of attacks on Pentecostal institutions. These began with the individuals and groups who had accused him of sexual misconduct in 1973. Ralph Wilkerson, the head of Melodyland, was "the Illuminati's top infiltrator," Todd said, and he claimed to have been present when Wilkerson received $10 million in Rothschild bribes. In addition, he added, "I saw $35 million go into the Charismatic Movement to build the four biggest churches in the United States." Demos Shakarian, head of the the Full Gospel Businessmen's Fellowship International and an early patron of Todd's, received "a $10 million check signed by [alleged Illuminatus] David Rockefeller" (Hicks and Lewis 1979:93–110).

Some of his rhetoric incorporated anti-glossolalia language similar to that used by Kurt E. Koch against the Pentecostal movement. At one point, Todd said, "I came from witchcraft and witches talk in tongues" (Hicks and Lewis 1979:118). This statement is close to Koch's belief that glossolalia was often demonic and spiritistic in nature. But Todd continued *ad hominem*, naming Oral Roberts, Pat Robertson, Jerry Falwell, and Jim Bakker, then leader of the charismatic PTL Network, as equally controlled by the Illuminati. Darryl E. Hicks and Dr. David A. Lewis, writers associated with the PTL, began wondering how Todd had managed to do all the things he'd claimed—undergoing intensive training and initiations into the inner circles of the Illuminati, managing major rock groups, traveling internationally to attend Illuminati meetings, dealing drugs, and giving orders to politicians—during the two years between his discharge and his emergence as reformed ex-Satanist in San Antonio. They began digging into his verifiable past.

It soon emerged that after he had been sent packing by Melodyland, Todd had gone to Dayton, Ohio, where he managed an occult book store called "The Witches Cauldron," using "Lance Collins" as his witch name. During this time he had organized a coven of teenagers that met at his house and store, and obtained a charter as the Watchers Church of Wicca from a neo-pagan organization in North Carolina. Eventually, one of the participants complained to police that Todd not only had her disrobe for rites (in the orthodox Gardnerian way), but he had forced her to perform oral sex on him. Charged with statutory rape, Todd appealed to the Wiccan network for legal assistance, and his situation was researched by Gavin Frost[23] and Isaac Bonewits, then acting as a civil rights consultant for neo-pagan groups. Their findings were blunt: "We found absolutely no foundation for the charges of persecution made by the Todds; rather we found a very negative situation conducted by an ex-Satanist, ex-Christian priest as a cover for sexual perversion and drug abuse. Todd is armed and dangerous, and any activity by him should immediately be reported to the Church of Wicca" (Plowman 1979:42). Todd pleaded guilty to a lesser charge and served two months in jail before a lawyer hired by the steadfast Jack T. Chick got him released early.

Rasmussen called Todd before the deacons of his church on May 27, 1978, and confronted him with the witchcraft tape. Todd admitted to having been in a temporary "backslidden" state during this time but did not give any other explanation. As he walked out, he stopped to retrieve an automatic pistol that had slipped out of his back pocket. The following day the church voted unanimously to expel Todd from membership and rescind its endorsement of his claims (Plowman 1979:39). His supporters met shortly after and issued a statement admitting that he was "vulnerable" in some areas, mainly because he had associated with Pentecostals during his early ministry and hence did not "receive a proper Biblical and theological foundation." Even so, his supporters felt, his accounts of the Illuminati were "reliable reports" and his ministry "has been successful in willing many of those in the occult, including many witches, to Christ." The statement was accompanied by an order blank for cassette tapes of Todd's lectures (Hicks and Lewis 1979:89–91).

Nevertheless, investigators commissioned by the PTL continued to uncover evidence of additional sexual scandals. On January 6, 1979, he told one of the PTL's investigators, "I don't care whether people believe me or not so it doesn't matter. Helter skelter has already started. . . . It's going to happen so it doesn't matter to me, I'm taking off" (Hicks and Lewis 1979:93–94). He was never heard from again (at least not under the name John Todd) and rumor had it, variously, that he was assassinated by the Illuminati, or that he had moved to Montana to sell freeze-dried food for those preparing for the millennium. The PTL-commissioned exposé appeared soon after his disappearance, complete with an approving prefatory statement by Mike Warnke, who warned that Todd "could possibly turn into another Jim Jones." Warnke concluded, "We as Christians have to be careful of those who take the name of the Lord in vain" (Hicks and Lewis 1979:9).

The Todd story has an ironic rider: in 1992, nearly twenty years after *The Satan-Seller* had reached print, the fundamentalist journal *Cornerstone* commissioned a detailed investigation into the truthfulness of Warnke's story. As with John Todd, reporters Mike Hertenstein and Jon Trott found it impossible to fit Warnke's career as a high-level Satanist inside the documented events of his life. The time from his entry to college to his entry into the navy occupied less than nine months, during which time he would have had to have been introduced to Satanism, initiated and promoted to high priest, gone to several training meetings in various parts of the country, and then finally expelled and nearly murdered. Acquaintances who knew him during this period repeatedly contradicted his stories of his extravagant, drug-using lifestyle.

The journalists also found a pattern of fabrications in Warnke's later church activities, which were tarnished by frequent sex and money scandals. They found that Warnke had even been ordained as a bishop of a splinter "Holy Orthodox Catholic Church" in Kentucky. Acquaintances recalled that he enjoyed carrying out elaborate rituals in this persona, wearing ornate jewelry and robes (Hertenstein and Trott 1993: 317–22). *Cornerstone* concluded that his confessions had been fabricated, and expressed concern that this in turn influenced the ways in which Christians viewed the actual menace of contemporary Satanism. The magazine called on him to either produce evidence for his claims or else publicly confess to lying and remove *The Satan-Seller* and his related products (including cassette tapes) from the market. "The secular press may scoff, and those who consider themselves *real* Satanists may snicker," their exposé concluded, "but the Jesus of the Bible is still the God of truth" (Hertenstein and Trott 1993:30).

Conclusions

Like Doreen Irvine, Warnke and Todd described an elaborate multilevel satanic operation; but the three systems are quite different in virtually every detail. Irvine describes a two-tier system, a "Black Lodge" of Satanists and a sex-hungry coven of witches. Mike Warnke's multilayer Satanism starts with something like Anton LaVey's Church of Satan, continues with media speculation about murderous hippie "commune-ists," and ends with John Birch Society world-domination theories. John Todd's description of cult organization goes in yet another direction, describing multigenerational witchcraft families who socialize their children into Satanism before handing them over to agents of the Illuminati for intensive indoctrination. Apparently there is no recruiting; instead, teenagers are directly influenced by evil occult symbols like the Star of David or by Druid-produced rock music.

Likewise, Irvine, Warnke, and Todd each had different ways to explain why such an elaborate network was never exposed by police action, even though police sources were a major source of information on satanic cults. With her characteristic supernaturalism, Irvine says that Satanists could call up a "green swirling mist" to make their activities invisible to observers (1973:97–98). Warnke more pragmatically suggests that certain police were paid off by powerful figures (1972:70–71). Todd more bluntly called all police "enemies" who were controlled by Freemasonry, a wing of the Illuminati, and urged his followers to resist them, with bullets if necessary, to protect their liberty. In such a progress we can see how the anti-Satanism crusade evolved from an explicitly supernatural narrative useful for evangelism but too vague even to suggest verification, to a call for explicit, immediate social action by believers.

It is now clear why Charismatics challenged Todd's story so immediately. The literal historicism of these "confessions" was not important until Satanism was defined as a *secular* problem. For Irvine and Warnke, and for the Todd of 1972–1973, the most important thing was their transformation, their becoming "new creatures in Christ." Dysfunctional individuals had become active functioning counselors with the help of supernatural gifts of the spirit. Strong magic had been replaced with stronger, and the power of their charismatic metamorphosis was made more dramatic by the high status they both had previously achieved within their cults' hierarchies. But as soon as a confession held secular importance as evidence, then its literal truth or falsehood became crucial to evangelicals. Thus, initially only Todd's entirely secular claims of Illuminati actions positively *required* either confirmation or denial, the more so as he repeatedly made "helter-skelter" prophecies that were to be fulfilled (or not) within the next few months. Warnke's half-secular, half-supernatural scenario had no such short-term prophecies and hence could be tolerated in spite of its improbability. But as the Satanism Scare took on force in the law enforcement community, and as Warnke's information became used as "evidence" for cult activities, evangelicals then found it necessary to check on his truthfulness, for fear that their credibility might be challenged with Warnke's.

However, the two exposés had strictly limited agendas. In revealing the fraudulent nature of Warnke's story, Trott and Hertenstein pointedly did not continue to say that the scare it provoked was likewise fraudulent. Similarly, while Hicks and Lewis show why Todd could not have been a member of the inner circle of the Illuminati, they also take pains to say, "it is very possible that the Illuminati still exists . . . secretly guided by a small group of powerful, wealthy men throughout the world." The authors advise "serious Christian" readers interested in examining conspiracy theories to read Pat Brooks's anti-Semitic *Return of the Puritans*, a "careful" documentation of the Illuminati that "outlines a program of prayer, good works, and involvement." Brooks, for her part, maintained even after Todd's exposure as a fraud that "God is blanketing the nation with his message" (Hicks and Lewis 1979:20–22, 35). And in the 1981 third edition of *Return of the Puritans*, Brooks singled out the Chick Publication comics containing Todd's information as "especially helpful for teenagers." Jack T. Chick continues to market anti-Masonic and anti-Catholic conspiracy theories and remains faithful to John Todd's cause. His Christian comics citing Todd as an authority on cults remain in print to this day, just as some of Todd's cassette tapes continue to circulate through the anti-occult conduit.

Overall, the value of "confessions" such as these lies not so much in their credibility as evidence but their utility. They dramatized and transmitted a belief system that could be used to construct contemporary stresses in terms of mythological concepts. As Daniel Wojcik (1997) has observed, end-of-the world predictions such as Hal Lindsey's allowed fundamentalist Christians to see social factors such as nuclear proliferation and international unrest in terms of an approaching Second Coming. Thus, there was a positive dimension to seeing adolescent crime and drug use as evidence for satanic conspiracies, since demonic activities such as these could signify the imminence of the end-times. But mythologizing secular society in this way, as we will soon see, has unfortunate side effects. If those involved in any activities that equated with Satanism in right-wing politics are part of a subversive conspiracy, then the response includes not only religious revival but secular witch-hunts. Worse, Todd's call for "retreat" and armed action against Satan-controlled authorities clearly anticipates the Waco self-immolation and the Oklahoma City bombing.

8

The Highgate Cemetery Vampire Hunt

Grave-Robbing and Rumor Panic

It must have been the flash which gave us away.
—Martine de Sacy,
to a *Hampstead & Highgate Express* reporter

By 1970, Satanism was a growth industry in Great Britain's popular and institutional culture. The Wheatley novels were being actively reprinted and inspiring a series of sensational horror movies. But many police and religious officials were convinced that Satanism was more than a fiction: they explained church desecrations as "black magic" ceremonies and warned that cults were capable of "hypnotising" and abducting unwary youths. Even occultists conceded that such evil cults probably operated alongside them. Sexual perversions, especially against small children, were assumed to be part of the Black Mass. And the members of such cults were said to be ordinary-seeming people who mingled freely with other Britons—except when a rite was due.

Despite confessions from ex-witches such as Alex Sanders and Doreen Irvine, the topic still did not inspire widespread concern. Contemporary press articles and editorials defined youth problems in terms of drug use, rock and roll, and gangs such as the ubiquitous "mods and rockers," the subject of a current British moral panic (see Jenkins 1992:6). Police reported numerous drug deals and seized quantities of cannabis (or marijuana), while local sermons stressed what was seen as a deluge of "child problems"—i.e., abusive parents and children left abandoned and neglected. Signs of Satanism, while obviously good press material for an occasional tabloid-style exposé, simply did not inspire a moral crusade at this time.

Similarly, in the United States, concern over occult groups was secondary to a broader media-based concern over the emerging youth counterculture. Mike Warnke and John Todd provoked considerable attention within the charismatic network, but their influence in mass culture was at the moment limited to occasional local press features. Much more concern was paid to youth and minority groups protesting the Vietnam conflict, still a political hotbed. Campus unrest and the growing popularity of mind-altering drugs were far more threatening to parents than the risk of satanic cults.

In both the U.S. and Great Britain, Satanism emerged as a more pressing moral concern through a series of media-influenced *rumor panics*. These phenomena are brief but intense events in which rumors about a menacing person or group circulate in a community. This menace involves some imminent act against humanity, and the only defense is a strong offense by concerned citizens. Usually the phenomenon climaxes with a series of vigils or hunts, and often tails off into punitive action against some scapegoat associated with the menace. Jeffrey S. Victor (1989, 1990) has detailed a number of such rumor panics about satanic cults that occurred in rural areas of the United States during the late 1980s, and several others have occurred more recently in Northeastern Pennsylvania. The most dramatic of these occurred in May 1987, fueled by rumors that a satanic cult would commit mass murder or suicide during a local high school prom. Although nothing tragic occurred, the rumors led to a show of strength by school and police authorities. These actions were a form of "therapeutic magic," in which the pressures and anxieties affecting a community were brought to a head and banished through some kind of collective action.

A closer analysis of the event showed that it was driven by concern about an unexplained teen suicide earlier that year. The rumor panic suggested a reason for this death—dabbling in the occult—and while no evidence ever emerged that the teen had in fact been involved in Satanism, the rumor allowed community members to "name" a previously undefined threat and exorcise it with collective action. However, such events bring large amounts of official and unofficial lore about Satanism to the surface, and the collective nature of such events ensures that virtually everyone in the community becomes aware of such lore. The event led to a series of local workshops by cult cops and effectively introduced Satanism as an ongoing social threat in the area. Rumor panics therefore are a primary means of moving contemporary mythologies out of the specialized conduits that generate them and into mass culture (Ellis 1990).

While the phenomenon does help communities bring threatening events like teen suicides to closure, it may also, paradoxically, encourage the very actions it claims to deter. In fact, the same area experienced another rumor panic in September 1996, involving many of the same ideas and participants (Ellis 1996). Rumor panics are essentially forms of telling a story through *ostension*, or through literally enacting part of a narrative. That is, people may be caught up in emergent stories in ways that urge them to act out parts in a cultural drama. In some cases, this may involve perpetrating hoaxes to frighten others and create excitement. However, ostensive behavior may be entirely sincere and well-intentioned: those who participate in the communal show of strength or in punishing scapegoats may be fully convinced that they are doing the right thing for society. By pointing out the traditional nature of rumor panics the motives of those who become involved are not being called into question. However, it is important to see the ways in which legends form maps for behavior, particularly how they may actually create the problem that is allegedly being solved.

The next two chapters will discuss how rumor panics in Great Britain, the United States, and Canada provided means for disseminating beliefs and legends about Satanism in these countries. The Highgate Cemetery Vampire Hunt was an especially long-lived phenomenon, beginning with a brief but highly visible "flap" over ghostly encounters in a ruinous cemetery but developing into lasting concern over allegedly satanic grave-robbing. Paradoxically, the incident tailed off into a highly visible court case in which one of the most devoted "hunters" in fact became the scapegoat blamed for "cult" activities. As this affair was winding down, a parallel series of rumor panics was developing in the United States over cattle mutilations. Less focused but more widespread, this series of panics introduced lore about satanic cults into a variety of communities and likewise gave rise to ostensive behavior. Together, these rumor panics disseminated information about satanic cults throughout Anglo-American culture through virtually every channel of communication, official and unofficial.

Ḥunting Spring-Ḥeeled Jack and Other Monsters

In January 1838, *The Times* published an unusual letter received anonymously by the mayor of London. The letter complained that a series of sinister events was occurring in Peckham and other villages on the outskirts of London, which the newspapers were perversely refusing to cover. At least seven ladies had been frightened out of their right minds by opening their doors to find horrific bogies just outside. The letter suggested that "some individuals (of, as the writer believes, the higher ranks of life) have laid a wager with a mischievous and foolhardy companion (name as yet unknown) that he durst not take upon himself the task of visiting many of the villages near London in three disguises—a ghost, a bear and a devil" (Dash 1996:44). Within a few days, the same paper printed a report that the wager was even more serious: "the bet is, that the monster shall kill six women in some given time." Other papers soon printed more elaborate versions: one claimed, "the object of the villains is to destroy the lives of not less than thirty human beings! viz. eight old bachelors, ten old maids, and six lady's maids, and as many servant girls as they can, by depriving them of their reason, and otherwise accelerating their deaths." The perpetrators, who were blamed for a whole series of scares in the London area, were said to be the delinquent sons of noble families competing to win a wager of the then fabulous sum of £5000, or close to $400,000 in modern currency (1996:48–51).

Chief among the suspects was the character who became known as "Spring-Heeled Jack" because authorities who failed to capture him believed that he wore boots with coiled springs in their heels, with which he could make otherwise impossible leaps over walls. The situation soon turned into a panic when a number of women began reporting being accosted by figures covered with sheets, often breathing fire. By March, *The Morning Herald* noted that "many silly young men" were beginning "to enact the ruffian in a small way, considering it something clever to frighten women and children out of their wits, under the belief that 'Spring-heeled Jack' was attacking them" (1996:57). The firsthand witnesses quoted in papers describe costumes and effects that could be produced easily by hoaxers, a number of whom were indeed apprehended and charged with minor offenses. The real "monster" was never apprehended, and the panic died down by the next spring, but the name

"Spring-Heeled Jack" entered tradition as a general term for any mysterious ghost or bogie.

In May 1873, the same "wager" legend reappeared in Sheffield, and a similar series of stories circulated about women accosted and badly frightened. The focus of this panic, however, was a cemetery where the victims of a recent cholera epidemic had been buried in a mass grave. Bands of amateur "ghost-hunters" began to haunt the area, much to the discomfort of local residents. On the night of May 22, an especially large group gathered at the locked entrance of the cholera burial ground. One witness described the scene:

> Soon we fell in with a crowd, all, like ourselves, bound on a ghost hunt. . . . Most of the would-be captors were armed with bludgeons of portentous thickness; some half score or so had with them bull terriers of truculent aspect, one man had over his shoulder a double barrelled gun, with a dose of No. 4 in each barrel, which he had benevolently prepared for the special benefit of his ghostship. . . . Loud and deep were the threats indulged in, for confident in numbers the most timid waxed valorous, and if the ghost had appeared he would, I fancy, have had a warm reception. No ghost was, however, encountered. (1996:92)

Indeed, the crowd, impatient at seeing no sign of an apparition, began "to scale the railings in order to explore the graveyard and discover the 'ghost.'" Police sent out in force to keep order intervened, and a full-scale conflict broke out during which two officers were wounded. No "well organised supernatural being" would be pleased by such a fracas, the local paper commented ironically: it could "only afford pleasure to a morbid-minded evil spirit unfit for decent society" (1996:89). Similar events in various towns were documented in British newspapers over the next decades. In 1877, mobs armed with sticks and stones gathered nightly in Lincoln, watching for Spring-Heeled Jack, and similar panics occurred in Liverpool in 1904 and in Bradford in 1926.

Great Britain was not alone in hosting such ghost hunts. In July 1951, a similar rumor panic occurred in the lower-class O'Donnell Heights district of Baltimore, Maryland. There a teenage girl claimed to have been slashed by a black-robed prowler who was able to leap easily over walls and off roofs. Residents stayed awake nights, armed with makeshift weapons such as baseball bats, and posses began to roam the neighborhood streets at night. On July 25, a crowd gathered outside an old German cemetery, claiming to have surrounded the prowler. Five teenagers were arrested inside, hiding behind tombstones, but they maintained that they were only helping to track the phantom. "Publicity about the prowler is drawing prowlers and youngsters from all over town," a policeman complained, adding, "They only aggravate the situation and it is very dangerous for them. Those people out there are angry and really aroused. Somebody is very likely to get hurt." However, by August the panic had passed without any prowler being apprehended (1996:102–8).

On the afternoon of September 23, 1954, homeowners in a lower-class Glasgow suburb complained about a clamor coming from a local cemetery. Police found hundreds of children, armed with sticks and stones, swarming over the graveyard. "Their excited shouts and screams became so loud," a local paper reported, "that normal conversation was impossible." When a constable arrived on the scene, he was surrounded by children who explained that they were hunting for a "vampire with iron teeth" who had already killed and eaten "two wee boys." "This I could handle," the constable told the press, "but when grown-ups approached me and asked earnestly, 'Is there anything in this vampire story?' it made me think" (Hobbs and Cornwell 1988:117). Glasgow papers described the event, which was repeated the following night, as an unhealthy hysteria brought on by too many American comic books and horror movies. But Hobbs and Cornwell found that similar children's hunts had been occurring regularly in Glasgow and other parts of Scotland; in fact, even larger crowds had gathered in the same neighborhood in the 1930s to hunt for Spring-Heeled Jack. Further, they note that participants were less frightened than curious, even eager to corner a threatening entity.

Hobbs and Cornwell suggest that some hunt-activating legends might be peculiar to children, who preserve them longer than do adults. But the investigating policeman in the 1954 vampire hunt noted that some adults also asked "earnestly" if there was anything to the rumor. And rumor panics can provoke a variety of reactions even among young people. Norine Dresser describes a panic that occurred in a small town in the southern U.S. on February 29, 1988, a day when the ghost of a suicide victim was supposed to return to her high school as a "vampire." Although many students took this scare as an opportunity for adventure, local police had to take stern measures to prevent others from carrying weapons to class on that day (Dresser 1989:42–44). Such legends seem to appeal to a broad spectrum of ages, and even those of the same age may respond to them quite differently.

The Beginnings of "Satanism" Rumor Panics

Such "monster hunts" also draw from the adolescent ritual termed *legend-tripping* by folklorists. This ritual involves a set of cautionary legends that warn of the danger of a site, which then functions as a dare to visit the very place and carry out the ritual that leads to danger. The content of such legends is extremely diffuse, some explaining why the place is haunted to begin with, others warning against trespassing on its boundaries. The film *The Blair Witch Project*, a surprise hit during the summer of 1999, is based on a number of common legend-trip motifs. But as folklorist Gary Hall (1973) has observed, the narratives are a means to an end, creating "an atmosphere of fear" that makes the trip itself an exciting event. Kenneth A. Thigpen (1971), who also studied a number of legend-trips in the Bloomington, Indiana, area, also observes that the orally narrated legend serves only to enhance "the receptive psychological state of all involved." That is, the story prepares the participants to experience something "supernatural" when they arrive at the site.

The trip itself, therefore, is a form of imaginative play that challenges the boundaries of reality and fantasy. Sociologist Ikuya Sato (1988) has made a similar observation about the activities of adolescent gangs. Previous analyses of youth crime, he noted, attributed delinquency to peer pressure, forcing individuals to conform to a group norm. But Sato's interviews with members of a Japanese motorcycle gang showed that gangs were rarely stable enough to enforce rules of behavior in the way that adolescent "cults" are often said to do. Gangs do not gain or "ensure long term commitments from followers," he concluded (198).

Sato concluded that *play* theory provided the best match for many of their activities. Play, he argued, provides groups with a loosely constructed set of rules for generating excitement. These rules create a liminal middle ground between conformity to norms and chaotic actions by defining the situation in terms of an alternate reality. Such a system of rules and goals for action can become quite complex; nevertheless, Sato notes, "It includes a great latitude for improvisation and often constitutes a loose dramaturgical system on the basis of which youngsters can generate their own 'street corner myth' or other narratives with more or less distinctive plots and themes. The dramaturgical system is flexible enough to allow each of the youngsters a considerable degree of improvisational performances" (201–2).Such "street drama" includes exaggerated and distorted images of adult roles, and Sato suggests a parallel with Third World initiation rituals, in which "some of the values, norms, and styles in ordinary life are presented dramatically, comically, and grotesquely" (200).

In many cases, the experiences that teens have during such rites do not have significant impact on their worldview; in fact, on some level they may be a form of homage to adult norms. But this type of play can also reveal serious forms of protest against repressive role models, and as such it can have serious motives. Ikuya Sato observes that when there is "a precarious balance between the two standards," and youngsters are not fully committed to official definitions of everyday life, a "corruption of play" may take place. Individuals, at heart ambivalent about adult mores, may become intensely involved in a group situation that generates its own momentum. Such events may lead to serious consequences: participants may breach social rules beyond the point of no return. Thus, play may cease to be play and generate real anxiety or physical actions that lead to serious consequences (203–5). It follows that the dramalike scenario of hunting a monster may easily lead the participants into criminal acts of vandalism and even grave-robbing.

When such acts occurred in the United States before the early 1970s they were seen as teenage play gone too far. As early as 1966, legend-trippers had fallen afoul of the law: three adolescent males were arrested for hanging the body of a German Shepherd dog on a tree near a gravesite at Stepp Cemetery, near Bloomington, Indiana. Investigation showed that the dog had not been killed in a ritual, but had been accidentally run over by the car in which the teens were cruising. After unsuccessfully trying to locate its owner, the youths told police, they decided to take it to the cemetery, where a mysterious woman in black was said to appear. There they hung the dog's body from a tree to frighten other visitors. Rumors spread quickly about the "sacrificed" dog, and when police arrived, they found a crowd of teens around the hanged dog eagerly waiting for the "witch" to appear.

Police discounted the significance of the event as a prank in bad taste, but the hanged dog quickly became a standard item in local legends. The lady in black was said to go after, kill, and hang dogs (primarily German Shepherds) in the cemetery, in order to provide herself with a supernatural pet to keep her company. And teenaged motorists began to refer to "white wolves" that appeared to them in the Stepp Cemetery area, trying to startle them into wrecking their cars. This tradition strikingly prefigured a rumor that gained currency among American anticult investigators some ten years later. Maury Terry, investigating the Manson/ Son of Sam connection in cults, in 1976–1977, also encountered rumors that Satanists collected and ritually sacrificed German Shepherds (Terry 1987:162).

In 1966, the Stepp Cemetery "dog-hanging" incident was correctly linked to adolescent legend-tripping and did not create any local panic. Official concerns about Satanism were quicker to develop in Great Britain, where occasional flaps about "black magic rings" had developed from the 1930s onward. So when grave desecrations occurred there, they were apt to be defined as a form of cult activity. A series of 1963 grave desecrations at Clophill (Bedfordshire) quickly passed into popular culture as evidence of devil worship. Yet the events were cut from the same cloth as American legend-trips.

A number of minor incidents led up to the Clophill case. In February 1959, vandals entered a churchyard in North Cray, Kent, knocking over and smashing ten crosses. The caretaker commented, "Something very strange is going on and I would not be at all surprised to learn it was devil worship. It is not the first time crosses have been smashed here." At the same time, though, the local rector blamed "hooligans"; while black magic could not be ruled out, he felt it was unlikely. Villagers too said they had heard sounds of partying from the churchyard and nearby woods during the night.[1] This relatively minor kind of vandalism was repeated in Elthan late in 1962, where crosses were also overturned (Maple 1966:171).

At the time, Bedfordshire was experiencing a dramatic rise in juvenile delinquency. The chief constable for the county reported an overall 6 percent increase in crime and an even more dramatic jump in numbers of cases involving juveniles—from 672 in 1960 to 1,027 in 1961 and 1,104 in 1962. An increasing problem was caused by gangs of youngsters who vandalized vacant houses, stripping lead and other materials that could be sold as scrap metal. News articles also reported on a variety of youth problems, especially in the urban center of Luton, where teens complained about boredom and a lack of employment and social facilities. Letters to editors of local papers also continually referred to the current rivalry between "mods" and "rockers."[2]

But the immediate trigger for the incident came from a column written by journalist Peter Castle for the local paper, the *Bedfordshire*

Times & Standard. Titled "I met a witch and a ghost!" it ran on December 7 as a spooky story, a traditional Christmas-season feature in British papers and magazines. The column began conventionally by placing the reader by a "warm-haloed fireside" to encourage indulgence in speculation over whether witches exist. Even though most of his colleagues felt that witchcraft was a thing of the Dark Ages, Castle related, he floored his colleagues one lunch with an account of meeting an attractively dressed twenty-eight-year-old "real witch" who had come to his office. "I don't practice Black Magic, so you needn't look so scared," she began, then described a typical Gardnerian-style Wiccan coven that held ritual dances and festivities before serving cakes and wine. Asked if they really undressed before their rituals, the witch admitted that they did because clothing impeded the mental vibrations that they used to improve situations or charm away illnesses. The human body is "a very mundane thing when completely unclothed," she added.

Gardner's *Witchcraft Today* had been published in 1954, so Castle's discovery of what he claimed was a living tradition of Murray-style pagan religion was not news among occultists. But Wicca had not yet emerged as a legitimate (or even alternative) religious movement, so Castle's news that there was an active group of pagans in Bedfordshire holding ritual dances in the nude provoked much reader interest. On February 1, the same paper ran a feature allegedly following up on the story, describing the 1667 witch trial of Elizabeth Pratt, who had confessed to making a pact with the Devil and ritually hexing villagers and their children. For all the assurances of Castle's visitor that her coven was not involved in such rites, interested readers inevitably inferred that black magic might still be a reality in the countryside.

Whether devil-worshipping cults existed in Bedfordshire or not, the media interest and teenage mischief created a real-life tradition near the village of Clophill, located midway on the main road between Luton and Bedford. On the afternoon of Saturday, March 16, 1963, a local couple encountered two Luton youths rambling through the streets playing with a human skull.[3] When the couple stopped the boys and asked where they had gotten it, the boys replied that they had taken a bicycle ride into the countryside and had visited the ruined tenth-century chapel of St. Mary's. This building, abandoned for ten years, stood well outside the town and more than a half mile from the nearest house; already its roof had been stripped of lead by vandals. On arriving at the chapel, the boys said they had looked in the window and found the skull impaled on a metal spike that the vandals had pulled out of a window frame and stuck in a crack in the church wall. In front of the skull were the skeleton's breastbone, pelvis, and leg bones, which police announced had been arranged "in the pattern used for the Black Mass."

It is unclear what this phrase means, except that police suspected some ritual significance to the placement of the bones.[4] No historical or occultist source, including Montague Summers's detailed reconstruction of the Black Mass, mentions anything about laying bones in patterns as part of a black magic rite. The Reverend Leslie Barker, the rector responsible for the disused church, noted that six other graves had been damaged before the vandals had managed to dislodge the stone slab above the remains of one Jenny Humberstone and pry open her coffin. "Satan-worshippers are known to always use a female at the centre of their ceremonies," Rev. Barker told the press, adding that each grave disturbed was that of a woman. Feathers were also discovered scattered inside the building, and police considered it possible that they had come from "a sacrificial cockerel," since accounts of satanic rites often did mention animal sacrifices. More likely, the idea came from Wheatley's *The Devil Rides Out,* where a black cock and a white hen are prepared for a satanic sacrifice in the book's first episode (1954:17).

Finally, close investigation revealed two tracings of a Maltese cross inside a circle on the church wall, one weather-beaten, the second fresh. The four arms of the cross were colored red, possibly with animal blood, police said, though the rector felt it looked more like paint. Although again no such symbol appears in occult or cabalistic sources, police felt this detail confirmed that a ritual had been performed with the bones. It was unclear when the grave had been opened, since the church had virtually been cut off from the community during a cold spell, but the rector recalled that "Sunday week was the night of the full moon, the traditional time for evil spirits and black magic to come into their own."[5] Rev. Barker recalled that someone had phoned him sometime during the previous months to ask if the church had ever been used for occult purposes, and police also noted that someone had come through nearby Ampthill "making inquiries about Black Magic on which he said he was writing a book." The rector concluded that he found some aspects of the damage inexplicable except in terms of Satanism. His churchwarden agreed: "We think the gang were fanatics who have done this terrible thing for black magic rites—some kind of devil worship."

The week the damage was reported, St. Mary's began to see more visitors. Even as Rev. Barker and his superior surveyed the damage, a man with a "foreign accent" and a London license plate drove up to express interest in black magic. On March 23, Jenny was reinterred with a brief service; by Monday her tomb was open again. By April 2, the grave had been disturbed twice more, and the site was attracting a constant stream of outsiders. "It is not only by day that the churchyard is being visited," a reporter observed. "Scores of young people have been going there after dark. One of the 'attractions' is the still open grave of Jenny." And although the grave was recemented, on the night of the next full moon it was opened yet again. At Luton Central Library there was "quite a run" made on the few non-fiction books held on black magic, though the librarian expressed skepticism about how genuine the Clophill "Black Mass" had been. Showing surprising knowledge, he commented, "If it were a real Black Magic ceremony, why did they leave the bones out in the open. . . . And authentic rituals usually involve the bodies of naked girls."

The incident swept up other mysterious happenings in the area. On April 9, a twelve-year-old boy visiting "Bluebell Wood," a remote but popular summer haunt near Caddington, just south of Luton, found the decapitated heads of six cows and a horse under a thicket. Oddly, authorities found that no animals had been reported missing anywhere in the Luton area. An inspector for the Royal Society for the Prevention of Cruelty to Animals noted that the heads were arranged on the edge of a circular clearing and that all but two were missing their jawbones—a part he claimed was sometimes used in black magic.[6] Estimating that the animals might have been killed at the time of the Clophill incident, he concluded, "There is absolutely no sensible or logical reason for the heads being hidden in the wood. . . . The only thing that I can think of is that it is tied up with the Clophill 'Black Magic' in some way."

Meanwhile, a local paper had made inquiries among young males and found a former forestry student readily admitted that he had visited St. Mary's two years earlier. He described the trip:

> He and about a dozen students from the Agricultural College, Silsoe [the next village over], slaughtered a cockerel, scrawled a Celtic cross, and left trails of blood and feathers. Only it rained— and the practical joke failed.
>
> "It was just a huge joke," explained the informant, "only it doesn't seem so funny now! . . . I'm fairly sure that the present ceremonial was a similar stunt, which badly blundered and broke the law."

This interpretation was given support when in Ivinghoe, a town west of Luton, police found a burnt cross surrounded by bones and other paraphernalia. Two young men admitted responsibility, commenting, "It was all a harmless joke, and neither of us has ever taken part in any voodoo rite or anything of that sort."

Curious visitors, however, were more apt to see black magic than juvenile hoaxes in the continuing desecrations. Eric Maple, author of a popular book on rural witchcraft traditions, visited Clophill and first suggested "a hideous ceremony akin to necromancy" (1966:171) then the mysterious "Devil's Pinch." In a later coffee-table book on witchcraft, he published several grisly photographs of broken monuments and decomposed corpses inside shattered coffins. He advised, "Those who feel the inclination for a truly Gothic experience should visit desolate Clophill to savour its wilderness of desecrated and looted tombs, symbols of the revival of black magic in the twentieth century." Many clearly did so; on his retirement in 1969, Rev. Barker said that since 1963 "not a month has gone by without one of the graves or tombs in the churchyard being dug up and some sort of rite performed" (Maple 1973:97).

This sensation was followed in July by a series of apparent desecrations in Lancashire; then in December 1963 and January 1964 a huge media flap erupted over ritualistic graveyard vandalisms all over Great Britain. Some involved no more than the smashing of gravestones and dumping of remains from coffins. But when "magical symbols" were left painted on the porch of a church in Bramber, Sussex, experts were called in, who affirmed that they had been left not by dabblers "but by someone with deep, detailed knowledge of witchcraft" (Lefebure 1970:25). The rector was impressed enough that he performed a counterritual, pronouncing a curse on the vandals, praying that "their days be of anguish and sorrow" (Maple 1966:171–72).

Some elements of these desecrations did in fact suggest knowledge of traditional folk magic. In the graveyard of St. Clements, in Leigh, Essex, a sheep's heart pierced with thirteen thorns was found on a tomb inside a chalked letter "A" and beside a pentagram. The rector called in police "because of similar incidents in churches up and down the country. I presume the letter A is the initial of the person who is intended to die." During the panic, similar finds of pierced animal hearts were made in the counties of Surrey (Guildford), Sussex (Jevington), Essex (Leigh-on-Sea) and Norfolk (Castle Rising and Sandringham) (Kobler 1966:76; Maple 1966:172, 177; Lefebure 1970:7, 20, 27). The British tabloid *TV*

Times called making such an object "the traditional Black Magic death curse."

Indeed, folklorists have recorded such a practice as a means of casting a spell: but the context is not witchcraft but witch-hunting, and the pierced heart is supposed to be a substitute for the witch's own heart. Yorkshire folklorist William Henderson collected nineteenth-century accounts of witch masters who used the technique to identify who had cast a hex on a client's child or animal (1866:184–85), and Ozark folklorist Vance Randolph likewise found the practice still in use in this century (1947:298–99). The rector at St. Clements observed that the tomb on which the heart was found belonged to a "supposed witch." So it seems more likely that the intent of the ritual was not to enlist the powers of evil but to defy or neutralize the powers of the alleged witch's tomb.

By the end of 1964, British police claimed to have linked more than two hundred acts of graveyard vandalism to black magic (Kobler 1966:76). In the United States, as cult awareness became a staple among local police networks, the "new awareness" of such practices began to focus on Satanism. In March 1972, for instance, police in Valhalla and in Johnson City, two small towns in New York State, discovered that they had been investigating "nearly identical" cases of grave-robbing in which dried bones had been removed from cemeteries. One of the police chiefs commented that their mutual investigation "has taken us into strange places to talk to strange people.... They have really weird ideas, most of them— if you know what I'm getting at." Further checking led to recognition that police departments in other parts of the country had similar cases, "and coincident with these have been rumors of Devil cults." Witches or Satanists might be responsible, suggested Roger Elwood, a science fiction author and New Jersey youth counselor, adding that he had sources that indicated that local police were repressing information to prevent a panic. "Undoubtedly, there would have been a lot more mentioned about these cults," Elwood's source told him, "but news of their weird practices would scare people out of their wits" (1973:32–33).

Men in Black: Cemetery Adventures

Highgate Cemetery was created during Victorian times to provide burial space for the thousands of London residents who could no longer be held in the burial plots of parish churches. Set in a hilly district, Highgate is divided into an older section dating to 1839, and a newer section opened later in the century, with Swains Lane, a sharply ascending street, running through the middle. Over one hundred thousand Londoners were buried there, including many of the Victorian Age's eminent people. Dickens's first wife, along with Elizabeth and Christina Rossetti lie in the older section; novelist George Eliot and economist Karl Marx rest in the newer.

The original owners of Highgate provided a variety of plots, ranging from the Columbarium, a complex of ornate crypts in pseudo-Egyptian styles, to densely packed rows of plots for those of humbler means. By the early twentieth century, the cemetery was filled, and complaints were already being made that even the newer plots were not being maintained. Conditions deteriorated rapidly after World War I, and when German bombing further damaged the vaults in World War II, many of them were simply left open, covered only by rotting tarpaulins.[7]

By the mid-1960s, the ruinous state of Highgate had become notorious. American scholar Richard D. Altick visited it then as part of his research into Victorian popular culture and left a vivid description:

> Highgate Cemetery, by its very nature, is warranted to convert what begins as a mere visit into an Adventure.... [It] represents what would result if the accumulated monuments of Westminster Abbey were transferred, in their full marmoreal extravagance, to the Amazonian rain forest. Although the guide maintains that the lush growth is systematically eliminated during the winter by the use of billhooks and wholesale burning, one cannot believe it has been curbed for years. Thick "cuckoo grass" rises to a height of four or five feet.... Trees, saplings, wild shrubs, weeds, all the rank vegetation that a weeping English climate can bring forth, swallow up every tombstone that does not front directly on a path.... To reach [one grave] requires plunging from the path through the brambles and burrs and hip-high undergrowth and tough, ground-clinging vines that constantly trip up the explorer fresh from the London pavements. A machete is not ordinarily part of one's traveling equipment in England, but it would come in handy here. (1969:194–95)

At the same time, the area surrounding Highgate was affected by a less obvious decline. Though Highgate and neighboring Hampstead were fashionable suburbs of London, the local newspaper reported numerous cases of youth gang violence and confrontations between self-styled "mods" and "rockers." Swains Lane, the road through the cemetery, already had its name in the nineteenth century, when it was used as a meeting place for sweethearts, or a "lovers' lane." Even then, young men were in the habit of walking their companions past or through the graveyard in much the same way that American couples have more recently used spooky sites as parking spots. By 1970, the gates around the cemetery itself had deteriorated to the point that groups of adolescents were freely using the space after dark for their own purposes. The cemetery groundskeeper complained that human intruders were a constant problem: "tramps" and "schoolboys climbing on graves at night as a dare" made keeping up the monuments difficult.[8]

Even after the 1963 Clophill "black magic" grave disturbances faded from view, British papers continued to blame Satanists for disturbing cemeteries throughout the 1960s. On the night after Halloween 1968, for example, police found "black magic symbols" around an opened communal grave in London's Tottenham Park Cemetery. The following February, police near Tunbridge Wells blamed witchcraft when a cross was upturned and a mysterious sign daubed on gravestones.[9] And the London tabloid *News of the World*, having created national concern in 1967 over drug use by rock groups such as the Rolling Stones, followed in February and March 1969 with weekly "exposés" of witchcraft circles. These were mainly researched by having reporters approach Wiccans and offer to be initiated. The stories emphasized ritual nudity and flagellation and hinted darkly that young girls and children were being "lured" by occultists (Smyth 1973:21). People soon attributed the Highgate intrusions to "black magic rings." One elderly woman complained of feeling uncomfortable visiting relatives' graves in the dense undergrowth. She added that on at least five occasions she had been molested by groups of strange visitors who followed her and stood silently behind her. "This may well be part of . . . strange ceremonies," she concluded, "and I feel that sooner or later someone will be murdered there."[10]

Much of this activity was clearly harmless, but some of it also involved vandalism and grave tampering, much of which could not immediately be easily detected in the dense undergrowth. Into this scene came two psychic investigators, Sean Manchester and David Farrant, both of whom were to make repeated visits to the cemetery to investigate claims of the paranormal. The two quickly agreed that the damage was tied to

Satanism, and their rivalry over how best to deal with it made good press and led to the publication of a great deal of private and official lore about what came to be called "the Highgate Vampire."

Farrant had witnessed no major damage during his early visits, but when he returned to Highgate Cemetery early in 1969, he immediately saw signs of increased vandalism. "Vaults had been broken open and coffins literally smashed apart," he later recalled. "One vault near the top gate ... was wide open and one could see the remains of a skeleton where it had been wrenched from a coffin" (1991:6). Another early visitor recalled seeing gangs of thirteen–fourteen-year-old youths smashing monuments and setting fire to coffins. Later he found corpses that had been pulled out of opened vaults and left on the path.[11] It seems likely that, as with the Clophill vandalism, most of the damage was caused by adolescent gangs expressing rebellion to adult norms or carrying out dares and hoaxes. Nevertheless, damage to markers and vaults had become a major problem for the local police.

The public sensation was sparked by a rash of mysterious sightings, which drew attention to the vandalism as signs of something more sinister than adolescent rebellion. Farrant records that members of his Society received two specific reports from people walking in or by Highgate Cemetery who had met a "tall dark spectre" that temporarily hypnotized or paralyzed the bystander. Intrigued by their stories and concerned about the escalating vandalism, Farrant decided to spend a night in Highgate, choosing December 21, 1969, the winter solstice. He arrived at the top gate shortly before midnight, but before he climbed the gate, he saw what at first seemed to be a tall person wandering in the cemetery. Then he realized that the shape was over seven feet tall, and he saw "two eyes meeting my gaze at the top of the shape ... [which] were not human, rather reflecting some 'alive presence.'" Recognizing that he was "under psychic attack," Farrant tore his eyes away, and the figure vanished (1991:7–8).

These encounters fit a widespread supernatural experience, in which a person feels paralyzed or overcome by fear in the presence of a sinister entity. David Hufford (1982) has studied such a phenomenon that occurs as a disruption of sleep: such "bedroom intruders" appear when a person is halfway between sleep and wakefulness, and a similar phenomenon may underlie the UFO abduction experiences that often occur at similar times. Peter Rojcewicz (1986, 1987) has made a similar suggestion about encounters with "men in black," frequently reported by UFO investigators. All three seem to be based in empirical experiences shared by many cultures. In any case, Farrant's circle of investigators was intrigued by the phenomenon and began to seek additional data. As one step, Farrant drafted a letter to the *Hampstead & Highgate Express* to ask for other unusual experiences in the cemetery. The letter was published on February 6, 1970, under the heading "Ghostly walks in Highgate":

> Some nights I walk home past the gates of Highgate Cemetery.
> On three occasions I have seen what appeared to be a ghostlike figure inside the gates at the top of Swains Lane. The first occasion was on Christmas Eve. I saw a grey figure for a few seconds before it disappeared into the darkness. The second sighting, a week later, was also brief.
> Last week the figure appeared, only a few yards inside the gates. This time it was there long enough for me to see it much more clearly, and now I can think of no other explanation than this apparition being supernatural.
> I have no knowledge in this field and I would be interested to hear if any other readers have seen anything of this nature.

The letter touched off a sequence of events that brought a spectrum of stories and beliefs into print and give us an unusually detailed look at Highgate's place in urban folk culture.

Friday, March 13: The First Vampire Hunt

A week later, on February 13, the paper printed four responses confirming that there was a local tradition about the Highgate "ghost": one said that the apparition had been appearing for several years, showing itself nightly for about a week at intervals of about a month. Another noted, "Many tales are told . . . about a tall man in a hat who walks across Swains Lane and just disappears through a wall into the cemetery." "Local superstition," this correspondent added, "also has it that the bells in the old disused chapel inside the cemetery toll mysteriously whenever he walks." A third writer added that he had seen the ghost cross a cemetery path while he and his "fiancé," were walking there: "I am glad somebody else has spotted it: I was convinced it was not my imagination." This series of responses provoked considerable attention in the area, as the February

20 issue included a front-page comment on the letters and an appeal for more material. The five letters published that week (as "Spooks!") included two more memorates concerning mysterious forms seen moving about behind headstones or inside the cemetery's gates. Also mentioned was a ghostly bicyclist said to chase women down Swains Lane; the next week, a patron of local pubs noted that this figure had collected several names in local lore: The Wild Eggman, Mad Arthur, the White Ghost.

On February 27, the paper ended a front-page feature by directing readers to "the latest letters," indicating that readers were still looking forward to contributions on the topic. Inside, six more correspondents related their mysterious encounters, expanding the range of paranormal experiences reported in the area. One told of seeing a figure wade into a viaduct pond, motioning for the witness to follow. Oddly, the figure made no ripples, but as it disappeared, it made a "terrible cry." Two others described observing a woman in white who went through a locked gate and hearing a mysterious voice calling "Hugo!" deep in the cemetery. Finally, David Farrant himself appeared to express thanks and relief that his ghostly experience had been corroborated by others.[12]

These letters provide an interesting cross section of traditions about the cemetery. Many of these have analogs in other complexes of adolescents' ritual behavior. The ghostly cyclist suggests widespread legends about the "headless horseman" who haunts by-roads in England, with his parallel, the "headless motorcycle man," who haunts roads in the American Midwest, chasing teens bold enough to invoke him (Rudinger 1976; Ellis 1982–1983; Scott and Norman 1986). The phantom "white lady" and the figure who appears to drown in the pond have cognates in many traditions attached to rivers, lakes, and holy wells in Great Britain (Bord and Bord 1986) and to teenage traditions about meeting "the white witch" on parking roads in the U.S. (Samuelson 1979; Bronner 1990:167–68). Even the odd detail of the voice calling "Hugo!" suggests the equally fey traditions of college students about ghosts who wander campuses at exam time, calling "Pedro!" or "Rinehart!" (Hankey 1944; Dorson 1959:259–60; Bronner 1990:38).

But the most impressive detail is the sheer amorphousness of the Highgate traditions; apart from the ghostly cyclist, hardly two informants gave the same story. Yet in all, young people seem compelled to walk by or even enter the cemetery in male/female couples or in unisex groups. The idea that "Something is supposed to happen" is coupled with the lack of a definite threat; in the same way, eerie-looking places in the

American Midwest generate legend-trips made up of beliefs and legends so variable that European-trained folklorists like Linda Dégh were initially puzzled. She and her students argued for a time over whether such bodies of lore were stable enough to constitute "a legend" (see Dégh 1969, Clements and Lightfoot 1972). But variability is the constant in the tradition: the trip, not the legend, is the thing. That is, any story, so long as it produces a willing suspension of disbelief, can be used to justify a trip to any site (Ellis 1982–1983). Samuel Menefee likewise has studied British ritual visit traditions, commenting both on the extreme divergence in story and belief and the "youthfulness" of most informants (Menefee 1985). Good ethnographic studies of adolescents' lore in Great Britain remain to be done; in the meantime, it seems likely that the Highgate legends fit into a much larger tradition of cemetery visits and dares.

At this point, Sean Manchester came forward with, as he put it, "a certain amount of reluctance as most forms of publicity put investigations of this kind to considerable risk" (1975:106). Nevertheless, he told a local reporter, he was concerned about the numbers of carcasses of foxes and other large animals that were showing up with "lacerations around the throat and . . . completely drained of blood." His conclusion: a vampire was at work. *The Hampstead & Highgate Express's* next weekly issue featured Manchester's warnings under the wry headline "Does a wampyr walk in Highgate?" Residents should know, Manchester said, that the spirit reported was far worse than expected: he speculated that it was a King Vampire from Wallachia that had been brought to England in a coffin by his supporters at the start of the eighteenth century. Installed at a fine house (Manchester later said a castle) in London's West End, this site became the traditional focus of England's vampire plagues.

In later times, the spot became the location of Highgate Cemetery. Manchester continued, ". . . now that there is so much desecration of graves by Satanism, I'm convinced that this has been happening in Highgate Cemetery in an attempt by a body of Satanists to resurrect the King Vampire. . . . We would like to exorcise the vampire by the traditional and approved manner—drive a stake through his heart with one blow just after dawn between Friday and Saturday, chop off his head with a gravedigger's shovel, and burn what remains. This is what the clergy did centuries ago. But we'd be breaking the law today" (*HHE* [27 February 1970]:1). Manchester, years later, recalled with some satisfaction that he had wakened the morning of this item's publication and found himself "famous."

To be sure, his theory was at first not taken seriously. One "expert" consulted was Christopher Neil-Smith of Hampstead, one of several Church of England ministers involved in exorcism and other forms of parapsychological research (see Neil-Smith 1974, Watkins 1984). Even he called Manchester's vampire theory "a novelistic embellishment." Another skeptic ironically applauded his "brave last-ditch battle on behalf of the romantics" but concluded, "alas, regretfully it is too late, by at least three generations."[13]

Even if few people thought the idea of a vampire believable, still, Manchester focused discussion of the happenings in Highgate Cemetery onto a definite narrative. The "vampire" being raised by occultists did provide an explanation both for the paranormal events seen and for the very obvious physical signs of intrusion and vandalism. However campy the idea of a "King Vampire from Wallachia" might have been, many were quite willing to believe that occultists were using the grounds for weird rituals. And Manchester's description of how to "lay" the vampire, likewise indebted to the numerous vampire movies then in production, also suggested to many people that a cemetery "hunt" might not be a bad move. At worst, a spooky good time could be had by all; at best, one might get to spy on a black magic ritual.

David Farrant, when contacted by reporters, preferred to say that if the being he had seen turned out to be a vampire, "I for one am prepared to pursue [it], taking whatever means might be necessary so that we can all rest."[14] The next weeks were dominated by an escalating rivalry between Farrant and Manchester. Both were contacted by the British network ITV for an interview, to be broadcast on Friday, March 13. Standing in front of the cemetery's gates, Farrant claimed to have received "threatening letters with black magic symbols on them" warning him to stay away from things he could not understand. Manchester repeated his description of how to destroy a vampire and warned Farrant indirectly, "He goes against our explicit wish for his own safety. We feel he does not possess sufficient knowledge to exorcise successfully something as powerful or evil as this Vampire, and may well fall victim as a result." The program also aired a series of ghost stories from a group of young neighborhood children, one of whom asserted, "I actually saw its face and it looked like it had been dead for a long time."

The television program aired at 6 P.M.; two hours later Swains Lane was packed with a crowd of would-be vampire-hunters who arrived by foot, car, van, and bus. By ten o'clock, a witness said, the onlookers resembled "a football crowd," with several squads of police unsuccessfully trying to control the mob that shook cemetery gates and scaled the walls. One participant who managed to attract the press's attention was a Mr. Alan Blood, a twenty-five-year-old history teacher who had come forty miles from Essex with several students in tow to participate, commenting, "I have taken an interest in the black arts since boyhood. . . ." About a hundred spectators successfully got into the old part of the cemetery before being routed out by police with searchlights. Manchester (who claimed to have been present) told a reporter, "It was like the end of a Frankenstein film when the monster was chased. People had weapons and looked as if they could have turned nasty if they had seen a tall lean person in dark clothing."

Many of the vampire-hunters in Highgate took the event as a lark. The Friday mob scene was followed by smaller incidents: on Saturday night, five "youths" were found inside the cemetery and ejected. "We were hoping to see an occult ceremony and got lost," one explained to police. But other Londoners treated the affair rather seriously: the *Evening News* stressed the cult connection in a story titled "Satan Riddle of Open Tomb." This cited Alan Blood as an authority, insisting that the "vampire . . . must be Satan-like in character." *The Hampstead & Highgate Express* likewise quoted Manchester at length on the "abominable desecration" he found: "It is too much to be merely the work of vandals. There are black magic signs and symbols, limbs and even entire bodies missing from graves. It all points to something very evil."[15]

Exorcisms and Nude Rites

A few months later the "vampire" was back in the news. Three adolescent girls visiting the cemetery on Friday, August 1, found the headless and charred remains of a woman's corpse lying outside a broken vault. Police took the incident seriously, noting that similar desecrations had occurred in Southwark in July. A spokesperson commented, "We are working on the theory that this may be connected with black magic. The body could well have been used for that reason."

The Hampstead & Highgate Express again quoted Manchester at length: "These same Satanists that desecrate Highgate Cemetery are disciples of 'The Evil One,' the vampire, and intend to spread the cult in the hope of corrupting the world." Stealing a human skull, Manchester warned, was a step toward resurrecting the King Vampire with the help of the powers of darkness and increasing the numbers of the cult with his aid. Though a cemetery employee differed, claiming he saw no signs of black magic, both police and caretakers promised intensified patrols in Highgate.[16]

Farrant was one of those caught up in these patrols: on August 17 he was arrested in St. Michael's Churchyard, adjacent to the upper end of the cemetery, and police found paraphernalia that they described as a crucifix and a sharp wooden stake. Authorities released a lengthy statement that they attributed to Farrant, explaining that he had gone to Highgate to watch for a vampire rising from its grave. "I would have entered the catacombs in my search," the statement continued, "—and upon finding the supernatural being I would have driven my stake through its heart and then run away."[17] Farrant later said that this statement had been fabricated by the police; in fact he had been there with other members of his Society to conduct a séance intended to establish a psychic link with the dark spectre he had seen. Farrant was reluctant to name the other members or give details of the séance (which involved using the "stake" with string attached to cast a magic circle for the ritual). So he gave an assumed name ("Alan Farrow") and chose not to deny the statement. Instead he allowed his solicitor to defend him on the grounds that hunting a vampire in itself was no crime and was akin to searching for the Loch Ness Monster.[18] And Farrant was exonerated: his case was dismissed on September 30 by the presiding judge. After the vindication, he promised to continue his effort to exorcise the "earthbound" spirit, conjured up by the "evil practices that have taken place at the cemetery among Black Magic followers."[19]

Simultaneously, his supporters had returned to Highgate Cemetery, standing on watch during the morning hours, hoping to spot and photograph the evil spirit, which he described as "not exactly a ghost, but something like a vampire that has taken on human form." Soon Farrant announced that he had found one body removed from a coffin and placed "in the middle of a black pentagon drawn on the floor of a vault." Remains of candles proved that the body had been the focus of a Black Mass. He hoped that the Society's efforts would help police catch the black magic circle "red-handed."[20] Shortly after, he took an *Evening News* reporter to Highgate for a midnight vigil on the night after a full moon in October 1970. There they surveyed the damage done: graves opened, skulls stolen, vaults defaced with strange scrawls. Farrant, the paper reported, claimed to be on watch at the cemetery "every night" for them and their evil master "who must be stalked." [21]

Within a week of Farrant's arrest, Manchester was at the Columbarium near where the headless corpse was found, burning incense, sprinkling "four cups of holy water from a Catholic Church," and reading an exorcism service in Greek, Latin, Hebrew, and English. This ceremony, however, was conducted outside the vaults in the middle of the afternoon at a time when visitors were few. He too asserted that a coven of devil-worshippers were using the cemetery and told reporters that his Society also held exorcisms in places where black magic meetings had been held. As for Farrant, Manchester said he "was lucky the police got to him. Had he met with the Satanists first, I feel we would not have heard more of him." [22]

By mid-October, BBC's *Twenty Four Hours* had become interested enough to bring a film crew to Highgate. The program included an interview with Manchester and a "documentary reconstruction" of his exorcism. The host began the segment, "We have a film report of a secret and Satanic ritual being practised in Britain in October 1970. *Twenty Four Hours* is building up a case history of the occult. We've heard of ghost hunters, psychic researchers, covens of witches dancing naked around bonfires in the middle of winter and even the odd black mass.... sometimes the fascination with the black arts leads its adherents to more sinister rituals." The program proceeded to show "evidence of a vampire cult in which diabolists worked to raise the undead to contaminate a society whose Christian values they despise." [23]

Later, Manchester revealed more details about his exorcism: he had followed Lusia, a London girl possessed by demonic spirits, to the vaults. Entering the crypt, he discovered an extra coffin with no nameplate, and opened it to find "a body which appeared neither dead nor alive." Manchester took up his stake and "placed the point between the seventh and eighth rib on the left. Grabbing my arm [one of my assistants] pleaded with me to desist saying that it would be sacrilege. If what lies before us is an undead, I replied, it would be an act of healing. Consternation grew among the group in the vault and the consensus of opinion was that the stake remained unsoiled until, at least, proper permission had been obtained from the correct quarter." So Manchester described how he was content to sprinkle salt, holy water, and garlic in the vault and read the exorcism while the sun dramatically came closer and closer to setting and "deep, voluminous booming sounds began vibrating through the tombs" (Manchester 1975:117–19; cf. Manchester 1991:82–90).

Indeed, Manchester's new fame as a vampire-hunter made him useful in the area. When a church in neighboring Islington was vandalized the following February and the reserved sacrament taken from the altar, the priest issued a warning, saying, "I immediately connected the incident with the body-snatching reported at Highgate Cemetery last year. I believe those concerned took the Blessed Sacrament to use in their devil-worship." Manchester immediately contacted the priest, offering to hold a special service to exorcise the evil from the desecrated objects. The ceremony included Bible readings, after which Manchester "uttered a number of incantations over the objects. Then he threw a handful of powder into a tiny flame burning in a small bowl and flames shot into the air." The local bishop, understandably upset that the priest had carried out the service without asking permission or checking Manchester's credentials, ordered an inquiry, the results of which were not publicized.[24]

Both Manchester and Farrant, from the start, seemed eager to carry legend making into ostension, and the stories they publicized encouraged ostensive activities on the part of other youngsters. Cemetery vandalism appears to increase as more public attention is given to it. The acts of desecration at Clophill and Highgate were real enough, but they needed no cult to explain why youths were drawn to the area. Clearly, increasing media attention was spreading the claims about Satanists to broader and broader audiences, many of whom were responding with concern, curiosity, or simple desire to perpetuate the sensation. Certainly other actual cases of "Black Masses" clearly derive from media warnings. One eighteen-year-old was arraigned in February 1971 after she and two friends stole a skull from a grave in a Walsall church. Daubing it with her own blood and red candle wax, she placed it on an inverted cross and placed it on an "altar" inscribed "Long live Manson. Kill the Pigs."[25]

Manchester, like many vampire "practitioners," chose ostensive behavior that looked more like harmless analogs to movie plots than illegal trespasses of this sort. By contrast, Farrant's activities continued to focus on late-night watches in the cemetery, where he competed with less savory visitors and a special police "ghost squad" formed to combat the continuing vandalism. Eric Maple, the folklorist who had evaluated the Clophill vandalism, also visited the cemetery in 1971 and wrote a detailed account for *Man, Myth, and Magic*, an encyclopedic popular work on pagan religion and the supernatural. In it, he noted that Farrant's visits were now imitated by "groups of youths . . . searching frantically for clues among the graves." The headless corpse, however, was almost certainly used for a "sacrificial rite" of necromancy, and he also felt that increasing numbers of graffiti were using "voodoo inscriptions." One in particular, a dot in a circle inside an acute angle, suggested to him homage to "Aida Wegg," a voodoo goddess (1971:2844+). Later, Maple told local reporters he believed that "more sinister happenings have occurred in the cemetery after bodies have been tampered with by black magic covens."[26]

Meanwhile, the police vigils were beginning to have some results. Two youths were caught on July 24 with a sharpened stake and a rucksack with sandwiches and coffee. Although the prosecutor demanded that the two be sent for a formal trial at the Old Bailey, the judge dismissed the case after hearing from the father of one of the youths, who said he was quite aware of his son's activities. In fact he had been invited along: "We often go on expeditions. He has a sense of atmosphere and I have always encouraged it." Manchester, responding to the event, warned "freelance vampire-hunters" to stay away from the cemetery as this activity impeded "serious research" carried out by him and his supporters. He also noted that such events "strained" relationships between the police and psychic researchers like himself.[27]

Indeed, police were less pleased to find Farrant and his girlfriend, Martine de Sacy, inside Highgate Cemetery that same night. At first suspecting the two possessed marijuana, detectives took the two in for questioning, then released them with a warning when the suspected pot turned out to be chamomile used in an exorcism carried out by Farrant's Society. The group, Farrant explained to reporters, had found evidence that black witches had broken into a mausoleum and painted a pentagram on the floor, decorating it with black magic symbols representing Jupiter, Mars, and the Moon. A bust of the deceased had been placed at the head of the pentagram, and burnt-out candles suggested that a ritual had been performed, perhaps to summon the dead man's body. "There was no doubt it was not the work of amateurs," Farrant concluded, "—in fact I know who was responsible for the desecration."

He and de Sacy explained that eight of the Society members had entered the cemetery after midnight with a Bible, a crucifix, holy water, and magical herbs. Entering the already-opened mausoleum, they joined hands, and the girls removed their clothes "as symbols of purity." After reading from the Bible and "spells taken from ancient books," the group felt the icy cold atmosphere of the crypt warm up, as a sign that the evil had been dispersed, and they prepared to leave. But Farrant remained to take a few documentary photographs, intending to show them to police and keep as a record of the exorcism. One showed de Sacy, still naked, at the vault: "It must have been the flash which gave us away," she commented.[28] This picture, which later became known as the "Nude Rites" photograph, later resurfaced to cause Farrant additional problems.

After this, the Highgate affair disappeared from public comment for some time, but police had to be called on Halloween night to control a mob that formed outside the cemetery at midnight, an event that was to become a yearly tradition (Farrant 1992). For popular writers, secret covens remained the most plausible—and interesting—part of the new tradition. When Peter Underwood included Highgate Cemetery in his 1973 book *Haunted London*, he gave prominent mention to the headless corpse, commenting, "almost certainly some kind of sacrificial rite had taken place." He also noted the numbers of intruders who had opened coffins in vaults and left mysterious symbols daubed on the walls (1973:122–23). Somewhat later, Jack Hallam's *Ghosts of London* also alluded to the incident, repeating Alan Blood's claim of "undead Satan-like beings appearing in the cemetery" (1975:148).

In the meantime, journalists continued to air rumors and beliefs about black magic cults. A *Daily Mirror* feature solemnly estimated that there were some 40,000 practicing witches in Great Britain. Of these, the *Mirror* warned, "10,000 are 'black' witches who worship evil." The feature that followed, however, was long on rumor and short on details about these thousands of evil-worshippers. Ray Bogart, who claimed leadership of a rather tame Manchester branch of "Satanic Templars," described his coven's emphasis on "good" Satan-worship, aimed at magical healing and banishing of unwelcome relatives. He admitted that his group did practice blood sacrifice (chickens and pigeons only), but not often, as it "upsets everyone in the coven." There were "bogus" occult groups in the Liverpool area, however: he heard about one in which members "started getting in prostitutes dressed in rubber gear and there was wife swapping, too. It gave Satanism a bad name."[29]

Dennis Wheatley was characteristically quick to exploit this popular interest with a glossy coffee-table anthology, *The Devil and All His Works* (1971). This cobbled together information and misinformation on a whole range of allegedly satanic topics and combined it with images drawn largely from allegedly diabolical Third World religions. When the

American publishing consortium American Heritage picked up the rights to this work, it became Wheatley's only work to be widely distributed in the United States. In Britain, the book's success inspired folklorist Eric Maple's equally glossy *Witchcraft: The Story of Man's Search for Supernatural Power* (1973). While the text of this work arguably contains more reliable information on rural magic and witch beliefs, its graphics appealed to a more sensational *Daily Mirror* audience. A closing section on Wicca prominently featured Alex Sanders, his nude and shapely wife, and an acolyte wearing a shaggy goat's head prominently decorated with a pentagram.

Hammer Studios was also quick to pick up on the popular interest in black magic. A series of films nominally updated the horror theme of the vampire Dracula (usually played by the veteran character actor Christopher Lee), but in fact these movies were vehicles for a wide range of popular and folk beliefs about Satanism. *The Satanic Rites of Dracula* (1972), for example, is a pointedly contemporary film about a group of influential businessmen who (like the Illuminati) are secretly planning to destroy civilization. Adapting age-old traditions linking witches and Jews to spreading diseases, the satanic businessmen are genetically engineering a new breed of plague germ which they intend to release into the world to decimate humanity (see Waller 1986:123–34; Everman 1993:188–89).

More significantly, *Dracula, A.D. 1972* (1972) picked up on the current use of satanic themes to express adolescent rebellion. It opens with a scene in which a posh party is trashed by a group of gang members as a band plays rock and roll in the background. The gang references apparently were meant to suggest the "mods and rockers," while the band alludes to the frequently occult themes being introduced by groups like the Rolling Stones and Black Sabbath, with its flamboyant lead singer Ozzy Osbourne. The plot continues as a young girl, intrigued by references to "Black Masses" in her father's library, falls into the power of an occult-oriented gang. Their activities climax when they desecrate a deserted London church to hold a Black Mass and so raise a satanic vampire (Christopher Lee again), who pursues them to their deaths.

The plot thus picks up on an idea that had been a right-wing cliché at least since the British Fascist "Lady Queenborough" had aired her concern in 1933 that young people were being drawn into the vortices of "vice rings and secret societies." Anti-Illuminati crusaders took it for granted that the popular media was dominated by subversives attempting to undermine family ties. William Guy Carr, for instance, argued that one of the Illuminati's goals was to foster adolescent rebellion against parents as a first stage into introducing them to petty crime "and then lead them deeper into the jungle of the Communist organized underworld." "Crime and Sex Comics" and movies containing explicit violence and pornography, in Carr's view, demoralize youth "so they can be recruited into revolutionary organizations" (1958:126–27).

Farrant followed this construction of Satanism in two summaries of his Highgate activities in local papers. For the *Camden Journal* (1972a) he recounted several personal experiences with tall, dark spectres that his Society had collected, and expressed concern that Satan worship and grave violation were on the increase. He and Society members had themselves observed "Satanic Masses" being conducted in the cemetery, and he added, "The people concerned are not youngsters 'out for kicks,' but genuine Satanists who take part in bizarre rites, and include sexual practices as part of their worship. It would be wrong to mistake their rites for harmless orgies. They are, on the contrary, using this tremendous sexual power—generated by many people—to direct and help them in the practice of their magic. Although the motive is not clear, their main aim seems to be invoking certain spirits to establish contact with the devil." In a similar piece published in the *Islington Gazette* (1972b), Farrant said that Highgate "has become a haven for the black magician who requires ancient relics for use in his rituals." Some of the damage, he conceded, was the work of "sheer vandalism," but other acts showed "planned and precise method." Farrant emphasized the "sexual activity ... of a highly organized form" that comprised the Black Mass and concluded on a moralistic note, ". . . the young, with their tendency to think they are invulnerable, . . . are the most prone to the evil influences of Satanism. . . . many young people, attracted by sexual promise or a daredevil instinct, are quite unaware of the hidden dangers. Consequently they dabble on the surface and are soon dragged down to become hopelessly entangled in a web of corruption from which there is virtually no escape. Yet surprisingly enough, the majority of the general public still live in complete ignorance of this dangerous religion." Farrant's campaign against the "vampire" and his satanic followers was less cautious than Manchester's, and as he became more involved in the Highgate lore, his exploits tended more and more to imitate the "necromancers" he claimed he was observing and exorcising. If one could truly say that the British general public was still "ignorant" of the dangers of Satanism in 1972, Farrant's next adventures educated them.

Farrant at The Old Bailey: A Police Exorcism

Early in 1973, flyers began to appear in North London underground stations advertising a "magicians' duel" between Manchester and Farrant. Farrant later recalled that his rival kept telling reporters he was challenging him to a "magical duel." At first Farrant disregarded these statements as publicity stunts, but when Manchester persisted, he finally agreed, providing that the "duel" would be privately witnessed, with only Manchester's and Farrant's seconds present. The affair was set for Friday, April 13, 1973 on top of Parliament Hill in Hampstead. Shortly before the event, a tabloid press article muddied the water by claiming that both Manchester and Farrant intended to slaughter a cat in front of an assembly of naked witches. The RSPCA naturally objected and said it would "take strenuous action to stop this medieval practice." The paper printed this as Farrant's explanation, "I have been approached by the police and have been advised not to go ahead with the duel, but I can't back down now. The cat, probably a stray, will be anaesthetised before it is slaughtered. When I agreed to take part in this duel I didn't realise there would be so many difficulties. At these ceremonies our members are usually naked because the ritual has to be done authentically. I am a white witch and I do not use evil powers."[30]

Actually, according to Farrant, the whole "cat sacrifice" story was based on media rumors and misquotations. "Well, the posters went up," he recalled in 1992, "but the thing is . . . the posters were worded—'blood sacrifice'—'naked virgins'—and the other thing was, he called me 'black magic practitioner David Farrant.' Of course he was referred to as a big 'white magician.'" In fact, no animal sacrifice had ever been planned by either party, and in any case the "magician's duel" turned out to be a non-event. Fearing that he would be "lynched" if he showed up, Farrant chose to stay away, and Manchester was content to perform an exorcism for the media to banish the powers of Farrant's magic.

In August 1973, Highgate Cemetery was closed to all but relatives of the buried, while caretakers evaluated the increasing damage caused by intruders. But the anesthetized cat sacrifice story refused to go away. Keepers at Highgate Woods, a nearby park, discovered an elaborate occult symbol painted on the pavement, along with three burned candles, a blood-stained knife and stockings, and a pool of blood. The *Hornsey Journal* at once laid the event to a witchcraft coven led by David Farrant, and a lead article described the alleged ritual in detail. The victim, the paper claimed, was a stray cat, anesthetized and sacrificed to celebrate "the festival of the Black Moon." The rite had been conducted with the help of a "naked High Priestess," and after each member of the coven had been smeared in the cat's fresh blood, "an orgy followed."[31] Local coverage led to a sensational piece in the tabloid *News of the World*, headed "UNMASKED—this evil high priest of witchcraft." Both of these articles contained lengthy statements attributed to Farrant justifying the ritual. To the *Hornsey Journal*, Farrant supposedly explained, "Hundreds of years ago a naked virgin would have been sacrificed but obviously we couldn't do this now so we had to have an animal for the important ritual. . . . We rarely sacrifice animals at rituals but this sacrifice was essential to our belief as we derive power from blood." And *News of the World* quoted the "evil high priest" as saying, "I do not see animal sacrifice as drastic as people have made it out to be. Thousands of cats are used annually for medical research. The very livestock we eat have their throats cut. And, at least, I anaesthetised the cat before I had to kill it." This article also contained a lurid description of the orgy by Martine de Sacy, now estranged from Farrant:

> On the stroke of midnight as the group chanted in a circle, David Farrant sacrificed a cat. It was drugged and he held it up and severed the head with a dagger. Blood spurted and he passed the body round the circle until every person was smeared. Then they each stepped forward to have an arm cut. The chanting began again and one man stepped forward and chose a partner. They made love in the middle of the circle. Then others took partners. Some made love to more than one. . . . Dozens of men made love to me in rituals, when you are so turned on you don't even know who your partner is and it seems so exciting and natural—at the same time. . . . I was afraid what the group might ask me to do. You are bound by oaths and supposed to obey even if they ask you to lie, steal or even kill. (September 23, 1973)

Farrant, who successfully sued *News of the World* for libel in 1980, explained that the truth was considerably more mundane. Long John Baldry, a rock musician of some eminence,[32] had a cat that failed to come home one day. Baldry publicly blamed Farrant of having abducted it for sacrifice. In the heat of the moment, Farrant's explanations to reporters and to call-in radio programs were misinterpreted and garbled into print. But the "sacrificed" cat's body was nowhere to be found, the Highgate Woods ritual, if it was one, never was linked to Farrant, and Baldry's own cat wandered home unscathed a few weeks later. Police never pressed charges in the matter and no other papers ever documented the alleged sacrifice; even Manchester says that his rival only "claimed responsibility for blood sacrifices" (1991:111). It seems clear that the affair was a media legend drawn from local rumor and Wheatleyesque models.

But Farrant, upset with how he had been portrayed in the press, pressed his case. When an RSPCA inspector and a doctor's wife called for his prosecution for cruelty to animals, Farrant sent both of them black boxes containing voodoo dolls with pins stuck in their heads, accompanied with a rhyming threat:

> Once this gift has passed your hand
> Your power to us you'll understand
> And be it understood by you
> We thus control all that you do
> LEAVE US ALONE—BEFORE WE MAKE YOU DO SO.

Each note bore a "voodoo seal" and Farrant's signature in red ink. A few days later, a TV crew from BBC's *Nationwide* news series was at the scene of the ritual, interviewing the two "voodoo victims" and Farrant, who explained that he intended no supernatural harm but only to turn their malice against themselves. Two miniature coffins also went to Long John Baldry, who was worried enough to ask Graham Bond, of the heavy metal rock group Cream, to neutralize the "spell." Bond, who had a keen interest in magic, did perform a protective ritual at Baldry's house, but the following year he fell in front of an underground train under odd circumstances, which Baldry took to be a result of Farrant's "curse."[33]

While the media were increasingly billing him as a black magician, Farrant was not deterred from continuing his occult investigations. By December he had agreed to help John Pope, a Barnet laborer who had fallen afoul of the law and been roughly handled during questioning. Farrant agreed to send out two more dolls to the detectives in charge to prevent them from doing Pope any more physical harm and warning them, "Your evil will be returned to you before another month is through."[34] Meantime, Pope was included in some of the Society's newer projects. On December 7, the *Hornsey Journal* had run an article describing a dilapidated house in Crouch End, the focus of many schoolchildren's spooky tales as "The House of Dracula." A reporter going to investigate found evidence of witchcraft ceremonies and a Star of David inscribed on the floor of one room (cf. Manchester 1985:91–92, 1991:127). On December 13, police found both Farrant and Pope, naked, inside the house beside a plate of glowing embers. Charged with arson, the two were tried on March 11. Farrant explained that he and other Society members were conducting a Wiccan ceremony to try to contact the spirit haunting the house, and they needed the elements of fire as well as air, water, and earth. Although the judge warned that the two were "clearly asking for trouble," again the jury exonerated Farrant.[35]

But local police had found the continuing vandalism in Highgate too much to endure and were convinced that Farrant was their scapegoat. On January 12, a Swains Lane resident woke to find what he first thought was a log of wood propped up in his car. Closer investigation proved it to be the remains of an embalmed, headless corpse. Police visited Farrant, the usual suspect, who admitted holding monthly meetings with his Society in Highgate Cemetery "if the weather was fine." A search uncovered a mass of photographs showing desecrated vaults, "necromantic" symbols on tombs—and the flash photo of de Sacy standing nude outside the vault. With this evidence in hand, authorities prepared charges against Farrant ranging from body snatching to threatening a witness to a criminal trial.

Farrant went to trial at London's Old Bailey on June 10.[36] Choosing to conduct his own defense, he described himself as a persecuted Wiccan who had never carried out any necromantic ceremonies. He conceded that he and his followers had entered the cemetery many times, but he insisted that all the physical damage and body snatching was caused by satanic cults. Secrecy was needed because whenever one of their meetings was publicized, "hundreds of people turned up . . . and this caused a lot of work for the police." He denied that his investigations had anything to do with vampires and concluded, "our beliefs have nothing to do with dead bodies. Our beliefs are pure. We do not desecrate coffins. That is done by satanic cults. When people don't understand, they fear, and automatically condemn."

His credibility was damaged by the photographs, which he tried to explain as documentary evidence intended for police and newspapers. De Sacy could not be found to give testimony about the 1971 incident, and the judge laid particular stress on the nude photograph of her. "It is a full frontal nude," the judge told the jury, "showing everything she has got, with her eyes raised toward the heavens." And the prosecution even produced Francis King, author of a popular history of ritual magic in Great Britain (1970), to interpret graffiti in the photographs. One pattern shown, King told the jury, was obviously "part of a necromantic ceremony," the object being "to bring life temporarily back to a dead body so that it could tell the future, or find hidden treasure . . . or to send the body on an evil mission."

The verdicts were a partial victory: Farrant was acquitted of the most serious charges. He received a surprise boost when a self-confessed robber came forward and admitted the body-snatching. He and five others (including three girls) had gone into Highgate Cemetery that night and found the body lying beside a smashed coffin. After leaving the body in the car "for a laugh," he took the head home and kept it on his mantelpiece as a trophy of his visit until it "began to smell a bit." The man also recalled seeing a friend pull another corpse from an opened coffin and dance with it. He and his friends had no interest in necromancy, the thief testified: "They were just playing the fool."

In the end, however, Farrant was found guilty of damaging memorials at Highgate and threatening detectives with the voodoo dolls, along with other minor offenses. A physician asked to evaluate Farrant's mental health judged him sane but in need of "guidance because there was a possibility of his beliefs taking him into a condition of mental disorder." After a tour of the vandalized cemetery, the judge sent Farrant to prison for four years and eight months, a sentence that even his enemies characterized as unnecessarily harsh. Farrant appealed the charge of grave tampering, eventually producing de Sacy and other witnesses to confirm that the vaults he visited were already damaged, but the appeal resulted only in a modest reduction of his fine. "When one looks at the photographs in the case," the appeal judges said, "it is quite clear that a gross indignity was shown by the conduct of the appellant being in this private place where the remains of the dead lie, supposedly in peace, and there conducting ceremonies, in which he no doubt believed, together with a girl who was almost nude. This Court has difficulty in imagining any greater indignity being done to the remains of the dead short of actually scattering the remains about."[37] And the Highgate adventures did not end with Farrant's conviction. On the following Halloween, rumors circulated that John Pope, Farrant's last client, was going to sacrifice a cockerel at Highgate and "spread its blood on naked coven members." Adolescents arrived from all over the London area:

> A group of rockers lounged on their "beat-up" Zephyr Six, parked outside the main gates with car radio blaring, and told the Journal: "We've come down from Bracknell, but it's a bit dead like, and we're going now. . . ."
> One blonde girl dressed in black with a crucifix round her neck ("I borrowed it from my Granny"), had come from Notting Hill Gate with friends "to see what it was all about." [38]

Police were ready for the "revelers," however, and when an advance party trying to scale the gates was ejected, the teens remained on the street side, annoying local residents.

Nor was this the last adolescent trip to Highgate: in September 1978, the Wessex Association for the Study of Unexplained Phenomena announced that it would hold a dusk vigil outside a tomb suspected to hold a vampire: "What happens then is anybody's guess." Soon after, a group of adolescents were arrested inside the cemetery and fined for "riotous and indecent behavior." Police learned that they had read the earlier article "and after a few drinks decided to join the hunt." The police officers found them banging on tombstones with stakes and shouting, "Come out vampire, we are coming to get you."[39] On subsequent Halloweens, teens have continued to reenact the original hunt to the present day (Farrant 1992).

Peter Castle, author of the "real witch" article that sparked the Clophill cemetery rumor panic, made a perceptive comment on such ostensive practices. In "The Shadow and the Mask," a feature article published on March 29, 1963, in the *Bedfordshire Time & Standard*, he recalled that earlier persons who practiced so-called black magic did so to parody Catholicism and other "standing customs of the day." Yet, Castle wondered, "Why do people today indulge in a Black Magic ceremony, when there is no enforced religion to rebel against?" Paraphrasing Jung, he answered that all people have a dual side, a shadow to hide and a mask to show society. In mature people, the two are integrated, but when the artificiality of modern existence becomes too much for some people, "The mask is temporarily thrown down and the primitive personality stalks abroad."

This is particularly true when groups act together, Castle continued, for when they become aroused by the spirit of their actions, they "suddenly become controlled by the emotion they have conjured ... as if it had taken them over with a personality of its own." Unintentionally, Castle anticipates Ikuya Sato's analysis of gang behavior, arguing that people normal enough in everyday life can readily commit criminal acts when they take part in deviant play, which can easily be corrupted in the excitement of the moment. Castle concludes:

> ... when people gather together for the sake of mischief, the corporate body can release aspects of the mind which are terrifying and often bestial. Some of the worst cases of hooliganism or mass hysteria can be explained in this way.
>
> So, one cannot help feeling with regard to Black Masses and similar rituals, that if the participants are wholly evil (a rarity indeed!) then they are to be pitied.
>
> But, if they are just out for "kicks," mischief, and rebellion against convention, then they should stop playing with fire, before they get their fingers nastily burned.

Conclusions

The story of the Highgate Vampire Hunt has a happy ending of sorts: after Farrant's trial gave added attention to the state of the cemetery, an organization was founded to put the site in better shape. The Friends of Highgate Cemetery, after fifteen years of fund-raising and restoration work, were able in 1990 to reopen the Victorian monuments to the public. Some Londoners grumbled over new restrictions: a fee is now charged, and visitors must enter as part of guided tours. But the coffins are back in the vaults, no more persons, living or dead, have lost their heads, and the jungle has been beaten back.

Farrant and Manchester remain active in the British occult scene. Released on parole after two years in prison, Farrant did win a number of vindications. A 1980 libel suit against *News of the World* was successful.[40] And in 1985, the European Commission of Human Rights, while failing to consider his complaints about the trial, did rule that Farrant's rights had been infringed because letters from prison had been intercepted and because he had not been able to practice Wicca in jail.[41] As head of the reorganized British Psychic and Occult Society, he continues to receive and investigate accounts of supernatural phenomena. Sean

Manchester has continued to serve as head of vampire-oriented societies, most recently the International Society for the Advancement of Irrefutable Vampirological and Lycanthropic Research.[42] Claiming ordination as a bishop of the Old Catholic Church, he has also increasingly devoted his efforts to organizing the Apostolic Church of the Holy Grail (Manchester 1991:14–15, 187–88).

A similar, more influential rumor panic occurred again in Great Britain in 1989, when a Central Television special program on devil worship was broadcast on *The Cook Report*.[43] Manchester claimed to have provided research for this program, and the show's co-producer, Tim Tate (see Sandell 1992), provided a blurb for Manchester's own book on the dangers of Satanism (Manchester 1991:42). On October 3, 1990, a presentation on Great Britain's Channel 4 (ITV) promised viewers solid evidence of Satanism "for the first time on British television." The show was based on stories elicited from children, describing bizarre ceremonies that included cooking babies in microwave ovens, killing sheep and drinking their blood, and sexual abuse conducted in tunnels beneath cemeteries. The feature's climax was a "torchlight visit" to The Rock Cemetery, a dilapidated graveyard in Nottingham, where viewers were taken into alcoves and tunnels to see half-burned candles, graffiti, and "something that looks like a little altar."

The same year, more than twenty children in a lower-class housing project near Manchester were taken into protective custody by authorities convinced that their parents were devil-worshippers. Another group of children in South Ayrshire, Scotland, were removed from their parents' custody and not returned until 1995. In March 1991, several children in the Orkney Islands were taken from families by social workers over fears of ritual abuse. Meanwhile, the press and Channel 4 traded bitter blows over whether televised specials on Satanism were fact or sensation. The child abuses in Nottingham were genuine enough, but local police found the link to Satanism tenuous. An official report gave a scathing account of the way social workers had solicited stories of ritual abuse from children. The cemetery, authorities added, was located in a "red-light district" of Nottingham and was used by many younger people as a secluded spot for sex, drinking, and drug use, but not— to police knowledge—for underground rituals.

The other incidents proved even less substantial, leading to a series of scandals over coaching of child witnesses and shoddy investigation. In the wake of these, the British Health Secretary ordered an investigation of the ritual abuse claims. The official report of this study, written by anthropologist Jean S. La Fontaine (1994), concluded that ritual abuse "was not happening and is not happening." American therapists, who had conducted a seminar for child care specialists in Reading in September 1989,[44] received much of the blame. But the Satanism Scare was hardly an American invention. Rumor panics such as the Highgate Cemetery vampire hunt brought into the public eye claims that underground cults were carrying out sinister rituals in underground cemetery vaults. Information such as this had disseminated easily into police and social work conduits as much as two decades before the ritual abuse scares. And British themes were exported to the United States, where similar panics broke out in the years following the Highgate affair.

9

The Great Plains Cattle Mutilation Panic

Satanism Becomes News

> I mean, this mutilation phenomenon is an *orphan* —
> *nobody* will take it. Even the craziest researchers that
> don't care about their reputations ... will not *touch* it.
> I mean they just can *not* get a handle on it
> —David Perkins, *Altered Steaks*

The Cattle Mutilation Panic began in the American Great Plains in the early 1970s, when ranchers reported strange deaths among their cattle. The animals appeared to have been killed, then drained of their blood; in many cases, sex organs, udders, eyes, or tongues seemed to have been cut off with scalpels. Most veterinarians agreed that the cattle had died natural deaths, then been attacked by common predators like coyotes and vultures. But many ranchers and private investigators preferred to believe that hippie witchcraft cults killed the cattle as part of weird religious rites, drinking the blood and eating and using the organs during devil-worship ceremonies.

The panic from time to time referenced stories similar to those described in the Highgate Cemetery affair: weird rites in cemeteries and grave desecrations along with dark rumors of bizarre sexual acts. However, in the United States, no obvious scapegoat like David Farrant emerged in the press: in fact, no one was ever publicly apprehended for the mutilations. As the panic developed, therefore, the phenomenon quickly developed into political scenarios inspired by the Illuminati mythology. That is, the mutilators were assumed to be undetectable because they were wealthy and had high connections in police, military, and governmental circles. One possibility was that the mutilators were similar to Mike Warnke's hippie families, organized by wealthy occultists out of adolescent drifters. As this possibility proved less likely, two others replaced it. One, initially developed among left-wing groups in response to the Satanism claim, held that the U.S. government itself was killing the cattle as part of a secret project. A second popular theory linked the animal deaths to aliens from outer space, asserting that the cattle were being killed as part of a complex series of biological experiments. And, as the affair moved away from broad-based rumor panics into specialized media-enhanced conduits, these three possibilities tended to merge into a single subversion myth presenting the U.S. government as corrupt and diabolical in nature.

This chapter will give a brief overview of the situation as it periodically emerged in the popular mass media over the decade from 1973 to 1982. Then each of the three rival scenarios will be examined individually to see where and how it developed. In each case, we see that the mutilation panic served to introduce important conspiracy themes to a broader public. Particularly, we learn how satanic cult mythologies began to be networked and disseminated broadly among local and state law enforcement agencies and right-wing antiestablishment groups. By the end of the period, the seeds of further panics and confrontations had been sown throughout the American rural landscape.

The Cattle Mutilation Panic: An Overview

The typical mutilation incident, as it developed in the 1970s, involved finding a bull or cow dead without any previous sign of illness. The carcass, moreover, was not like that of a normal livestock death: certain body parts were missing, usually the sexual organs (male or female), one or both eyes or ears, or the tongue. In some more elaborate cases, the head might be stripped of flesh and internal organs like the heart cut out and removed. More oddly, no blood was found at the site, and the animal's body appeared to have been drained of its blood. Normally, cattle-owners might assume that rustlers had killed the animal for its beef, or that it had been partially dismembered by natural predators like birds of prey or coyotes. But in the "classic" mutilation no tracks were visible anywhere around the carcass. In fact, ranchers often reported that predators visibly avoided touching the dead animal. And the mutilations seemed to show not only human ingenuity but also extraordinary skill. Often, the incisions were described as "surgically precise." Moreover, the parts apparently taken—the blood, penises, eyes, ears, and so on—had no commercial or food value, so the motive of the "mutilators" could not have been profit.

The underlying phenomenon is probably universal among cultures with domesticated animals. The incidents shade into legend, however, as soon as observers begin to tailor facts to link what they observed to some basic theory of who or what was responsible. Discussion of the mutilations regularly connected one mystery to other puzzling phenomena seen in the area. Such links received wide publicity and to some extent led ranchers and police investigating unusual cattle deaths to look for the same details in new cases. The perceived pattern that emerged from this combination of facts and implied scenarios helped produce the major competing contemporary mythologies that grew up around the cattle deaths. Like the "vampire" scenarios behind the Highgate Cemetery affair, these mythologies spread on the crest of a series of panics and media reports. Newspaper features, radio talk shows, and television spots all helped lend warrant to the claims being made about the mutilations and their significance.

In the United States, small-scale scares based on animal mutilations probably occurred in many different places but did not come to national attention. In September 1966, for instance, a woman from the Gallipolis, Ohio, area complained to the FBI after a number of her cows were killed: "The cow carcasses had been expertly butchered in part and the bodies were bloodless." The same year some thirty cattle were found dead in the Scranton, Pennsylvania, area, and the following year, a veterinarian was left puzzled by cows found dead near Allentown: "Parts of their hides had been removed and all of their blood and blood marrow was inexplicably missing" (Spencer 1976:102–4). A group of farmers attempted to organize and try to halt the incidents, but they received no official support, and the effort led to nothing (*Stigmata* 19 [Fourth Quarter, 1984]:110).

The nationwide wave of mutilation reports began in 1973, when rashes of animal deaths began to show up in newspapers. In parts of Pennsylvania, something killed a number of domestic pets and livestock including chickens and sheep; some had been brutally dismembered, while others had had their throats "expertly" slit (Clark 1974:89). In November, farmers in rural counties of Minnesota and Kansas found some of their cows dead with no sign of a fatal wound; yet their genitals, udders, or sometimes an eye, ear, or tongue had been cut off with no sign of blood or bleeding. A veterinarian in Canby, Minnesota, suggested that the culprit had paralyzed the cattle with a tranquilizer gun, immediately drained out their blood, and then returned about six hours later to cut off parts of the bodies. But why?

Barroom gossip in the nearby town of Ivanhoe quickly concluded that a "cult of devil-worshippers" was responsible. A local veterinarian had told authorities that the animals had died of natural causes and that "varmints" such as foxes had subsequently gathered to feed on the soft parts of the carcasses. Ranchers who had lost cattle scoffed: "Yeah, it was a varmint all right," one said, "a two-legged varmint." Authorities were concealing the truth, many suspected, because they were afraid to investigate further. Several said, "Who knows? Maybe it'll be a human being next time." Rumor went so far as to implicate a high school senior girl whose family had come to the rural area from New York City. A non-Catholic in a heavily Catholic region, she had been seen reading a book that was reputed to be occult in nature. Stories soon circulated that she was "the head of a coven of bloodthirsty, devil-worshiping teen-agers who were collecting cow parts for use in orgiastic rites." While the girl proved to be the victim of a slander campaign, residents continued to fear that a teenage blood cult was at work (Clark 1974).

In Kansas, a university likewise concluded that cattle had died naturally, but local police were not so sure: Deputy Sheriff Gary Dir said: "I've spent all of my life except the last eight months on a farm and I know when a critter's been cut." He confirmed the deaths as suspicious and suggested that the animals had been drugged with an untraceable tranquilizer and then drained of their blood. In other places, autopsies turned up traces of chemicals like nicotine sulfate, suggesting that the animals had been drugged before the mutilation. In some cases, investigators claimed to have seen puncture marks in the animal's jugular vein, suggesting that its blood had been sucked or pumped out. One theory that spread among rural law agents was that witches or hippies tranquilized cattle with PCP, a common veterinarian drug, but also a hallucinogen known as "angel dust" by drug users. The blood was then drained and drunk by the witches, "which caused them to trip out" (Donovan and Wolverton 1976:33–37).

Noting that most of the animals had been Black Anguses, ranchers speculated that members of an unknown religious cult had sacrificed them in much the same way that black cats and cockerels had been killed in Great Britain. One such cow was owned by Kansas State Senator Ross Doyen. An autopsy conducted at Kansas State University concluded that the animal had died of natural causes and then been mauled by a coyote, but Doyen remained convinced that a cult was responsible. "If that ear hadn't appeared cut, I wouldn't have thought anything about it. Whoever's cutting on them always cuts an ear off, that's their trademark." Authorities were baffled by the events. No suspects were apprehended, although it was observed that most mutilations took place within a few miles of U.S. Highway 81, a major north-south thoroughfare. Eventually the Kansas office of the FBI became involved, and the Kansas Farm Bureau offered a five-hundred-dollar reward for information, but the incidents remained mysterious (Randolph 1975:17; Albers 1979:6–7).

The Doyen cattle investigation might have died out, as had earlier investigations, except that it was made the subject of a major article in the *Kansas City Times* on December 22, 1973. The piece reported that many slaughtered cows "bore knife marks . . . including the apparent butchering of the sex organs from both bulls and heifers," and implied that "satanic cultists" were responsible (Randolph 1975:17). Although an official inquiry suggested that coyotes were responsible, this article laid the foundation for an even more extensive panic the following year. After cattle deaths were reported in Custer County, Nebraska, a rumor panic spread across the entire state in August 1974, reaching a peak in mid-September (Albers 1979:12–13; Stewart 1977:56–57). As ranchers began forming CB-radio-coordinated vigilante groups that patrolled pastures nightly with guns at hand, a statewide investigation was ordered (Davidson 1975:62). The official report again blamed natural predators, but the satanic cult theory again proved more popular out on the plains.

The belief was given additional credibility when folklorist Richard Thill told a reporter, "It could be someone setting up a fertility cult of some kind . . . or it could be someone putting you on. If they [sic] are putting you on, they are pretty sick." This quote was reproduced in the September 30 issue of *Newsweek*, the first to bring the events to nationwide attention. On November 25, Thill expanded his remarks for the tabloid *Midnight*. "The mutilations may have a ritualistic significance," he speculated, adding, "The only explanation that makes sense is some kind of pagan motivation. There is strong worldwide belief in the practice of magic. It wouldn't surprise me if what we are seeing is the result of some devil cult's rituals."

Mutilations then began to be reported in several other Great Plains states. South Dakota experienced a short-lived panic in October, climaxing on October 3, when the director of male admissions at the state's mental hospital stated that a psychopath was most likely at work. Warning that "such individuals often graduated to humans as their next victims," he publicized a probable description of the mutilator: "a young male from a farm background with high levels of hostility toward his parents and other authority figures" (Davidson 1975:71; Stewart 1977:56–57). In November, the phenomenon took hold in eastern Colorado, Oklahoma and North Texas, and in central Minnesota. By early December, the American Humane Association had endorsed the "cult ritual" theory, and one rural Colorado District Attorney was blaming "people . . . who believe they can cast spells on other people" (Davidson 1975:76).

By November 1974, too, the scare had evolved into a full-fledged rumor panic in Swift County in western Minnesota. Officials there learned that farmers had placed loaded guns at the ready and in some cases even told children to use them if a stranger appeared. Authorities worried that a disabled traveler who had long hair, a beard, or a mustache might be shot if he approached a farmhouse. A news release made brief mentions of the rumors circulating, chief among them the story "that a 13– or 14–year-old girl, in place of an animal, will be the next target." The report also mentioned "notes left on the carcasses" and "observations of hooded men running through pastures carrying candles" (Davidson 1975:73).

On January 9, 1975, a widely published AP press release termed three cattle deaths in Texas "ritualistic" and cited a Texas Ranger as saying that a tranquilizer gun could have been used to immobilize the animals before mutilating them (Davidson 1975:57). By February, reports were widespread in the eastern part of the state. In Dallas, a woman claiming to be part of the Wicca movement met with reporters in front of shelves of occult books and jars of herbs. She was sure the incidents were committed by a large Satanist group operating out of Fort Worth, she said, adding, "this is consistent with their rituals. . . . The blood is used for drinking and the sex organs of the animals are used in sex ceremonies. They do evil things. They're into drugs and other things, desecrating churches and such" (Davidson 1975:49). By the end of February, the governor of Oklahoma had appointed a special task force to investigate the rumors. John Dunn, president of the Oklahoma Cattlemen's Association, said that the first cow in the area had probably been sacrificed at midnight on November 12, "the Equinox of Pandaa." "After that," he continued, "they began killing them for the blood and sex organs and are probably saving up the stuff for their ceremonies on Easter" (Davidson 1975:36; *NYT* 2 Mar.75:33). The "Equinox of Pandaa" was not immediately identifiable, but this scenario probably owes much to the anti-Semitic Blood Libel, according to which Jews were thought to collect blood and vital organs from children to prepare for a diabolical ritual on Good Friday.

By June 1975, the panic had spread to counties in eastern Colorado, where officials said they had heard about "a cult in witchcraft" that had spread into the state from Kansas. A reporter for the *Colorado Springs Gazette Telegraph* suggested that the mutilations were "medicinal murders" of a sort that had originated in Africa. "If one wants sexual prowess," she explained, "he removes the sex organs of the human or animal; if he wants keener eyesight, he removes the eyeball or the brain." Others suggested, "Those hung up on drugs may be mutilating the livestock, starting unexplained fires and desecrating graves" (Davidson 1975:8). By August, the mutilations were attracting so much attention in Colorado that Governor Richard Lamm called them "one of the greatest outrages in the history of the western cattle industry."

In late September and early October, another full-scale rumor panic occurred in parts of Montana and Idaho. Police there reported clusters of mutilated carcasses, while rumors similar to those circulating earlier in Minnesota circulated. In Idaho, for instance, a group of mysterious hikers in black-hooded robes were seen in an area where dead cattle had been found. Soon after, a driver claimed that a group of people in masks had stood across Highway 95 with locked arms, trying to stop his car. The area of Missoula, Montana, had been affected by cult rumors as early as 1974, when a five-year-old and a middle-aged woman who had worked in a Christian bookstore were found brutally murdered. These were supposed to be the first two in a series of "devil worship" sacrifices, with a third soon to follow. Sociologists Robert W. Balch and Margaret Gilliam (1991) observed that this rumor was most actively circulating among conduits of Pentecostal Christians. They also collected several accounts of cult members trying to stop motorists by blocking the roadway, all set in various locations of western Montana and northern Idaho. Such was the degree of concern that a local paper in Driggs, Idaho, published this official warning, "Parents, please be sure you know where your children are at night and especially Halloween night. On Halloween night, with the happenings in our own area, it would be advisable to have the younger children home before dark and the older ones home immediately after the football game scheduled on that night" (Sanders 1976:120). In all, seventeen states were affected by the panic, which in Colorado was voted the Associated Press's top story of 1975.

The following year, the phenomena continued to spread to new states, eventually touching twenty-three in all. In August and September, rural areas of Minnesota and North Dakota were plagued by reports of mysterious white-robed individuals standing by roads or near mutilation sites. Police scrambled in Kindred, North Dakota, when a teenaged boy ran into a "hooded figure in white" near a local granary. But the strange figures proved as elusive as Spring-Heeled Jack: intensive searches by police failed to turn up any suspects (Albers 1979:86). Meanwhile, "classic" mutilation stories circulated widely and often proved difficult to verify. One of the most widespread held that a note had been found next to a mutilated animal, warning "Next time it will be a human being" (Randolph 1975:19) or, more pointedly, "This time it's a cow, next time it'll be your daughter" (*Minneapolis Tribune* 20 April 1975:18A). Even cases that had been discredited or disowned by the original researcher took on a life of their own in the media-enhanced conduits of researchers that sprang up. By 1976, at least one researcher was complaining that mutilation enthusiasts were circulating stories without any indication of names, dates, or sites. "Nothing is harder to disprove than a rumor," he noted, that happened "somewhere at sometime involving some witnesses" (Bonham 1976:55).

A series of influential debunking reports then began to drive the debate out of the popular press. In 1975, the Oklahoma state probe found no evidence for human or supernatural involvement (Rommel 1980:241–44), and in January 1976, the Colorado Bureau of Investigation, which had initially favored the cult theory, reported that natural scavengers and public hysteria accounted for all but one of the cases reported there (Albers 1979:61). Experiments conducted in Texas and South Dakota exposed carcasses to predators like buzzards, foxes, and coyotes under close surveillance; the resulting damage was similar to that blamed on "surgical" incisions (Wolfe 1976:10).

In 1978–1979, a series of new mutilation scares in the Southwest occurred (Clark 1980a, 1980b). Media attention over these incidents attracted the attention of the junior senator from New Mexico, the ex-astronaut Harrison Schmitt. Arguing that the federal government should be investigating the matter, Senator Schmitt held a day-long mutilation conference in Albuquerque on April 20, 1979, inviting law enforcement agents from New Mexico, Nebraska, Colorado, Montana, and Arkansas (Lebelson 1980). Shortly afterward, the U.S. Department of Justice allowed the FBI to join the investigation, and the Santa Fe District Attorney's office was granted $50,000 for its study. The result was bitterly disappointing for the mutilation investigators: Kenneth M. Rommel, a former FBI agent and vocal skeptic, was appointed project director. His report, issued in June 1980, blamed natural causes and predators for all the professionally investigated cases and castigated amateur investigators for perpetuating the scare. The publicity following the release of this report (Rorvik 1980; Randi 1980) virtually closed the case so far as the national mass media was concerned. In 1983, Daniel Kagan and Ian Summers published *Mute Evidence,* a detailed debunking of the phenomenon, but attention had already waned to the point that the book sold poorly.

By this time a strong conduit of mutilation researchers had developed, however, including amateur UFO investigators, local police agents fascinated by the phenomenon, and a range of others drawn to the affair by interest or the desire for self-protection. Lacking any concrete evidence to identify the perpetrator of any individual mutilation, these conduits tended to explain what they saw in terms of "usual suspects."

Suspect 1: Mystery Helicopters and Extraterrestrial Rustlers

The earliest explanation that arose for the mutilations was not immediately connected with Satanism. Rather, it was associated with a nationwide interest in UFOs that had arisen from a wave of sightings and popular books during the mid 1960s. Some investigators claim precedents for the phenomena as far back as 1897, when a Kansas newspaper printed a report from a local rancher that an "airship" (in this case, a dirigible) had passed over his farm and lassoed one of his calves. The next day, the report claimed, the mutilated carcass was found miles away with "no track of any kind" around it. The rancher, a member of a local "liar's club," soon admitted that his letter was a hoax inspired by a nationwide "mystery airship" panic, but the letter was rediscovered and reprinted as authentic in a number of UFO books during the mid-1960s (Clark 1998:I:102). Soon after the reprinting of the 1897 case, similar accounts of animal mutilations began to appear in ufologists' reports. In September 1966, John A. Keel found that a wave of UFO sightings in the Gallipolis, Ohio, and adjacent West Virginia area coincided with a rash of missing, bloodied, and killed dogs. Similarly, he found that the woman who had complained about her cows being "expertly butchered" had also seen, on a number of occasions, "strange luminous objects hovering at tree-top level above her pastures" (Spencer 1976:102–3).

Probably there were many small-scale affairs of this sort, but the so-called "Snippy" incident in southern Colorado brought the issue of animal mutilation to a broader audience. On September 8, 1967, rancher Larry King discovered a horse mysteriously killed and partially skinned. There were no tracks near the carcass, although close by there were strange circular marks and indentations as if some kind of aircraft had landed there. The ranch was adjacent to the Great Sand Dunes National Monument, which had become notorious for mysterious aerial lights. These bright white lights were sighted below the rims of the surrounding mountains and appeared to move steadily along before vanishing suddenly into the air. Such "mystery lights" are a common motif in many locations across the United States, where they may seem like globes of light above mountains or move along a stretch of railroad tracks or a highway. Some such "spook lights" have attracted generations of visitors and become tourist attractions in their own right. The Missouri Spook Light near Joplin, in fact, inspired its own regional museum. Others, such as the Headless Motorcyclist of northern Ohio, are the subjects of adolescent legend-trips, in which participants "dare" the light to appear by carrying out a prescribed ritual.[1] Therefore, it made sense to link the horse's mutilation to this phenomenon. A U.S. Forestry ranger interviewed recalled seeing strange "jets" flying near the place where the animal was found, and the rancher's mother also thought she had seen something large fly over the ranch shortly before the discovery of the dead horse.

Coincidentally, authorities found Dr. John H. Altshuler, a Denver hematologist, spending the night in the National Monument, where he had come to observe the mystery lights. He agreed to examine the horse's remains and found, to his surprise, that her blood and internal organs had apparently been removed. Local ufologists quickly publicized the case as evidence for extraterrestrial contact, and the story eventually found its way into the *Denver Post.* By this time, many of the details of the case had been garbled (the horse's name, "Lady," for instance, was always reported as "Snippy," presumably more appropriate for a mutilation victim.) The University of Colorado was at the time sponsoring a project investigating the reality of UFOs, and members of this team agreed to examine the case. Veterinarians found that the animal had apparently been shot in the flank, presumably by vandals, and that her throat had afterwards been slit, perhaps to put her out of her misery. While the case was never fully resolved, the Colorado team found no reason to think that Lady's death was paranormal in nature, although a number of ufologists continued to stress the bizarre and mysterious nature of the case (Clark 1998:I.103–4; Howe 1989:1–6).

Mysterious aircraft of a different kind also formed a background for the early mutilation panic. The first incidents occurred at a time when inflationary pressures were driving up beef prices dramatically. Recognizing the appreciating value of their cattle, ranchers were unusually sensitive to rustling, and in 1973, some months before mutilation rashes came to public notice, there had been a number of panics in the Great Plains when farmers began reporting strange unmarked helicopters hovering over their cattle herds. In one of the most dramatic incidents, a Baptist minister from Mark, a tiny settlement in southeastern Iowa, awoke one April morning when an intercom installed for security purposes picked up a two-way radio message in which "there was plenty of use of the Lord's name in vain." Suspicious after a strange car had been seen the night before, he and a friend decided to drive around to see if any mischief was going on. When he came to a local rancher's place, he told authorities, "this helicopter started to raise out of the field right in front of us." He continued:

> It hovered over our heads for a few seconds, and when we got out of the car, we could see the tail structure and the fuselage structure. It wasn't one of those bubble-type copters. It had an enclosed fuselage that I would guess could carry four or five men. And there were no visible numbers on the helicopter. . . . When we got over the shock of what we had seen, we realized that Francis's cattle were bawling and running all over the pasture. It was like they were scared. . . . Now whether there were cattle rustlers in that helicopter or not, I can't say. But it's strange that a helicopter would be out in a farm pasture that late at night for any *good* purpose.

Highway patrol troopers received scattered reports of an aircraft in the area and attempted to follow it toward the Missouri border, but they found no traces of it: "It's like it vanished at the Iowa border," one said (Davidson 1975:94). When the occurrence was reported on the front page of the Des Moines *Register*, lawmen were soon "besieged" with similar reports across the state.

In August, similar excitement occurred in southern Missouri and adjacent areas of southern Illinois. On August 19, Illinois State Police issued a bulletin asking police to watch for "an olive drab helicopter with its identification numbers painted out" that was suspected to be involved in rustling operations. A few days later, a farmer near Jonesboro told authorities that he had fired a shotgun at a copter he had found hovering above his herd and shining a bright light on them. The helicopter's motor, his wife added, "was quiet running and apparently muffled by some device" (Davidson 1975:96). While no cattle were found missing there or anywhere else, another rancher who had found thirty-five animals missing "remembered he had seen a green helicopter without markings" nearby a few days before. Authorities speculated that the aircraft were used to spot cattle and provide radio directions to accomplices driving trucks. While the cattle were being loaded, the helicopter would serve as a lookout. Alternatively, one sheriff's deputy suggested, the rustlers would "shoot the animals with tranquilizer guns, then lower a cable and hoist them aboard." Reports of these encounters appeared in local papers, and then appeared on nationwide press services such as the Associated Press and UPI (Davidson 1975:95–97).

Thus, the "mystery helicopter" motif was available to ranchers and investigators during the early mutilation panics. It was slow to enter, however. When Jerome Clark, who was aware of the airborne rustler stories, asked if this might explain the new incidents, authorities acknowledged that they had received many such reports, but did not see any connection. "I think these may have been secret military exercises out of Fort Riley," one said, "and I don't think this has anything to do with these mutilations" (1974:87–88). But the link between two mysteries was too logical to miss, and when the panic broke out in Nebraska in 1974, mysterious helicopters were regularly associated with cattle deaths. Ranchers rode regular patrols in pickup trucks equipped with CB radios, watching for helicopters, and so many authorized aircraft were fired on that the Nebraska National Guard ordered its pilots to double their cruising altitudes to avoid damage or injury (*Newsweek* [30 Sept.74]; Davidson 1975:62–63).

However, even though such craft ought to have been easy to track, no helicopter was ever reliably traced to rustling or mutilation. "This thing is getting to be like sighting those Unidentified Flying Objects," a California official noted (Davidson 1975:95). And UFOs refused to stay out of the picture. A December 1974 mutilation at a farm in Meeker County, Minnesota, attracted the attention of Terrance Mitchell, a young UFO researcher. Mitchell had been investigating a bright aerial light seen by highway patrolmen in Wisconsin, when he became aware of the link between mystery aircraft and mutilations. Called to the farm by officials, Mitchell noticed that while the dead cow lay in a field covered with snow, there were no prints around it, and the ground around the carcass had melted into a circular pattern. He quickly concluded that the cow had been mutilated by "surgical instruments never seen before on earth." An aerial photograph showed a series of circular impressions, which he interpreted as landing sites, and a ground-level survey found a series of broken tree branches and holes apparently punched into the ice of a farm pond. These could be further signs of a UFO landing to pick up provisions and water. The cow, he concluded, was killed with an "electro-mercuric gun." This weapon, part of the space visitors' advanced technology, killed the cow with an intense electrical burst of energy that also instantaneously drained it of blood.

In other ways, however, he believed that the extraterrestrials were similar to humans in appearance, mentality, and tastes. "They're just like us," he said. "Everyone likes a good steak." The animal would be killed and taken inside the spacecraft, he theorized, where parts of its body were removed to test for "quality." If it did not measure up, he thought that the animal would simply be dropped back to the ground from the spacecraft. Some of the portions might also be used for "preliminary scientific information." His background research suggested that the aliens were creatures much like humans "and therefore might not want to harm a fellow humanoid." Despite the mutilations, therefore, he expressed faith that when contact was finally made, "we'll find they are very, very nice extraterrestrial visitors" (Davidson 1975:54–55, 58).

Mitchell was part of a lecturers' bureau provided by the University of Minnesota's Department of Concerts and Lectures to community groups, so he was able to use these contacts and his university ties to promote his theories. By January 1975, he was receiving national publicity on the TV news series *Tomorrow*, hosted by telejournalist Tom Snyder (Albers 1979:19–21; Howe 1989:16–17). The Meeker County circles eventually proved to be snow-covered silage, and the other "landing" signs had mundane explanations (Albers 1979:22). Still, Mitchell's visibility helped bring the cattle mutilations to popular attention. Another key person in publicizing UFO theories was radio talk show host Michael J. Douglas, news director of WYOO, a major radio station in Eagan, Minnesota, a suburb of St. Paul. Like Mitchell, Douglas was a UFO buff who personally interviewed ranchers who reported strange cattle deaths and devoted airtime to theories about their causes and talks with residents who had seen flying saucers (Albers 1979:23–24). Although Mitchell recanted the UFO theory in April 1975 (*Minneapolis Tribune*, 20 April 1975:18A) and Douglas later concluded that occultists were responsible, both were influential in establishing the outlines of what became the "black helicopter" scenario.

This held that the aircraft came not from ordinary airfields but was hypertechnological in nature—either a secret government experiment or else an extraterrestrial object launched by a UFO. Unmarked helicopters with mystifying powers were at the heart of the 1975 rumor panic that affected much of eastern Colorado, where again official surveys using such craft had to be curtailed because ranchers were regularly shooting at passing copters. Telltale signs of rotor wash were supposedly found near dead animals, and in one widely reported case, three teenaged girls claimed to have been chased by an unmarked helicopter. The craft were regularly reported to show up hovering over houses or near herds and beaming an intensely powerful light on the ground. This was generally understood as a surveillance device, but some reports held that it had mystifying effects. Allegedly it could wilt grass around the dead animal and in some cases shut down automobile ignition systems just as UFOs were said to do. Many ranchers were convinced that the animals had been picked up, mutilated in mid-air, and then dropped back to the ground inside padlocked pens, between large rocks, or in sandy beds without even the cow's prints to explain how the carcass had gotten there. Such an aircraft, experts noted, would have to be extremely powerful and hence extremely noisy in operation. But, strangest of all, many of the helicopters observed were now said to be not just muffled, but in fact silent in operation (Smith 1976:5, 16, 20–22, 74).

The UFO explanation could explain (or at least gracefully fail to explain) how the cattle were mutilated so mysteriously: they were killed and biopsied with technology too far advanced for humans to understand. Similarly, if the mystery helicopters did not use known aerodynamic principles, it stood to reason that they could fly silently, teleport animals from the ground, and seemingly disappear from the skies when sought by authorities. Frederick Smith suggested that the extraterrestrials were already living among us and so presumably already flying helicopters as they pass for ordinary humans.

> They could very easily take as many of them as they wanted, and of any type. And they wouldn't have to power them as ours are powered, or base them where ours are based. They could support them from above, make them invisible when necessary, and hangar them at the top of the sky so that there would never be any need for their planes or helicopters to touch down or refuel. They can simulate anything we have and thereby make themselves even more unidentified than any of us had previously suspected. Who knows what's in the aircraft overhead, or what government could risk shooting one out of the sky? (1978:iv)

However, this theory could not provide a credible reason for *why* the mutilations were happening. This difficulty was amusingly illustrated when Michael D. Albers, one of the most thorough investigators, located a hirsute Satanist, who adamantly blamed "Martians" for the killings. But when asked why creatures from outer space would take only small parts of the cattle's body, he looked perplexed, saying, "Maybe they're going to clone cattle and only need small pieces" (Albers 1979:50).

Suspect 2: Blood Cults

From the beginning, however, police and religious figures presumed that the mutilations were being carried out by cults. The claim that Satanists were killing cows and taking their blood, after all, was no different from similar claims made about the hippie witches in California who had for years been rumored to kill dogs and drink their blood. Because an existing subversion myth is precisely a way of finding and explaining relationships among events, it is not surprising that the cult theory quickly became the dominant explanation. Bizarre religious groups worshipping the principle of evil provided both a structure and malign motivation for apparently random excisions. Alleged "ritualistic" elements were observed: for instance, some linked the cattle deaths to the dates of the full moon (Donovan and Wolverton 1976:18). Others speculated that the agents took only the left eye of females and only the right eyes of males (Owen 1980:13). Police also could easily connect mutilations to other traditional signs of rural "Satanism" such as church desecrations, graffiti, and the discovery of "altars" in remote areas. Captain Keith Wolverton, for instance, visited an apparent worship site known as "The Montana Site," where cult members, dressed in long robes, were rumored to hold ceremonies. Wolverton admitted that the site "could be interpreted different ways," but he notes that the god "Isis," prominently mentioned in inscriptions, was an ancient god who demanded cattle sacrifices.

The "satanic" explanation was consistently the most plausible theory among the general public and was most often endorsed by authority figures such as police, university professors, and psychologists. James R. Stewart, polling residents of South Dakota in 1974–1975, some months after the initial panic had passed from the media there, found that close to two-thirds of those who believed that the deaths had some extraordinary cause endorsed the cult theory (1977). The only weak point was that it did not explain how groups of Satanists could carry out their work and leave no tracks or clues. For this reason, authorities were unusually willing to investigate a bizarre story presented by a group of convicts who claimed to have inside knowledge of the satanic mutilators.

This story came out of an odd collaboration between the U.S. government and UFO researchers. In January 1974, A. Kenneth Bankston, an inmate of the Federal Penitentiary at Leavenworth, Kansas, contacted Jerome Clark, whose investigation of the 1973 mutilations had been published in the paranormal magazine *Fate*. Bankston, a convicted bank robber, had been in the habit of developing pen pals outside of prison, and had also read about Kansas State Senator Doyen's belief that cults were responsible for the Kansas mutilations. He wrote to Doyen, claiming to have inside information on the mutilations, and repeated his story to Clark, "I did . . . relate to the Senator that a 'Cult' was responsible for these killings and that I and two other inmates had been told the whole bit and the sick trip behind the whole thing. I also correspond with some people in Minnesota and in the world of hippies. This cult is of Satan and blood is drawn from the cattle by hypo and their sex organs are taken for their fertility rites. . . . I will say that this is a prelude to human sacrifice" (23 Jan. 74). If he were transferred to a county jail in Minnesota to protect himself from Satanists, Bankston said, he would be happy to cooperate with authorities in exposing the cult.

Subsequent letters repeated this request, with escalating warnings that quick action was necessary to avoid the mayhem the cult had planned: "the sacrifice of the small animals . . . first, then the cow, now the People small People first (children) then teens then the older ones. It sounds far out but I asure [*sic*] you very real, very true, very near" (19 Feb. 74). In fact, Bankston said, Clark's very life might be at stake if he did not do something quickly to get him transferred out of Leavenworth:

> After a conversation with one of the people in here that is indirectly with the Cult I feel that you should forego any further investigation due to the fact that it could become dangerous to you and your friends. . . . the people that are now in your area and in the Mpls. Area are the same people that were with the movement at the U. of Wisc. and Madison. But as you will recall that ended up in a Death and a Bldg. being blown up with a fertilize compound known as Ammonia nitrate.[2] As you will well see your investigation could very well end in rubble of your business home and person. However as I said before I would feel a lot safer and could be of more help to you in [the jail at] Yellow Medicine County. . . . I am sure that you and the people in Minn. and who want to see the end of all this stupid Cult [*sic*]. (24 Feb. 1974)

Clark at first was skeptical about these stories; but as other sources related similar details, he became concerned that there was some truth behind them.

Meanwhile, as the mutilation panic began to spread through the Great Plains late in 1974, UFO networks became more involved in trying to explain the phenomenon. Dr. J. Allen Hynek, director of the Astronomy Department at Northwestern University and head of the Center for UFO Studies, was one person who felt that the cattle mutilation link detracted from responsible study of verifiable "close encounters" with UFOs. He contacted Donald E. Flickinger, an agent for the Federal Bureau of Alcohol, Tobacco, and Firearms (BATF), who had for some time investigated UFO incidents for him on a private basis. Hynek asked Flickinger to look into the Meeker County cattle mutilation being promoted by Mitchell to see if any extraterrestrial connection could be verified. Flickinger found no basis for the UFO theories, but he concluded that "a certain pattern existed, . . the animal would be found in the middle of an open field, various parts of the body had been surgically removed such as the sex organs, eyes, ears, lips, tongue, teats, etc. In many of the cases the blood had been drained from the animal and in several cases, veterinarians were unable to determine cause of death . . . most concurred that the removal of the various organs was surgical with some sort of sharp instrument."[3] Clark learned of Flickinger's investigation and passed on Bankston's letters to the agent. Flickinger contacted the Minneapolis U.S. Attorney, who agreed that the case should be pursued officially. Bankston was transferred to a Minnesota jail along with another Leavenworth inmate, Dan Dugan, who claimed to have been a member of "the occult" for some years.

In March, 1975, Flickinger interviewed Dugan, who spun out a complex tale of a cult he had joined in the Fort Worth, Texas, area, which enlisted members through their "unlimited access to drugs." Dugan told Flickinger, "The group would regularly conduct rituals and ceremonies and would use parts of small animals in the rites. He described the killing of dogs, cats and rabbits in various areas which would be bled, the sex organs would be cut off and all of these parts would be used in the rites." He then explained how the mutilations were accomplished: the cattle would be shot from a distance with "tranquilizer pellets," and he and other cult members would then move up to the animal, laying down large pieces of cardboard ahead of them to avoid leaving tracks. Having reached the animal, the cult members would then hold amyl nitrate ampoules to its nose, which would speed up its bodily functions, and the blood would be removed with "large veterinarian syringes." Once the animal was dead, its sex organs would be removed, and if there were snow, cult members would use a blowtorch to melt it in a circular area so authorities would blame the event on a UFO.

Clearly, Dugan had encountered the Meeker County mutilation promoted by Terrance Mitchell and had adapted its details for their purposes. In fact, at the same time that Dugan was giving his confessions to Flickinger, Michael J. Douglas was promoting his newest theory of the mutilations on his radio talk show: "the killers had first disabled the animal by shooting it with a tranquilizer dart, then injected a heart stimulant and allowed the animal to pump out most of its blood through a punctured artery. . . . the killers had used large sheets of cardboard to distribute their weight. They would lay out one sheet, walk across it, lay out another and pick up the first . . . without leaving behind telltale footprints" (Albers 1979:23). It is not clear whether Dugan picked up his story from Douglas's radio show, directly or indirectly through fellow convicts, or whether Douglas broadcast a version of Dugan's story leaked to him by UFO investigators privy to the interviews. Whatever the case, the sheets-of-cardboard explanation became one of the most highly publicized theories. Douglas soon after received several anonymous telephone threats, which led him to drop the subject from his radio shows but also, in his mind, "provided the final proof for the theory" (Albers 1979:24)

While the cult focused mainly on animal sacrifices, Dugan told Flickinger, he added, "It was believed by all the members of the group that their 'religion' called for sacrifices of human life later on." In fact, Dugan described in detail how he had seen four transient teenagers killed and ritually mutilated. Additional human sacrifices would occur sometime around the end of 1975, when the world would enter "the Age of Aquarius." Dugan and Bankston provided Flickinger with a list of names of people associated with the cult, and he then asked various local law enforcement agencies to compile dossiers on these people. Flickinger found that a number of these agencies had already begun their own investigations into the occult link with cattle mutilations.

The Texas Rangers in Kilgore, Texas, for instance, had interrogated suspects there and learned that a mass meeting of Satanists had been planned in August 1975 to mark the "end of the 10 year cycle and the age of the coming of Aquarius." They referred to the group as "The Church of Satan," which also matched the details Flickinger was getting from Bankston and Dugan. "The name 'Church of Satan,'" Flickinger told his superiors, "according to Texas DPS, has never been publicized until recently so it would be unlikely Bankston or Dugan could have picked the name up by reading about it in some newspaper."

Actually, Dugan was also corresponding with reporter John Makeig of the *Fort-Worth Star-Telegram* (Cockburn 1975:64). Makeig, who had previously reported at length UFO investigator Terrance Mitchell's views on mutilations,combined these stories and other rumors into a dramatic series of articles advocating the satanic cult theory.[4] On April 5, he reported that "an occult-type group containing 600 or more members" had been mutilating cattle since 1967. The name of this group, he claimed, was the "Sons of Satan." The most extensive basic information on this group had come to law officers through a theme paper allegedly submitted by a student at Kilgore Junior College. Teachers supposedly destroyed this paper "because it was so obscene and gory and disgusting they didn't want anybody else to see it," but Makeig said police had traced its author, who freely repeated its contents:

> In it, the man wrote that, in following the group's beliefs, the cattle must be mutilated "between midnight and sunrise . . . and the ritual must be completed as sunlight starts to filter down on the animal through the branches of a tree."
>
> If no tree is near where the mutilation occurs, branches torn from trees are held above the dying animal as the sun rises, federal and state investigators said.
>
> Portions removed from the cattle, a lawman explained, have been used by group members in their initiations of new members, both men and women. (Davidson 1975:18)

Further information on the "Sons of Satan" came through themes submitted to an English professor at the University of Pennsylvania, who was attending a conference on "Literature and the Occult" at the University of Texas at Arlington. He was quite familiar with the group, he told a reporter; in fact, he had had some cult members in his classes. While he had not heard about their involvement in cattle mutilations, he conceded that a "primary thrill" was eating their own flesh. "I've seen some girls who'd cut off their fingers and pieces of their ears and things like that," he commented (Davidson 1975:18).

Although Makeig (and to some extent Flickinger) took such information at face value, all this indicates is that the mythology of satanic cults had permeated the American media. Texas law agents were puzzled over how Bankston and Dugan could have heard about Anton LaVey's Church of Satan and the motorcycle gang "Sons of Satan," but Ed Sanders's *The Family* or one of the popular media's handlings of his theories was an easy source for these details. And Mike Warnke's cult exposé, *The Satan-Seller*, which had been a best-seller among charismatic groups for more than a year, was the logical source for the details about self-mutilation and cannibalism. Indeed, Warnke was then residing in Tulsa, Oklahoma, and was quite willing to talk to reporters about the satanic elements of the mutilations. "Well, I would have to look into the circumstances," he told a *Denver Post* reporter in June 1975, "but when blood has been drained from the animal and the sexual organs removed, it's highly likely that it was a satanic cult. They use the organs in fertility rites, you know" (Davidson 1975:7)

The mysterious Kilgore Junior College term paper, like the University of Pennsylvania English themes, simply showed that satanic cult folklore had trickled down to American adolescents just as it had a few years earlier in Great Britain. The Kilgore term paper in fact was itself a sort of legend. In an article that appeared a day after Makeig's article, sheriff's deputies in the Kilgore area, reacted angrily. No reports of mutilations had been made anywhere in the county, they said, no theme paper had been brought to their attention, and no suspects had ever been formally questioned (Davidson 1975:17). The theme and its author, it seems, were as difficult to trace as the cult it described.

Flickinger conceded that it was possible that the two convicts had "concocted a fantastic, bizarre and grisly story which is so complicated that they could never be proven as liars." But he added that the claim was not so fantastic if compared to the career of the Manson Family. "I must admit to having mixed emotions about such a horror story being true," he concluded, "but at the same time cannot help but feel such an investigation would be justified." In response, Flickinger was relieved of his usual duties by the U.S. government so that he could pursue the case full time. The story continued to grow. "The Occult's" leader was "a confirmed racist convinced that the white race is superior to any other." This mysterious leader supposedly had contacts with wealthy patrons and drug dealers, whom he relied upon to obtain the tranquilizer guns and other paraphernalia used in the mutilations. He also had a fleet of black, unmarked helicopters in which he traveled around. His agenda included a period in the near future during which his followers would abduct and mutilate humans and also assassinate liberal politicians like Hubert Humphrey and Edward Kennedy as well as prominent blacks, including Barbara Jordan, Senator Edward Brooke, and the Reverend Ralph Abernathy. In the end, they would seize a nuclear warhead or use plutonium stolen from a nuclear fuel plant in Oklahoma to commit a terrorist act and usher in a one-thousand-year reign of darkness.

Bankston's story was taken seriously enough that in 1975 the federal government apparently did initiate a nationwide investigation of satanic organizations, contacting and questioning well-known occultists. One of the first contacted was Anton LaVey, who, in his own defense, began compiling a "complete, centralized file . . . on the cattle mutilation hoax." This file was later shared with his biographer, Burton H. Wolfe, who used it to respond to several sensationalized media accounts of the scare that appeared in San Francisco-area papers. The alleged mutilations, Wolfe said, were the result of "hysterics, psychotics and frauds" (1976:10).[5] Isaac Bonewits, another of the logical suspects put under federal investigation, took a more serious approach. Already notorious because of publicity over his "witchcraft" degree from Berkeley, Bonewits was then editor of a monthly publication for occultists, titled *Gnostica: News of the Aquarian Frontier*. "If you put the KKK in black robes instead of white ones," he told Makeig, "you'd have most of the Satanist groups pegged."

To fellow pagans, he was more serious. In a lead editorial for the May 1975 issue of *Gnostica*, Bonewits called the federal investigation "sheer scapegoating, since only a rank amateur would believe it possible to get usable psychic energy out of such mutilations." Nevertheless, he expressed concern that the cattle deaths had in some places been accompanied by incidents of grave desecration during which corpses had allegedly been mutilated. "Whoever or whatever is responsible for the animal and/or corpse mutilations," he continued, "may not have intended to induce a state of anti-occult hysteria by the Powers That Be, but this seems to be the rapidly growing result. If the Aquarian community doesn't figure out what the hell is going on, and fast, we may well wind up being officially blamed for this hideous mess." Like LaVey, Bonewits called for a central data pool that could be used to try to identify reliable links between mutilation events and other phenomena, including grave desecrations, UFO and mystery animal sightings, and "unusual psychic phenomena." Such information would then be shared with authorities. "The reasons we wish to cooperate with the police are simple," he concluded. "Firstly, we wish to prevent further occurrences of these horrible killings, and secondly, if indeed any agency connected (however tenuously) with the occult is responsible for the incidents, it is far better public relations for the Aquarian community if occultists and other Aquarians *themselves* make this discovery, rather than some outside, hostile group."

The so-called Flickinger Report, which summarized Bankston's and Dugan's confessions, traveled far beyond the BATF and Minnesota police channels that commissioned it. The report was distributed to police departments throughout the affected states. The Aerial Phenomenon Research Organization, a major UFO network based in Tucson, Arizona, summarized it in a public statement (Spencer 1976:111–12), and in other cases details from the report were published in local newspapers (Smith 1976:38; Donovan and Wolverton 1976:97). It caused several local panics, one in Mayflower, Texas, after a sheriff's deputy told townspeople that cult members planned to murder and mutilate two humans (Sanders 1976:113). On May 25, John Makeig summarized the report in the *Star-Telegram*, blaming a "super, super wealthy group of amateur Satanists" for the mutilations. To the cast of suspects, Makeig added The Process, already notorious from Sanders's work, and a local gang called "The Flaming Stars." He implied a link with a series of allegedly satanic murders committed in Florida and New Mexico during the past three years. Flickinger, who had by now appeared on several radio talk shows, reported that he had received death threats and that blood had been smeared on the front of his door (Davidson 1975:10–11).

But the report's credibility lasted barely a week more. Claiming that his life was still in danger, Bankston had asked to be transferred to a yet smaller jail, and on May 31 he escaped from this low-security facility with another prisoner. Meanwhile, Dugan was transferred to a small jail in Texas where he was supposed to cooperate with officials in tracing the cult there; he too broke jail on June 1 and was recaptured during a hold-up attempt less than a month later. On recapture, both men initially claimed they had been trying to hide from Satanists, but eventually police concluded that their story had been a fabrication compiled from rumors and legends circulating among fellow convicts. Bankston departed the scene, still writing letters to Makeig protesting his sincerity and begging to be "transferred to a county jail in Texas" so he could help police put the real occultists in prison (Davidson 1975:4).

Even though authorities abandoned the case as a hoax, the Flickinger Report took on a life of its own in the media. In the fall of 1975, a column in *Esquire* paraphrased the report sympathetically, adding lurid details. After threats had been made on Flickinger's life, the magazine darkly added, the investigation came "to an abrupt end"—presumably because powerful Satanists had shut down the inquiry (Cockburn 1975:64). The November issue of the men's magazine *Saga* contained another account of the Bankston/Dugan stories under the sensational title, "The Killer Cult Terrorizing Mid-America." This article concedes that the federal investigation had ended "because of the continual conflicting testimony of one of its key informants," but otherwise presents the story as credible. Indeed, *Saga* accentuated the Illuminati-like elements of Bankston and Dugan's scenario. Randolph claimed that the cult had been founded by a "brilliant, charismatic" person whom he called "Howard."[6] This person had collected a large sum of money from drug deals and from his followers and had plans to "help drive the world into another dark age, where violence and madness would rule, and the Earth would become like hell itself."

The group developed into "a loose confederation of satanist cults," whom he told to begin a series of mutilation killings of small animals, gradually working up to larger and larger beasts and then to human sacrifices. This was to be done "in such a manner that nobody would understand how it was being accomplished. The resulting panic would lead farmers and others to wonder if they were not the victims of supernatural forces." As the cult grew, it recruited a person familiar with helicopters, who trained others to fly them into otherwise inaccessible places to mutilate cattle. He also formed chapters among the "new hippie drug cultures" on college campuses. Randolph suggested that the cult had an overall membership of 400–700 persons, including members of wealthy families who secretly financed the group. Moreover, he added, "the cult may have infiltrated police forces and the local political power structure." Other lawmen, an ominous screamer for the piece implied, have backed off the investigation, "afraid to probe any deeper," because they fear that "they are up against the devil himself." The failure of state and federal officials to apprehend the cult leaders, as with many subversion myths, ironically became one of its key proofs: they had become powerful enough to defy detection. But if that was true, then the U.S. government, no less, was an integral part of the mutilation conspiracy.

Suspect 3: "The Great Satan"

Thus, as police investigations into cults came up blank, the government conspiracy explanation began to gain popularity. In 1973, when the mutilations began, covert operations in Vietnam remained fresh in memory, along with scandals that rocked President Nixon's first term when secret bombing missions were exposed by the press. When the Watergate scandal unraveled in a series of sensational hearings over the summer of 1973, it became clear that Nixon had used both the FBI and the CIA to carry out "dirty tricks" against political enemies. Clearly the technology needed to elude ranchers and police had to be expensive, and if wealthy "patrons" of the cults could not be identified, it followed that they were being shielded or even supported by government agents. It was therefore plausible that the Flickinger Report was no more than "a very high level government propaganda plant," as one investigator put it (Smith 1976:38).

Remote areas of the American West, furthermore, had been affected by a number of sensitive government projects. Open-air nuclear testing had dusted local communities with radioactive fallout, and, during the Vietnam conflict, the Defense Department began working with even more frightening weapons. In March 1968, an experimental open-air release of deadly nerve gas at the Dugway Proving Grounds in Utah went astray when high winds blew it into neighboring fields. Ranchers later found sixty-four hundred of their sheep dead from the gas, and the U.S. military initially tried to deny responsibility. Eventually the truth came out, and the government paid the landowners $376,000 in damages. As a result of this scandal, the U.S. Congress formally banned active military research into poison gas and germ warfare in 1970, but rumors persisted that such experiments were still going on covertly (Albers 1979:99).

The main attraction of this explanation is that it explained how the mutilators had access to advanced technology; it had simply been shifted from Vietnam to domestic military bases. The cattle were being exposed to toxins, allowed to die naturally, and then biopsied to check on how well the agent worked. The mutilators left no traces because they used super-secret military helicopters, and any traces that were left were covered up by officials. This scenario built into the period's paranoia about the Nixon administration, which obligingly was caught in scandal after scandal throughout the peak time of the mutilation reports. During the politically bizarre months leading to Nixon's resignation in August 1975, Ed Sanders reappeared as one of the primary theorists of cattle mutilation. Sanders was then developing a theory of "investigative poetry," in which avant-garde artists would reclaim their role in interpreting history. "This is the Age of Investigative Poetry," he proclaimed at a New Year's Day reading in 1975, "When verse-froth again will assume its prior role as a vehicle for the description of history—and this will be a golden era for the public performance of poetry: when the Diogenes Liberation Squadron of Strolling Troubadors and Muckrakers will roam through the citadels of America to sing opposition to the military hit men whose vision of the U.S.A. is a permanent War Caste & a coast-to-coast cancer farm & a withered, metal-backed hostile America forever" (1987:137).

Sanders had noted and filed away some of the early media coverage of the mutilation scare, but did not have a particular interest in the events until June, when Dutton, publishers of *The Family*, forwarded a package sent to his care. It contained a large cow's tongue, which made Sanders recall that in his clippings the tongue had often been removed from mutilated cattle. The following month he traveled to Boulder, Colorado, for a poetry reading, and he decided to travel down to Elbert County, the focus of Colorado's rumor panic. There he discussed the mutilations with sheriff George Yarnell, who confirmed that they were associated with mysterious, untraceable helicopters. The pilots, he explained to Sanders, "had learned to hug the landscape even in rugged terrain so as to muffle their own sound." Implicit in Yarnell's account and those of his assistants was the belief that "Somehow, in some way, the Government is involved in the mutilations."

Yarnell's opinion was shared by other lawmakers. Leroy Yowell, sheriff at Lincoln County, commented:

> Look at the timing of the mutilation reports. They started in the spring and summer of 1975, right after we closed out Saigon and ended the war and brought all those combat helicopter pilots back home. . . . I think it's possible that some of those hotshot combat pilots were bored after all the action they had over there. I think maybe they were sitting around with nothing to do, and these mutilation reports started coming in. And I think it's possible some bright boy got the idea that they could play a little war game, you know, secret night operations against the local ranchers and sheriffs, and that some of them started using their combat skills to hop around the pastures killing cattle and cutting parts off them, just for a lark and to feed their need for action.

This scenario was given added credibility when local authorities found a government-issue satchel in the driveway of a local rancher, which contained a scalpel, a cow's ear, and part of a tongue (Kagan and Summers 1983:331–33).

Sanders's investigative instincts drew him back repeatedly to Colorado, where he found numerous rumors about the mutilators' agenda. In a detailed report published in the soft-core girlie magazine *Oui!* (1976), he related several of the scenarios being proposed by investigators. The most credible, in his view, was the theory that the incidents were related to a top-secret experiment using biological warfare agents. The animals were being deliberately exposed to genetically altered bacteria or natural toxins, and then autopsied to test the results. "I had long heard it rumored that there had been a Government germ-warfare program that had been targeted against Orientals," Sanders said. He added, "Is it unreasonable to think the United States is capable of developing a germ, or toxin, or nerve agent that picked on the enzymes of a particular race?" (1976:118). In fact, advocates of poison gas as a war weapon had for years suggested that certain agents had different effects on different races. J.B.S. Haldane, in 1925, had suggested that East Indians and Africans were less affected by mustard gas, and seriously suggested that armies of black soldiers could be used along with these weapons to gain advantages over troops made up entirely of Europeans. "The American Army authorities," he said, "made a systematic examination of the susceptibility of large numbers of recruits. They found that there was a very resistant class, comprising 20% of the white men tried, but no less than 80% of the negroes." This, he suggested, was explained by their dark skin, which also resisted sunburn. It should therefore be possible, he suggested, "to obtain colored troops who would all be resistant to mustard gas blistering in concentrations harmful to most white men" (qtd. in Gould 1998:81–82).

If this theory was taken seriously by American and British military personnel in 1925, why not its mirror image fifty years later—an agent that would selectively harm ethnic people and leave persons of European descent relatively unharmed? Sanders said, "One of the grim possibilities is that, while once supposedly targeted against Orientals, the research may now be aimed against a different human target. One hears talk among mutilation investigators that the mucous membranes of a cow's eye possess properties similar to the mucous membranes of a particular race, and that the cow, therefore, is a perfect subject on which to test the effects of a bacteriological agent" (Sanders 1976:118). Such a rumor would have been credible in the wake of the public outrage emerging in 1972 over the Tuskegee Study, in which the U.S. Public Health Service withheld antibiotics from four hundred black males suffering from syphilis so that they could document the progress of the disease (Jones 1981). Since a government agency had openly treated African Americans as "guinea pigs," there would have been nothing unreasonable about this situation's flip side: treating livestock as preparation for making African Americans expendable. Certainly the same historical facts have tended to validate rumors current among blacks concerning AIDS being a CIA-developed weapon against their race (Turner 1993).

Sanders suggested two reasons why such a project might be kept secret. First, government involvement in nominally illegal experiments might become one more campaign issue against the Republican presidential candidate, Gerald Ford. A second and more unsettling possibility, he continued, was that "some of these researchers, whatever their credentials, are insane." Certainly he associated it with fanatics in the military-industrial complex who were irritated over the ban on biological weapons and took advantage of the scandals affecting the country to continue their work on their own. Such a conspiracy, like Watergate, obviously involved a huge number of people, he conceded, and the costs of helicopters (and the fuel to run them) must amount to hundreds of thousands of dollars. Thus, even though the military could use its power to stop local police from discovering the truth, Sanders expressed faith that sooner or later the mutilators would, like Nixon, make a fatal mistake and allow investigators to follow their trail (1976:122).

In 1977, Sanders taught at the Naropa Institute, a Buddhist college in Colorado, along with his fellow beat poet Allen Ginsberg. Because of its non-standard religious orientation, this colony was the target of suspicion, especially when two mutilations were reported nearby. Sanders promoted his concept of "investigative poetry" and continued collecting information on the mutilations. In the same year, he briefly circulated a newsletter titled *The Cattle Report* in which he described cases that suggested U.S. military involvement with the mystery helicopters. In one case, a spotter plane rented by a county sheriff followed a "phantom copter" only to lose it when it descended to the ground. When the spotter plane followed it, passengers found only a missile silo. "Sad to ask is this," Sanders ended, "Is the United States Air Force involved in supplying cover for the mutilators?" (rptd. in *Stigmata* 9 [1980]:21–23; Adams 1991:33).

Counterculture writer David Perkins, who had been at the Naropa Institute since the sixties, recalled that Sanders and Ginsberg had come to Colorado in 1977 determined to get to the bottom of the mutilation:

> . . . at that time opinion seemed to be divided between the mutilations being caused by the government doing clandestine tests, or biological warfare exercises, or training exercises, or experimenting with new forms of death germs or whatever, nerve gases, lasers, rays, incapacitating devices. I've had several law officials look right at me and tell me they thought the govern-

ment was doing the whole thing, and that I should probably just forget about it. So that theory had a lot of proponents, and Ed Sanders put a lot of weight behind that theory with various articles and ideas he was spreading at that time. That was Ginsberg's idea at the time. You know, he's always collected those files on the CIA—always collecting information on what's going on in the government, and so on. So, to them, they thought, oh boy! We're going to nail them now! If we can catch the government running some illegal testing program, there's going to be a big scandal. (1982:6)

The government conspiracy mythology appealed strongly to both the far left and the far right, who shared a worldview based on opposition to presidential and military power. Perkins later became a committed mutilation investigator and had gathered so much information supporting the conspiracy theory that in 1979 he was invited to participate in Senator Schmitt's conference on the problem. Newspaper reporters paid special attention to his version, which suggested that the government was secretly testing the side effects of released radioactivity on animals. In support of his theory, he compiled a map showing a close relationship between nuclear facilities and mutilation reports (Rommel 1980:24–25). This theory, interestingly, gained unanimous support from psychics who were invited to handle photographs of mutilated cattle and interpret the vibrations they could detect (Jordan 1982).

The helicopter sightings (increasingly described as "black" in coloring) remained a focus of investigation through the 1980s and were increasingly assumed to be military in origin. Tom Adams, editor of *Stigmata,* the most widely distributed newsletter among mutilation specialists, published a detailed list of mystery copter sightings appropriately titled, *The Choppers — and the Choppers* (1980; rev. ed. 1991). He admitted that it was impossible to say whether the aircraft crews were actually carrying out the mutilations or simply observing the actual mutilators. Whatever the truth, he concluded, "The operatives and their superiors are very knowledgeable about the identity and motives of the mutilators and, by their presence, they are diverting our attention to the possibility of direct involvement by the military or the U.S. government, for whatever the reason might be" (1991:8). In ultra-right-wing conduits where William Guy Carr's and John Todd's Illuminati mythology held that the government itself *was* the "Great Satan," controlled by Jews and devil-worshippers, these antiestablishment ideas made perfect sense as well.

Suspect 4: Killer Jews from Outer Space

Although the Flickinger Report was officially retracted, local rumor panics based on similar claims continued to flare up during the next years. Near Dixon, Missouri, for instance, police investigation into a series of cattle deaths led to a panic when local police issued warnings that a cult was present. On October 19, 1978, the county's deputy sheriff told the local paper that the mutilations matched descriptions found in Anton LaVey's *Satanic Bible*[7] and that he expected that the cult would soon abduct and sacrifice a thirteen-year-old unbaptized girl on Halloween. School superintendents sent notes home with students with the warning, and parents responded with fear, followed by anger when no sacrifice followed (Albers 1979:74–75). Similar panics occurred the following year in Arkansas, where cattle deaths were linked to seven "witchcraft altars" found in Benton County (Owen 1979). By August 14, 1979, Arkansas police were circulating a "survivor's" account of a cult composed of doctors, lawyers, veterinarians, and other wealthy people who reportedly used unmarked helicopters and, on occasion, a van truck with a telescoping lift that would reach two-hundred feet over fields. The Satanists "would use that to extend a man out to the cow, and he would mutilate it from a board platform on the end of the boom and would never touch the ground. The apparatus would telescope back into the vehicle much as a wheelchair lift and not be noticed." (Sananda 1989:157–58). In Iowa, the state's Department of Criminal Investigations claimed to have located "satanic groups" and fought an unsuccessful battle with the Iowa Civil Liberties Union to find out who was checking out books on Satanism from the Des Moines Public Library (*Newsweek*, 21 January 1980:16).

Similarly, in western Canada, a rumor panic occurred in 1979, to be followed the next year with a rash of rumors concerning a group known as "Sons in Satan's Service" or SISS. A Saskatchewan investigator heard that this cult regularly sacrificed human babies during their services, and that a potential member was expected to "go out and bring back various parts of an animal" as part of his initiation requirements (*Stigmata* 11 [Fourth Quarter 1980]:10–11). This set of rumors recalls the contemporary legend usually termed "The Castrated Boy" (Dorson 1981:228;

Toelken 1979:178). Here the members of an ethnic gang are said to hide in public restrooms and cut off the penis of a young child who enters as part of their initiation. And the abbreviation of the cult looked ahead to a common belief among anticult crusaders that the name of the popular rock band KISS stood for "Kids (or Knights) In Service to Satan" (Lyons 1988:169).

The Flickinger Report inspired an even more elaborate story in 1979, when New York Times Books published *Jay's Journal*. According to an introduction, it was found among the effects of a sixteen-year-old suicide victim and edited by Beatrice Sparks (1979). Sparks had previously published *Go Ask Alice*, a diary documenting the downfall of a girl ruined by LSD, and *Voices*, alleged interviews with confused teens, including one "deprogrammed" by her parents after falling prey to a charismatic cult leader. This book too warns what happens to innocent adolescents who dabble with non-standard practices. Introduced to transcendental meditation by "Pete," a child-molesting "missionary" for a mysterious underground group called "The Occult," Jay soon finds himself practicing nightly rituals that help him see auras and levitate small objects. Before long he is encouraged to take the hallucinogen PCP and participate in sadomasochistic orgies at the home of a local witch. He later "marries" Tina, the coven leader, in a graveyard ceremony that includes strangling a kitten.

The climax of the book describes how Jay and three pals travel to Colorado to collect cattle blood and organs for a ceremony in an occult tradition called "Bootan." Mel, the initiated leader, fells a bull with an "electric arrow," then makes "precise little surgical cuts in exactly the right places" (1979:145). A few days later the coven meets to drink and bathe in the blood, which, not surprisingly, has been spiked with some kind of drug that removes Jay's ability to resist. "I couldn't hold back!" Jay writes. "I remember feeling like a prisoner of war or something, that they had taken my will away." The remainder of the book resembles a campfire story usually called "The Fatal Initiation," in which the members of a group who have carried out a forbidden ritual die one by one, until only the narrator of the story is left. Jay relates how each of his friends, tormented by demons who make them listen to rock music and look at pornography, all die from a blow to the temple just before they are to meet with the local bishop to expose "The Occult." An epilogue placed after Jay's final entry relates how he too placed the barrel of a gun to his temple and killed himself.

J. Gordon Melton, an encyclopedic observer of the American cult and occult scene, reviewed *Jay's Journal* and termed it "the ultimate magical mystery tour," realistic enough at the start but eventually filled with "improbable and finally outrageous elements." Any similarity to modern-day Wiccan groups, he said, was "purely coincidental," although, he conceded, "it's possible that a small group of weirdos might copy the rituals the book describes" (1980:104). On the other hand, the book received a warm review from *America*, the U.S. Catholic Church's weekly magazine, which called it "An obligatory book for those who minister to youth" (2 June 1979:459). *Jay's Journal* was also praised highly in *The Chronicle of Higher Education*, a respected weekly newspaper for college professors and administrators. The book "has the ring of authenticity and truth," said Allen Lacy, a California professor of philosophy, adding: "The account of the ritual killing of livestock is convincing. . . . *Jay's Journal* gives credence to those who have attributed this bizarre butchery to a resurgence of Satanism and witchcraft" (20 February 1979:R11).

Ed Sanders's investigative poetics, however, did not lead to any Watergate-style scandal, and after Rommel's 1980 debunking report, serious discussion of the U.S. military involvement theory faded from the mass media back into specialized conduits. Still, the antiestablishment theme was strong enough that it inspired a feature movie. *Endangered Species*, released by Warner Brothers in 1982, was made by Alan Rudolph, a young director with three major releases, who also co-authored the script after consulting with a number of mutilation investigators. It starred Robert Urich, acclaimed for his work on the prime-time soap *Vega$*, as a New York City cop tired of (in his character's own words) "kicking the shit out of bad guys so faggot judges could let them go." He travels to a small town in Colorado, where he is attracted to a newly elected female sheriff. After getting nailed in the groin during a drunken pass at her, the city cop agrees to help her solve a puzzling series of cattle mutilations. These turn out to be part of a secret government project in human-engineered anthrax germs, being field-tested in a mock-up of Moscow. The movie effectively introduces numerous special effects of high-tech cattle capture and biopsy and a plausible mystery black helicopter with a muffled jet engine that hovers and lands silently in a field. However, it was released well after the peak of the panic and grossed barely enough to cover theatre expenses in big cities. It was pulled from circulation almost immediately and packaged for the less expensive TV rerun and video rental markets (*Stigmata* 19 [Fourth Quarter, 1982]:2–9).

As investigations into flesh-and-blood conspirators grew less and less productive, two realistic alternatives remained: that the incidents had natural explanations after all, or that they were caused by creatures with superhuman powers of avoiding detection. Even UFO researchers who were initially struck by the anomalous features of early mutilations began to disclaim the mutilation-UFO link and join the skeptics. Jerome Clark, whose 1974 discussion of the Minnesota and Kansas mutilations was influential in attracting attention to them as mysteries, by 1982 had concluded that the mystery was non-existent.

Yet among some circles the quest continued, and in an unexpected way it validated Ed Sanders's faith that government officials would slip up and incriminate themselves. In May 1980, as Rommel's debunking research was drawing to an end, Paul Bennewitz, an Albuquerque businessman with scientific training, became interested in the newly discovered concept of "Close Encounters of the Third Kind"—i.e., actual contact with aliens. The publication of *The Interrupted Journey* in 1966, followed by Stephen Spielberg's landmark movie in 1977 had introduced the idea that humans were being abducted aboard UFOs and subjected to medical testing by extraterrestrials. Memories of these experiences were erased by the aliens' technology, but often spontaneously returned later on or could be recovered through a process of hypnotic regression. A number of cases had been reported in western states, where APRO had made a specialty of investigating them (see Lorenzen and Lorenzen 1976, 1977).

Bennewitz was convinced that abductees were being controlled by extra-low-frequency (ELF) communications and constructed a device to monitor such frequencies, sharing his finds with officers at the nearby Kirtland Air Force Base. During this work, he came across a woman who claimed a UFO encounter followed by a four-hour "loss of time," a frequent indicator of abductions. In May 1980, Bennewitz contacted Dr. Leo Sprinkle, a University of Colorado psychologist who had conducted several hypnotic regression sessions to recover abduction memories. Bennewitz and Sprinkle were well aware of the mutilation theories; Sprinkle's initial notes include the entry "Cattle mutilations in the area? She said that there were many cows in the pasture." And two months earlier, Sprinkle had conducted another hypnotic regression session with a woman who had described the simultaneous abduction of a cow and a child (Howe 1989:300–39). This case had come to the attention of Linda Moulton Howe, a documentary journalist for the Denver TV station KMGH who was working on a special show on mutilations, titled *A*

Strange Harvest. Howe was developing the idea that extraterrestrials might be carrying out the mutilations as part of biological experiments, perhaps to monitor the effects of fallout on the environment. She believed that alien abductions, which involved invasive medical procedures and possibly biopsies, were as part of the same extraterrestrial agenda. She videotaped the earlier hypnosis session and made it the centerpiece of the show, which aired on May 25, 1980, and subsequently received a regional Emmy award as an outstanding TV documentary.

The new hypnosis session, conducted with Bennewitz present, produced a sensational eyewitness account of aliens who wore long robes and had huge, slit-shaped "burning eyes, like the Devil" (Howe 1989:347). Led by a mysterious "Man in White," they abducted a cow and the woman's six-year-old son, slicing off the cow's genitals while it was still struggling and simultaneously performing some unseen medical operation on the child. In a subsequent session, the woman also recalled being taken to an underground alien base where she saw a tank full of blood-red liquid with body parts floating in it, in which one of the aliens was apparently bathing (Howe 1989:372–73). By this point, Sprinkle recalls, Bennewitz had become so anxious that he was carrying both a rifle and a handgun to protect himself from extraterrestrials, and he forced Sprinkle to break off the sessions, fearing the psychologist was a CIA agent (Clark 1998:I:304).

In the meantime, Bennewitz's ELF experiments had attracted the attention of personnel in the U.S. Air Force Office of Special Investigations (AFOSI) at the nearby Kirtland Air Force Base. In fact, ELF frequencies were being tested there as part of the Reagan-era "Star Wars" defense program, and researchers, finding that Bennewitz's equipment could monitor their experiments, apparently became concerned that he might inadvertently pass classified information to foreign agents. Consequently, a group of agents decided to infiltrate the circles of ufologists, first, to find out exactly what he was doing and, second, to discredit him so that whatever information he had would not be taken seriously. On October 24, Sgt. Richard Doty and another agent went to Bennewitz's house, ostensibly to look at evidence he had collected to prove that UFOs exist. They listened to tapes of the electronic pulses that he had recorded, and, while the agents concluded that they were "inconclusive," Bennewitz was invited to the base to explain his research to officers and researchers there. Meanwhile, a Kirtland agent had contacted William L. Moore, author of *The Roswell Incident*, a book claiming that the U.S. government had covered up recovery of an extraterrestrial spacecraft that had crashed in 1947. Moore was promised exclusive access to secret government documents proving that the crash had occurred and that contact had been made with space aliens. In return, Moore was to help inundate Bennewitz with "disinformation" that would discredit his work.

The situation was, as Moore later recalled, "the wildest science fiction scenario anyone could possibly imagine," but in essence it took the "body parts" elements implicit in the abduction story and made them even more explicit. In return for advanced technology, the officers told Bennewitz, the government had made a deal that allowed aliens to mutilate as many cattle as they needed. Now, however, the creatures had graduated from animals to humans, "whose organs they need to lengthen their lives." They were now living off of human flesh and working in underground bases alongside depraved human researchers to make soulless robots out of animal and human body parts, and also abducting Americans to implant them with mind-control devices. When air force agents confirmed this story, Bennewitz, driven even more frantic, suffered a mental collapse and had to be institutionalized (Clark 1998:I:303–5).

Sgt. Doty (who remained associated with the USAF until 1989) and at least one other AFOSI officer continued to leak alleged information about the "secret alien treaty" to ufologists, including Moore and Howe. This included copies of documents relating to a "Project Aquarius" that secretly handled UFO contacts. Howe, then under contract to produce a documentary for the American cable network Home Box Office (HBO) on UFOs, was repeatedly promised government footage of extraterrestrials and shown an alleged paper briefing a U.S. president on the aliens and their agenda. The footage never materialized, and Howe eventually lost her contract with HBO. She continued to show *Strange Harvest* at UFO conferences throughout the midwest and developed a small business in marketing copies of the film (1988) as well as a coffee-table format hardcover book, *Alien Harvest* (1989), which included facsimiles of many of the photographs of mutilated cattle and alleged government documents. Her work helped keep lore about the various suspects—Satanists, aliens, and government agents—circulating in various conduits well into the 1990s.

Conclusions

The mutilation mythologies cut deeply through American culture, revealing some of its priorities and anxieties. The idea that the mutilators were following some sort of religious rite or scientific agenda provided structure and motivation for apparently random acts. Thus, the implied cult members were mirror images of the investigators. Paranormal investigator R. Martin Wolf was the first to observe that law enforcement agents favored the cult mythology because it linked the mutilations to a group bound together with strict rules of conduct and procedure like their own. A cult committing crimes was, in this mythology, the exact inverse of a police force preventing crimes (Wolf 1977:25). And in fact, the cult scenario continues to be the dominant police explanation for animal mutilations, as the data collected by Jeffrey Victor on more recent rumor panics shows. References to animal deaths appear in 75 percent of newspaper reports of such cult scares, more than any other single motif (Victor 1990).

Similarly, the government conspiracy mythology was initially attractive to both the far left and the far right because it reflected an impersonal central government absolutely insensitive to the needs of individuals and bent on scientific and military success at any cost. Albers, like others maintaining the UFO link, could provide no more detailed theory than this and sought comfort in what he called the "reflective factor" of paranormal events—namely, that unexplained phenomena "appear to transform themselves to reflect the beliefs and expectations of witnesses" (104). The "dark side" UFO mythology incorporated this and the government conspiracy mythology into a single coherent one: the aliens, like fairies and vampires in earlier mythologies, harm cattle and steal children, so they are in some form diabolical in nature. The U.S. government's collusion is a kind of Faustian bargain, making military and scientific personnel into technologically enhanced witches and Satanists. This was yet another inversion: it explained ambiguous scientific data by turning to a power beyond science, or using the unknown one more time to comprehend the unexplained.

The alternative, though, was to concede that the mutilations could not be explained because the answer was in some way beyond human understanding, or because the agents had not yet agreed to share the secret with the American people. Frederick Smith said that the aliens "leave their calling cards but no one has ever surprised them at their work. They leave too much evidence for any rational person to deny they exist, but never enough to be identified. . . . They're obviously playing with us like a cat plays with a mouse" (1976:9). *The Mute Strategy,* a popular novel inspired by the scare expressed a similar view. "We are confronting forces we cannot hope to totally comprehend," the author wrote. "There are relationships among all the bizarre events, but uncovering those relationships will be far more difficult than the physical capture of the mutilators" (DeWitt 1979:168).

After a decade of involvement in the investigation, Jerome Clark concluded that there *was* no relationship among the claims being made by "mutologists." In a positive review of Kagan and Summers's skeptical history, he found himself disturbed by their suggestion that the "UFO subculture" was responsible for the panic. This was partly true, he conceded, "Unfortunately many persons are attracted to ufology not out of scientific curiosity so much as an adolescent fascination with mystery for its own sake. They aren't seeking answers; what they really want are more questions—as if there weren't enough of these already. It was in the end only natural that even after Kagan and Summers' thorough demolition of a mystery that never existed, cattle mutilations will remain, to some, yet one more of the world's unfathomable enigmas" (1984:102). But David Perkins countered that refusing to allow for any mystery behind the mutilations was itself mysterious. "I mean, this mutilation phenomenon is an *orphan* — *nobody* will take it," he commented. "Even the craziest researchers that don't care about their reputations in paranormal research, and UFO research, will not *touch* it. I mean they just can *not* get a handle on it, they don't want to think about it—they shut it off completely. To me this is very strange" (Perkins 1982:21).

Folklorists may perhaps be able to find the handle. The temporary presence of a mysterious conspiracy is *necessary* to give the proper therapeutic magical power both to healing acts and also to symbolic communal acts like rumor panics. Thus, rumor panics like the Highgate Vampire Hunt and the cattle mutilation scare are secular revivals, helping participants believe that their faith in themselves and their mythologies is justified. Anticult crusades challenge us to see details not as random accidents but as vehicles of *transcendent* mythic meaning. This is why Fredrick Smith (1976) insisted that the mutilators ultimately are sent by Jesus Christ, trying to wake Americans up to the imminence of the apocalypse.

> What makes Sodom memorable is that its tragedy has such clear
> sexual overtones. The same is true of cattle mutilations. A
> number of tongues, eyes, ears, skin and rectums have been
> excised. But the headlines that jostled the bells in everyone's mind
> was the removal of sex organs. . . .

For some reason extraterrestrials must be extremely interested in sex. But why? They do in fact have a very profound
interest in sex, but it isn't in any way pornographic as it is with
many earthlings. Sex is the one point, and the only point, where
mortality can reach immortality, where this finite principle can
reach an infinite principle . . . and where a merely animal nature
can effectively work in an eternal and transcendent nature.
(1978:65)

Perkins seems also to be driving at the same principle in a New Age fashion when he comments,

> . . . this mutilation phenomenon could be a *multitude* of things
> happening, for our benefit. See, it has an element of *show* to it.
> And that reflective quality, that mirror quality, intrigues me. That
> it could be beckoning us into this other area—that we're *supposed*
> to go there, we're *supposed* to pay attention to it. . . .
>   What if, you know, man's future involves traveling to the
> stars? . . . It's the next frontier. We're like going into the Pacific—
> we can't go nowhere, so we're going up! So we need a mythology
> to cling to or to attach ourselves to that will draw ourselves up. . . .
> And a cattle mutilation could be a stigmata—a spontaneous
> manifestation of faith and belief, which feeds a belief system—
> which adds fuel, which gives the whole thing its energy and
> transforming power. So whatever it takes to provide that image,
> it's gonna give it. And a cattle mutilation is the perfect thing.
> (1982:13–15)

Likewise, the actions taken by communities affected by rumor panics
(such as patrolling fields in pickup trucks) are like adolescents' legend-
trips and Ouija rituals, in that all are ways of participating in myth. They
are *transcendent* in nature, in that they reaffirm that the universe may be
frightening but is not random, and by engaging in ritual actions we exorcise evil and regain control over the forces that threaten us.

Interestingly, as with other rumor panics, the absence of any tangible result of these ritual actions is paradoxically a sign of their effec-
tiveness. Senator Harrison Schmitt defended his sponsorship of a 1979
conference on cattle mutilations, which led to Kenneth Rommel's harsh
debunking of the investigation, by noting, "after the meeting, we found

that there was almost no mutilation activity in the state of New Mexico. So that if nothing else, it appears that the conference had the purpose of protecting the property of many small ranchers and farmers for that period of time" (*Stigmata* 19 [Fourth Quarter 1982]:12). In other words, after the conference, the cattle mutilators just went away, as if by magic. If a dead cow or satanic symbol is a breakthrough of supernatural power into everyday life, then the skeptical point of view is willfully oblivious to the human quest for significance. One exasperated veterinarian, pressed for rational explanations of various mutilations, finally said, "So what? ...I can't explain it. Big deal. I have seen lots of things I can't explain, that doesn't mean they *mean* anything" (Kagan and Summers 1983:467). But for most people the inexplicable is the source of meaning, not the absence of it.

Skeptical responses have the effect of driving cult theories from the forefront of the national media, but they do not convince people. In the end, the cattle mutilation rumor panic, like the Satanism Scare as a whole, was driven by the belief that a messy affair can be seen as part of some larger, divinely ordained time scale. The presence of existential evil powerfully validates belief in ultimate divinity.

10

Conclusions

Was the Satanism Scare "Folklore"?

> No matter how strongly a folklorist argues against
> what we might feel to be false or even dangerous
> belief, we stand as one opinion in many. It is by
> knowing about the construction, world-view, and
> maintenance of belief that we can truly do some good.
> —Diane Goldstein, "Belief and Disbelief"

Jeffrey A. Victor has argued that the ritual abuse memories recovered by
some professional therapists make a "fit" with at least one definition of
"contemporary legend." For him, legends are "symbolically true emotional messages" that emerge in similar ways whenever an underlying
social stress is expressed in metaphoric form by a group of people who
stand to gain prestige or social benefits by exposing a social problem. We
might therefore classify all aspects of the Satanism Scare, as does Jeffrey
S. Victor, as "contemporary legend," a symbolic expression of unresolved
social tensions. Yet others have argued that issues of the ultimate truth or
fiction of such stories ought not to be questioned by folklorists. David
Hufford and Thomas E. Bullard have argued that "legend" is a prema-
ture and inappropriate label to describe how individuals construct encounters with extraordinary psychological events. In commenting on an
early draft of one of this book's chapters, Hufford said:

> What you have to say . . . could be a useful contribution to the
> history of modern, anti-occult Christian belief. But as your own
> evidence shows, Koch did not create this belief, nor is this belief
> entirely unreasonable. Much occult belief competes with Chris-

tianity, and within Christianity, much healing belief competes with the authority of specific denominations. Universally, ideas of magic compete with devotion. Religious ideas of evil do not map perfectly onto the evil that you and I find in the world, but then neither do modern moral theories or the ideas of clinical psychology. But in the end, those who believe that there is evil in the world, that sometimes evil uses ritual, that evil is opposed to religion (their religion, someone else's, whatever), and that it sometimes hurts people, have reasons for their belief that are not addressed *at all* in the contemporary legend things written on the "Satanism Scare." As a result, that literature is probably incapable of having any practical effects on what is an important social issue.

I concede that not everyone who reports or investigates cult activity is hysterical or deluded. In fact, for such people satanic cult beliefs may well be cultural language that allows them to express emotions and experiences that they might otherwise not be able to handle. Ironically, when societies *lack* traditions of belief that describe such events, persons there may often experience greater psychological trauma because they fear that describing their experiences will label them as deviant.

Nevertheless, even those willing to credit the core premises of the cult scenario have to admit that folklore intruded into the information they received. "We got an interesting phone call on the hotline this morning from a girl who says her father is a Satanist," a youth crisis hotline operator told Mark A. Galvin, director of DIOS in San Diego. DIOS, or Dunamis Impact Outreach Services, is one of many anti-occult organizations formed in the San Diego area to combat Satanism and its alleged partners, Wicca, Santería, and Rastafarianism. Galvin, interested, asked for details.

> "She says she's tired of the abuse and ready to run for help."
> "Where is she?"
> "Oregon. . . . She wants someone to pick her up tonight. Do you know of someone in that area?"
> "Well, wait a second. Do you know anything about this girl? Name? Date of birth? Address?"
> "She says her name is Julie. She won't give us any more information because she says her father will find out. He is an FBI agent."
> "How do you know that?"

"Well, that's what she said. Mark, I talked to her for a long time, and I believe her. Several times she began to cry uncontrollably. I knew she was hurting; I could hear it in her voice. I believe her."

Galvin was unsure what to do next: on the one hand, he realized that the girl might give him "the first incident of hardcore, organized ritual abuse we can actually document." On the other hand, the lack of details made him suspect a "a joke ... or a setup." He chose instead to call around to other hotlines to see if "Julie" had talked to other crisis interventionists. Within days, Galvin collected enough information to convince him that the call was a fraud. Women had been calling anticult hotlines such as Mike Warnke Ministries with similar but unconfirmable stories for at least the previous two years. But the story did not end there. Two months later another crisis operator called DIOS with a follow-up: "Julie" was dead. She had run away from her family, but they had caught up to her in Anaheim and cut her heart out, the report went. Finding that the Anaheim Police had no record of the murder, Galvin knew what to expect next, "When we called back the crisis hotline operator who originally gave us the information, we asked where she heard it. Our questioning led us to another crisis hotline operator in San Diego, then to another police officer in Idaho, then to a free-lance writer in Florida . . . and then to a crisis hotline supervisor also in Florida. She heard it from someone while on the hotline! This whole story started and ended within the conversations of those who are asking for help and those who attempt to give it." The case of "Julie" circulated widely because the caller(s) were constructing a message that the anticult hotline operators wanted to hear and pass on. Her message confirmed that the FBI (a noted skeptic of SRA claims) was not only wrong but also contaminated with evil. To doubt the story might strike to the heart of the crusade at the very moment when success was at hand. The "Julie" legends thus complement each other and reinforce in metaphoric form the mission of the anticult networks. The bottom line, though, is that "Julie" did not exist.

Galvin is typical of intelligent, undeluded people committed to the cause of combating dangerous cults. Aware that not all claims about ritual abuse are true, he properly criticizes Christian "professionals" (the facetious quotation marks are his) who "assume what they hear is true and run with it." He would rather have people criticize his organization for "not believing everything," he concludes, "rather than believing anything"

(1991:1, 5). That is, even anticult crusaders recognize the need to sort out fact from non-fact. In much the same vein, the Christian journalists who exposed Mike Warnke and John Todd as frauds did so in the name of preserving the cause of opposing Satanism and the Illuminati.

As argued in this book, there is a substantial grain of truth behind the anticult crusade. Occult-oriented folklore such as communication with spirits and ritual visits to uncanny sites is common among adolescents. Exorcism, a means of temporarily inducing an alternative personality, is an empirical form of religious experience. Further, the ritual may be beneficial to some persons for whom conventional psychological or psychiatric therapy fails. Finally, rumor panics, in the way that they create avenues for collective action against poorly defined threats, may be therapeutic in the way that they create a sense of community. For all the apparent "hysteria" and "delusion" involved in such scares, then, we must try to recognize the way in which a phenomenon such as the Satanism Scare was *beneficial* to many of its participants. Only then can we begin to sort out in what ways it may have been socially detrimental.

I raised the Devil, and the Devil raised me

In 1895, the British folklorist Sidney Oldham Addy published an account of a Derbyshire man who announced that he intended to raise the Devil. He went at dusk to a crossroads accompanied by a crowd and rattled together a frying pan and a key, repeating the cryptic rhyme:

> I raised the Devil, and the Devil raised me,
> I never shall forget when the Devil raised me.

Suddenly, the story continues, the Devil appeared in a clap of thunder, "but nobody saw him except the man who had raised him." He fell on his knees, saying "'Get thee behind me, Satan, for it is written that thou shall worship the Lord thy God, and him only shalt thou serve,'" and the Devil vanished (1973:75).

This little story, with its cryptic riddle, embodies many of the traditions we have studied. Crossroads are traditional places to meet the Devil, and the dusk setting and group participation recall the dynamics of legend-trips. The Ouija ritual too relies on a dimly lit environment and a small but intense group as audience. When we compare other rituals mentioned in early accounts (e.g. Thorpe 1851:3:16), we see that the key and the frying pan were an early form of the Ouija board, with the key used as a kind of planchette to construct diabolical messages. The clap of thunder represented the expected sign of the Devil's presence, and the incident, like legend-trips, concluded with the participants reaffirming their faith rather than concluding a bargain with the Devil. Raising the Devil raises those who raise him; their doubts about the world of myth are resolved; in a spiritual way they are healed by commanding the Devil to come and then instantly leave again.

The Satanism Scare, fundamentally, was a form of psychological healing founded on such folk roots. Early crusaders like Kurt E. Koch saw the healing as a process in which some kind of genuine power entered the patient and drove away the cause of the disease. Folk-healing traditions can produce medically valid results, and Koch saw that the folk healer was a rival to the professional role he was attempting to carry out as priest. From an institutional point of view, folk healing must itself be a form of Satanism in that it tempted people to make use of supernatural powers outside of the control of the Church. Further, Koch reasoned, such a healing ritual must introduce demons that later caused mental illness.

Grappling with the fact that folk healing did produce medically valid results, Koch was methodologically far ahead of the folklorists of the 1940s and 1950s. For academics, it often was seen indulgently as "usually amusing and a pleasant folklore study . . . one of the foibles of an ancestry which we with our modern science and invention have left far behind" (Bomberger 1950:7). By the 1970s, a growing number of academics were conceding that a diagnosis of "evil supernaturalism" may be valid within some cultures' traditions of belief. Felicitas Goodman (1988) in fact has suggested that the nearly universal practice of exorcism points to real psychological states that western physicians operating within the scientific medical tradition cannot treat nearly as well. This is as true for patients in Anglo-American cultures as for those in supposedly "primitive" third-world cultures.

Any patient consulting any therapist has first to absorb a field of reference, made up of numerous beliefs and scenarios. The patient contributes a willingness to compose a unique story within this field of reference; the therapist, a willingness to hear and make sense out of this story. Together, much like two adolescents holding either end of a Ouija board planchette, they construct a "grammatical" explanation for the patient's disorder, which includes a name and a strategy for overcoming it. When the patient and therapist share beliefs and story elements dealing with Satanism, subversive cults become part of one such explanation in their shared cultural grammar. If the therapist specializes in detecting and treating SRA cases, such an explanation becomes a likely outcome. The motifs and formulas that went into such recovered memories became available in specialized media-enhanced conduits in the early 1960s and were disseminated in the popular media in the wake of the rumor panics of the early and mid-1970s.

The recovered memory is not a "legend," although it may borrow from their content and imitate their structure. The concept "contemporary mythology" provides a much sharper fit for SRA accounts, particularly when one considers it in the context of folk healing. Both SRA and folk healing rely on Satan as the source of mental illness, often blame deviant neighbors or relatives as the immediate agents of the "spell," and offer psychological relief in the form of intensive counseling (often resembling interrogation). Conversion to the therapist's field of reference is logically followed by public testimony to the power of the healing that has occurred. The experience thus constructed is thus parallel to the transformative mythology that underlies folk healing.

Are we professionally obligated, as Hufford suggests, to give institutions the same "right to believe" if their beliefs, if not "scientific," are also not new and not entirely unreasonable? If they heal sick patients and create community, why should folklorists call them into question? Might we consider, at least for a while, that the Satanism Scare might have had therapeutic value? Could we concede that, in many ways, raising the Devil also allows people to raise themselves? By directly participating in myth, by "naming" their illnesses and casting them out, and by participating in ritual activities that provide reassurance that social evils can be neutralized by communal activities, those who engage in anticult activities achieve personal transcendence.

I never shall forget . . .

The folklorist's answer must at first seem paradoxical: we must support and value *folk* beliefs such as Ouija board rituals while at the same time criticizing the efforts of *institutional* therapists and religious groups who crusade against Satanism. Folk mythologies are a historically stable safety valve for social aggression. Groups may use them to justify scapegoating deviant individuals, but such myths do not lead to panics. Over the long term, these traditions play a positive role in communities' moral systems. We must hold institutions to a *higher* standard of proof than folk subcultures. When they lend credence to some mythologies and privilege special interpretations of these beliefs, their actions function as cultural catalysts, causing community-wide or nationwide crusades against persons or issues blamed for social problems.

Institutional mythologies like the Satanism Scare are *not* folklore, even though they appropriate folk ideas and practices that have been preserved in a given community because they have proved functional for that community's needs. Once appropriated by an institution for a different use, however, such ideas and practices may become dysfunctional. Historically, crusades that have been based on appropriated folk beliefs have done more damage than good, whatever truth or good intentions may lie behind them. Sadly, it is easy for institutions to forget this.

And this is what we see in the development of the contemporary satanic cult panic. Some adult survivors may in fact have been traumatized by child abuse, and it is not unreasonable to suspect that some of this abuse may have been ritual in nature as in the fatal Cunningham exorcism of 1976. But to assume that such practices are widespread and highly organized, despite the lack of hard evidence, involves a leap of faith into subversion myth. These myths, as we have seen, cannot be *disproved* but they also cannot be proved and are self-confirming. Hufford is right: individual evil can and does hurt; but corporate evil, backed by legal and political clout, can and does hurt far more people. This difference in power alone, as Gustav Henningsen found in the seventeenth-century investigations, distinguished witch beliefs, which might result in the scapegoating of a few individuals, from witch crazes, which killed by the thousands. Doubtless some of the witches executed in Europe, perhaps even in Salem, were guilty of practicing self-consciously maleficent sorcery. But the craze, once begun, swept up far more innocent persons than guilty. And while the exorcism of cults and the evil they represent may help heal an individual or community, the reverse of the same coin may involve hurt to others who are not "one of us."

Michelle Smith was as much the culmination of a mythmaking process as the beginning of one. Her story would not have been as credible and coherent without the preceding decade's theological debate. The demonic origin of certain mental illnesses, the contagious multigenerational effects of occultism, the power of The Blood, the Jekyll-and-Hyde multiple personality nature of exorcism, the undetectable omnipresence of subversive occultists—all of these themes needed to be stated, publicized through conduits, and worked into testimonies and cautionary illustrations first. To be sure, the deliverance ministry was not made up of credulous, irrational observers, and deliverance works because demon possession is often an empirical experience, for both exorcist and victim. And many individuals were helped by projecting their present problems onto a demonic part of their personality and ritually renouncing it. They raised the Devil, and by so doing, they raised themselves.

But we should not lose sight of the cultural stakes involved. Once a belief has been sanctioned by powerful groups, widely disseminated, and reinforced by frequent airing in the media, it may take on the status of a truism. Official anti-occult beliefs may thus mirror the way that anti-"superstition" beliefs held sway in the academy without being confirmed by direct observation. "Superstition," Koch argued, "is not only a sign of stupidity, credulity and a lack of knowledge and enlightenment, but it is also a sign of a bias toward God-opposed forces." To opt for a purely objective, neutral position here suggests that some kinds of folklore are so negligible in value that we should allow politically powerful groups to define them as forms of devil worship and systematically eliminate them. I agree with Phillips Stevens Jr. (1989), that a folklorist is morally obligated to confront institutions when they misrepresent subcultures that we claim to value.

In addition, when contemporary mythologies lead to ostension, they involve real-life, irreversible consequences. When a group of teens vandalizes a "witch's" tombstone to free themselves of the threat she symbolizes, the result is corruption of play, and a "street-corner myth" turns into a real crime. In the case of violent gang activity, satanic play can lead even to murder. Such tragedies may not prove the existence of satanic networks orchestrating such crimes; nevertheless, the folklore of Satanism can kill. But when a group of crusaders channels an institution's power and energy into punishing scapegoats for the problems of society, the result is something even more dangerous than these street dramas. Folklorists Linda Dégh and Andrew Vázsonyi concluded their discussion of ostensive behavior (1983) by saying that the word "dog" can bite: in other words, institutional myths, once put into cultural language, can hurt by becoming the model for future actions. If this is true for the copycat vandals who use the folklore of Satanism as a guide for real crimes, it is true at an exponential level for politically powerful networks and organizations of therapists. An old legal principle holds that a dog is entitled to one bite before it is ruled vicious. How many bites do we allow a dysfunctional myth?

In modern times, as before in the witch-hunts, ostension grew out of divisive and unproductive theological discussion, with even exorcists unable to decide who is an agent of Satan and who of God. To generate a sense of common purpose out of such disorder, participants progressively emphasized their dark alter ego, the devil-worshippers. And having gradually gathered and publicized what passed as concrete evidence for witches' illegal acts, the size of their database eventually became itself warrant for a secular crusade to oppose Satan's agents in this world. Regrettably, those who pressed the crusade hardest did not recall the historical outcome of the previous witch trials, where justification of diabolical medicine led to judicial murder on a megascale.

Happily the cost of the modern Satanism Scare in human lives is relatively small. Anneliese Michel, David Weilbacher, Christine Taylor, and other victims of exorcisms gone wrong number perhaps no more than a few dozen, compared with the thousands of witchcraft executions of the 1600s. Still, the ritual abuse investigations and trials of the 1980s and early 1990s represented a similar waste of expense and needless ruin of reputations and livelihoods. Reviewing the often disheartening material that came out of researching this book, I can readily agree that there is evil in the world, that sometimes evil uses ritual, and that it sometimes hurts people. I would also caution Hufford and similar-minded readers that evil is *not* always opposed to religion. Indeed, when evil appropriates the ideals and institutions of religion, the results are far more damaging than when individuals carry out self-consciously evil acts.

Anticult crusaders might have heeded the 1975 warnings of Christian historian John Warwick Montgomery:

> Man wants to carry out God's functions; he wants to build new towers of Babel to reach heaven. Not satisfied with the areas of civil and legal control given to him . . . man tries also to subdue hell. In the case of the witch trials, irony is piled upon irony, for in an effort to conquer the devil by whatever means, man falls directly into the clutches of the evil one. . . . Thus were the Christians who played God in the witch trials historically tainted with the mark of the beast they endeavored to subdue.

Even after all appropriate qualifications have been made, the Devil achieved more through the witch trials than he could possibly have gained by demonic activity apart from them. (1976b:102–3)

Notes

1. Christian Magic and Diabolical Medicine

1. I recognize that choosing the term "mythology" presents problems, even for academics. Richard Dorson noted that even among folklorists the term suggests a "fuzzy sense indistinguishable in common usage from 'legend' or 'folklore'" (1968:84). One problem is that terms like "myth," "legend," and indeed "folklore" for most popular readers imply untruth or lack of rational thought. Therefore, we hesitate to apply such terms to the culture and religion of educated, politically powerful groups in western industrial cultures. I follow scholars in using the term in a non-judgmental way to refer to a body of knowledge that defines this world as one that is directed and continuously informed by divine power.

2. Some folklorists have suggested "folk ideas" (Dundes 1971) or "worldviews" (Toelken 1979, Dundes 1989) for global concepts that combine and link many beliefs, legends, and customs. These concepts are valid, so far as they go. But they describe unspoken preconceptions that are not controversial within the culture that uses them. By contrast, the scenarios I describe are fully part of the legend process and spark hot debate.

3. *Belasten* is literally "to load or burden," but in Koch's field of reference it has the special sense of "to enslave," "to place in bondage [to Satan]," or, by extension, "to oppress [with demons]." *Besprechen*, literally "to discuss," is the usual German euphemism for working folk magic by using a charm and thereby "talking it over [with the spirit of illness]"; hence, a *Besprecherin* is a woman who practices charming, or, in Koch's worldview, an enchantress or witch. See Yoder 1976:246 and the entry on Besprechen in the *Handwörterbuch des Deutschen Aberglaubens*, 1:1156–72.

4. The concept of the "engram," or memory track, was popular among psychologists earlier in this century. It lost ground after neuropsychologist Karl Lashley failed to locate any specific location in the brain where memories were stored (Lashley 1950; Gregory 1987:223, 428). The concept was also used by the occultist L. Ron Hubbard in formulating his theory of dianetics, now advocated by the Church of Scientology.

5. For folk analogs, see Hand 1961–64: nos. 5581–85; Goldberg 1974:101–2.

6. Compare the folk analogs catalogued by Baughman 1966 under Motif G 03.25.21.4: *Witch bears devil child.*

7. Indeed the very word "blood" is etymologically related to the word "bless," because of the historical connection between blood sacrifice and religious ceremonies.

2. The Jesus of Satan

1. Good reviews of this material are given in Rogo 1987 and in Eugene Taylor's reconstruction of William James's 1896 public lectures on the topic (1984:73–112 and 186–93).

2. Malachi Martin also gives a detailed overview of the typical stages of exorcism in the conservative Catholic tradition, which will be discussed in a later chapter. He names these stages *Presence, Pretense, Breakpoint, Voice, Clash,* and *Expulsion.* This structure is similar to that of the Protestant deliverance tradition, except that the latter is based largely on the possessed person's experience of his release from demonic influence, while the former is based on the exorcist's reactions to the ritual. *Presence* and *Voice,* for instance, are steps in the exorcist's growing certainty that he is confronting existential evil, and his success in negotiating *Pretense* involves overcoming the victim's initial denial that he or she is in fact possessed (1976:17–21).

3. Dr. Smith is best known otherwise as one of the leading proponents of the notorious Tuskegee Study. Nine months before his spirit baptism, he had argued that medical treatment should continue to be withheld secretly from a group of African Americans with syphilis so that he and other physicians could study the damage the disease was causing to their eyes. See Jones 1981:194–97. Smith went on to a lengthy career at the Bascom Palmer Eye Institute of the University of Miami School of Medicine. In retirement, he continues to write for *The Trumpeter,* an interdenominational Christian magazine published in Miami (see *http://www.elink.net/trumpeter/staff.htm*).

4. Only Brooks's initials are given at the end of this letter in the original publication, but she is later identified in Basham's list of individuals networking in the deliverance ministry (1972:222). As we shall see, Brooks later relocated to the Asheville, North Carolina, area and became prominent in an anti-Semitic survivalist Christian movement. Basham's tapes continue to circulate through conduits of Charismatic lending libraries such as that run by Manna Ministries in El Paso, Texas; see *http://www.christianaudiotapes.com/basham.htm*.

3. Speak to the Devil

1. Anti-occult crusader Hobert E. Freeman likewise observes that whenever users asked for the source of the board's power, they received answers such as "the god of Hell," "Hell," "Satan," or the "Devil" (1969:17). Evangelist Gary Wilburn records similar answers to the query: "Satan," "Father of Lies," "God of this World," and "Deceiver" (1972:195).

2. In the Ohio State Folklore Archive, Ryan (1991) describes one very elaborate hoax of this sort: "So what we did is we took, um, we took thread and had it hooked up for example to a radio in the bathroom; the door was closed, so all I had to do was sit in the corner of the living room. . . . And I had to pull the string and the radio would go off. Or I could pull a string and a bible would fall off the shelf and open to a page of Revelations. *[Laughter] Oh wow! Wow, that's great! . . .* And people just screamed. And got the room—cleared out of there. *Wow!*"

3. American demonologists Ed and Lorraine Warren took an even stronger stance: mere possession of a board may expose women to sexual assault by demons. As protection, they advised owners not simply to burn the device but to sprinkle it with holy water and then bury it at least a foot-and-a-half deep (Hunt 1985:69–78).

4. Not surprisingly, this procedure also parallels Basham's instructions for learning to speak in tongues in private. This required a quiet preparation in which believers confessed Jesus as their Savior and reviewed Bible passages describing tongues. Basham then advised his readers to say a brief prayer inviting the Holy Spirit in: "You may experience a tingling sensation or a gentle vibration as if touched by an electric current." Then, no matter how awkwardly or shyly, he tells believers simply to open their mouths and speak: the Spirit will miraculously provide the language (1967:177–85).

5. The case is discussed in detail in Goodman 1981. See also Goodman 1988:114–22 and Watkins 1983:138–40.

6. For more details of this procedure, in the context of a transcribed exorcism in which Satan himself manifested and was compelled to speak nothing but the truth before the exorcist, see Ensign and Howe 1984:17ff. They admit, tellingly, that the "test for truth" was not 100 percent accurate, perhaps because Satan took advantage of inadvertent verbal slips in speaking the formula. Nevertheless it has proven "remarkably reliable in detecting the truth or falseness of [a demon's] statement" (171).

7. See Harrell 1985:199–206

8. This event does not appear in Harrell's biography of Roberts (1985), but seems to have been a widespread rumor among Roberts's opponents. The flamboyant "confessing Satanist" John Todd took it a step further, saying that Roberts had attended séances held by a "Cherokee medium," who taught him how to heal (Hicks and Lewis 1979:128).

9. Koch writes about this case briefly in 1973b:144–46 and in 1980b:30–38. I quote here a version presented in 1971 to a live audience in Minneapolis. This version, circulated in the deliverance conduit on audiocassette, is his earliest, fullest, and most detailed rendering of this incident. In his German autobiography (1980b), he observes that the demons understood every European language he used to address them, but the possessed victim spoke only Filipino and English. Koch consistently quotes the demons' words in English, and then translates to German, so presumably Koch conducted the exorcism in English. The exact rendering of the demons' answers, however, differs somewhat from version to version.

4. Putting the Pieces Together

1. Among these are Jenkins and Katkin 1991, Mulhern 1991, Nathan 1991, and Nathan and Snedeker 1995. Hicks 1991 and Victor 1993 also devote lengthy chapters to this controversy.

2. Lindsey later became a patron of Lauren Stratford, a controversial "survi-

vor" of Satanic ritual abuse during the 1980s (see Passantino, Passantino, and Trott 1990).

3. Several critical surveys of the emergence of the ritual abuse claim in the early 1980s exist, including Jenkins and Katkin 1991, Mulhern 1991, Victor 1991a, Hicks 1991:138–270, Jenkins 1992, Nathan and Snedeker 1995.

4. Goodman (1988) has noted that hypnosis, as it has developed from eighteenth-century mesmerism in western industrialized cultures, does not seem to exist in Third World cultures. However, she suggests that such cultures preserve and teach other means of switching between normal and altered states of consciousness (31).

5. Dr. Benjamin Simon, a specialist in war-caused post-traumatic shock, used a variation of this same technique to treat Betty and Barney Hill, who thus produced the first highly publicized UFO abduction narrative. Dr. Simon did not consider the recovered memories reliable, although the incident created a growing literature of UFO abduction tales recovered both spontaneously and under hypnosis. Interestingly, abductees also report memories of child abuse and trauma on a significantly higher rate than the general population, though the relationship between this phenomenon and that of the phenomena we are studying remains unclear.

6. This idea was mainstreamed in the public media by William Peter Blatty's *The Exorcist*, a best-selling book (1971) and blockbuster movie (1973). The plot included an incident that attributed a young girl's casual use of a Ouija board to her psychic rape and possession by an obscene male demon. Blatty in fact maintained that confidential records kept by Catholic exorcists blamed a Ouija board for the 1949 case that inspired his book (Gruss 1975:17). More public discussions of this case (e.g., Linson 1951) do not include this detail. Blatty's claim is ironic, as he admitted purchasing and using a Ouija board to contact his dead mother during the last stages of writing his book (1973).

7. Similarly, in *Venture Inward*, trance medium Edgar Cayce gave an example of a woman who lived through a similar progression from dabbling with a Ouija board to automatic writing to experiencing a vulgar spiritual voice and "a sexual stimulation which resulted in orgasm" (qtd. in Gruss 1975:163). Presumably this experience is similar to that which gave rise to traditions of the incubus, or demonic spirit that sexually stimulates women.

8. This account follows Watkins 1984:143–50, a full and accurate summary of the British press's extensive coverage of the event. See also Lee and Moore 1975:117–21 for a more popular summary.

9. Rogo notes that Allison's experience was paralleled by other psychic researchers' experiences with multiple-personality cases and cites an example from the 1890s. Interestingly, the concept of "psychic attacks" is commonplace in occult literature. As early as 1930, Dion Fortune wrote a substantial monograph on *Psychic Self-Defense* (1992) describing how to identify such attacks and defend against them. For more on this work and the dealings with British occultists that occasioned it, see King 1989:141–51.

10. We will hear more about this odd motif, which appears to derive from Mike Warnke's "confession," *The Satan-Seller*, in chapter 7.

11. Quotes and details on the Cunningham case are taken with permission from E. Ann Neel's unpublished paper (1990), which cites official court records. See also Watkins 1984:128–31 for a popular account of the affair.

5. The One-World Demonology

1. Good historical studies of what can be ascertained about the Bavarian Illuminati include Stauffer (1918) and Roberts (1972).

2. Presumably a misprint for "Judenstrasse" or "Street of the Jews."

3. Carr credits some of his information to "a man who was extremely well informed" (i.e., about military gossip and conspiracy theories) whom he met in 1917 while serving as King's Messenger (1958:82).

4. Cf. Carr 1958:61–63, which explicitly terms this an International Banker plot to cause World War I.

5. Wilgus (1978) is a popular but useful survey of the enormous popular literature inspired by this myth in the 1960s and 1970s.

6. I.e., Nelson Rockefeller (1908–1979), son of multimillionaire John D. Rockefeller and at the time of the prophecy the first non-elected vice president of the United States. William Guy Carr had already indicated, "The Rockefellers have replaced the Rothschilds as far as the manipulation of finances is concerned" (1958:xix). In his unsuccessful bid for the Republican Party's nomination for the presidency in 1964, supporters of Barry Goldwater successfully demonized him as a liberal with links to a mysterious group of international financiers called the "Bilderburgers." See Phyllis Schlafly's notorious campaign book for Goldwater, *A Choice, Not an Echo* (1964). After Nixon resigned and his successor Gerald Ford designated Rockefeller as his vice president, conspiracy theorists widely believed that the Illuminati were preparing to assassinate Ford, thus putting ultimate power in Rockefeller's hands.

7. The Christian Identity Movement and its history is fully discussed in Barkun (1994).

6. Brits and the Black Mass

1. King (1989:53) says that Crowley was "inspired by some dark hints given in the introduction to [Waite's] book" but does not mention which. Probably it was Waite's *Devil-Worship in Modern France* (1896) or, more likely, its immediate successor, *The Book of Black Magic and Pacts* (1898), which implies indirectly that Waite had experimented with some of the magickal procedures included and found them effective.

2. Robert Anton Wilson, in the forward to *Portable Darkness* (Crowley 1989), notes that this story still frequently circulates in oral tradition, despite the lack of any trace of such an event in Crowley's well-documented career. Wheatley also adapts the scene in the climax of *Strange Conflict* (1941), where an evil voodoo priest is unwise enough to summon Pan and is driven insane by the power of the entity.

3. See *FOAFTale News* 19 (October 1990):10 for a husband/wife version; the more common version, circulated during the British "white slave" panic of a few years earlier and still around today, has a father encountering his own daughter.

4. *Bolton Evening News* [20 Oct.1958]:1.

5. Contemporary press accounts include the London *Evening News* (18 December 1958) as well as local (and more detailed) coverage in the *Brighton and Hove Herald* (20 December 1958) and *Brighton and Hove Gazette* (20 December 1958). Additional information is provided by Doreen Valiente (1989:138–44).

6. Gardner held that the word "witch" was derived from a term denoting "wise one." He may have bypassed the historically correct "wicca" to highlight the superficial similarity of "wica" to "wise." In any case, "wicca" later became the standard spelling among his followers.

7. Wayne State University Folklore Archives 1969 (128) Canadian, Canada and U.S., Ontario and Michigan, Iroquois Falls and Houghton Lake, Roy D. Smith, 1962–1965, witchcraft.

8. The political implications of race are particularly clear in Wheatley's last occult novel, *Gateway to Hell* (1970). Set in Central America, it associates black magic with the Black Power movement. One of the head Satanist's henchmen admits, "Well, man, my buddy here an' me, we's bin doin' a lot of thinkin' dese pas' few weeks. Dis bid to bring de world under Black Power seemed jus' fine to us when we was indoctrinated. But we's bin gettin' doubts. You whites got all der guns, tear gas an' that. Reckon we don' stan' no chance. You'll sure come out on top. Slaughter'll be bad as a first-class war; an' we poor bastards'll end up wors' off than we was before' (1972b:227).

9. This ambiguity exists in tradition. A North Carolina collection (Johnson 1974) includes two variants of the "devil baby" legend, one in which the devil child drags an unrepentant father into Hell, another in which the father repents and the child loses his horns to grow up to be a respected lawyer and politician.

10. The choice of name reflects, of course, her burlesque stage name "Daring Diana." But the entire scene, even to the title, is heavily dependent on Leo Taxil's nineteenth-century "memoirs" of the fictitious Diana Vaughan, who was designated the "grand-priestess" Diana by Lucifer himself at the Satanic Masonic Temple in Charleston, South Carolina.

11. Cf. Summers: "'You may well suppose,' writes Boguet, 'that every kind of obscenity is practised there, yea even those abominations for which Heaven poured down fire and brimstone on Sodom and [G]omorrah are quite common in these assemblies.' ... To-day the meetings of Satanists invariably end in unspeakable orgies and hideous debauchery" (157–58) His follower Wheatley has de Richleau comment: "When these swine have recovered their wind the next act of this horror will be the baptism of the Neophytes and after that the foulest orgy, with every perversion which the human mind is capable of conceiving" (1954:95).

7. Hippie Commune Witchcraft Blood Rites

1. *San Francisco Examiner* [1 Feb.67]:41; *San Francisco Chronicle* [1 Feb.67]:5
2. *Los Angeles Herald-Examiner* [20 Dec.69]:A-6.
3. To be sure, Sanders was not anti-religious; in fact a few years later he wrote an apology of sorts:

Forgive me God if that I ever
wrote a book called *Fuck*
God in the Ass, which I did
indeed....

But I think of this, O God,
a movie I heard someone
made in the '60s (I never saw it):
a shot of the orphans
of Vietnam perhaps,
splashed with a demon barrel
of jellied gasoline, burning,
sizzling, demoted to tissue.
And then: the sound track (sing it with me please)
"Jesus loves the little children
all the children of the world"

& you will understand
the title of my book.... (1987:147–48)

4. Anthologized in Sanders 1987:49–51.
5. This last possibility was dramatized in the satirical novel *Illuminatus!* (1975) by counterculture figures Robert Shea and Robert Anton Wilson.
6. Mailer adds characteristically, "it had taken him[self] through three divorces and four wives to decide that some female phenomena could be explained by no hypothesis less thoroughgoing than the absolute existence of witches" (123).
7. See Sanders 1971a:302; Steiger and Smith 1971:135. Police records identified the object as a light-colored face towel stained with Sebring's blood.
8. To be sure, "Lucifer" in Anger's film is not the traditional Devil but a benevolent god who brings illumination to mankind, as in Albert Pike's Masonic cosmology; nevertheless, Anger had other direct links to popular culture Satanism. His previous film, *Invocation of My Demon Brother,* had featured Anton LaVey (again portraying Satan). Background music was provided by controversial rock musician Mick Jagger of the Rolling Stones, whose then-current album, *Their Satanic Majesties Request,* was decorated by Crowley's interpretation of the tarot card "The Devil." See Sanders 1971a:47–48; Lyons 1988:167; and Chapman 1991:9, 51.
9. This theory had previously been advanced, with variations, in the wake of a 1963 "human sacrifice" affair in Mexico. According to a popular report, the

cult, centered near Monterrey, was in the habit of drinking human blood mixed with marijuana to produce euphoria and mystic hallucinations (Starr 1965). In the wake of the scare that followed, hippie guru and LSD advocate Timothy Leary was asked to leave the country.

10. As late as 1973, the Reverend James Stowe and High Priestess Dolores Stowe of the Karnak Grotto of the Church of Satan, Santa Cruz, were complaining to reporters that officials were still harassing them despite their lack of any evidence to link cults and dog-skinning (*San Francisco Chronicle* [1 Apr.73]:B5).

11. *Los Angeles Times* [10 July 1970]:1:3, 19. Other contemporary accounts of this crime are in the *Los Angeles Times,* 2 July 1970:2:1–2 and 11 July 1970:2:1, 5. The case became a "classic" in the anti-occult literature: see Steiger & Smith 1971:7–8; Freedland 1972:199; Cerullo 1973:72. Hurd, diagnosed as a paranoid schizophrenic, was committed to a California hospital for the criminally insane (Lyons 1988:96).

12. The Baker case became another "classic": see Steiger & Smith 1971:10–12; Freedland 1972:199; Cerullo 1973:68–69. Baker, sentenced to life, eventually became an inmate counselor for drug problems at a maximum-security prison in Illinois and in 1976 unsuccessfully applied for membership in the Church of Satan (Lyons 1988:97–98). Baker's case was embellished by Hal Lindsey in his immensely popular *Satan Is Alive and Well on Planet Earth* (1974:6), and further embellished in Jack T. Chick's anti-occult comic book *The Broken Cross* (1974).

13. *Los Angeles Times* [17 July 1970]:1, 24–25.

14. William Sims Bainbridge (1978) gives a detailed ethnographic portrait of this group, based on interviews with Process members.

15. For descriptions of these issues in various shades of outrage, see Sanders 1971a:92–93; Terry 1987:177; and Lyons 1988:91–92.

16. Diane Speakman confirmed the general outline of this part of Warnke's conversion but also stated, "he has added comic things, unreal things. . . . The way Mike described our conversations, that wasn't the way we had them. And Mike said he started in ministry later; he actually started in ministry the night he was baptized in the Holy Spirit. He sat there and wrote down just what the Lord wanted him to do" (Hertenstein and Trott 1993:140).

17. Cerullo's chapter, although published slightly after Warnke's own book, was actually written first: see Hertenstein and Trott 1993:145. Unless otherwise stated, this discussion follows Warnke's second version, which became a modest best-seller among Christian books and was far more influential than Cerullo's work.

18. This work, presumably, is Erich Neumann's *The Great Mother: An Analysis of the Archetype* (1955). This Jungian analysis of goddesses in world mythology was an influential source for the emerging women's spirituality movement and contains nothing attributed to "Satan," nor is it mentioned in any other early discussion of Satanism as a black magic book. Perhaps the notion of a female deity was Satanic enough for Warnke's purposes.

19. This motif, which finds no earlier place in occult literature, must derive immediately from Stanley Baker, who removed his victim's fingers and took them with him. On some level, though, it may reflect a Native American practice in

which mourning females cut off the first joint of a finger out of respect for the dead. The practice was noted with disgust by General Custer, and Baker, who came from the state of the Battle of Little Bighorn, may have encountered a reference to this practice. See Connell 1984:54.

20. These meetings are not included in Warnke's *Satan-Seller*, probably because someone pointed out that Manson was still in prison during the time when Warnke claims he was active in his own cult activities.

21. Presumably an allusion to Peter, Paul, and Mary's 1963 hit song "Puff, The Magic Dragon," which was widely rumored to contain a coded encouragement for teens to try marijuana.

22. Unless otherwise noted, details on Todd's career come from Hicks and Lewis (1979).

23. Frost, like Sybil Leek, was a British-born Wiccan who emigrated to the United States and married a Southern Californian psychic. Together, they founded a "School of Wicca" in 1969 that provided correspondence courses in Gardnerian witchcraft. The Frosts are best known for producing *The Witch's Bible* (1972), which was issued in a black-covered paperback mimicking LaVey's *Satanic Bible*.

8. The Highgate Cemetery Vampire Hunt

1. *Daily Telegraph* (28 February 1959).

2. This information is gleaned from *Bedfordshire Times & Standard* (15 March 1963):16–17 and *Beds and Herts Pictorial Notes* (12 March 1963):10–11 and (19 March 1963):1.

3. The account given is based on the more detailed and objective coverage of the event in local newspapers, including: *Bedford Record* (19 March 1963) (2 April 1963):3; *Luton News* (21 March 1963):1, 4, (28 March 1963):2; (11 April 1963):1, 13; and *Beds and Herts Pictorial* (9 April 1963):1. The Clophill desecrations were also reported in the London papers, most notably *The Times* (18 March 1963):6, (25 March 1963):6, and (27 March 1963):6; and *The Daily Mirror* (18 March 1963). See also Maple 1966:171 and 1973:97, Lefebure 1970:7, Cavendish 1969:377, and Kobler 1966:76–78.

4. Maple says only that the bones were arranged in a circle (1978:97).

5. In fact, as Richard Cavendish notes, the *dark* of the moon is the phase most propitious for black magic (1969:251–52).

6. I have found no mention of animal jawbones used in any kind of folk magic, white or black.

7. *Hampstead & Highgate Express* [*HHE*] (28 January 1948).

8. *HHE* (31 October 1969):26, (6 March 1970):1.

9. *The Times* [*TMS*] (2 November 1968):4; (6 February 1969):2.

10. *TMS* (4 July 1974):4.

11. *HHE* (28 June 1974).

12. This issue marked the climax of legend swapping initiated by Farrant's letter. Two additional issues of the *Hampstead & Highgate Express* included letters discussing the "Highgate ghost," but little new material was received, and

many of the letters expressed openly skeptical points of view. No further letters on the topic were published after 20 March.

13. *HHE* (20 March 1970):23.

14. *HHE* (6 March 1970):1. Farrant later said that this remark was intended to humor "some over-zealous reporter" (1991:14).

15. The fullest account of this event is *HHE* (13 March 1970):1, although the *Evening News* also covered the event (14 March 1970:1). Manchester (1975:115) and Farrant (1991:14) also discuss this public "vampire hunt." *TMS*, interestingly, did *not* mention the incident, but on 13 March the paper's lead editorial, "The Threat of Drugs," commented that drug abuse "is becoming one of Britain's most disturbing social problems" and urged tough new laws to curb "the cult of cannabis" (11).

16. *HHE* (7 August 1970):1; *Camden, Hampstead & Highgate Record* [*CHHR*] (7 August 1970):1.

17. *HHE* (21 August 1970):1; *CHHR* (21 August 1970):1.

18. *CHHR* (28 August 1970):1, (2 October 1970):1; Farrant 1991:16–18.

19. *TMS* (30 September 1970):4; *HHE* (2 October 1970):1; *CHHR* (2 October 1970):1.

20. *Hornsey Journal* [*HJ*] (9 October 1970):9.

21. *Evening News* (16 October 1970):C3.

22. *HJ* (28 August 1970):36.

23. *HJ* (16 October 1970):40; Manchester 1975:119–20; Manchester 1991:93–94.

24. *Islington Gazette* [*IG*] (22 February 1971):1, (29 January 1971):1, (19 February 1971):3.

25. *Guardian* (28 February 1971):7.

26. *HJ* (31 August 1973):3.

27. *CHHR* (1 October 1971):1; *HHE* (1 October 1971):1; *HJ* (8 October 1971):31.

28. *HHE* (15 October 1971):3; *HJ* (15 October 1971):10.

29. *Daily Mirror* (28 February 1972):11.

30. *Sunday People* (8 Apr.1973).

31. *HJ* (31 August 1973):3; (2 September 1973); *News of the World* (23 September 1973).

32. His single "Let the Heartaches Begin" was number one on the British rock music charts in November 1967, briefly eclipsing the then-dominant Beatles (Taylor 1987:252).

33. *HJ* (2 September 1973):1; *Daily Express* (26 June 1974):9; *HJ* (5 July 1974):10; *CHHR* (5 July 1974):7.

34. *TMS* (2 July 1974):4; Farrant 1992.

35. *HJ* (25 January 1974), (15 March 1974):3.

36. Local press covered the case in loving detail: see *HJ* (11 February 1974):1, (22 March 1974):5; *HHE* (14 June 1974):60; *HHE* (21 June 1974):4; *Daily Express* (26 June 1974):9; *HJ* (28 June 1974):7, (20 August 1976):11. Additional press coverage of the trial and verdict included *TMS* (12 June 1974):5, (13 June 1974):4, (15 June 1974):3, (2 July 1974):4, (4 July 1974):4, (18 July 1974):3; *Daily*

Telegraph 18 July 1974; and *Daily Mail* 18 July 1974. See also Underwood 1975:80 and Manchester 1985:77–81.

37. *Reports on Sentencing from the Criminal Division of the Court of Appeal* 61 (17 March 1975):200–205.

38. *HJ* (8 November 1974).

39. *Daily Express* (9 September 1978):14, (12 September 1978):11.

40. An earlier suit against the *Daily Express* came first to a hung jury, then failed on retrial.

41. *City Limits* (6–16 April 1987):C1.

42. Or simply The Vampire Research Society, P.O. Box 542, Highgate, London N6 6BG.

43. For details on the British scare, see *FOAFTale News* 20 (December 1990):6–7 and 37 (June 1995):2; *Magonia* 38 (January 1991), Bennett 1991a and 1991b, Hobbs and Ellis 1991, Bennett, Hobbs, and Ellis 1991, *Fortean Times* 57 (Spring 1991):46–62, Sandell 1992. Jenkins 1992 is a sociological discussion of the construction of Satanic cult and associated social problems in Great Britain during the 1980s.

44. *FOAFTale News* 16 (September 1989):8.

9. The Great Plains Cattle Mutilation Panic

1. Popular handlings of these lights include Coleman 1983:261–63 and 1985:82–86, and Gaddis 1967:69 ff. Folkloristic treatments, which are less detailed but better at discussing the context and significance of such beliefs, include Montell 1975:141 and Rudinger 1976:52–62.

2. This alludes to the terrorist bombing of August 24, 1970, in which antiwar extremists destroyed an army research center at the Madison campus of the University of Wisconsin. Ammonium nitrate, widely available as a commercial fertilizer, was the explosive used in the 1996 bombing of the Oklahoma City Federal Building as well.

3. This and following quotes are from Flickinger's report, "Occult Activities in U.S.," submitted April 10, 1975 to the BATF. This affair is also summarized in a number of popular sources, including Randolph 1975:52–57; Cockburn 1975:64–65; Smith 1976:38–39; Sanders 1976:52, 92, 113; Albers 1979:31–36; and Vallee 1979:178–83.

4. These are also summarized in Sanders 1976:113–14 and in Albers 1979:36.

5. Ultimately this file went to ex-government agent Rommel to use in his debunking report. As before, when targeted by officials looking for hippie Satanists, LaVey characteristically ended up collaborating with the government to make the case for skepticism.

6. "Howard" was a real person named in the Flickinger Report. The *Esquire* column notes that he and all the other persons implicated by Bankston and Dugan were trailed and eventually detained by federal agents, who subjected them to polygraph tests. No evidence ever emerged to link them with cult activities. "Howard," it turned out, had been in jail on other charges during the

time when Bankston and Dugan claimed he had been active in organizing the cult (Sanders 1976:113).

7. LaVey specifically instructed his followers to respect animals and children and consistently denied encouraging any of his followers to carry out blood sacrifices (1969:89).

Bibliography

Adams, Thomas R. 1991 [1980]. *The Choppers—and the Choppers: Mystery Helicopters and Animal Mutilations.* Rev. ed. Paris, Tex.: Project Stigma.

Adler, Margot. 1986. *Drawing Down the Moon: Witches, Druids, Goddess-Worshippers and Other Pagans in America Today.* 2d ed. Boston: Beacon.

Addy, Sidney Oldall. 1973 [1895]. *Household Tales with Other Traditional Remains.* Totowa, N.J.: Rowman and Littlefield.

Albers, Michael D. 1979. *The Terror.* New York: Manor Books.

Allen, Denna, and Janet Midwinter. 1990. "Michelle Remembers: The Debunking of a Myth." *The Mail on Sunday* [London] 30 September 1990: 41. Available: *http://www.angelfire.com/or/ASTAROTH/michelle.html*

Allison, Ralph B. 1974. A New Treatment Approach for Multiple Personalities. *The American Journal of Clinical Hypnosis* 17:1 (July). Available: *http://www.dissociation.com/index/published/NEWRXMP.txt*

———. 1984 [1978] Psychotherapy of Multiple Personality. Unpublished paper presented at the Annual Meeting of the American Psychiatric Association, Atlanta, Georgia. Available: *http://www.dissociation.com/index/unpublished/psyofmpd.txt*

———. 1985. The Possession Syndrome on Trial. *American Journal of Forensic Psychiatry* 6 (1): 46–56. Available: *http://www.dissociation.com/index/published/POSTRIAL.txt*

———. 1991. Satanic Ritual Abuse and Multiple Personality: The Negative Side of the Argument. Unpublished paper presented at the Annual Conference of the Society for the Anthropology of Consciousness, Fallbrook, California. Available: *http://www.dissociation.com/index/unpublished/SAPMPD.txt*

———. 1998. The Human Essence: Manual for Six Week Workshop at Unity Christ Church, San Luis Obispo, California. Available: *http://www.dissociation.com/index/manuals/unindex.html*

Allison, Ralph, with Ted Schwarz. 1980. *Minds in Many Pieces: The Making of a Very Special Doctor.* New York: Rawson, Wade Publishers, Inc.

Altick, Richard D. 1969. *To Be in England.* New York: Norton.

Anderson, Peter. 1973. *Talk About the Devil.* London: Word Books.

Ankarloo, Bengt, and Gustav Henningsen, eds. 1990. *Early Modern European Witchcraft: Centres and Peripheries.* Oxford: Clarendon Press.

Bainbridge, William Sims. 1978. *Satan's Power: A Deviant Psychotherapy Cult.* Berkeley: University of California Press.

Balch, Robert W., and Margaret Gilliam. 1991. Devil Worship in Western Montana: a Case Study in Rumor Construction. In Richardson, Best, and Bromley 1991: 249–62. New York: Aldine de Gruyter.

Barber, Paul. 1988. *Vampires, Burial, and Death: Folklore and Reality*. New Haven, Conn.: Yale University Press.

Barkun, Michael. 1994. *Religion and the Racist Right: The Origins of the Christian Identity Movement*. Chapel Hill: University of North Carolina Press.

Baroja, Julio Caro. 1965 [1961] *The World of the Witches*. Trans. O.N.V. Glendinning. Chicago: University of Chicago Press.

Barrett, Sir William F. 1914. On Some Experiments with the Ouija Board and Blindfolded Sitters. *Proceedings of the American Society for Psychical Research* 8: 381–94.

Barstow, Anne Llewellyn. 1996. *Witchcraze: A New History of the European Witch Hunts*. San Francisco: Pandora.

Bascom, William. 1965. The Forms of Folklore: Prose Narratives. *Journal of American Folklore* 78: 3–20.

Basham, Don W. 1967. *Face Up with a Miracle*. Springdale, Pa.: Whitaker House.

———. 1971a. *Can a Christian Have a Demon?* Monroeville, Pa.: Whitaker House.

———. 1971b. *A Handbook on Tongues, Interpretation and Prophecy: 27 Questions and Answers on the Inspirational Gifts of the Holy Spirit*. Monroeville, Pa.: Whitaker House.

———. 1972. *Deliver Us from Evil*. Washington Depot, Conn.: Chosen Books.

———. 1986. *Lead Us Not into Temptation*. Old Tappan, N.J.: Chosen Books.

Basham, Don W., and Dick Leggatt. 1974. *The Most Dangerous Game: A Biblical Exposé of Occultism*. Greensburg, Pa.: Manna Christian Outreach.

Baughman, Ernest W. 1966. *Type and Motif-Index of the Folktales of England and North America*. The Hague: Mouton.

Bennett, Gillian. 1987a. The Rhetoric of Tradition. *Talking Folklore* 1:3 (spring 1987): 32–46.

———. 1987b. *Traditions of Belief: Women, Folklore and the Supernatural Today*. New York: Viking Penguin.

———. 1991a. Sex and Cannibalism in the Service of Satan: A Checklist of Articles about Satanic Abuse in the British Quality Press February 1989 to October 1990. *Dear Mr. Thoms* 20 (April): 36–44.

———. 1991b. Satanic Ritual Abuse in the United Kingdom: A Checklist of Newspaper Reports, Part Two: The Rochdale and Nottingham Affairs. *FOAFTale News* 23 (September): 7–11.

Bennett, Gillian, Sandy Hobbs, and Bill Ellis. 1991. Satanic Ritual Abuse in the United Kingdom: A Checklist of Newspaper Reports in England and Scotland. Part Three: The Orkney Islands Ritual Abuse Case Continued. *FOAFTale News* 24 (December): 1–4.

Berger, Peter L., and Thomas Luckmann. 1967. *The Social Construction of Reality: A Treatise in the Sociology of Knowledge*. New York: Anchor Books.

Best, Joel. 1991. Bad Guys and Random Violence: Folklore and Media Constructions of Contemporary Deviance. *Contemporary Legend* 1: 107–22.

Best, Joel, and G.T. Horiuchi. 1985. The Razor Blade in the Apple: The Social Construction of Urban Legends. *Social Problems* 32: 488–99.

Blatty, William Peter. 1971. *The Exorcist.* New York: Harper & Row.

———. 1973. *I'll Tell Them I Remember You.* New York: Norton.

Bomberger, C.M. 1950. Braucherei. *Pennsylvania Dutchman* 2:11 (1 November): 7

Bonewits, P.E.I. 1989 [1971]. *Real Magic: An Introductory Treatise on the Basic Principles of Yellow Magic.* Rev. ed. York Beach, Maine: Samuel Weiser.

———. 1975. The Case of the Mysterious Mutilations. *Gnostica* (May): 2.

———. 1997 [1975]. My Satanic Adventure 2.1.3: or I was a Teenaged Satanist! Available: *http://www.qed.net/bonewits/SatanicAdventure.html*

Bonham, James Butler. 1976. Cattle Mutilations and UFOs: Satanic Rite or Alien Abduction? *Official UFO* 1:13 (December): 26–27, 54–55.

Bord, Janet and Colin. 1974. *Mysterious Britain: Ancient Secrets of the United States and Ireland.* London: Grenada.

———. 1978. *The Secret Country: More Mysterious Britain.* London: Grenada.

———. 1980. *Alien Animals: A Worldwide Investigation.* London: Grenada.

———. 1985. *Sacred Waters: Holy Wells and Water Lore in Britain and Ireland.* London: Grafton Books.

Bronner, Simon J. 1990. *Piled Higher and Deeper: The Folklore of Campus Life.* Little Rock, Ark.: August House.

Brooks, Pat. 1972. *Out! In the Name of Jesus.* Carol Stream, Ill.: Creation House.

———. 1978. *Healing of the Mind.* Fletcher, N.C.: New Puritan Library.

———. 1981a. *Hear, O Israel.* Fletcher, N.C.: New Puritan Library.

———. 1981b. *The Return of the Puritans.* Fletcher, N.C.: New Puritan Library.

Brunvand, Jan Harold. 1986. *The Mexican Pet: More "New" Urban Legends and Some Old Favorites.* New York: Norton.

Bullard, Thomas E. 1989. Hypnosis and UFO Abductions: A Troubled Relationship. *Journal of UFO Studies* N.S. 1: 3–40.

———. 1995. *The Sympathetic Ear: Investigators as Variables in UFO Abduction Reports.* Mt. Rainier, Md.: Fund for UFO Research.

———. 1998. Abduction Phenomenon. In *The UFO Encyclopedia, 2nd Edition: The Phenomenon from the Beginning,* ed. Jerome Clark. Detroit: Omnigraphics.

Burl, Aubrey. 1985. *Megalithic Brittany: A Guide to Over 350 Ancient Sites and Monuments.* London: Thames and Hudson.

Campion-Vincent, Véronique. 1990. The Baby-Parts Story: A New Latin American Legend. *Western Folklore* 49: 9–25.

Carlson, Shawn, et al. 1989. *Satanism in America: How the Devil Got Much More Than His Due.* El Cerrito, Calif.: Gaia Press.

Carr, William Guy. 1958. *Pawns in the Game.* Willowdale, Ontario: Federation of Christian Laymen.

Cavendish, Richard. 1969. *The Black Arts.* London: Pan Books.

Cerullo, Morris. 1973. *The Back Side of Satan.* Carol Stream, Ill.: Creation House.

Chapman, Douglas. 1991. Celluloid Crowley: The Mage and the Movies. *Strange Magazine* 8: 6–9, 51.

Chick, Jack T. 1974. *The Broken Cross*. Chino, Calif.: Chick Publications.

———. 1978. *Angel of Light*. Chino, Calif.: Chick Publications.

Clark, Jerome. 1974. Strange Case of the Cattle Killings. *Fate* [27:8] (August): 79–90. Reprinted in Ebon, ed. 1979: 115–26.

———. 1980a. Cattle Mutilations—The Deepening Mystery: Part I. *Fate* 33:2 (February): 61–68.

———. 1980b. Cattle Mutilations—The Deepening Mystery: Part II. *Fate* 33:3 (March): 66–72.

———. 1984. Reality Mutilation. *Fate* 37:10 (October): 99–101.

———. 1998. The *UFO Encyclopedia: The Phenomenon from the Beginning*. Detroit: Omnigraphics.

Clason, Clyde B. 1960. *I Am Lucifer: Confessions of the Devil*. Philadelphia: Muhlenberg Press.

Clements, William M., and William E. Lightfoot. 1972. The Legend of Stepp Cemetery. *Indiana Folklore* 5: 92–141.

Cockburn, Alexander. 1975. Rippers of the Range. *Esquire* (December): 62–65.

Cohn, Norman. 1967. *Warrant for Genocide: The Myth of the Jewish World-Conspiracy and the Protocols of the Elders of Zion*. New York: Harper & Row.

———. 1975. *Europe's Inner Demons: An Enquiry Inspired by the Great Witch-Hunt*. New York: New American Library.

Coleman, Loren. 1983. *Mysterious America*. Boston: Faber and Faber.

———. 1986. *Curious Encounters: Phantom Trains, Spooky Spots, and Other Mysterious Wonders*. Boston: Faber and Faber.

Connell, Evan S. 1984. *Son of the Morning Star: Custer and the Little Bighorn*. San Francisco: North Point Press.

Covina, Gina. 1979. *The Ouija Book*. New York: Simon and Schuster.

Crosby, Rev. John R. 1927. Modern Witches of Pennsylvania. *Journal of American Folklore* 40: 304–9.

Crowley, Aleister. 1989. *Portable Darkness: An Aleister Crowley Reader*. Ed. Scott Michaelsen. New York : Harmony Books.

Crowther, Patricia and Arnold. 1976. *The Witches Speak*. New York: Samuel Weiser. (Orig. pub. 1965.)

Cruz, Nicky. 1973. *Satan on the Loose*. Old Tappan, N.J.: Fleming H. Revell.

Dash, Mike. 1996. Spring-Heeled Jack: To Victorian Bugaboo from Suburban Ghost. *Fortean Times* 3: 7–125.

Davidson, Jacob A. 1975. *Cattle Mutilation Special Report*. Seattle: Jacob A. Davidson.

Dégh, Linda. 1969. The House of the Blue Lights Revisited. *Indiana Folklore* 2: 11–28. Reprinted in Dégh, ed., 1980: 179–95.

———. 1971. The "Belief Legend" in Modern Society: Form, Function and Relationship to Other Genres. In *American Folk Legend: A Symposium*, ed. Wayland Hand, 55–68. Berkeley: University of California Press.

―――. 1979. Conduit-Theorie. In *Enzyklopädie des Märchens,* ed. Kurt Ranke et al., 3:1: 124–26. Berlin: Walder de Gruyter.

―――, ed. 1980. *Indiana Folklore: A Reader.* Bloomington: Indiana University Press.

―――. 1990. Are Sectarian Miracle Stories Contemporary American Folk Legends? In *Storytelling in Contemporary Society,* ed. Lutz Röhrich and Sabine Wienker-Piepho. Tubingen, Germany: Gunter Narr.

―――. 1994. *American Folklore and the Mass Media.* Bloomington: Indiana University Press.

―――. 1995. *Narratives in Society: A Performer-Centered Study of Narration.* Helsinki: Academia Sciantiarum Fennica.

Dégh, Linda, and Andrew Vázsonyi. 1975. The Hypothesis of Multi-Conduit Transmission in Folklore. In *Folklore: Performance and Communication,* ed. Dan Ben-Amos and Kenneth A. Goldstein, 207–52. The Hague: Mouton. Reprinted in Dégh 1995: 173–212.

―――. 1983. Does the Word "Dog" Bite? Ostensive Action: A Means of Legend-Telling. *Journal of Folklore Research* 20: 5–34. Reprinted in Dégh 1995: 236–62.

Devil Rides Out, The. 1996. Jacket notes to videocassette release SV10266. Troy, Mich.: Anchor Bay Entertainment.

DeWitt, Dave. 1979. *The Mute Strategy.* Albuquerque, N.Mex.: Sunbelt Press.

Dieffenbach, Victor C. 1976. Powwowing Among the Pennsylvania Germans. *Pennsylvania Folklife* 25 (2): 29–46.

Donovan, Roberta, and Keith Wolverton. 1976. *Mystery Stalks the Prairie.* Raynesford, Mont.: T.H.A.R. Institute.

Dorson, Richard M. 1959. *American Folklore.* Chicago: University of Chicago Press.

―――. 1968. Theories of Myth and the Folklorist. In *Myth and Mythmaking,* ed. Henry A. Murray, 76–89. Boston: Beacon Press.

―――. 1973. *America in Legend: Folklore from the Colonial Period to the Present.* New York: Pantheon.

―――. 1981. *Land of the Millrats.* Cambridge: Harvard University Press.

Dresser, Norine. 1989. *American Vampires: Fans, Victims, Practitioners.* New York: Norton.

Dundes, Alan. 1971. Folk Ideas as Units of Worldview. *Journal of American Folklore* 84: 93–103.

―――. 1989. Defining Identity through Folklore. In his *Folklore Matters,* 1–39. Knoxville: University of Tennessee Press.

―――. 1991. The Ritual Murder or Blood Libel Legend: A Study of Anti-Semitic Victimization through Projective Inversion. In his *The Blood Libel Legend: A Casebook in Anti-Semitic Folklore,* 336–76. Madison: University of Wisconsin Press.

Ebon, Martin, ed. 1971. *Witchcraft Today.* New York: New American Library.

―――. 1974. *Exorcism: Fact Not Fiction.* New York: New American Library.

————. 1979. *The World's Weirdest Cults*. New York: New American Library.

Ellis, Bill. 1982–1983. Legend-Tripping in Ohio: A Behavioral Survey. *Papers in Comparative Studies* 2: 52–69.

————. 1990. The Devil-Worshippers at the Prom: Rumor-Panic as Therapeutic Magic. *Western Folklore* 49: 27–49.

————. 1991. Legend-Trips and Satanism: Adolescents' Ostensive Traditions as "Cult" Activity. In Richardson, Best, and Bromley 1991: 279–95. New York: Aldine de Gruyter.

————. 1996. Satanic Déjà vu in Northeastern Pennsylvania. *FOAFTale News* 40–41 (December): 4–8.

Elwood, Roger. 1973. *Strange Things Are Happening: Satanism, Witchcraft, and God*. New York: Family Library.

Ensign, Grayson H., and Edward Howe. 1984. *Bothered? Bewildered? Bewitched? Your Guide to Practical Supernatural Healing*. Cincinnati: Recovery Publications.

Erikson, Erik. 1970. Reflections on the Dissent of American Youth. *International Journal of Psycho-Analysis* 51:11–22.

Ernest, Victor H. 1970. *I Talked with Spirits*. Wheaton, Ill.: Tyndale House.

Estes, Leland L. 1986. The Medical Origins of the European Witch Craze: A Hypothesis. In *A Lycanthropy Reader: Werewolves in Western Culture*, ed. Charlotte F. Otten, 200–19. Syracuse, N.Y.: Syracuse University Press.

Evans, Hilary. 1989. *Alternate States of Consciousness : Unself, Otherself, and Superself*. Wellingborough, Northamptonshire, England : Aquarian Press.

Everman, Welch D. 1993. *Cult Horror Films: From Attack of the 50 Foot Woman to Zombies of Mora Tau*. Secaucus, N.J.: Carol Publishing Group.

Fabian, Robert. 1953. *Fabian of the Yard*. New York: British Book Center.

————. 1954. *London After Dark*. London: Naldrett Press.

Farrant, David. 1972a. Vampires—Fact or Fiction? *Camden Journal* (5 May): 4.

————. 1972b. Has the Stone Cast Its Magic Spell? The "Black History" of Highgate. *Islington Gazette* (29 September).

————. 1991. *Beyond the Highgate Vampire*. London: British Psychic and Occult Society.

————. 1992. Personal interview, London, 24 July.

Farrar, Stewart. 1971. *What Witches Do: The Modern Coven Revealed*. New York: Coward, McCann & Geoghegan.

Fortune, Dion. 1992 [1930]. *Psychic Self-Defence*. York Beach, Maine: Samuel Weiser.

Frazier, Ian. 1989. A Reporter at Large: Great Plains II. *The New Yorker* (27 February): 35–65.

Freedland, Nat. 1972. *The Occult Explosion*. New York: Berkeley Medallion.

Freeman, Hobart E. 1969. *Angels of Light?* Plainfield, N.J.: Logos International.

Gaddis, Vincent H. 1967. *Mysterious Fires and Lights*. New York: Dell.

Galvin, Mark A. 1991. Testing the Truth. *The D.I.O.S. Informant* 2:3 (July–August): 1, 5.

Gardner, Emelyn Elizabeth. 1937. *Folklore from The Schoharie Hills, New York.* Ann Arbor: University of Michigan Press.

Gardner, Gerald. 1954. *Witchcraft Today.* London: Rider.

———. 1951. *The Meaning of Witchcraft.* London: Aquarian Press.

Gasson, Raphael. 1966. *The Challenging Counterfeit.* Plainfield, N.J.: Logos International.

Georges, Robert A. 1971. The General Concept of Legend: Some Assumptions to be Reexamined and Reassessed. In *American Folk Legend: A Symposium,* ed. Wayland Hand, 1–19. Berkeley: University of California Press.

Ginzburg, Carlos. 1990. Deciphering the Sabbath. In Ankarloo and Henningsen 1990: 121–38.

———. 1991. *Ecstasies: Deciphering the Witches' Sabbath.* Translated by Raymond Rosenthal. New York: Pantheon.

Goldberg, Christine. 1974. Traditional American Witch Legends: A Catalog. *Indiana Folklore* 7: 77–108.

Goldstein, Diane. 1989. Belief and Disbelief: Is Neutralism Really the Issue? *Talking Folklore* 6 (April): 64–66.

Goodman, Felicitas. 1981. *The Exorcism of Anneliese Michel.* New York: Doubleday.

———. 1988. *How About Demons?: Possession and Exorcism in the Modern World.* Bloomington: Indiana University Press.

Gould, Stephen Jay. 1998. This View of Life: Above All, Do No Harm. *Natural History* (October): 16–24, 78–82.

Goy, Michael J. 1976. *The Missing Dimension in World Affairs.* South Pasadena, Calif.: Emissary Publications.

Graves, Thomas E. 1992. Powwowing in Pennsylvania: An Ancient Tradition Refuses to Die. *The World & I* 7 (January): 636–45.

Graves, Tom. 1986. *Needles of Stone Revisited.* Glastonbury (Somerset): Gothic Image.

Gregory, Richard L., ed. 1987. *The Oxford Companion to the Mind.* New York: Oxford University Press.

Grider, Sylvia. 1973. Dormitory Legend-Telling in Progress: Fall 1972–Winter 1973. *Indiana Folklore* 6: 1–32. Reprinted as "The Hatchet Man" in Dégh 1980: 147–78.

Gruss, Edmond C. 1975. *The Ouija Board: Doorway to the Occult.* Chicago: Moody Press.

Gumaer, David Emerson. 1970. Satanism: A Practical Guide to Witch Hunting. *American Opinion* (September): 41–72.

Hall, Gary. 1973. The Big Tunnel: Legends and Legend-Telling. *Indiana Folklore* 6: 139–73. Reprinted in Degh, ed. 1980: 225–57.

Hall, Manly Palmer. 1951. Dangerous Doctrines. *Horizon* 10 (Spring): 42–54.

Hallam, Jack. 1975. *Ghosts of London.* London: Wolfe.

Hand, Wayland D., ed. 1961–1964. *Popular Beliefs and Superstitions from North Carolina.* Durham, N.C.: Duke University Press.

Hankey, Rosalie. 1944. Campus Folklore and California's "Pedro!" *California Folklore Quarterly* 3: 29–35.

Harper, Michael. 1970. *Spiritual Warfare*. Plainfield, N.J.: Logos International.

Harrell, David Edwin Jr. 1985. *Oral Roberts: An American Life*. Bloomington: Indiana University Press.

Henderson, William. 1866. *Notes on the Folk Lore of the Northern Counties of England and the Borders*. London: Longmans, Green.

Henningsen, Gustav. 1980. *The Witches' Advocate: Basque Witchcraft and the Spanish Inquisition (1609–1614)*. Reno: University of Nevada Press.

———. 1990. "The Ladies from Outside": An Archaic Pattern of the Witches' Sabbath. In Ankarloo and Henningsen 1990:191–215.

Hertenstein, Mike, and John Trott. 1993. *Selling Satan: The Tragic History of Mike Warnke*. Chicago: Cornerstone Press.

Hettinger, Virginia A. 1982. The Ghost at Stepp Cemetery and Related Events. Unpublished student paper submitted during the Indiana University course "Midwestern Folklore." Now in Penn State University, Hazleton, Folklore Archive.

Hicks, Robert D. 1991. *In Pursuit of Satan: The Police and the Occult*. Buffalo, N.Y.: Prometheus.

Hicks, Darryl E., and Dr. David A. Lewis. 1979. *The Todd Phenomenon: Ex-Grand Druid vs. the Illuminati, Fact or Fantasy*. Harrison, Ark.: New Leaf Press.

Hitchcock, James. 1982. *The New Enthusiasts and What They Are Doing to the Catholic Church*. Chicago: Thomas More Press.

Hobbs, Sandy, and David Cornwell. 1988. Hunting the Monster with Iron Teeth. In *Monsters with Iron Teeth: Perspectives on Contemporary Legend 3*, ed. Gillian Bennett and Paul Smith, 115–37. Sheffield: Sheffield Academic Press.

Hobbs, Sandy, and Bill Ellis. 1991. Satanic Ritual Abuse in the United Kingdom: A Checklist of Newspaper Reports in England and Scotland. Part One: The Orkney Islands Case. *FOAFTale News* 22 (June): 1–3.

Hoekema, Anthony A. 1972. *Holy Spirit Baptism*. Grand Rapids, Mich.: William B. Eerdmans.

Hohman, John George. 1992. *Pow-Wows: Or, The Long Lost Friend*. State College, Pa.: Yardbird Books.

Hole, Christina. 1947. *Witchcraft in England*. New York: Scribner's.

Howe, Linda Moulton. 1988. *A Strange Harvest*. Video documentary originally broadcast 25 May 1980 on KMGH-TV (Denver, Colo.). Littleton, Colo.: Linda Moulton Howe Productions.

———. 1989. *An Alien Harvest: Further Evidence Linking Animal Mutilations And Human Abductions to Alien Life Forms*. Littleton, Colo.: Linda Moulton Howe Productions.

Hufford, David J. 1982. *The Terror That Comes in the Night: An Experience-Centered Study of Supernatural Assault Traditions*. Philadelphia: University of Pennsylvania Press.

———. 1995. The Scholarly Voice and the Personal Voice: Reflexivity in Belief Studies. *Western Folklore* 54: 57–76.

Hughes, Pennethorne. 1965 [1952]. *Witchcraft*. Baltimore: Penguin.

Hunt, Stoker. 1985. *Ouija: The Most Dangerous Game*. New York: Harper & Row.

Hyatt, Harry Middleton. 1965. *Folk-Lore from Adams County Illinois*. Rev. ed. Hannibal, Mo.: Alma Egan Hyatt Foundation.

Irvine, Doreen. 1973. *From Witchcraft to Christ*. Cambridge, UK: Concordia Publishing House. [Published in US as *Freed from Witchcraft* (Nashville: Thomas Nelson).]

Jackson, Bruce. 1976. The Other Kind of Doctor: Conjure and Magic in Black American Folk Magic. In *American Folk Medicine: A Symposium*, ed. Wayland D. Hand, 259–72. Berkeley: University of California Press.

Jenkins, Philip. 1992. *Intimate Enemies: Moral Panics in Contemporary Great Britain*. Hawthorne, N.Y.: Aldine de Gruyter.

Jenkins, Philip, and Daniel Maier Katkin. 1991. Occult Survivors: The Making of a Myth. In Richardson, Best, and Bromley 1991: 127–44.

Jobes, Gertrude. 1962. *Dictionary of Mythology, Folklore, and Symbols*. New York: Scarecrow Press.

Johns, June. 1969. *King of the Witches: The World of Alex Sanders*. New York: Coward-McCann.

———. 1971. *Black Magic Today*. London: New English Library.

Johnson, F. Roy. 1974. *Supernaturals among Carolina Folk and Their Neighbors*. Murfreesboro, N.C.: Johnson Publishing Company.

Johnson, Henry. 1906. *Stories of Great Revivals*. London: Religious Trace Society.

Johnson, Jerry. 1989. *The Edge of Evil: The Rise of Satanism in North America*. Dallas: Word Publishing.

Jones, James H. 1981. *Bad Blood: The Tuskegee Syphilis Experiment—A Tragedy of Race and Medicine*. New York: Free Press.

Jordan, Peter A. 1982. Psychometry & Cattle Mutilation: Four Psychics & Their Readings. *Fortean Times* 38 (Autumn): 4–14.

Kagan, Daniel, and Ian Summers. 1983. *Mute Evidence*. New York: Bantam.

Kelly, Aidan A. 1991. *Crafting the Art of Magic, Book I: A History of Modern Witchcraft, 1939–1964*. St. Paul, Minn.: Llewellyn.

Kelly, Reverend Clarence. 1974. *Conspiracy Against God and Man*. Boston: Western Islands.

Kenyatta, Jomo. 1965 [1938]. *Facing Mount Kenya: The Tribal Life of the Gikuyu*. New York: Vintage Books.

King, Francis. 1989. *Modern Ritual Magic: The Rise of Western Occultism*. Rev. ed. Bridport, Dorset: Prism Press.

Kittridge, George Lyman. 1929. *Witchcraft in Old and New England*. Cambridge: Harvard University Press.

Kobler, John. 1966. Out for a Night at the Local Cauldron. *Saturday Evening Post* (5 November): 76–78. Reprinted in Ebon 1971: 21–30.

Koch, Kurt E. 1962. *Between Christ and Satan*. Grand Rapids, Mich.: Kregel.

———. 1969. *The Strife of Tongues*. Grand Rapids, Mich.: Kregel.

———. 1970 *The Devil's Alphabet*. Berghausen, Germany: Evangelization Publishers.

———. 1971. *Occult: The Christian Perspective*. Six- cassette sound recording. Minneapolis: Greater Minneapolis Association of Evangelicals.

———. 1972. *Christian Counselling and Occultism: The Counselling of the Psychically Disturbed and Those Oppressed through Involvement in Occultism*. Grand Rapids, Mich.: Kregel.

———. 1973a. *Demonology, Past and Present*. Grand Rapids, Mich.: Kregel.

———. 1973b. *Revival Fires in Canada*. Grand Rapids, Mich.: Kregel Publication.

———. 1978. *Satan's Devices*. Grand Rapids, Mich.: Kregel. Reprinted 1980 as *Occult ABC*.

———. 1980a. *Gottes Treue: Aus Meinem Liebe, Teil 1*. Lavel, Quebec: Association for Christian Evangelism.

———. 1980b. *Besessenheit und Exorzismus: Aus Meinem Liebe, Teile 7–8*. Lavel, Quebec: Association for Christian Evangelism.

Koch, Kurt E., and Alfred Lechler. 1970. *Occult Bondage and Deliverance. Advice for Counseling the Sick, the Troubled and the Occultly Oppressed*. Grand Rapids, Mich.: Kregel.

La Fontaine, Jean S. 1994. *Extent & Nature of Organized Ritual Abuse*. London: [Great Britain] Department of Health.

Lanning, Kenneth V. 1989. *Satanic, Occult, Ritualistic Crime: A Law Enforcement Perspective*. Quantico, Va.: FBI Academy.

Lashley, Karl S. 1950. In Search of the Engram. In *Symposia of the Society for Experimental Biology IV: Physiological Mechanisms in Animal Behaviour*, 454–82. New York: Academic Press.

LaVey, Anton Szandor. 1969. *The Satanic Bible*. New York: Avon.

Lebelson, Harry. 1980. Death on the Range. *Omni* 2:4 (January): 28, 116–17.

Lee, John, and Barbara Moore. 1975. *Monsters Among Us: Journey to the Unexplained*. New York: Pyramid Books.

Leek, Sybil. 1968. *Diary of a Witch*. Englewood Cliffs, N.J.: Prentice-Hall.

Lefebure, Charles. 1969. *The Blood Cults*. New York: Ace Books.

———. 1970. *Witness to Witchcraft*. New York: Ace Books.

Levin, Ira. 1967. *Rosemary's Baby; A Novel*. New York: Random House.

Lewis, I.M. 1989. *Ecstatic Religion: A Study of Shamanism and Spirit Possession*. 2d. ed. New York: Routledge.

Lewis, Richard Warren, and Lawrence Schiller. 1967. *The Scavengers and Critics of the Warren Report*. New York: Dell.

Licht, M[ichael]. "Some Automotive Play Activities of Suburban Teenagers." *New York Folklore Quarterly* 30 (1974): 44–65.

Lindsey, Hal, with C.C. Carlson. 1974 [1972]. *Satan Is Alive and Well on Planet Earth*. New York: Bantam Books.

Linson, D.R. 1974 [1951]. Washington's Haunted Boy. In Ebon, ed. 1974:13–17.

Lloyd-Jones, D. Martyn. 1988. Body, Mind and Spirit. In his *Healing and the Scriptures*. Nashville, Tenn.: Oliver-Nelson Books. [Originally delivered 1974.]

Long, Martha. 1985. Is Satan Alive and Well in Northeast Arkansas? *Mid-America Folklore* 13 (2): 18–26.

Lorenzen, Coral, and Jim Lorenzen. 1976. *Encounters with UFO Occupants*. New York: Berkley Medallion.

———. *Abducted! Confrontations with Beings from Outer Space*. New York: Berkley Medallion.

Lueken, Veronica. 1991. *The Incredible Bayside Prophecies on the United States and Canada!* Lowell, Mich.: These Last Days Ministries.

Lyons, Arthur, Jr. 1988. *Satan Wants You: The Cult of Devil Worship in America*. New York: Mysterious Press.

McClenon, James. 1994. *Wondrous Events: Foundations of Religious Belief*. Philadelphia: University of Pennsylvania Press.

MacHovec, Frank J. 1973. *Exorcism: A Manual for Casting Out Evil Spirits*. Mount Vernon, N.Y.: Peter Pauper Press.

Mailer, Norman. 1968. *The Armies of the Night: History as a Novel, The Novel as History*. New York: New American Library.

Manchester, Sean. 1975. The Highgate Vampire. In *The Vampire's Bedside Companion: the Amazing World of Vampires in Fact and Fiction*, ed. Peter Underwood, 82– 121. London: Leslie Frewin.

———. 1985. *The Highgate Vampire: The Infernal World of the Undead Unearthed at London's Highgate Cemetery and Environs*. London: British Occult Society.

———. 1991. *The Highgate Vampire: The Infernal World of the Undead Unearthed at London's Highgate Cemetery and Environs*. Revised edition. London: Gothic Press.

Maple, Eric. 1966. *The Domain of Devils*. New York: A.S. Barnes.

———. 1971. London's Graveyard Ghouls. *Man, Myth, and Magic*, 2844+.

———. 1973. *Witchcraft: The Story of Man's Search for Supernatural Power*. London: Octopus Books.

Martin, Malachi. 1976. *Hostage to the Devil: The Possession and Exorcism of Five Living Americans*. New York: Reader's Digest Press.

Masters, Anthony. 1978. *The Devil's Dominion: The Complete Story of Hell and Satanism in the Modern World*. New York: G.P. Putnam's Sons.

McCarty, John. 1984. *Splatter Movies: Breaking the Last Taboo of the Screen*. New York: St. Martin's Press.

Meade, J. Russell, ed. 1963. *Victory Over Demonism Today*. Wheaton, Ill.: Christian Life Publications.

Melton, J. Gordon. 1980. Books, News & Reviews. *Fate* 33:8 (August 1980): 103–5.

———. 1990. *New Age Encyclopedia*. Detroit: Gale Research.

Menefee, Samuel Pyeatt. 1985. Circling as an Entrance to the Otherworld. *Folklore* 96: 3–20.

Milligan, Linda. 1983. The Cult of the UFO: Middle America in Search of Itself. Paper presented at the Annual Meeting of the American Folklore Society, Nashville, Tenn.

———. 1990. The "Truth" about the Bigfoot Legend. *Western Folklore* 49 (1990): 83–98.

Milspaw, Yvonne J. 1978. Witchcraft in Appalachia: Protection for the Poor. *Indiana Folklore* 11: 71–86.

Montell, Lynwood. 1975. *Ghosts Along the Cumberland : Deathlore in the Kentucky Foothills.* Knoxville: University of Tennessee Press.

Montgomery, John Warwick, ed. 1976a. *Demon Possession: A Medical, Historical, Anthropological and Theological Symposium.* Minneapolis: Bethany Fellowship.

———. 1976b. Not Suffering Witches to Live. In Montgomery 1976a: 91–104.

Muchembled, Robert. 1990. Satanic Myths and Cultural Reality. In Ankerloo and Henningsen. 1990: 139–60.

Mulhern, Sherrill. 1991. Satanism and Psychotherapy: A Rumor in Search of an Inquisition. In Richardson, Best, and Bromley 1991: 145–72.

Murray, Margaret A. 1921. *The Witch-Cult in Western Europe.* Oxford: Oxford University Press.

———. 1931. *The God of the Witches.* Oxford: Oxford University Press.

Nathan, Debbie. 1991. Satanism and Child Molestation: Constructing the Ritual Abuse Scare. In Richardson, Best, and Bromley 1991: 75–94.

Nathan, Debbie, and Michael Snedeker. 1995. *Satan's Silence: Ritual Abuse and the Making of a Modern American Witch Hunt.* New York: BasicBooks.

Neel, E. Ann. 1990. Accounting for Horror: When the Rod Killed the Child. Unpublished paper presented at the Society for the Study of Social Problems.

Neil-Smith, Christopher. 1974. *The Exorcist and the Possessed.* St. Ives, Cornwall: James Pike.

Neumann, Erich. 1955. *The Great Mother: An Analysis of the Archetype.* New York: Pantheon.

Nevius, John. 1968 [1895]. *Demon possession.* Grand Rapids, Mich.: Kregel Publications.

OSUFA. Ohio State University Folklore Archive, Columbus, Ohio. Dr. Patrick Mullen, Archivist. Student projects are accessed by the collector's last name.

Owen, Alex. 1990. *The Darkened Room: Women, Power and Spiritualism in Late Victorian England.* Philadelphia: University of Pennsylvania Press.

Owen, Nancy H. 1980. *Preliminary Analysis of the Impact of Livestock Mutilations on Rural Arkansas Communities.* Report prepared for the Arkansas Endowment for the Humanities, Little Rock, Ark.

Passantino, Gretchen and Bob Passantino with Jon Trott. 1990. Satan's Sideshow. *Cornerstone* 18(90): 24–28.

Pedigo, Jess. 1971. *Satanism: Diabolical Religion of Darkness.* Tulsa, Okla.: Christian Crusade Publications.

Perkins, David. 1982. *Altered Steaks: A Colloquium on the Cattle Mutilation Question*. Santa Barbara, Calif.: Am Here Books.

Petitpierre, Dom Robert, ed. 1972. *Exorcism: The Report of a Commission Convened by the Bishop of Exeter*. London: SPCK.

Philpott, Kent. 1973. *A Manual of Demonology and the Occult*. Grand Rapids, Mich.: Zondervan.

Pimple, Kenneth D. 1985. "It's Because I Believe in It": History, Beliefs, and Legends of the Ouija Board. Unpublished graduate term paper (Bloomington, Ind.).

Plowman, Edward E. 1979. The Legend(s) of John Todd. *Christianity Today* (2 February): 38–42.

Price, Harry, with Ian D. Coster. 1931. "I know that Black Masses are being celebrated to-day." *Nash's Pall Mall Magazine* (February): 26–29, 92–93.

Queenborough, Lady (Edith Starr Miller). 1968. *Occult Theocrasy*. Hawthorne, Calif.: The Christian Book Club of America.

Randi, James. 1980. Mutilation Madness. *Omni* 2:10 (July): 35.

Randolph, Keith. 1975. The Killer Cult Terrorizing Mid-America. *Saga* (November): 16–19, 49–59.

Randolph, Vance. 1947. *Ozark Superstitions*. New York: Columbia University Press.

———. 1953. Nakedness in Ozark Folk Belief. *Journal of American Folklore* 66: 333–39.

Raschke, Carl A. 1990. *Painted Black*. New York: Harper & Row.

Raupert, J. Godfrey. 1918. The Truth About the Ouija Board. *American Ecclesiastical Review* (November): 463–78.

Ray, Linda McCoy. 1976. The Legend of Bloody Mary's Grave. *Indiana Folklore* 9: 175–87.

Real Witches at Work. 1964. *Life* (13 November): 55–62.

Reimensnyder, Barbara. 1989 [1982]. *Powwowing in Union County: A Study of Pennsylvania German Folk Medicine in Context*. New York: AMS Press.

Rhodes, Henry T.F. 1954. *The Satanic Mass: A Sociological and Criminological Study*. London: Rider and Company.

Richards, John. 1974. *But Deliver Us from Evil: An Introduction to the Demonic Dimension in Pastoral Care*. New York: Seabury Press.

Richardson, James T., Joel Best, and David G. Bromley, eds. 1991. *The Satanism Scare*. New York: Aldine de Gruyter.

Roberts, J.M. 1972. *The Mythology of the Secret Societies*. New York: Charles Scribner's Sons.

Roberts, Jane. 1966. *How to Develop Your ESP Power*. New York: F. Fell.

Robertson, Pat. 1991. *The New World Order*. Dallas: Word Publishing.

Rogo, D. Scott. 1985. *The Search for Yesterday: A Critical Examination of the Evidence for Reincarnation*. Englewood Cliffs, N.J.: Prentice-Hall.

———. 1987. *The Infinite Boundary: A Psychic Look at Spirit Possession, Madness, and Multiple Personality*. New York: Dodd, Mead.

Rojcewicz, Peter M. 1986. The Extraordinary Encounter Continuum Hypothesis and Its Implications for the Study of Belief Materials. *Folklore Forum* 19: 131–52.

———. 1987. The "Men in Black" Experience and Tradition: Analogues with the Traditional Devil Hypothesis. *Journal of American Folklore* 100: 148–60.

Rommel, Kenneth M. 1980. *Operation Animal Mutilation.* Report of the District Attorney, First Judicial District, State of New Mexico, Santa Fe.

Rorvik, David. 1980. Cattle Mutilations: The Truth at Last. *Penthouse* (September): 121–22, 142–43.

Rosik, Christopher H. 1992. Conversations with an Internal Self Helper. *Journal of Psychology and Theology* 20:3 (Fall): 217–23.

Rudinger, Joel D. 1976. Folk Ogres of the Firelands: Narrative Variations of a North Central Ohio Community. *Indiana Folklore* 9: 52–62.

Ryder, Daniel. 1992. *Breaking the Circle of Satanic Ritual Abuse: Recognizing and Recovering from the Hidden Trauma.* Minneapolis: CompCare Publishers.

Samuelson, Sue. 1979. The White Witch: An Analysis of an Adolescent Legend. *Indiana Folklore* 12: 18–37.

Sananda. 1989. *Satan's Drummers: The Secret Beat of Evil— "Satan" Is Alive and Well.* Carlsbad, Calif.: America West Distributors.

Sandell, Roger. 1992. Desperately Seeking Satan. *Magonia* 42 (March): 8–13.

Sanders, Ed. 1967. *Fuck God in the Ass.* New York: Fuck You Press.

———. 1971a. *The Family: The Story of Charles Manson's Dune Buggy Attack Battalion.* New York: E.P. Dutton.

———. 1971b. Charlie and the Devil. *Esquire* (November): 105–12, 235–59.

———. 1976. The Mutilation Mystery. *Oui* 5:9 (September): 51+.

———. 1987. *Thirsting for Peace in a Raging Century: Selected Poems 1961–1985.* Minneapolis: Coffee House Press.

Sargant, William. 1961. *Battle for the Mind.* Rev. ed. Baltimore: Penguin.

Sato, Ikuya. Play Theory of Delinquency: Toward a General Theory of "Action." *Symbolic Interaction* 11:2 (1988): 191–212.

Schlafly, Phyllis. 1964. *A Choice Not an Echo.* Alton, Ill.: Pere Marquette Press.

Scott, Beth, and Michael Norman. 1986. *Haunted Heartland.* New York: Warner Books.

Sebald, Hans. 1978. *Witchcraft : the heritage of a heresy.* New York: Elsevier.

———. 1995. *Witch-Children: From Salem Witch-Hunts to Modern Courtrooms.* Amherst, N.Y.: Prometheus Books.

Seth, Ronald. 1969. *Children Against Witches.* New York: Taplinger Publishing Company.

Shaner, Richard H. 1961. Living Occult Practices in Dutch Pennsylvania. *Pennsylvania Folklife* 12:3 (Fall): 62–63.

———. 1972. Recollections of Witchcraft in the Oley Hills. *Pennsylvania Folklife* 21 (Folk Festival Supplement): 34–44.

Shepherding Movement - Discipleship Movement. 1999. BELIEVE Religious

DataBase Program. Available: *http://www.mb-soft.com/believe/txc/shepherd.htm*

Sherman, Harold. 1969. *Your Mysterious Powers of ESP: The New Medium of Communication.* New York: World Publishing.

Simpson, Jacqueline. 1969. Legends of Chanctonbury Ring. *Folklore* 80: 122–31.

———. 1994. Hecate in the Primrose Wood: The Propagation of a Rumour. *Contemporary Legend* 4: 91–118.

Smith, Fredrick W. 1976. *Cattle Mutilation: The Unthinkable Truth.* Cedaredge, Colo.: Freedland Publications.

Smith, Michelle, and Lawrence Pazder. 1981. *Michelle Remembers.* New York: Pocket Books.

Smith, Oswald J. 1933. *The Revival We Need.* London: Marshall, Morgan & Scott.

Smyth, Frank. 1973 [1970]. *Modern Witchcraft: The Fascinating Story of the Rebirth of Paganism and Magic.* N.p.: Castle Books.

Sparks, Beatrice. 1979. *Jay's Journal.* New York: New York Times Book Company

Spraggett, Allen. 1967. *The Unexplained.* New York: New American Library.

St. Clair, David. 1987. *Say You Love Satan.* New York: Dell.

Spencer, John Wallace. 1976. *The UFO Yearbook.* Springfield, Mass.: Phillips Publishing Company.

Starr, Bill. 1965. Mexican Cult of Human Sacrifice. In *Strange Fate,* ed. Curtis and Mary Fuller, 132–36. New York: Paperback Library.

Stauffer, Vernon. 1918. *New England and the Bavarian Illuminati.* New York: Columbia University Press.

Steiger, Brad. 1969. *Sex and Satanism.* New York: Ace Books.

Steiger, Brad, and Warren Smith. 1971. *Satan's Assassins.* New York: Lancer Books.

Stevens, Phillips, Jr. 1989. Satanism: Where Are the Folklorists? *New York Folklore* 15: 1–22. Reprinted in *Contemporary Legend: A Reader,* ed. Gillian Bennett and Paul Smith, 341–62. New York: Garland.

———. 1991. The Demonology of Satanism: An Anthropological View. In Richardson, Best, and Bromley 1991: 21–39.

Stewart, James R. 1977. Cattle Mutilations: An Episode of Collective Delusion. *The Zetetic* 1: 55–66.

Stewart, Susan. 1976. Rational Powwowing: An Examination of Choice among Medical Alternatives in Rural York County, Pennsylvania. *Pennsylvania Folklife* 26:1 (Fall): 12–17.

Stine, Scott Aaron. 1999. The Snuff Film: The Making of an Urban Legend. *The Skeptical Inquirer* 23:3 (May/June). Available: *http://www.csicop.org/si/9905/*

Summers, Rev. Montague. 1956 [1926]. *The History of Witchcraft and Demonology.* New Hyde Park, N.Y.: University Books.

Taylor, Derek. 1987. *It Was Twenty Years Ago Today.* New York: Fireside Books.

Taylor, Eugene. 1984. *William James on Exceptional Mental States: The 1896 Lowell Lectures.* Amherst: University of Massachusetts Press.

Terry, Maury. 1987. *The Ultimate Evil: An Investigation of America's Most Dangerous Satanic Cult.* Garden City, N.Y.: Doubleday.

Tertullian. 1931. Apology. Trans. T.R. Glover. In *Tertullian/Minucius Felix. Loeb Classical Library*, vol. 250. Cambridge: Harvard University Press.

Thigpen, Kenneth A. 1971. Adolescent Legends in Brown County: A Survey. *Indiana Folklore* 4: 141–215.

Thoreau, Henry David. 1985. *A Week on the Concord and Merrimack Rivers*. New York: Library of America.

Thorpe, Benjamin. 1851. *Northern Mythology Comprising the Principal Popular Traditions and Superstitions of Scandinavia, North Germany, and the Netherlands*. London: E. Lumley.

Tippett, A.R. 1976. Spirit Possession as It Relates to Culture and Religion: A Survey of Anthropological Literature. In Montgomery, ed. 1976a: 143–74.

Toelken, Barre. 1979. *The Dynamics of Folklore*. Boston: Houghton Mifflin.

Townsend, Barbara Ann. 1971. String Measurement: Additional Accounts. *Indiana Folklore* 4: 89–94.

Townsend, Barbara Ann, and Donald Allport Bird. 1970. The Miracle of String Measurement. *Indiana Folklore* 3: 147–62.

Trachtenberg, Joshua. 1943. *The Devil and the Jews: The Medieval Conception of the Jew and Its Relation to Modern Antisemitism*. New Haven: Yale University Press.

Trevor-Roper, H.R. 1969. *The European Witch-Craze of the Sixteenth and Seventeenth Centuries, and Other Essays*. New York: Harper & Row.

Turner, Patricia A. 1993. *I Heard It Through the Grapevine: Rumor in African-American Culture*. Berkeley: University of California Press.

Underwood, Peter. 1973. *Haunted London*. London: Horrop.

———. 1975. Vampires and Highgate Cemetery. In *The Vampire's Bedside Companion: The Amazing World of Vampires in Fact and Fiction*, ed. Peter Underwood, 75–80. London: Leslie Frewin.

Unger, Merrill F. 1971. *Demons in the World Today: A Study of Occultism in the Light of God's Word*. Wheaton, Ill.: Tyndale House.

Valiente, Doreen. 1989. *The Rebirth of Witchcraft*. London: Robert Hale.

Vallee, Jacques. 1979. *Messengers of Deception: UFO Contacts and Cults*. Berkeley, Calif.: And/Or Press.

Vargo, Beth. 1993. Satanism, Ritual Child Abuse and Urban Legends. *Believe the Children Newsletter* 10:3.

Victor, Jeffrey S. 1989. A Rumor-Panic About a Dangerous Satanic Cult in Western New York. *New York Folklore* 15: 23–49.

———. 1990. Satanic Cult Rumors as Contemporary Legend. *Western Folklore* 49: 51–81.

———. 1991. The Dynamics of Rumor-Panics about Satanic Cults. In Richardson, Best, and Bromley 1991: 221–36.

———. 1993. *Satanic Panic: The Creation of a Contemporary Legend*. Chicago: Open Court.

von Sydow, Carl Wilhelm. 1978 [1948]. *Selected Papers on Folklore*. New York, Arno Press.

Waller, Gregory. 1986. *The Living and the Undead: From Stoker's Dracula to Romero's Dawn of the Dead.* Urbana: University of Illinois Press.

Ward, Donald, ed. 1981. *The German Legends of the Brothers Grimm.* Philadelphia: ISHI.

Warnke, Mike. 1972. *The Satan-Seller.* South Plainfield, N.J.: Bridge Publication.

Watkins, Leslie. 1984. *The Real Exorcists.* London: Futura.

Webster, Nesta H. 1921. *World Revolution: The Plot Against Civilization.* London: Constable and Company.

Welch, Robert. 1966. More Stately Mansions. In his *The New Americanism And Other Speeches and Essays,* 115–52. Belmont, Mass.: Western Islands.

Westwood, Horace. 1949. *There Is a Psychic World.* New York: Crown Publishers.

Wheatley, Dennis. 1954 [1934]. *The Devil Rides Out.* London: Hutchinson.

———. 1956 [1953]. *To the Devil—A Daughter.* London: Hutchinson.

———. 1959 [1948]. *The Haunting of Toby Jugg.* London: Hutchinson.

———. 1962 [1960]. *The Satanist.* London: Hutchinson.

———. 1971. *The Devil and All His Works.* New York: American Heritage Press.

———. 1972a [1941]. *Strange Conflict.* New York: Ballantine Books.

———. 1972b [1970]. *Gateway to Hell.* London: Arrow Books.

Whyte, H.A. Maxwell. 1973a *The Power of the Blood.* Springdale, Pa.: Whitaker House.

———. 1973b. *Dominion over Demons.* Springdale, Pa.: Banner Publishing.

———. 1973c. *The Kiss of Satan.* Monroeville, Pa.: Whitaker House.

———. 1989. *Demons and Deliverance.* Springdale, Pa.: Whitaker House. [A combination of *Dominion over Demons* and *A Manual on Exorcism.*]

Wickland, Carl A. 1968 [1924]. *Thirty Years Among the Dead.* London: Spiritualist Press.

Wilburn, Gary. 1972. *The Fortune Sellers.* Glendale, Calif.: G/L Regal Books.

Wilgus, Neal. 1978. *The Illuminoids.* New York: Pocket Books.

Wiloch, Thomas. 1984. Sanders, (James) Ed(ward). *Contemporary Authors* 13: 447–50.

Wojcik, Daniel. 1996. "Polaroids from Heaven": Photography, Folk Religion, and the Miraculous Image Tradition at a Marian Apparition Site. *Journal of American Folklore* 109: 129–48.

———. 1997. *The End of the World as We Know It: Faith, Fatalism, and Apocalypse in America.* New York: New York University Press.

Wolf, R. Martin. 1977. Chaos in Quiescence. *Pursuit* (Winter): 19–27.

Wolfe, Burton H. 1976. Demystifying all the satanic conspiracy stories on "The Cattle Mutilations." *San Francisco Bay Guardian* (14 May): 10–11.

Wyckoff, Donna. 1996. "Now Everything Makes Sense!": Complicating the Contemporary Legend Picture. In *Contemporary Legend: A Reader,* ed. Gillian Bennett and Paul Smith, 363–80. New York: Garland.

Yoder, Don. 1962. Witch Tales from Adams County. *Pennsylvania Folklife* 12:4 (Winter): 29–37.

———. 1965–1966. Official Religion versus Folk Religion. *Pennsylvania Folklife* 15:2 (Winter): 36–52.

———. 1972. Folk Medicine. In *Folklore and Folklife*, ed. Richard M. Dorson, 191–215. Chicago: University of Chicago Press.

———. 1976. Hohman and Romanus: Origins and Diffusion of the Pennsylvania German Powwow Manual. In *American Folk Medicine: A Symposium*, ed. Wayland D. Hand, 235–48. Berkeley: University of California Press.

Index